Knowledge before Action

Studies in Comparative Religion
Frederick M. Denny, Series Editor

Knowledge & before Action

Islamic Learning and Sufi Practice in the Life of Sayyid Jalāl al-dīn Bukhārī Makhdūm-i Jahāniyān

Amina M. Steinfels

The University of South Carolina Press

Published by the University of South Carolina Press
Columbia, South Carolina 29208

www.sc.edu/uscpress

Manufactured in the United States of America

21 20 19 18 17 16 15 14 13 12 10 9 8 7 6 5 4 3 2 1

Library of Congress Cataloging-in-Publication Data

Steinfels, Amina M.
Knowledge before action : Islamic learning and Sufi practice in the life of Sayyid Jalāl al-Dīn Bukhārī Makhdūm-i Jahāniyān / Amina M. Steinfels.
p. cm. — (Studies in comparative religion)
Includes bibliographical references and index.
ISBN 978-1-61117-073-3 (cloth : alk. paper)
1. Makhdūm Jahāniyān Jahān Gasht, Jalāluddīn, d. 1383. 2. Sufis—Biography. 3. Muslim scholars—Biography. 4. Sufism—History. I. Title.
BP80.M29S74 2012
297.4092—dc23
[B]2011048947

This book was printed on a recycled paper with 30 percent postconsumer waste content.

CONTENTS

List of Illustrations *vii*
Series Editor's Preface *ix*
Acknowledgments *xi*
Note on Transliteration *xiii*

Introduction *1*

Part One ❧ The Education of a Sufi Shaykh
One Initiation into the Sufi Path *15*
Two Pilgrimage and Travel *37*

Part Two ❧ Teaching and Practice
Three Book-Learning and Islamic Law *63*
Four Ritual and Practice *81*
Five Money, Non-Muslims, Women, and Saints *103*

Part Three ❧ Served by the Inhabitants of the World
Six A Public Figure *125*
Seven Legacy *144*

Conclusion *154*

Appendix A: Jalāl al-dīn Bukhārī's *Khirqas* *157*
Appendix B: The *Malfūẓāt* of Jalāl al-dīn Bukhārī *165*
Appendix C: Works Attributed to Jalāl al-dīn Bukhārī *169*
Appendix D: *Taẕkira* Entries on Jalāl al-dīn Bukhārī *173*
Appendix E: Jalāl al-dīn Bukhārī's Bibliography *181*
Notes *191*
Bibliography *221*
Index *223*

ILLUSTRATIONS

Maps

South Asia *11*
Jalāl al-dīn Bukhārī's Travels *38*

Tables

Table 1: Genealogy of the Bukhārī Sayyids *18*
Table 2: Books Read under Bukhārī's Supervision *67*
Table 3: Suhrawardī *Khirqas* from the Shaykhs of Multan and Uch *157*
Table 4: Suhrawardī *Khirqas* from the Shaykhs of Hejaz, Yemen and Iran *158*
Table 5: Suhrawardī *Khirqa* from Amīn al-dīn al-Balyānī *159*
Table 6: Chishtī *Khirqas* *160*
Table 7: Kubrawī *Khirqas* *161*
Table 8: Qādirī *Khirqas* *162*
Table 9: Kāzarūnī *Khirqas* *163*
Table 10: Rifā'ī *Khirqas* *164*
Table 11: Ahistorical or Miraculous *Khirqas* *164*

SERIES EDITOR'S PREFACE

This is the "first ever critical academic evaluation of a figure exceedingly significant for understanding Islamic intellectual history in South Asia," according to a distinguished scholar of Sufism in an external review of the manuscript as it was being considered for publication. Another leading scholar's external review stated that "the main contribution of this work to the field is twofold: (1) it provides a detailed and richly textured portrait of a major Sufi figure of South Asia on the basis of careful and searching analysis of appropriate primary sources, and (2) it offers the readers quite possibly the most focused and comprehensive glimpse into the daily lives of institutionalized Sufis of the medieval period that I have read. Once published, this will easily become one of the major 'go-to'works for anyone interested in social, economic, political, and especially ritual aspects of Sufism of the early Middle Period (roughly the thirteenth through the fifteenth centuries). This is quite an accomplishment, and the manuscript makes a key contribution to scholarship on this score."

It is always a delight for a series editor to read supportive external reviews of proposed manuscripts that are based on rigorous analysis and profound understanding of what the author has been aiming to achieve. The main title phrase, "Knowledge before Action," clearly characterizes both the great Sayyid Jalāl al-dīn Bukhārī's dedication to disciplined and thorough study leading to action in his context as a major Sufi master and the author's rigorous and extensive research, which one reader characterized as "exceptionally thorough, both in terms of her coverage of all the relevant dimensions of Bukhārī's long life and career as a Sufi master and in her thorough attention to all previous scholarship on the topic." This final comment particularly applies to her productive use of "hitherto unutilized or underutilized primary sources on this major Sufi master," as the reviewer concludes.

This book fills a huge gap in our understanding of Islam and Muslims, and particularly Sufi Muslims in South Asia during the period when al-Bukhārī (1308–1384) was a principal player there.

It stands as a solid companion to a range of excellent works on Islam and Muslims that have been published over the past quarter century in this series.

Frederick M. Denny

ACKNOWLEDGMENTS

I would like to express my profound thanks to my mentor, Professor Gerhard Böwering, for his guidance, encouragement, and generosity, without which this project would have foundered long ago. Jamal J. Elias introduced me to the academic study of Sufism more than twenty years ago, and I am deeply grateful that he has continued to be my teacher, friend, and colleague.

This project has benefited greatly from the comments, criticism, and conversation of my colleagues in the fields of Islamic studies and South Asian studies, especially Shahzad Bashir, Kavita Datla, Tariq Jaffer, Suleiman Mourad, Andy Rotman, and Walid Saleh. My colleagues in the Religion Department at Mount Holyoke, Jane Crosthwaite, Larry Fine, John Grayson, Susanne Mrozik, Michael Penn, and Susan Rusiecki, have been unstinting in their support and encouragement. I owe a debt of gratitude to them as well as to many other faculty, staff, students, and colleagues at Mount Holyoke College, Yale University, Amherst College, Gettysburg College, and the Five Colleges consortium.

I would like to thank the Urdu Pundit at the Government Oriental Manuscripts Library, Madras; Mrs. Tanvir Fatima and Mrs. Rafat Rizwana at the Andhra Pradesh Government Oriental Library, Hyderabad; Dr. Muhammad Hussain Tasbihi and Dr. Muhammad Mehdi Tavasoli at Kitābkhāna-yi Dātā Ganj-bakhsh, Islamabad; and the librarians at the Punjab University Library, Lahore; Yale University Library; Musselman Library at Gettysburg College; the British Library; and the Mount Holyoke College Library. My research in South Asia would not have been possible without the generous hospitality and practical assistance of Dr. T. J. Jayaraman and Tara Srinivasan in Chennai. Research at the British Library was supported by a grant from Mount Holyoke College. Shaji Ahmed kindly helped me with the maps. Kristin Hansen spent many hours working on the formatting. I am very grateful to the anonymous scholars who carefully read an earlier draft of this manuscript and provided extremely insightful and useful comments. I would also like to thank Bill Adams, Jim Denton, and the University of South Carolina Press.

I am grateful to my parents, Jane Steinfels Hussain and Faheemullah Hussain, and my brother, Nadeem Hussain (and Pauline Larmaraud), for their support, their interest in my work, and their constant willingness to discuss and debate religion, South Asia, and Islam. My late father facilitated my research in Pakistan and India, and his company (and that of Sara Monticone) enlivened my *ziyārat* to Uch Sharif. My mother, herself an expert in South Asian history, took time out of her busy schedule (with Al

Levenson's help) to read and comment on portions of this work. My uncle, Martin Steinfels, and my dearest friend, Francis Guévremont, read and re-read many early drafts and came to know more than they ever dreamed possible about medieval Sufism. Their insightful comments and questions kept alive my own interest in the project. My friends, Shana Brown, Herschel Farbman, Dan Friedman, Adinah Miller, Jenny Robertson, and Jackie Urla, have challenged me, entertained me, fed me, and generally preserved my sanity.

NOTE ON TRANSLITERATION

Persian, Arabic, and Urdu words have been transliterated according to the following chart. Arabic words used in Persian texts have been transliterated as Persian. Apostrophes have been used to distinguish some aspirated consonants in Urdu words such as "Lak'hnawī." Words appearing in the Oxford American Dictionary have not been transliterated nor italicized but I have retained the *'ayn* (') in words such as "Shi'a."

Transliteration Chart

Urdu	Arabic	Persian		Urdu	Arabic	Persian	
gh	gh	gh	غ	'	'	'	ء
f	f	f	ف	b	b	b	ب
q	q	q	ق	p		p	پ
k	k	k	ك	t	t	t	ت
g		g	گ	ṯ			ٹ
l	l	l	ل	s̱	th	s̱	ث
m	m	m	م	j	j	j	ج
n	n	n	ن	ch		ch	چ
ṉ			ں	ḥ	ḥ	ḥ	ح
w	w	w	و	kh	kh	kh	خ
h	h	h	ہ	d	d	d	د
y / ī / ē	y / ī	y / ī / ē	ي	ḏ			ڈ
ē			ے	ẕ	dh	ẕ	ذ
				r	r	r	ر
				ṟ			ڑ
ā	ā	ā	ا	z	z	z	ز
ā	ā	ā	ىٰ	zh		zh	ژ
ū / ō	ū	ū / ō	و	s	s	s	س
a	a	a	ـَ	sh	sh	sh	ش
i	i	i	ـِ	ṣ	ṣ	ṣ	ص
u	u	u	ـُ	ż	ḍ	ż	ض
a / t	a / t	a / t	ة	ṭ	ṭ	ṭ	ط
aw	aw	aw	او	ẓ	ẓ	ẓ	ظ
ay	ay	ay	اى	'	'	'	ع

Introduction

Sufis tell stories. They tell stories to teach moral points or religious ideas, they tell stories of the pious or miraculous actions of past saints, and they tell stories of their own journey on the Sufi path. Anecdotes, myths, fables, hagiography, and personal reminiscences are all constant features of Sufi teaching. It is fitting, therefore, to explore medieval Sufism and its place in an Islamic society by telling a story, the life story of a Sufi master (a *shaykh*, to use the Arabic word, or a *pīr* in Persian). This book is a critical retelling of a formative period in Sufism in the form of a biography of one individual, Sayyid Jalāl al-dīn Bukhārī (1308–1384). Bukhārī, a shaykh of the Suhrawardī order, is widely known in Pakistan today as Makhdūm-i jahāniyān Jahāngasht (served by the inhabitants of the world, world-traveler), and his tomb in the Punjabi town of Uch attracts a constant stream of pilgrims. As part of his instruction of students and disciples, Bukhārī told and retold episodes from his life and anecdotes about his spiritual masters. His disciples wrote down these vignettes and embedded them in their own reminiscences of their encounters with him. Story-tellers of a different kind, the chroniclers of courts, kings, and wars, mentioned Bukhārī when his life intersected with those of the rulers. Later hagiographers built upon these brief anecdotes to tell, on the one hand, more dramatic tales of wonders performed and, on the other, to pin down more definitively details of time, place, and genealogy. It is from all these strands, then, that I weave together his biography and a picture of the world he inhabited.

The society in which Bukhārī lived, the Muslim community of medieval South Asia, is one that has been unduly neglected in academic studies. In general, the later middle period of Islamic history, that is, after the end of the ʿAbbāsid Caliphate at the hands of the Mongols in the thirteenth century and before the rise of the "Gunpowder Empires" in the sixteenth century, has been overlooked. This is even more true for historical work on the Indian sub-continent, where interest tends to be focused on the British period or, at the earliest, the Mughal Empire. Furthermore, in the study of Islam, the religion as practiced in South Asia has also often been viewed as marginal from a Middle East–centered perspective and, therefore, its pre-modern formations have not been seen as crucial to an understanding of the religious tradition as a whole. There is good reason to associate the Indian sub-continent with "Hinduism," rather than Islam, as the overwhelming majority of the population has continued to identify with Indic religious traditions. However, in relation to the global Muslim population, South Asian Muslims today account for about a third of the total, perhaps the single largest cultural grouping of Muslims in the world. The Islamic traditions of South Asia have never been cut off from the rest of the Islamic world but instead have participated in, influenced, and been influenced by the various religious movements and developments that have arisen in global Islam.[1]

The period of the Delhi Sultanate, 1206–1526, was when Indo-Islamic culture began to develop its distinctive characteristics, characteristics that were to come into full bloom under the Mughal Empire.[2] The segments of Indo-Muslim society about which we have the most information, the military ruling class and the religious and cultural elite, prided themselves on their non-Indian descent, tracing their roots to Turkish, Afghan, Persian, or, less commonly, Arab progenitors. Persian was their lingua franca and in literature, the arts, government, and religion they followed the models developed in Central Asia and Iran, self-consciously participating in what Marshall Hodgson dubbed the Persianate world.[3] At the same time, perhaps less consciously, this was a culture gradually being indigenized—becoming Indian—through the absorption and appropriation of Indic models and ways of living, and through inter-marriage, conversion of local populations, and the inclusion of converts and non-Muslims into the military and governing structures.

Sufism had a particularly important place in this nascent Indo-Islamic culture.[4] From the days of the earliest Turkish conquests, representatives of the major Middle Eastern Sufi orders were active in the region, acquiring devotees among both the Muslim elite and the conquered population. Traditionally the Sufi orders have been credited with a major role in the spread of Islam in South Asia, though there is little clear evidence for this in the earliest textual sources. Many of the great Sufi shrines of South Asia, objects of pilgrimage and veneration to this day, belong to the saints of the thirteenth and fourteenth centuries. The two Sufi orders of greatest popularity and influence at this time were the Suhrawardīya, founded in twelfth-century Iraq, and the Chishtīya, which originated in Central Asia but only became important in India. Sayyid Jalāl al-dīn Bukhārī was primarily affiliated with the Suhrawardīya but was also initiated by the leading Chishtī shaykh of his time, as well as by representatives of numerous other lineages.

Despite the importance of the Sufi orders and shaykhs, they were by no means the only representatives of Islamic religious authority. The Delhi Sultanate supported an active madrasa-based tradition of scholarship on Islamic law, the Quran, and hadith, training clerics, judges, and other religious professionals. New texts, as well as commentaries and extracts of earlier works, were produced for use in the madrasas and for consultation by the ʿulama (the religious scholars) and other educated Muslims.[5] Relations between the ʿulama and the Sufi shaykhs seem to have been generally cordial, despite various struggles for preeminence as the ultimate authority on matters Islamic and periodic episodes of mutual condemnation for impiety.

Individual rulers followed different policies with regard to religion and, in particular, the degree to which they enforced or followed the dictates of Islamic law. However, any sultan had to engage, one way or the other, with the claims of both elements of the religious establishment, the ʿulama and the Sufi shaykhs. Both the madrasas and the Sufi shrines and hospices relied upon the patronage of the ruling political and military class, though the Sufis, in theory at least, attempted to keep themselves aloof from the taint of direct financial support. For their part, the rulers sought, on the one hand, to bolster the legitimacy of their rule through seeking the approval of the religious classes, and, on the other, to check the threat posed by alternate sources of popular authority by attempting to control and/or appease these classes. In other words, the ʿulama, the Sufi shaykhs, and the Sultan formed a sometimes tense triangle of rivalry and cooperation at the apex of Islamic society, a triangle often bound together by familial bonds and by ties of mutual respect and obligation. This was the milieu into which Bukhārī was born and in which he rose to the highest levels of political influence and religious stature.

In his own time and place, Bukhārī was a figure of both religious and political importance, commanding the respect and the devotion of a large segment of the South Asian Muslim community, including the Sultans of Delhi and the ʿulama. Sought out by students and disciples for religious instruction and Sufi initiation, he was a key link in the spiritual genealogies of saints from all the major Sufi orders, and different regions, of the Indian sub-continent. His teachings and reminiscences were recorded by several of his disciples in voluminous *malfūẓāt* texts covering every topic of Islamic religious practice.

Since much of the biographical information collected by Bukhārī's disciples and hagiographers was aimed at legitimizing his status as a religious authority, it details the steps by which he acquired that status and the ways in which it was recognized by his contemporaries. His biography thus illuminates the social practices by which medieval Islamic teachings were transmitted and through which the religious elite, both Sufi shaykhs and ʿulama, sustained and reproduced their positions in society. Islamic religious authority and charisma in pre-modern India could rest on a variety of different qualities or accomplishments: holy descent, textual scholarship, piety, mystical insights, and affiliation with a spiritual lineage, to name a few possibilities. This status was confirmed by the recognition of an individual by his (or, occasionally, her) contemporaries. One form of such recognition came from teachers and spiritual masters—both textual scholarship and initiation into the Sufi path required certification by authorities in those traditions. Such certification usually also included permission (*ijāzat*) to transmit the teaching or the Sufi affiliation to further students and disciples, thus opening the way for another form of recognition, that by the public in quest of knowledge or spiritual training. A final, more controversial, form of recognition came from relations with the temporal powers.

In Jalāl al-dīn Bukhārī, a number of these different modes of religious authority were brought together in a single individual. Bukhārī was a *sayyid*, a descendant of the Prophet Muḥammad, a status held in high respect. He was also the son and grandson of Sufi masters in the Suhrawardīya lineage, one of the most widespread Sufi orders in the Muslim world. Initiated into this lineage by his relatives, as well as by other shaykhs, Bukhārī became its leading Indian representative by the time he was forty years old. His status as an initiatory master did not rest on a single lineage, however, as he was affiliated with most of the other major Sufi lineages of the Islamic east, including the Chishtīya, the most popular Indian order, and had the ability to pass on these affiliations to his numerous disciples.

Bukhārī combined this role as initiatory master with that of teacher and transmitter of normative Sunni texts on law, hadith, theology, and Sufi practice. His teachings and daily activities were largely devoted to the reading and explication of books. As a scholar and teacher of traditional Sunni religious texts, and as an authority on correct Islamic practice, Bukhārī participated in some of the functions of the ʿulama, the traditional guardians of legalistic Islamic orthodoxy. At the same time, he was primarily known and sought after as a Sufi master. The Sufi path is often described as an alternative to Shariʿa-based orthodoxy or as acknowledging and then transcending it in pursuit of "higher" mystical truths. For Bukhārī, however, living up to the requirements of the Shariʿa was the primary task of any aspirant on the Sufi path, and instruction in the scholarly basis of the law was part of his own function as a Sufi master. One of his maxims was "first *ʿilm* (knowledge), then *ʿamal* (actions)," *ʿilm* being knowledge of the law and its roots in Quran and hadith while *ʿamal* are acts of devotion and piety.

For much of his education and for many of his Sufi affiliations, Bukhārī was indebted to a single voyage beyond the confines of the Indian sub-continent to Arabia to perform the hajj. Bukhārī stayed and studied in Mecca and Medina for seven years before traveling through southern Iraq and Iran on his way home. Very few of the great South Asian Sufi saints of this time period are known to have performed the hajj, and this trip gave Bukhārī great cachet, allowing him to speak as an authority on the "authentic" Islam practiced by the Arabs. A deeper knowledge of the Arabic language acquired in the holy cities also gave him greater mastery of the Arabic texts which were the backbone of the Islamic religious curriculum, even in a culture where Persian was the usual language in both speech and writing. The Middle East has often been envisioned as the Islamic heartland and the Arab as the most authentic Muslim, in contrast to supposedly marginal regions such as South Asia, Southeast Asia, or Africa, whose Islamic practices have been viewed as merely local or regional. Yet, it is often Muslims from these "margins," such as Bukhārī or the twentieth-century poet Muhammad Iqbal, who have played a crucial role in imagining this sacred geography.

Jalāl al-dīn Bukhārī's voyage to Arabia was partly motivated by his desire to flee the patronage and control of Sultan Muhammad b. Tughluq (r. 1325–1351), famous for his contentious relations with the religious classes. Bukhārī's relations with Muḥammad b. Tughluq's successor, Fīrōz Shāh (r. 1351–1385), were much more cordial, marked by mutual respect and frequent contact. For Bukhārī and his fellow Sufi shaykhs, the attention of the political rulers was never an unalloyed good. On the one hand, the patronage of the powerful and wealthy was one of their primary sources of sustenance, and it allowed them to intercede on behalf of their devotees for political and material benefits and to guide the ruler towards what they saw as more pious or more Islamic behavior. On the other hand, contact with the temporal powers might undermine the saintly model of absolute moral and spiritual independence and might suggest a condoning of dubious political, economic, and military practices.

The stereotype of the medieval Indian Sufi saint is of a figure engrossed in picturesque ascetic and meditative practices, attracting devotees by his display of ecstasy and mystic insight, disdaining the concerns of the world and religious orthodoxy to pursue a higher path of love and divine union. Jalāl al-dīn Bukhārī did not fit this model. Though he undertook and taught the standard Sufi practices of *ẕikr*, fasting, and retreats, the heart of his religious life was *namāz*, ritual prayer, multiplied and extended far beyond its obligatory core. Ecstatic or mystic experiences were not the explicit goals of his religious practices, though they might sometimes be the result. Rather, obedience and devotion to God and imitation of the Prophet Muḥammad were the motivation for all pious actions. The results to be legitimately expected from such devotional actions were concrete benefits in both this world and the next. Bukhārī fully participated in the pragmatic use of prayers, invocations, and amulets, often relegated by scholars of Islam to the realm of popular religion.

Today's romanticized image of Sufism, especially in South Asia, might lead one to wonder whether a personality like Bukhārī was a Sufi at all. Certainly the fact that Bukhārī did not fit the expected image of a Sufi saint may be one reason why he did not become as posthumously popular as some of his contemporaries (though the waxing and waning of a saint's cult over seven centuries cannot be explained so reductively). However, during his own lifetime his status as a great Sufi shaykh and an authority on matters Islamic was undisputed. Bukhārī and his disciples were Sufis not because they were love-intoxicated mystics but because they were initiated into Sufi orders, initiated others, participated in *ẕikr*, and taught and studied Sufi texts. Therefore, Bukhārī's success and fame requires us to rethink our understanding of Sufism, not as a strand of Islam clearly marked by particular intellectual, emotional, or theoretical content but as practice and social affiliation.

Jalāl al-dīn Bukhārī's variety of religiosity is also representative of a particular moment in South Asian Sufism. Bukhārī lived a century and a half after one of the most influential figures in the history of Sufism: Muḥyi al-dīn ibn al-ʿArabī (d. 1240), the great Andalusian theorizer of *waḥdat al-wujūd* or Unity of Being. Ibn al-ʿArabī's ideas became hugely popular in South Asia, such that much of Sufi thought since the fifteenth century has been dominated by debates over the validity of the theory of *waḥdat al-wujūd*.[6] During Bukhārī's lifetime, however, these ideas were barely beginning to be known in South Asia, though they had already spread throughout the Middle East.[7] Instead, it was the writings of a contemporary of Ibn al-ʿArabī, Shihāb al-dīn

Suhrawardī (d. 1235), especially his handbook *ʿAwārif al-maʿārif*, that formed the core curriculum for most aspirants on the Sufi path in fourteenth-century India.[8] If Ibn al-ʿArabī exemplifies the creative edge of Sufi thought, flirting with heresy and antinomianism, Suhrawardī represents institutionalized Sufi practice, built on a diligent adherence to the Sharīʿa and an accommodation of secular powers. Bukhārī, whose primary affiliation was to Suhrawardī's eponymous lineage, followed the latter model in his teaching and practice.

Such a rigid commitment to legalistic accuracy combined with a lack of interest in mystical ecstasy and speculative thought might suggest a sober and down-to-earth personality. Yet, Bukhārī did not live in a world devoid of enchantment. A central element of his worldview was a belief in the concrete efficacy of prayers and amulets, in the miraculous powers of saints, and in the presence of jinns and other supernatural beings. His autobiographical anecdotes recount communications from distant or dead saints and encounters with jinns, and his teaching included instruction in the use of particular prayer formulas to achieve practical goals. The later hagiographical tradition further expanded on this theme to recount more dramatic tales in which Bukhārī performs such feats as causing fish to leap from the sea, ready-cooked for his disciples to eat, and striking people dead or bringing them back to life.

Bukhārī did not himself produce a body of written work, neither poetry nor prose, mostly leaving it to his disciples to write down his teachings. He did not promulgate any new systems of either Sufi thought or practice. And yet, he continues to be one of the pantheon of famous South Asian Muslim saints, recognizable as "Makhdūm-i jahāniyān Jahāngasht" to most Pakistanis. Every account of South Asian Sufism or the history of the Delhi Sultanate mentions him, at least in passing. His name appears in the spiritual genealogies of Sufi saints throughout the Indian sub-continent, and his descendants continue to be prominent figures in Pakistani politics and culture. Though Uch, the city of his birth and his tomb, has dwindled over the centuries to little more than a dusty and provincial town, it still holds a place in the national consciousness as the city of saints, "Uch Sharif" (Uch the Noble), one of whose quarters is Uch Bukhāriyān.[9]

How did Jalāl al-dīn Bukhārī earn his place in the illustrious list of the most important saints in the region? One approach to this question would look to the hagiographic legends that grew up posthumously around his name, legends of a miracle-working saint who magically circled the earth seven times and converted numerous local tribes to Islam. That is not the approach of this book. Instead, I attempt to reconstruct Bukhārī's life and career from the earliest sources in order to discover how he achieved or earned the respect of his contemporaries during his own lifetime, thus laying the ground for a devotional cult that has lasted seven centuries.

In trying to tell the story of a medieval figure, from a limited number of sources, one might be tempted to extract whatever biographical information and anecdotes there are to be found and piece them into a coherent whole, explaining away discrepancies or choosing between alternate versions of events. Historiographical concerns would, of course, require some judgment of the relative reliability of textual sources and the plausibility of events. The problem with such an approach is that it presumes that it is possible to draw a clear line between the reliable and unreliable, to winnow the grains of historical fact from the chaff of hagiographical legend. My approach, though necessarily engaging in some broad judgments of this kind, is somewhat more complex. In reading the available sources, I have attempted to pay close attention to questions of genre and narrative context. For example, the concerns of dynastic chronicles are not those of Sufi hagiographies, and the differences in their depictions of a single event have a logic worth exploring. Furthermore, biographical anecdotes serve particular pedagogic and illustrative functions within Sufi texts and oral Sufi teaching. Thus, to view the existence of alternate narratives, contradictions, and implausible events as simple markers of "unreliability" is to overlook the ways in which such moments of textual difficulty are, in fact, windows onto the underlying concerns and themes of medieval Sufism. In writing this book, I have also attempted to make visible my process of reading these sources, so that the discussion of hermeneutical questions and genre concerns is not cordoned off to the realm of footnotes but is woven throughout the text.

The primary sources for this biography are the extensive records (*malfūẓāt*) of Jalāl al-dīn Bukhārī's teaching compiled by his disciples. *Malfūẓāt* were a popular form of Sufi writing in medieval South Asia in which a disciple would record his master's daily teaching sessions, discourses, and other activities.[10] In the immediacy of such a representation, *malfūẓāt* texts preserve both the intellectual content of medieval Sufi teaching and an image of the daily life of a Sufi master and his circle of disciples. Furthermore, the biographical information in *malfūẓāt* is not limited to the period in a shaykh's life observed by his amanuensis. In order to illustrate their points, Sufi shaykhs frequently recounted events from their lives, or those of their masters. Thus, as part of their teaching discourses they presented an autobiographical narrative, however fragmentary and focused on key moments in their careers.

Bukhārī's *malfūẓāt* are, by and large, authentic—that is, written by a named disciple in close contact with the living shaykh rather than posthumously imagined. In this they differ from some of the *malfūẓāt* of earlier saints whose authorship is doubtful and whose content is a retrospective reconstruction. The hermeneutical problem presented by Bukhārī's *malfūẓāt*, then, is not of tracking the development of a hagiographical legend over time but of understanding the context and purpose of Bukhārī's self-narration and his disciples' observation. Often, biographical and autobiographical anecdotes in *malfūẓāt* serve two related purposes. The first is the didactic function mentioned above: the illustration of ethical norms or religious truths through recounting the observed actions or words of past masters, either the disciple's observation of Bukhārī or Bukhārī's observation of his spiritual masters. The other function is the demonstration of Bukhārī's authority as a Sufi shaykh, and therefore the authenticity and importance of the teachings preserved in the *malfūẓāt*. This is demonstrated, on the one hand, through the disciple's depiction of Bukhārī's pious, saintly, or scholarly actions, and, on the other hand, through Bukhārī's recounting of his training and authorization at the hands of his own teachers and Sufi guides, whose religious status is again demonstrated through illustrative anecdote. While the biographical information in the *malfūẓāt* is thus limited to particular themes, this is the information most valuable for my purposes: the discovery of what it took—in terms of personality, activity, and authorization—to become a recognized religious authority in this context.

The use of hagiography as historical source material is notoriously problematic. In the case of *malfūẓāt*, this problem is complicated by the subject's own involvement in the hagiographical process—that is, Bukhārī's self-representation in the tropes of sanctity. His autobiographical narratives are, to a large extent, "autohagiographical" narratives, highlighting his own piety and spiritual greatness. *Malfūẓāt* are also quite different from other Sufi hagiographical genres, particularly the biographical dictionary or *taẕkira*, in their contemporaneity with their topic and reliance on mostly first-hand observation.[11] Yet, the *malfūẓāt* do share the problem that material and information are selected and shaped to serve the purpose of demonstrating sanctity. We might therefore suspect that the topoi of the stereotypical saint's life irredeemably distort or disguise the biography of the historical individual. Though true of many accounts contained in the *taẕkira*s, this would be an overly pessimistic assessment of the *malfūẓāt* based on a simplistic view of the relationship between text, life, and stereotype. We use the phrase "the life of a saint" to refer both to the text that records it and to the life that was lived. It is both of these that are shaped by models of sanctity. Someone like Bukhārī would consciously live his life, make choices, and pursue his career in conformation with certain standards of piety and religiosity, that is, models of sanctity. Furthermore, insofar as his actions and personality were recognized as pious and saintly by others, the particular contours of Bukhārī's life become a new example of sanctity, thus modifying or adding to pre-existing topoi. And, of course, the disciples who authored the *malfūẓāt* also played a crucial and creative role in the ongoing construction of sanctity by finding Bukhārī's life and teachings (or certain aspects of them) worthy of being recorded.

Finally, though the lives of saints as depicted in the *taẕkira*s do tend to blend into the generic, authentic *malfūẓāt* texts are remarkable for the very recognizable individuality and the detailed specificity of the figures they record. One reason for this is that the collective veneration of deceased saints embodied in the *taẕkira*s is quite different from the relationship of a *murīd* (aspirant) with his *pīr* (guide) reproduced in the *malfūẓāt*. The *pīr-murīd* relationship lay at the heart of medieval Sufi practice and was indispensable for any aspirant on the Sufi path. A *murīd* was expected to love and obey his *pīr* and treasure every moment in his presence and every word spoken by him. Since this is the attitude that underlies the writing of *malfūẓāt* by a disciple, the *pīr*'s words and deeds were recorded with as much fidelity and specificity as possible. The inclusion of every detail of time and place, of names of people present, of books read, of trivial conversation, can make *malfūẓāt* tedious reading. But these elements also make them treasure troves of historical information.

There are seven extant texts described as Bukhārī's *malfūẓāt* compiled by his immediate disciples. Four of these, *Khizānat al-fawā'id al-Jalālīya*, *Jāmi' al-'ulūm*, *Tuḥfat al-sarā'ir*, and *Sirāj al-hidāya*, have served as the source for most of the biographical information presented in this book.[12] *Khizānat al-fawā'id al-Jalālīya*, organized into topical chapters, was compiled by Aḥmad Bhaṯṯī in Uch during the 750s/1350s and 760s/1360s. It has never been printed but a number of manuscript copies are preserved in the British Library and libraries in Pakistan and India.[13] *Jāmi' al-'ulūm*, also known as *Khulāṣat al-alfāẓ-i jāmi' al-'ulūm*, is a day by day record of Bukhārī's ten-month stay in Delhi in 781/1379–1380 by Sayyid 'Alā' al-dīn Ḥusaynī. An edition of *Jāmi' al-'ulūm* by Sajjād Ḥusayn was published in 1987 by the Indian Council of Historical Research. Another edition by Ghulām Sarwar was published in 1992 by the Iran Pakistan Institute of Persian Studies.[14] *Tuḥfat al-sarā'ir* is a much shorter text, recording Bukhārī's discourses over a single week in 777/1376. It contains some interesting variations on the information from *Khizānat al-fawā'id al-Jalālīya* and *Jāmi' al-'ulūm*.[15]

Besides *Jāmi' al-'ulūm*, the only other compilation of Bukhārī's *malfūẓāt* to have been published is *Sirāj al-hidāya*, also edited by Sajjād Ḥusayn and brought out by the Indian Council of Historical Research in 1983.[16] Although *Sirāj al-hidāya*'s length and range of topics should make it a valuable resource and it does contain some incidents not found in the other texts, I have some reservations about its claim to directly represent Bukhārī's teachings. On one hand, it contains several contradictory accounts of its authorship and transmission—one of which also appears as the preface of a wholly different text.[17] On the other hand, it is largely consistent with Bukhārī's worldview and religious attitudes as represented by the other *malfūẓāt* collections, especially with respect to the texts quoted in it. I suspect that *Sirāj al-hidāya*'s core teachings do derive from Bukhārī and his disciples but that they have gone through several layers of transmission and transformation before acquiring their current textual form. Bukhārī's other *malfūẓāt* have been of less value for a number of different reasons. *Khizāna-yi jawāhir-i Jalālīya* consists largely of prayer formulas and instructions.[18] I have not been able to access the single incomplete manuscript of *Manāqib-i Makhdūm-i jahāniyān* at the Asiatic Society of Bengal. For further discussion of these texts, see Appendix B.

Much of the history of South Asian Sufism, especially in studies with a broad temporal sweep, has been derived from *tazkira* texts. A very large number of these biographical dictionaries of saints' lives were produced in South Asia, particularly during the Mughal period, usually with a focus on a specific region or Sufi lineage. Although I have drawn upon the *tazkira* entries about Bukhārī, his antecedents, and his disciples, I have treated the information contained in these texts with greater suspicion than my reading of the *malfūẓāt* and have tried to maintain a clear distinction between these two types of sources. One simple basis for this distinction is that while Bukhārī's *malfūẓāt* were compiled during his lifetime, the earliest *tazkira* entry on him (in Jamālī's *Siyar al-'ārifīn*) dates from the early sixteenth century, more than a hundred years after his death.[19] Thus, regardless of the veracity of the historical or biographical information in either set of texts, the relevant *tazkira*s are products of a later time period and therefore cannot illuminate or represent fourteenth-century Sufi thought and practice in the same manner as Bukhārī's *malfūẓāt*. Furthermore, most of the biographical information about Bukhārī in the *tazkira*s is derived from the *malfūẓāt* texts, sometimes in the form of direct and acknowledged borrowing, and other times through the development of a dramatic tale from the kernel of a brief remark in one of the *malfūẓāt* texts. Finally, to do justice to any single *tazkira* text would require trying to understand the vision of sainthood, Sufi history, Sufi lineages, Indo-Islamic history, and so on, that governs the structure of that text and its choices of organization, inclusion, and emphasis. Such a holistic approach is at odds with my concentration on a single figure and, again, would be more useful to the study of the time period of the *tazkira*'s composition rather than of the eras of the saints whose lives it is narrating.

Jalāl al-dīn Bukhārī has been the subject of two Urdu monographs, *Makhdūm-i jahāniyān Jahāngasht* by Muḥammad Ayyūb Qādirī[20] and *Tazkira-yi ḥazrat sayyid Jalāl al-dīn Makhdūm-i jahāniyān Jahāngasht* by Mirzā Sakhāwat,[21] both published in the early 1960s. Besides collecting much of the available information about Bukhārī from the hagiographical and historical traditions, Qādirī's work is invaluable for its detailed listing of all the *malfūẓāt* devoted to the saint and all the writings attributed to him. Although both works bring together much useful information on Bukhārī, they suffer from an overreliance on a limited range of sources and a sometimes uncritical approach to those sources, especially the *tazkira*s. Another flaw, present to a greater degree in Sakhāwat's biography though still noticeable in Qādirī's, is an unquestioned attitude of pious respect towards their subject. This leads not only to a credulous attitude towards the praises heaped on Bukhārī by his disciples and hagiographers but also to an interpretation of his personality that best fits twentieth-century Pakistani expectations for the true Sufi saint. Thus, for example, Qādirī describes Bukhārī as an indefatigable missionary for Islam to the largely Hindu population.[22] My investigation of the sources has not found much evidence to support this depiction.

Turning to scholarship in Western languages, one is struck by the absolute paucity of information about Jalāl al-dīn Bukhārī. *Encyclopaedia of Islam* contains a brief entry by Bazmee Ansari, and there are various references to Bukhārī in general works such as S. A. A. Rizvi's two-volume *History of Sufism in India*, Annemarie Schimmel's *Islam in the Indian Subcontinent*, Bruce Lawrence's *Notes From a Distant Flute*, and K. A. Nizami's numerous articles on pre-Mughal South Asian Sufism.[23] Here too, it is largely the *tazkira* tradition that has shaped Bukhārī's image. The one exception to this rule is the extensive use of Bukhārī's *malfūẓāt* by Riazul Islam in his *Sufism in South Asia: Impact on Fourteenth Century Muslim Society*.[24]

Lahore
Multan
Ajūdhān
Bhatnēr
Uch
Delhi
Bhakkar
Lucknow
Sehwan
Kichawcha
Jawnpur
Thatta
Iraj
Kara
Bihar
Lahārī
Sonargaon
Sarangpur
Ahmadabad
Chittagong

South Asia

PART ONE

The Education of a Sufi Shaykh

ONE

Initiation into the Sufi Path

By the time of his death in 784/1384, Makhdūm-i jahāniyān Sayyid Jalāl al-dīn Bukhārī[1] was a widely respected Sufi shaykh and a recognized authority on Islamic religious practice and the Islamic intellectual traditions. Bukhārī's later status was largely a product of his learning and Sufi affiliations. However, such acquired qualifications worked in concert with his inherited social status and group identity. Birth was insufficient to determine the ultimate place of an individual in society, but it was an important factor. As Roy Mottahedeh points out in his discussion of Iraqi society in the fourth/tenth and fifth/eleventh centuries, an individual's pedigree included both "biological ancestry" and the noble deeds of his ancestors. "The great majority of men took a man's genealogy, and the stockpile of honorable deeds that he inherited, into consideration both in estimating that man's capacities, and in assigning him a station in society."[2] Besides such an inherited social status, however, this principle also influenced an individual's choices in life, since he might feel compelled to live up to the nobility of his ancestors. Bukhārī's life can be seen as an example of this process.

Family Background

Genealogy

Jalāl ad-dīn Bukhārī was born in 707/1308 to a family with a definite social identity and status: sayyids (that is, descendants of the Prophet Muḥammad), originating in Bukhara, settled in the town of Uch, and affiliated with the Suhrawardī Sufi order. Bukhārī's grandfather, also named Sayyid Jalāl al-dīn Ḥusayn and known as Shēr Shāh Jalāl Surkh (or Surkh-pōsh), had emigrated to India from Bukhara sometime in the early thirteenth century. Unfortunately we have little reliable information about Jalāl Surkh and must depend upon somewhat contradictory sources from several centuries after his death. Furthermore, the identical names of grandfather and grandson have understandably caused some confusion in popular legend, such that tales told of one figure have become attached to the other. To the best of our knowledge, Jalāl Surkh was born in 595/1198 in Bukhara to a family that traced its descent to ʿAlī al-Hādī, the tenth imam of the Twelver (Imāmī) Shiʿa.[3] This family lineage also served as the chain of transmission for the *khirqa* (Sufi robe) with which Jalāl Surkh was initiated into the Sufi path by his own father, ʿAlī Abū al-Muʾayyad.

The family's descent from the Shiʿa imams and their use of the name Ḥusayn have lead to the suggestion that they were, in fact, Shiʿa.[4] Today, some branches of the Bukhārī family, including the one in control of the family tombs in Uch, identify as Imāmī (Twelver) Shiʿa, while others are Sunni. Support for the suggestion that Jalāl Surkh was Shiʿa can be found in *Maẕhar-i Jalālī*, a putative collection of his teachings and one that refers to him by the very Shiʿa title of Ḥaydar-i ṣānī (the second ʿAlī).[5] In contrast, his grandson Jalāl al-dīn Bukhārī Makhdūm-i jahāniyān presents himself as very definitely Sunni in his *malfūẓāt*; while his teachings contain a great veneration for the family of the Prophet and especially for the twelve Imams, it was the Sunni Ḥanafī creed that he taught and practiced. When asked by members of the sayyid community in Medina about his *maẕhab*, he answered, "the *maẕhab* of Abū Ḥanīfa, along with all my forefathers in Bukhara,"[6] thus asserting not only his own identification with Ḥanafism but also that of his whole lineage. Bukhārī's remarks on the Shiʿa identity of most of the sayyids that he met in Mecca and Medina, especially his use of the derogatory term *rawāfiż* (turncoats), assume that Shiʿism is foreign to himself and his audience.[7] Furthermore, Bukhārī was extravagantly praised by the historian Żiyāʾ al-dīn Baranī, a strident anti-Shiʿa bigot, and patronized by Sultan Fīrōz Shāh Tughluq, who boasted of suppressing and humiliating his Shiʿa subjects.[8]

Could the Bukhārī sayyids have been secretly Shiʿa, practicing *taqīya* (dissimulation) to avoid persecution? Might Jalāl al-dīn Bukhārī's statements be purposefully misleading? While this would be difficult to reconcile with Bukhārī's career as a very public and erudite expert in the Sunni scholarly and religious traditions, it is not impossible. Devin Stewart has documented numerous cases of Shiʿa legal scholars participating in the "Sunni legal system," mostly through public affiliation with the Shāfiʿī *maẕhab*.[9] During the 740s/1340s when Bukhārī was in Arabia, he studied with several leading Shāfiʿī scholars. Furthermore, as exemplified by his statement quoted above, it seems that he was obliged to answer questions about his sectarian affiliation from various sides, suggesting that his contemporaries were not always certain of his Sunni identity. At any rate, whether it was a matter of conversion or of coming out of the Sunni closet, the family's Shiʿa identity dates from after the eleventh/seventeenth century.[10]

Although the Bukhārī family's illustrious genealogy did not necessarily indicate a sectarian Shiʿa affiliation, it did place the family into a specific social category, that of sayyids (descendants of the Prophet Muḥammad through his daughter Fāṭima). Being a sayyid was a significant aspect of Bukhārī's public identity; in his *malfūẓāt*, he is often called *sayyid al-sādāt* ("sayyid of sayyids" or "master of sayyids") and eulogized for the purity of his descent. Sayyids constituted and, in some parts of the world, continue to constitute a high-status group among Muslims, associated with religious learning, piety, and charisma.[11] In eighth-/fourteenth-century India, the status of sayyids was formally recognized by the Delhi Sultanate. According to Ibn Baṭṭūṭa, sayyids and other religious dignitaries, such as judges, scholars, and Sufi shaykhs, took the "principal place" at Muḥammad bin Tughluq's royal banquets, ahead of his own relatives and the nobility.[12] One of the examples of Fīrōz-shāh Tughluq's piety, listed by the historian Żiyā' al-dīn Baranī, was his generosity to sayyids, as well as the 'ulama, Sufis, and other religious figures.[13]

It is worth noting that in these examples sayyids are listed with religious professionals, even though, as a group, they had no defined social or religious function and might in fact, as individuals, have careers as scholars, judges, or Sufi shaykhs. That is, since a sayyid is categorized by his or her blood descent while the other categories are defined by professional qualification, there is obviously opportunity for overlap and, as mentioned above, the religious careers were considered particularly suitable for sayyids. Many of the great South Asian Sufi shaykhs were said to be of sayyid descent, including most of the early Chishtī masters: Mu'īn al-dīn Chishtī, Quṭb al-dīn Bakhtiyār Kākī, Niẓām al-dīn Awliyā,' and Naṣīr al-dīn Maḥmūd Chirāgh-i Dihlī.[14] To this day, there is an assumption in South Asian Muslim communities that any saint or holy person is most likely a sayyid.

In the case of Jalāl al-dīn Bukhārī the status and label of sayyid tended to trump other acquired labels, a pattern found in other figures of the fourteenth and fifteenth centuries. One minor indicator of this is the seeming inalienability of the title sayyid from the name of any figure with the right to bear it, for example, Sayyid 'Alī Hamadānī, Sayyid Ashraf Jahāngīr Simnānī, Sayyid Gīsūdarāz. In general, medieval South Asian Muslim culture was quite flexible as to which elements of a person's name would be highlighted or forgotten, paying scant attention to the classical Arab distinctions of *ism* (personal name), *laqab* (honorific), patronymic, and so on. According to those distinctions, our subject would be more appropriately referred to as Ḥusayn or Abū 'Abdallāh or Ibn Aḥmad rather than Jalāl al-dīn Bukhārī. Furthermore, Sufi shaykhs and saints were given a plethora of hyperbolic titles and nicknames by their disciples such as *makhdūm-i jahāniyān* (served by the inhabitants of the world), *sulṭān al-mashā'ikh* (king of shaykhs), *shaykh al-akbar* (greatest shaykh), *quṭb-i 'ālam* (axis of the world). Yet, despite all this creativity and flexibility, we rarely find the name of a descendant of the Prophet without sayyid preceding it.

In order to preserve the purity of their lineage, sayyids frequently practiced endogamy—for a sayyida this was the only appropriate marriage since a Muslim, especially Ḥanafī, woman may only marry an equal or a better. Although the information on Jalāl Surkh's life is sketchy and despite the general neglect of women in medieval Sufi texts, the sources are careful to mention that all of his wives were sayyidas. His first wife, whom he married in Bukhara and by whom he had two sons, Awḥād al-dīn 'Alī and Ja'far, is variously described as belonging to a family of Medinan sayyids and as the daughter of Sayyid Qāsim Bukhārī.[15]

Given the nature of the sayyids as an endogamous descent group, with a fixed status above others, and a religious justification for this status, it is unsurprising that attempts to identify caste or a caste-like system among South Asian Muslims have

Table 1: Genealogy of the Bukhārī Sayyids

Muḥammad
|
ʿAlī ibn Abī Ṭālib
|
Ḥusayn
|
ʿAlī Zayn al-ʿĀbidīn
|
Muḥammad al-Bāqir
|
Jaʿfar al-Ṣādiq
|
Mūsā al-Kāẓim
|
ʿAlī al-Riżā
|
Muḥammad al-Jawād
|
ʿAlī al-Hādī
|
Jaʿfar al-Murtażż al-Āʿẓam
|
ʿAlī al-Ashqar
|
ʿAbdallāh
|
Aḥmad
|
Maḥmūd
|
Muḥammad
|
Jaʿfar
|
Abū al-Muʾayyad ʿAlī — Sayyid Badr al-dīn Bhakkarī

Jalāl al-dīn Ḥusayn Bukhārī Surkh :: Zahra :: Fāṭima — Dawla

Ṣadr al-dīn Muḥammad — Aḥmad Kabīr :: [daughter]

[daughter] :: Jalāl al-dīn Ḥusayn — Ṣadr al-dīn Muḥammad Rājū-qattāl

frequently listed sayyids as the highest caste.[16] However, the question of whether caste exists among Muslims is a vexed one whose answer depends on how caste is defined. And though it might be analytically useful to view sayyids in the context of caste, it would be unwarranted to take this as an example of the influence of Indic traditions on Islam, since sayyids have been a high-status group in many different regions of the world. Furthermore, unlike Hindu caste systems, sayyids do not form part of an overarching hierarchical scheme theoretically incorporating all of society. In some ways, they stand out as a unique phenomenon in Islam: a pan-Islamic descent group maintaining its status in a range of Islamic societies, each of which is made up of various competing social classes, factions, and ethnicities.

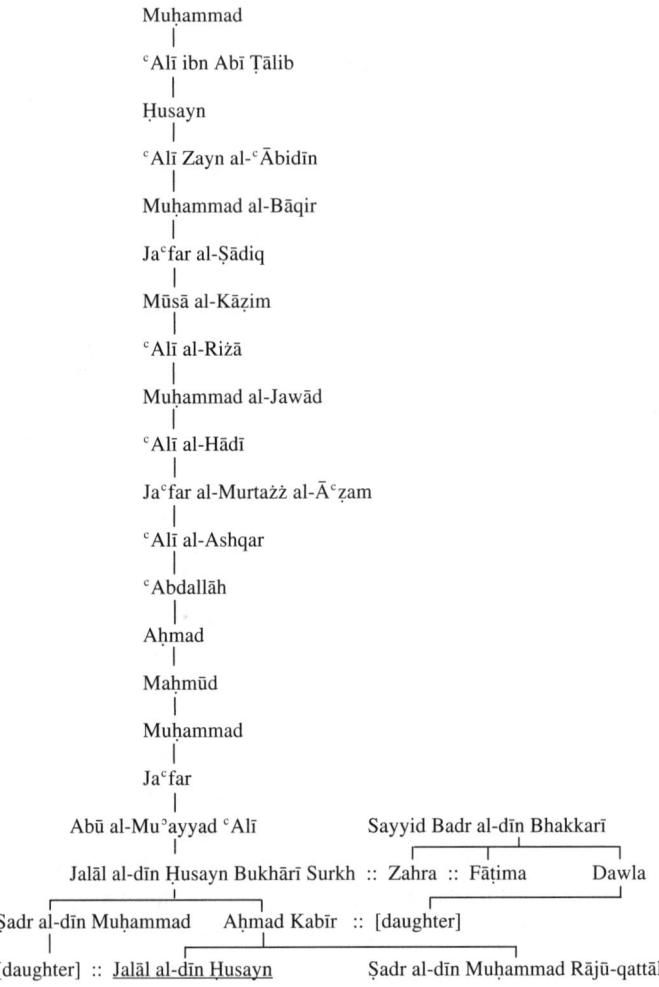

Sacred Geography

Though we have no definite information on the dates or motivations for Jalāl Surkh's emigration from Bukhara, it is probable that, like so many others, he fled the destruction and upheaval brought by the Mongol invasions of the 620s/1220s. He is said to have visited the holy cities of Mecca, Medina, and Mashhad before arriving in South Asia. His two eldest sons accompanied him to India but later returned to Bukhara.[17] In India, Jalāl Surkh first lived in Bhakkar (near the modern towns of Sukkur and Rohri in Sind), where his relative Sayyid Badr al-dīn Ḥusaynī was settled. Badr al-dīn gave him his daughter in marriage. According to one account this was in obedience to the Prophet Muḥammad's instructions given in a dream. The match lead to a rift with Badr al-dīn's brothers and Jalāl Surkh's departure from Bhakkar.[18] Another account gives the bride's name as Zahra and states that after her untimely death Jalāl Surkh married her sister Fāṭima.[19] The couple had three sons: Ṣadr al-dīn Muḥammad, Aḥmad Kabīr, and Bahā' al-dīn.[20] From Bhakkar, Jalāl Surkh moved to Multan to attach himself to the Suhrawardī saint Bahā' al-dīn Zakarīyā (577–661/1182–1262). Various dates are reported for his discipleship and his initiation into the Suhrawardī path; 'Abd al-Ḥayy Lak'hnawī asserts that this took place in 635/1237, but according to *Sawāl ō jawāb*, Jalāl Surkh came to Multan when the Sultan of Delhi was trying to conquer Thatta and Bhakkar. That would suggest the 650s/1250s when Sultan Nāṣir al-dīn b. Iltutmish (r. 644–664/1246–1266) was attempting to quell the Sumra tribe in Sind.[21] At any rate, Jalāl Surkh was eventually instructed by his spiritual mentor to move to the town of Uch, where he spent the rest of his life and where his tomb is still a site of devotional activity.

Today, Multan and Uch are part of the Pakistani province of Punjab, while Bhakkar is in Sind. At the time, however, the whole valley of the Indus and its tributaries, from Multan down to the sea, was referred to as Sind in contrast with Hind (the Gangetic plain and by extension northern India as a whole). Sind had been the first region in the sub-continent to come under Islamic rule with the Arab invasion in 92/711 and the ancient towns of Multan and Uch were both conquered by the 'Umayyad general Muḥammad bin Qāsim. Multan was also among the first cities taken by Maḥmūd of Ghazni in the early fifth/eleventh century and subsequently remained a significant possession of the Ghurids and the Delhi Sultans. By the eighth/fourteenth century, therefore, Multan and Uch had been under Muslim domination for over six hundred years and had become significant centers of Islamic learning and culture. As the two most important cities of upper Sind, they served as the administrative and political centers for their regions, although Uch was sometimes politically and culturally dominated by Multan. Control of these territories was a plum assignment for an ambitious military leader, one often given to a close relative or ally of the Sultan. The great distance from Delhi allowed local governors to rule with significant independence and, in times of dynastic instability, to either rebel, make a bid for the imperial throne, or play kingmaker.

In many respects, Uch was a frontier town, at the western edge of the territories of the Delhi Sultans, its location both profitable and perilous. On the one hand, Uch benefited from lying on a major route down the Indus valley to the Arabian Sea or west across the Indus to the Bolan Pass. On the other hand, it was also vulnerable to the depredations of the Mongols, who laid siege to Uch repeatedly during the seventh/thirteenth and eighth/fourteenth centuries. Furthermore, the authority of the Delhi Sultans grew increasingly tenuous southward from Uch, especially below the traditional Indus crossing at Bhakkar. Throughout this period the Sultans made repeated attempts at crushing the independence of the Samma and Sumra tribes of Thatta, but they were never able to achieve stable control over lower Sind for very long.

Jalāl Surkh settled in Uch on the directive of his *pīr* Bahā' al-dīn Zakarīyā, the famous saint of Multan, from whom he had received initiation into the Suhrawardī order.[22] Bahā' al-dīn Zakarīyā was a disciple of Shihāb al-dīn Abū Ḥafṣ 'Umar al-Suhrawardī (d. 632/1234) of Baghdad and the most significant representative of the Suhrawardīya lineage in thirteenth-century South Asia.[23] Jalāl Surkh was one of numerous disciples attracted to Bahā' al-dīn's wealthy *khānqāh* in Multan; the most famous is perhaps the Persian poet Fakhr al-dīn 'Irāqī. Under Bahā' al-dīn's leadership and that of his successors, the Suhrawardīya became the most prominent Sufi lineage in Sind during the pre-Mughal period. Just as Uch was often subject to Multan's authority in the political realm, so too was this the case in the spiritual realm—the city's two most important *khānqāh*s were each headed by a *khalīfa* of Bahā' al-dīn Zakarīyā or his descendants. This relationship between the Sufi establishments of the two cities was carried forward in successive generations, so that Jalāl Surkh's son, Aḥmad Kabīr, and grandson, Jalāl al-dīn Bukhārī, were disciples of Bahā' al-dīn's son, Ṣadr al-dīn 'Ārif (d. 684/1286), and grandson, Rukn al-dīn Abū al-Fatḥ (d. 735/1334–1335). Sind's most popular saint, 'Us̱mān Marwandī (Lāl Shāhbāz Qalandar, d. 673/1274) whose tomb at Sehwan attracts hundreds of thousands of pilgrims annually, is also described as a disciple of Bahā' al-dīn though any reliable information on his life is lost in legend.

The dominance of Bahā' al-dīn Zakarīyā and his successors in Sind was not just a matter of popularity or visibility but of perceived spiritual power over the territory and its inhabitants. Sufism in South Asia has often appropriated the language and symbolism of monarchic rule so that, for example, saints are referred to as kings and princes (*shāh*, *sulṭān*, *mīr*), and their tombs and hospices as courts (*darbār*, *dargāh*). The bestowal of an initiatory robe (*khirqa*) on a disciple parallels the bestowal of a robe of honor (*khil'at*) by a ruler on a vassal, and a saint's heirs struggled for control over his seat (*sajjāda*, *gaddī*), just as a ruler's heirs might contend for his throne. Just as the reign of a temporal king extended over a certain territory with rival powers ruling beyond the borders of his kingdom, so too did the powers of a saint.

The idea of a spiritual territory was expressed through one of the two possible words for sainthood, that is one of the two vocalizations of the abstract noun derived from *walī* (Ar. saint or friend, plural *awliyā'*): *walāyat* and *wilāyat*. *Walāyat* is usually understood as implying intimacy: sainthood as closeness to God. *Wilāyat*, in contrast, indicates power and authority and is often used in political contexts to mean rule or the geographical area being ruled. In the Sufi context, then, *wilāyat* is sainthood as power and the geographical extent of that power. Along these lines, Jalāl al-dīn Bukhārī explained *walāyat* as *maḥbūbiyat* (being beloved) and *wilāyat* as *taṣarruf fī 'l-aqālīm* (power over regions).[24] Saints, sainthood, and saintly miracles will be discussed in greater detail in Chapter 5. At this point, it is sufficient to note that the primary regional aspect of a saint's powers was the miraculous ability to protect it and its inhabitants from harm. The corollary of this was that the inhabitants of a region should logically seek the protection and guidance of its reigning saint. Thus, for example, when asked for protective amulets (*ta'wīẕ*) to lay in the four corners of a house, Bukhārī wrote them using the names of Bahā' al-dīn, Ṣadr al-dīn, Rukn al-dīn, and Jamāl al-dīn (a disciple of Bahā' al-dīn settled in Uch). If Bukhārī made a *ta'wīẕ* for someone from Sind he wrote Bahā' al-dīn Zakarīyā's name. But if it was for someone from Hind, Bukhārī wrote the name of the Chishtī saint Farīd al-dīn Mas'ūd (Bābā Farīd Ganj-i-shakar, d. 1265), thus demonstrating the zones of influence of each saint.[25]

According to Bukhārī, the *wilāyat* of Bahā' al-dīn Zakariyā' extended to Khurāsān.[26] Most of India, however, was the *wilāyat* of Farīd al-dīn Mas'ūd. The boundary between the two territories lay at Ajūdhān (modern Pakpattan), where Farīd al-dīn is buried, and at Udaypūr, presumably the modern city of Udaipur in Rajasthan. These territories were inherited by their successors so that Rukn al-dīn Abū al-Fatḥ, Bahā' al-dīn's grandson, became master (*mutaṣarrif*) of Sind and the Chishtī shaykh Naṣīr al-dīn Maḥmūd (Chirāgh-i-Dihlī, d. 757/1356) master of Hind.[27] This mapping of the Suhrawardī saints' *wilāyat* is obviously partisan in its extension of their territory all the way to distant Khurāsān and right up to the centers of Chishtī activity in Ajūdhān and Rajasthan where Mu'īn al-dīn Chishtī (d. ca. 630/1233), the eponymous founder of the Indian Chishtī lineage, is buried at Ajmer. But while the devotees of the Chishtī saints might have quibbled about where to draw the line, the general principle of an identifiable boundary between these territories was accepted by the Chishtīya as well.

Despite the rivalry between the Chishtī and the Suhrawardī lineages, later popular legend imagined Farīd al-dīn Mas'ūd and Bahā' al-dīn Zakarīyā as working together for the protection of the region. One indication of their place in the local sacred landscape is their appearance in Wāriṣ Shāh's famous eighteenth-century Punjabi romance, *Hīr*. In strophe 82 Wāriṣ Shāh identifies the *panch pīr*, the five tutelary saints venerated under different names throughout South Asia, as Khwāja Khiżr, Shakar-ganj, Zakariyā' of Multan, Sayyid Jalāl al-dīn Bukhārī, and Lāl Shāhbāz.[28]

In this list, Sayyid Jalāl al-dīn Bukhārī probably indicates the elder of that name, Jalāl Surkh, though it is possible that his grandson is meant. Khiżr is the secret deathless guide mentioned in the Quran, while the other three saints are foundational figures associated with the presence of particular varieties of Sufism in Pakistan: Lāl Shāhbāz ('Uṣmān Marwandī) is patron of the radically socially deviant *qalandar*s and *malang*s, Bahā' al-dīn Zakariyā' (d. 1262) brought the Suhrawardī order to India and was known for his wealth and political contacts, and Farīd al-dīn Mas'ūd Ganj-i shakar (d. 1265), the great Chishtī ascetic and poet, fled the ambit of the capital to live in the wilderness with his disciples. In this list, the geographical underpinning of these saints' power is apparent: the saints' respective tombs are strung in a row down the Indus valley from Pakpattan on the banks of the Sutlej River, to Uch and Multan at the confluence of the rivers of the Punjab, to Sehwan in lower Sind. The rivers, especially the Indus, are themselves personified by Khwāja Khiżr, master of the waters.

Hereditary Sainthood?

After Jalāl Surkh's death on 19 Jumādā I 690/20 May 1291, his tomb, *sajjāda* (prayer rug), and *khānqāh* passed into the hands of his son Sayyid Aḥmad Kabīr. Aḥmad Kabīr married a woman from the Bhakkarī sayyid family, that is, a maternal cousin, and had two sons, Jalāl al-dīn Ḥusayn and Ṣadr al-dīn Muḥammad Rājū-qattāl, both of whom went on to become Sufi shaykhs.[29] The pattern exemplified by the Bukhārī family and by the saintly dynasty of Multan is frequently, and somewhat misleadingly, understood as "hereditary" succession. Although affiliation with a Sufi order and advancement on the Sufi path were theoretically voluntaristic pursuits enabled by individual capacity and dedication, family traditions of Sufi participation also exerted a strong influence. However, while family affiliation with a Sufi order made it more likely that an individual would take on the same identity, descent from a well-known saint was neither a necessary nor a sufficient condition for succession to the same status. Thus, in contrast to the above example, the most widely recognized lines of spiritual succession in the Chishtī order in this period were not by biological descent.

Strictly speaking, the only aspect of Sufism automatically heritable by blood descendants and other legal heirs was real estate or other tangible property: ancestral tombs and shrines, *khānqāhs*, and religious paraphernalia such as prayer rugs. However, even for property such as this the laws of inheritance did not automatically apply or were preempted. Many Sufi establishments, like other religious institutions, were categorized as *waqf* (endowment) and therefore not governed by the same inheritance laws as private property. In that case trusteeship was often assigned, in perpetuity, to the descendants of the founding figure but succession might also be left to the discretion of the current holder. A Sufi establishment, especially one that attracted the donations of numerous pilgrims or had significant income-generating property, could provide its possessor with a very handsome living. At the same time, the maintenance of such a site, the hosting and feeding of pilgrims, and the organization of ritual activities were serious and time-consuming responsibilities. Regardless of personal inclination, inheritance of such responsibilities was likely to encourage participation in Sufi practice and cement one's Sufi identity and affiliation.

Religious paraphernalia, too, were usually not treated as normal household goods. In particular, the *sajjāda* of a saint was understood to be imbued with his *barakat* (spiritual blessing or grace) and as a symbol of his religious authority. The *sajjāda*, along with similar holy objects such as prayer beads (*tasbīḥ*), was therefore usually bestowed on a spiritual successor by the living saint rather than being treated as ordinary property. Possession of these objects, especially the *sajjāda*, was often used by a saint's disciples and/or his children to demonstrate and establish spiritual preeminence in the next generation.

Investiture into the Sufi Path

Unlike his inherited status as a sayyid, Jalāl al-dīn Bukhārī's affiliation with Sufism was ritually transmitted to him; *khirqa*s (Sufi robes) of the Suhrawardī lineage were bestowed on him in his youth by his father, Aḥmad Kabīr, and his uncles, Ṣadr al-dīn Muḥammad and Awḥād al-dīn ʻAlī.[30] Over the course of his life, Bukhārī was invested with the *khirqa*s of six different lineages by nineteen Sufi masters, as well as receiving permission (*ijāzat*) to invest others with them. A *khirqa* was not necessarily an actual robe; the term was used for any garment ritually bestowed by a shaykh, usually a hat (*kulāh*). And since *khirqa*s might be received in dreams or visions, there might be no physical garment involved at all. *Khirqa* was also used as shorthand for affiliation with a Sufi order and *khirqa pōshānīdan* (investiture) was the ritual through which that affiliation was created.[31] (For an extended discussion of *khirqa*s, see Chapter 4.)

Bukhārī received his *khirqa* of discipleship from his father, Aḥmad Kabīr, and it was also from him that he learned hadith, thus beginning his education in the traditional Islamic sciences.[32] As we will see, Bukhārī's training as a Sufi aspirant at the hands of various masters was accompanied, at every step of the way, by textual learning. Basic texts on hadith and Islamic law made up the core of his curriculum both as a student and, later, as a teacher. (Most of these texts were in Arabic, a language that Bukhārī would have been taught in addition to Persian, his primary language.) At his father's *khānqāh*, Bukhārī heard *Maṣābīḥ al-sunna*, the well-known compendium of hadith by Baghawī (d. 516/1122), and other texts read by a travelling scholar of law and hadith.[33] He also studied with the *qāżī* of Uch, Bahā' al-dīn ʻAllāma, who taught him portions of Pazdawī's *Kanz al-wuṣūl* and Marghīnānī's *Hidāya*, standard works on Ḥanafī law.[34] The relationship between Bukhārī's education in the texts of legalistic Ḥanafī orthodoxy and his affiliation by investiture with numerous Sufi orders will be discussed in depth in Chapters 3 and 4. At this point, it is sufficient to point out that this textual learning ultimately gave Bukhārī another source of religious authority—in his later years he was sought out for his ability to teach and transmit texts, and his *malfūẓāt* contain copious quotations from hadith and Quran and from works on law, Quranic exegesis, and theology. Education in the central texts of the Islamic religious sciences is a standard element in the biographies of most medieval Sufi shaykhs. For some of them this was merely a necessary preliminary to a Sufi discipleship focused on other matters such as various ascetic and contemplative practices. But for Bukhārī and the individuals who guided him on the Sufi path—Jamāl al-dīn Uchchī, Naṣīr al-dīn Maḥmūd Chirāgh-i Dihlī, ʿAbdallāh Yāfiʿī, and ʿAfīf al-dīn Maṭarī—the study and teaching of such texts remained central to their daily religious practice.

Shaykh Jamāl al-dīn Uchchī

Apart from Sayyid Aḥmad Kabīr's *khānqāh*, there were two other *khānqāhs* in Uch at this time, that of Shaykh Jamāl al-dīn, and that of the Kāzarūnī family.[35] The first of these played a major role in Jalāl al-dīn Bukhārī's early life and education as, besides his father, Jamāl al-dīn Uchchī was his primary teacher. Unfortunately we know little about him other than that he was a *khalīfa* (successor) of Ṣadr al-dīn ʿĀrif Multānī. It seems certain that if he had not had a student as famous as Bukhārī and one as determined to demonstrate his teacher's virtues, he would not be known at all. Though respected enough in his own lifetime to be sent gifts by Sultan Ghiyāṣ al-dīn Tughluq (which he refused), Jamāl al-dīn Uchchī appears in the Sufi hagiographies only as one of Jalāl al-dīn Bukhārī's *pīrs*.[36] In Bukhārī's *malfūẓāt*, he is frequently and affectionately remembered by his disciple as pious, humble, learned, and gifted with mystical insights. According to *Siyar al-ʿārifīn*, Bukhārī was placed under Jamāl al-dīn Uchchī's tutelage at the age of seven.[37] The *malfūẓāt* do not mention the period of their association but the numerous anecdotes about Jamāl al-dīn's teaching circle and the mention of books read with him imply a fairly extensive relationship.

The anecdotes supporting Jamāl al-dīn's piety are fairly typical of South Asian saints, and Bukhārī used them as teaching examples throughout his life. Shaykh Jamāl al-dīn was poor and lived humbly with nothing to offer guests but bread and *rōghan* (ghee). His humility was expressed not only in the simplicity of his dress and eating habits but also in his attitudes towards others. For example, when confronted by threatening *qalandar*s, angry because he offered them only bread, Jamāl al-dīn laid his own head on the dining cloth. Of course, this display of self-sacrifice and humility overcame the *qalandar*s—they dropped the iron skewers with which they were threatening him and fell at his feet.[38] That Jamāl al-dīn Uchchī is known as "Khandān" or "Khandān-rū" (laughing) suggests a cheerful personality to accompany his piety and humility.[39]

Despite this simplicity of life-style, the shaykh accepted offerings (*futūḥ*), at least in his old age, in order to follow the example of his masters (the Multan Suhrawardīs). Much has been made of the acceptance of land and gifts by the Suhrawardīs in contrast to the Chishtīs, and Jalāl al-dīn Bukhārī seems to have been aware of this criticism. He represents Jamāl al-dīn as accepting gifts only out of respect for his predecessors and emphasizes Jamāl al-dīn's acceptance of only legally acceptable, halal items. One reason why accepting gifts was an occasion of sin was the possibility that the gift originated from an unlawful, haram source. Shaykh Jamāl al-dīn never accepted haram property; if he was in doubt he would bow his head in concentration and a voice from God would tell him that the offered item had been made legal for him. His acceptance of gifts is a justification for Bukhārī's later practice of accepting *futūḥ*, as advised by his other teachers, particularly Yāfi'ī and Maṭarī.[40]

Jamāl al-dīn Uchchī's habit of bowing his head and receiving divine guidance is a recurring theme in Bukhārī's anecdotes about him. During his teaching sessions, if the text was unclear Jamāl al-dīn would bow his head and be given the answer by God. Such an interruption in the middle of a lesson could also indicate a more dramatic event. Once during a lesson, Shaykh Jamāl al-dīn put his head down, as if asleep, and when he returned to consciousness he said he had been to Aden, in Yemen, to save a sinking boat. His wet sleeve was the proof of this miracle. During his travels in Aden, Bukhārī was shown where this took place, as well as where Jamāl al-dīn supposedly did his ablutions.[41]

I doubt that Jamāl al-dīn Uchchī ever traveled to Yemen or Arabia—in the waking world. In his *malfūẓāt*, Bukhārī recounted both visionary or miraculous events and "normal" ones. Many of his interactions with his shaykhs, and their contacts with each other, were magical or visionary. Events were marked out as miraculous not only by their physical impossibility but also by the language used to describe them. For example, whenever Bukhārī mentioned meeting a saint in a vision or through the saint's ability to transport himself over vast distances, he said that he "saw" (*dīdam*) the saint.[42] This is not a construction he used for ordinary meetings or conversations.

One of the challenges facing the historian of medieval Sufism is the interweaving of mundane and supernatural occurrences in the lives of the saints and their disciples. The authors of our sources, though reporting both types of events as "real," were fully aware of the difference between a normal, unmarked conversation and one that required a narrative mark as taking place in a dream, in a vision, or in the "world of flight." To ignore these markers and treat all reported events as taking place on the same plane, governed by the usual rules of geography and synchrony, results in historical reconstructions that are neither plausible nor supported by our texts. Another, equally unsatisfactory, modern response to the supernatural events in Sufi sources is to dismiss them out of hand as impossible and therefore fictitious. This results in the peculiar situation in which some portions of a text are relied upon as historical documents while other intimately related portions of the same text are rejected as false, based solely on criteria of plausibility external to the text.

In Bukhārī's *malfūẓāt*, most first-person testimony of supernatural events, whether by the compiler of the *malfūẓāt* or by Bukhārī or by someone else present in his circle, recounts solitary experience, such as dreams or visions or private conversations with jinns and dead or distant saints. Or supernatural intervention is offered as the causal explanation for somewhat unpredictable or uncontrollable events, such as the outcome of a battle or a diplomatic negotiation, the course of an epidemic outbreak, and the arrival or failure of seasonal rainfall. By contrast, the kind of publicly visible and obviously supernatural event that is a central feature of some *tazkiras*—such as causing people to drop dead by glancing at them in a state of rage or concentration, bringing a corpse back to life, and conjuring up cauldrons of food in the wilderness to feed a multitude, along with pavilions to shelter it—is rare in the *malfūẓāt* texts. When it does appear, as in the above case of Shaykh Jamāl al-dīn Uchchī's rescue of a sinking ship, the eyewitness to the event is offstage, so to speak, and the compiler of the *malfūẓāt* is reporting something that neither he nor his direct informant saw happen. Bukhārī saw his teacher lost in concentration and was told by him that he had been in Yemen. Later in life, some unnamed Yemenis seemed to confirm this story, though the lack of detail given makes it difficult to assess the nature of that conversation.

Shaykh Rukn al-dīn Multānī

While Jamāl al-dīn Uchchī is a vibrant presence in Bukhārī's reminiscences, the *tazkira* tradition pays more attention to Bukhārī's association with Rukn al-dīn Abu al-Fatḥ (known as Rukn-i ʿālam). Rukn al-dīn had succeeded to his grandfather Bahā' al-dīn Zakarīyā's position as the head of the *khānqāh* in Multan and as the most well known Sufi shaykh of the region. Because he was a contemporary colleague and rival of Niẓām al-dīn Awliyā,' Rukn al-dīn is frequently mentioned in the *malfūẓāt* and biographies devoted to the latter. In most of the *tazkira*s the Suhrawardī lineage in India is traced through three generations of the Multan family, from Bahā' al-dīn to Rukn al-dīn, and then through the Bukhārī family in Uch with the unspoken assumption that Rukn al-dīn's descendants and other disciples were of less importance. Jalāl al-dīn Bukhārī is usually represented as being one of Rukn al-dīn's primary *khalīfa* and as having received his spiritual training (*tarbīyat*) from him.[43]

By his own account, Bukhārī went to Rukn al-dīn's *khānqāh* in Multan to complete his study of Pazdawī's *Kanz al-wuṣūl* and Marghīnānī's *Hidāya* which had been cut short by the death of the qāżī of Uch. However, because Bukhārī was there to study (*taḥṣīl-i ʿilm* or *ṭalab-i ʿilm*) he was not taken into the *khānqāh* nor was he allowed to eat the food from the *khānqāh* kitchens or property. Instead, Rukn al-dīn placed him under the tutelage of his grandson Shaykh Mūsa and of Mawlānā Majd al-dīn at the madrasa. Bukhārī was housed in a room over the city gates and supplied with food (bread and soup) from Rukn al-dīn's private property.[44] Bukhārī recounted the details of this setup to his disciples, and I repeat them here, because they are illustrative of the relationship between Sufi institutions and the other Islamic sciences. Although it made sense for the young man from Uch to seek to further his education in the larger city of Multan under the guidance of his family *pīr*, and Rukn al-dīn did fulfill his request, this type of textual instruction—the transmission of legal texts—did not fall under the mandate of a Sufi *khānqāh*. The acquisition of *ʿilm*, in the sense of orthodox legal learning, was an important component of a Sufi aspirant's education but it was a distinct activity, set apart institutionally and materially from the spiritual training and discipline that were the purpose of life in a *khānqāh*. By contrast, madrasas were the institutional bases for advanced education in the law, and for the ancillary religious sciences of hadith and Quran scholarship.

Furthermore, Bukhārī was not a common seeker after knowledge to be enrolled as a madrasa student, with room and board at the madrasa. As a sayyid and as the scion of a saintly family with ties of discipleship to Rukn al-dīn's family, he was treated more as a personal guest of Rukn al-dīn and his material needs were met from the shaykh's private wealth rather than through either of the institutions of madrasa or *khānqāh*. Rukn al-dīn instructed his womenfolk to send Bukhārī daily a cup of the same "soup" that that they made for him, containing various fruit cooked in ghee or milk. Bukhārī later recounted this detail as an example of Rukn al-dīn's generosity and affection for him. It was also, however, an occasion for Bukhārī to demonstrate his asceticism, to Rukn al-dīn at the time and to his own disciples when telling this anecdote: Bukhārī never touched the soup. Eventually Rukn al-dīn told the women to stop preparing it for either of them, apparently following Bukhārī's example in limiting his meals to bread.[45]

After about a year in Multan, when Jalāl al-dīn Bukhārī had completed the texts he was studying, Rukn al-dīn sent him back to Uch in a hurry without—as far as I can ascertain—taking him on as a disciple or giving him a *khirqa* or an *ijāzat*. Rukn al-dīn was in such a rush to send him home to Uch that he even lent Bukhārī his own boat for the voyage down the Chenab River. The reason for this rushed trip was that Rukn al-dīn wanted to send Bukhārī's father, Aḥmad Kabīr, an urgent message that he must defer to Jamāl al-dīn Uchchī's authority and put himself in his care. Without Jamāl al-dīn's care, Aḥmad Kabīr's liability to being overcome by *shawq* (desire) would drive him mad (or cause him to become *muwallah*, intoxicated or enraptured). Aḥmad Kabīr obeyed Rukn al-dīn's command and threw himself at Jamāl al-dīn's feet. Jamāl al-dīn told him that when he (Aḥmad) was born his father, Jalāl Surkh, had foretold his propensity for losing control and asked Jamāl al-dīn to take care of him.[46]

This incident makes clear that Sayyid Aḥmad Kabīr was a mystic of a rather different temperament than his son; while Jalāl al-dīn Bukhārī, in his *malfūẓāt* at least, was always sober and scholarly, his father was more emotional and less controlled. (One of the few expressions of deep emotion evinced by Bukhārī and witnessed by his disciples were the tears that ran down his face when he talked about his father.) Bukhārī described Aḥmad Kabīr's vulnerability to *shawq* as a habit of yelling and crying during prayers. A spiritual sensitivity that results in a strong emotional response to religious stimuli could be a valued trait in a Sufi. But it was not a trait that Bukhārī, despite his deep attachment to his father's memory, esteemed highly; he rarely if ever presented anecdotes of ecstatic experience or emotional response as evidence of someone's spiritual greatness. In Aḥmad Kabīr's case, spiritual sensitivity carried the risk of madness and, by requiring Rukn al-dīn's and Jamāl al-dīn's intervention and surveillance, reinforced his inferior position in the local hierarchy of Sufi shaykhs.

At any rate, one definite result of this incident is that Jalāl al-dīn Bukhārī was sent home to Uch, bringing his time under Rukn al-dīn's care to an abrupt and unsatisfying conclusion. While discussing these events with his own disciples, many years later,

Bukhārī remarked that another would-be disciple of Rukn al-dīn was also sent home unsatisfied, that is, without being given a *khirqa*, thus mitigating the unflattering possibility that the shaykh had not singled him out for rejection.[47] This seems to be the extent of Bukhārī's actual (rather than spiritual) relationship with Rukn al-dīn. Although the *malfūẓāt* record a number of anecdotes about Rukn al-dīn and quote his teachings, most of these anecdotes and quotations had been received second-hand by Bukhārī and very few instances are mentioned of their actually being in each other's company. It seems that the actual corporeal relationship between them was quite limited. I suspect that Bukhārī was not directly a *khalīfa* of Rukn al-dīn and that Rukn al-dīn did not, during his lifetime, give him a *khirqa*. No mention is made of any later attempt to spend time with Rukn al-dīn nor, according to the detailed lists in the *malfūẓāt*, did Bukhārī receive a *khirqa* from him during his life.[48] Rukn al-dīn died in 735/1334 but neither his death nor his funeral prayers are mentioned in Bukhārī's reminiscences.

The links between the Bukhārī family and the Multan Suhrawardīs were established by Jalāl Surkh and continued by Aḥmad Kabīr through their affiliation with Bahā' al-dīn Zakarīyā and his son Ṣadr al-dīn 'Ārif. It is logical to expect this series to continue and for Jalāl al-dīn Bukhārī to have been a disciple of, and receive a *khirqa* from, Rukn al-dīn. As mentioned above, in later *taẕkira*s Bukhārī is referred to as a *murīd* (disciple) and a *khalīfa* of Rukn al-dīn.[49] His own grandson, Burhān al-dīn 'Abdallāh (Quṭb-i 'ālam, d. 858 / 1454), also wrote that Bukhārī was Rukn al-dīn's *khalīfa* and that he received a *khirqa* from him in the waking world besides the two given in dreams.[50] This was no doubt the relationship Bukhārī was pursuing by traveling to Multan to study with Rukn al-dīn. However, as described above, Rukn al-dīn farmed him out to other teachers, sent him home as soon as possible, and during the course of his life never gave Bukhārī any *khirqa*s or *ijāzat*s.

It was only in the realm of visions and dreams that Rukn al-dīn truly acted as Jalāl al-dīn Bukhārī's master. It was from the grave that Rukn al-dīn instructed him to respect Tuesdays because Bahā' al-dīn Zakarīyā died on a Tuesday. When Bukhārī was put in charge of forty *khānqāh*s in Sīwistān (in Sind), Rukn al-dīn appeared to him in a vision (*dar wāqi'a*) and told him to flee to Mecca or face destruction. These events I discuss shortly; my point here is that Rukn al-dīn's influence on Bukhārī's life is mostly posthumous. When Bukhārī eventually received a *khirqa* from Rukn al-dīn it was also in a dream in Aden in 748/1347, thirteen years after Rukn al-dīn's death.[51] To point out that Rukn al-dīn was more accessible to Bukhārī as a *pīr* after his death is not to diminish his importance in Bukhārī's life nor Bukhārī's devotion to him and his memory. While he lived, Rukn al-dīn was *the* representative of the Suhrawardī lineage into which Bukhārī had been initiated. After his death, he joined his grandfather Bahā' al-dīn in continuing to be an object of veneration and a source of blessing and spiritual protection for the populace. Even in his old age, at the height of his fame, Bukhārī refused to be labeled a shaykh (master) in his own right, declaring instead that he was merely a representative (*wakīl*) of Bahā' al-dīn and that his disciples were not really his but rather Bahā' al-dīn's.[52]

An Encounter with Muḥammad b. Tughluq and Shaykh Naṣīr al-dīn Awadhī

When Shaykh Rukn al-dīn died in 735/1334, Jalāl al-dīn Bukhārī was twenty-six years old. Shaykh Jamāl al-dīn Uchchī and the Bukhārī elders had trained him in the disciplines of the Sufi path and his education had been supplemented by study with the best Islamic scholars available in Uch and Multan. Bukhārī was well on his way to a career much like his father's: a Sufi master within the local hierarchy of the Suhrawardī lineage in a provincial backwater at the edge of the Sultanate. Sometime in the year 741/1341 or 742/1342, however, Bukhārī was ordered to Delhi and the royal court by Sultan Muḥammad b. Tughluq.[53] This encounter with the Sultan was a turning point in Bukhārī's life, leading to his initiation into the Chishtī lineage by Shaykh Naṣīr al-dīn Maḥmūd Awadhī Chirāgh-i Dihlī, his appointment by the Sultan to official position, and his decision to perform the pilgrimage to Mecca. In his reminiscences in the *malfūẓāt*, Bukhārī used this meeting with the Sultan as a key marker in the narrative of his life and recounted several versions of the event.

An Audience with the Sultan

Muḥammad b. Tughluq, who reigned from 724/1324 to 752/1351, was "the wonder of the age" according to the historian and one-time royal boon companion Żiyā' al-dīn Baranī.[54] "Intellectually gifted and quixotic in personality and politics,"[55] he dazzled the Moroccan traveler Ibn Baṭṭūṭa by his munificence and appalled him with his cruelty.[56] Whether his schemes to introduce a token bronze currency and to move the imperial capital *en masse* from Delhi to the southern city of Dawlatābād were brilliant or foolhardy, they were certainly innovative. Such radical policies made Muḥammad b. Tughluq a target of criticism from various quarters and, combined with famine and military weakness, led to revolts by both peasants and the nobility. The Sufi community, particularly the shaykhs of the Chishtī order, grew disgruntled under his rule, objecting to his harshness, his lack of respect for their independence, his co-optation of their services, and his requirement that they accompany his court on campaign and during its sojourn in Dawlatābād.[57]

The relationship, sometimes hostile, sometimes mutually beneficial, between the major Sufi shaykhs and the Sultans of Delhi has attracted the attention of a number of scholars. Simon Digby has compiled a number of instances of conflict between the Sultans and Sufi shaykhs over who truly owed respect and obedience to the other. There are also instances in which the spiritual authority of the saints was credited with the rise of a particular ruler or the preservation of his realm.[58] Within the accounts of interactions between saints and sultans, it is perhaps useful to distinguish between two different elements. On the one hand, the saints are ascribed the supernatural ability to help, harm, or withstand the power of rulers and armies. Thus their prayers can protect a city from invasion and their disapproval can cause the death or downfall of powerful men. On the other hand, there was a more mundane side to the Sufi shaykhs' relation with secular powers in which they might interact with rulers as advisors or advocates or critics. These two elements, spiritual dominance and mundane political involvement, were intertwined, since whatever personal reverence a ruler might have for a shaykh, he was likely to pay attention to someone venerated by the local population, believed to have miraculous abilities beyond the control of the state, and frequently in control of significant wealth and property. (Of course, that wealth and property was itself a result and sign of elite patronage and popular offerings.)

Whether trying to remain aloof from secular politics or being active participants, the Sufi shaykhs claimed spiritual authority, sometimes over a specific territory or *wilāyat*, and expressed such claims through language, paraphernalia, and ceremony very similar to that used in the royal courts. All of this was "a source of vague and recurrent unease"[59] for kings who might see them as a challenge to the authority of the state and its monopoly on royal symbolism. The Sufi use of distinctive clothing seems to have been particularly objectionable to Muḥammad b. Tughluq.[60] The *khirqa*, so central to the production of Sufi relationships and hierarchies, had a direct parallel in the robe of honor (*khilʿat*) bestowed by rulers on nobles and diplomats.

The most extensive account of Bukhārī's command audience with the Sultan, found in *Khizānat al-fawā'id*, focuses precisely on the issue of ceremonial robes.

> Before he went to Mecca, in the era of the late monarch Sultan Muḥammad Shāh, the master of sayyids [i.e., Bukhārī] said to Shaykh Naṣīr al-dīn Maḥmūd Awadhī, mercy be upon him, "Master, I fear that these days the children of *darwēshes*[61] are being taken out of the *darwēsh* costume and dressed in hats (*kulāh*) and cloaks (*qabā*)."
>
> Shaykh Naṣīr al-dīn dressed [him] in a robe of blessing (*khilʿat-i tabarruk*), a turban (*dastār*) and his own cloak (*bārānī-yi khāṣṣ*). The shaykh said, "Go before the Sultan wearing these clothes so that you will not be taken out of the *darwēsh* garments." He went before the Sultan wearing these clothes.
>
> Responsibility for the role of *shaykh al-islām* of Sind, the Muḥammadī *khānqāh* in Sīwistān [modern day Sehwan], and forty additional *khānqāhs* were assigned to him. When he returned from the camp of the Sultan, he kissed the feet of the shaykh. He said, "The Sultan's command is to serve the *faqīrs* of the area of Sīwistān but I do not have permission (*ijāzat*) from Shaykh al-islām Rukn al-dīn." Shaykh Naṣīr al-dīn said, "From my side there is permission for you to serve the *faqīrs* and to give a *khirqa* if anyone seeks it."[62]

Elsewhere, Bukhārī describes the clothing that the Sultan was imposing on the "children of *darwēshes*" as the "dress of an office-holder" (*jāma-yi kārdārī*), that is, of a state appointee.[63] The threat felt by Bukhārī that he might be re-costumed by the king is thus a threat of being somehow co-opted by the governmental bureaucracy, being put to work in the service of the state. Royal appointment, unlike other kinds of remunerative work (*kasb*), was morally and spiritually problematic because of the often illicit and extortionist sources of the wealth of kings. In using the locution "the children of *darwēsh*es" Bukhārī emphasizes the familial nature of many Sufi identities. Muḥammad b. Tughluq's purposeful negation of this hereditary pattern suggests an interest in preventing the development of saintly dynasties, perhaps a greater threat to the authority of the state than individual charismatic figures.

The power of Sufi vestments to create identity, to challenge royal authority, and ultimately to protect their wearers is apparent in this passage. In this version of events, the primary garment bestowed by Shaykh Naṣīr al-dīn Maḥmūd on Bukhārī is described not as a *khirqa* but as a *khil'at*—an appropriation of the term used for robes conferred by royalty.[64] Through this act of investiture Naṣīr al-dīn Maḥmūd accomplished three things: he reaffirmed Bukhārī's Sufi identity, gave him an affiliation to the Chishtī lineage, and gave him the supernatural protection of objects imbued with saintly power. The robes acted as an amulet (*ta'wīẕ*) deflecting the Sultan's ill intentions. (According to a slightly different account, Bukhārī was protected by the power of a particular prayer formula. Worried about his upcoming audience with the Sultan, he spent the previous night in recitation of this formula.)[65]

Naṣīr al-dīn Maḥmūd and the Chishtī Order

Naṣīr al-dīn Maḥmūd (d. 757/1356) was the leading representative of the Chishtī lineage in northern India at this time. Based in the environs of the capital (his popular nickname Chirāgh-i Dihlī means Lamp of Delhi), he was a popular and influential shaykh although he never achieved the stature of his master Shaykh Niẓām al-dīn Awliyā' (d. 725/1325). As mentioned above, the Chishtīya and Suhrawardīya were the two Sufi lineages with the greatest followings and importance in South Asia during this period, and one of Bukhārī's claims to fame was his initiation, and his ability to initiate disciples, into both. As one source puts it, "*namak-i Chishtīyān dar dēg-i ni'mat-i Suhrawardīyān kardand*" (he put the salt of the Chishtīs into the pot of the grace of the Suhrawardīs).[66] The account of Bukhārī's encounter with Muḥammad b. Tughluq and Naṣīr al-dīn Maḥmūd quoted above is from a chapter in *Khizānat al-fawā'id al-Jalālīya* on Bukhārī's *khirqa*s and *ijāzat*s, therefore its purpose is to tell how he received the Chishtī *khirqa* and *ijāzat*.

Much of the secondary scholarship on Sufism in pre-Mughal India has explored the differences between the Chishtīya and Suhrawardīya orders and has suggested a rivalry between their leading shaykhs. However, I argue that while there may have been disagreements and tensions between individual figures, it is unwarranted to suggest serious, consistent, or long-lasting conflict between the two orders on the whole. Although the Chishtī sources contain criticisms, sometimes implicit, of the Suhrawardī saints of Multan, respectful and even cordial relations were maintained between the shaykhs of the two orders. The territorial understanding of *wilāyat* may have been instrumental in achieving amicable coexistence, as long as there was mutual recognition of the other lineage's sphere of influence.

I have found little evidence of significant theological or philosophical differences, in Bukhārī's lifetime, between the two orders; both relied on Shihāb al-dīn Suhrawardī's handbook of "orthodox" Sufism, *'Awārif al-ma'ārif*, as a primary teaching tool. In practice, the most important distinction, and one which has had the most long lasting effect on South Asian Sufism, lay in the attitude towards the use of music and dance. For the Suhrawardīya, as for most orders claiming a mainstream "orthodox" status, listening to musical instruments and dancing were forbidden except under highly controlled circumstances. The Chishtī shaykhs, in contrast, found these practices to be highly effective aids on the mystical path.[67] (Bukhārī did allow musical performances in his assemblies. For an account of one such occurrence, see Chapter 4.)

Another distinction lay in the attitudes towards the state taken by the early Chishtī and Suhrawardī saints. As Aziz Ahmed writes, echoing K. A. Nizami's argument: "The difference in attitude to the sultan and the sultanate was one of orientation. Should the saint be the sultan's advisor in the guidance of the Muslim state; or should the saint in his own right rule over the spiritual elite and the Muslim intelligentsia, an inward, unworldly rule which did not need the alliance of and did not brook any compromise with the state or its ruler? The Suhrawardīs chose the former path and the Chishtīs the latter."[68] This difference in attitude, to whatever extent it existed, was most apparent in the figures of the great early saints, Bahā' al-dīn Zakarīyā and Farīd al-dīn Mas'ūd. In the three generations separating these two from Bukhārī, however, the conditions of both *silsila*s and their relations with the rulers had changed. Under Niẓām al-dīn Awliyā''s leadership, the center of the Chishtī order had moved to Delhi and thus into closer, though still contentious, interaction with the Sultan. Muḥammad b. Tughluq's policies of attempting to co-opt, undermine, or disperse the Sufi shaykhs had also reduced their independence.

A related issue was the attitude towards wealth and the acceptance of land grants; the Chishtī shaykhs had a policy of refusing land grants and of distributing all donations immediately, while the Suhrawardīs accepted what was given, as long as the source was legitimate, and stored up wealth and grain.[69] This difference is not as important as it may seem; in actuality both orders depended on the patronage of the rich and powerful and both acted as conduits of charity to their local followers. In the case of political entanglements and economic dependence, there was often a gap between statements of principle and the actual activities of individual shaykhs and their establishments.[70]

Furthermore, although members of a Sufi lineage tried to adhere to the teachings and policies of past masters, personal temperament played a significant role in the practices of any individual figure. The shaykhs of the Chishtī lineage, who have been studied in greater depth than any other South Asian lineage, represented a fairly wide variety of personalities. Thus, Naṣīr al-dīn Maḥmūd is known as a sober and scholarly figure, committed to orthodoxy and (perhaps unavoidably) cooperative with the state. His fellow disciple Burhān al-dīn Gharīb (d. 738/1337) was more like their joint *pīr*, Niẓām al-dīn Awliyā,' in placing a greater value on poetry and mystical ecstasy than on traditional scholarship.[71] One cannot, therefore, use affiliation with a particular Sufi lineage as a wholly accurate predictor of a Sufi shaykh's beliefs and practices.

One of the difficulties in assessing the relationship between the Suhrawardīya and the Chishtīya is the ambiguity of the concept of "order" and, perhaps, its inapplicability to Sufi organization at this time. In Bukhārī's *malfūẓāt*, Sufi identity and affiliation are described in terms of a person's *khirqa*, the genealogy of that *khirqa*, and the shaykh who invested him with it. Did this create a corporate identity for all those invested by a particular shaykh or with a *khirqa* of a particular lineage? Would such a corporate identity be distinct from and in rivalry with those invested by a different shaykh or with a *khirqa* of a different lineage? The clearest example, in these sources, of distinction and rivalry is in the description of territorial *wilāyat*s. These *wilāyat*s, however, are described not as Suhrawardī territory and Chishtī territory but rather as the territories under the protection of Bahā' al-dīn Zakariyā' and Farīd al-dīn Mas'ūd, respectively, and of their successors. In other words, the line that is being drawn is not exactly between the members of two lineages or orders but between the protective power of two saints of the previous century.

Bukhārī's investiture with the Chishtī *khirqa* by Naṣīr al-dīn Maḥmūd is in itself an indication that, at least at this point in time, there was no insurmountable distance between the two orders. This investiture, as well as Bukhārī's later investiture with the *khirqa*s of the Kāzarūnī, Rifā'ī, Qādirī, and Kubrawī lineages, can also be seen as a symptom of a widespread change in the Sufi landscape of India. During the eighth/fourteenth century the pattern of Chishtī and Suhrawardī dominance and mutual exclusivity declined and was replaced by a greater variety of Sufi lineages and the rising importance of further regions of the Indian sub-continent. In the east, Shaykh Sharaf al-dīn Aḥmad b. Yaḥyā Manērī brought fame to the Firdawsī order in Bihar, in the north Sayyid 'Alī Hamadānī brought the Kubrawī lineage to Kashmir, and in the south the Deccan became the new center of gravity for the Chishtīya.[72] Furthermore, while some of Bukhārī's contemporaries and successors followed his pattern of acquiring *khirqa*s from numerous shaykhs and lineages, this practice is not apparent in the careers of Sufis of the previous generation. In general, biographical reports on the shaykhs of the seventh/thirteenth and early eighth/fourteenth centuries highlight their relationship with a single *pīr*. Accounts of figures from the mid-eighth/fourteenth continue to stress this primary relationship, but they also frequently record multiple *khirqa* investitures and carefully identify the various lineages and shaykhs from whom these *khirqa*s are derived.

Seemingly protected by the amuletic powers of Naṣīr al-dīn Maḥmūd's robe and a prayer formula, Bukhārī emerged unscathed from this encounter with Muḥammad b. Tughluq. On the contrary, his stature as a Sufi shaykh was recognized and confirmed by the Sultan's appointment of him as a *shaykh al-islām* in Sīwistān. *Shaykh al-islām* was the title given to the representative or head of the Sufi community at the royal court in Delhi but in Bukhārī's case probably signified no more than a similar position at the provincial or regional level.[73] That Muḥammad b. Tughluq demanded his presence in Delhi shows that Bukhārī must have already been a figure of some local importance, probably simply by virtue of being heir to the leading Sufi family of Uch. As the next in a line of Sufi shaykhs it made sense for him to be put in charge of the Sīwistān *khānqāh*s. In making such an appointment, Muḥammad b. Tughluq was following his usual policy of attempting to control or co-opt the Sufi community; this may also have been part of an attempt to integrate the rebellious region of Sind into the bureaucratic structures of the Sultanate. The position of *shaykh al-islām*, whether on a local or imperial level, was a royal appointment and a part of the bureaucracy, but it did not appear to carry quite the same negative implications and temptations for sin as a more secular post.

Bukhārī's quandary about not having permission from Rukn al-dīn "to serve the *faqīrs*" arose from the fact that Sīwistān fell under that shaykh's *wilāyat* and Bukhārī had not been made one of his *khalīfa*s with a *khirqa* and *ijāzat*. Bukhārī may have already received permission from his father to invest others with the Suhrawardī *khirqa*, but this was clearly insufficient authorization for the position offered by Muḥammad b. Tughluq. Naṣīr al-dīn Maḥmūd's permission (*ijāzat*) seems to have filled this lack, as well as accomplishing a great deal more. This *ijāzat* was not only permission to take up the post of *shaykh al-islām* and take charge of the forty *khānqāh*s. It was, in fact, also an *ijāzat* in the more technical sense of authorization to bestow the Chishtī *khirqa* on others—in other words, authorization for Bukhārī to act as a shaykh of the Chishtī lineage. This is evidenced by the placement of this anecdote in the context of a list of Bukhārī's *khirqa*s and *ijāzat*s and by his statement that he later received a written version of this *ijāzat*, at a point in his life when the question of this particular royal appointment was moot.[74]

In his *malfūẓāt*, *Khayr al-majālis*, Naṣīr al-dīn Maḥmūd remarked that if a shaykh meets someone else's disciple who has "traversed the path and reached the level of perfection," then he can give that disciple permission to initiate disciples into his (the shaykh's) lineage.[75] This was presumably his rationale for giving Bukhārī an *ijāzat*. Elsewhere, Bukhārī recounted a conversation in which he asked Rukn al-dīn about the legitimacy of one ascetic or scholar making another into a *khalīfa* and instructing him to take the oath of allegiance (*bay'at*) from people, without the other's *pīr*'s permission. Rukn al-dīn categorically replied that if one receives *bay'at* without the *pīr*'s permission, one becomes a *kāfir* (unbeliever). However, if another *pīr* gives his permission, one may "serve the people."[76] Later in life, Bukhārī did pass on the *khirqa* of the Chishtī order when it was requested by his disciples but this was not his standard practice: for every Chishtī investiture he bestowed ten times as many Suhrawardī *khirqa*s. He continued to consider himself primarily a member of the Suhrawardī order and followed the Suhrawardī practice of accepting gifts and of (mostly) rejecting music and dance.

Departure from India

At this point in Bukhārī's life, however, the question of initiating disciples was made irrelevant by his decision to leave India rather than taking charge of the Sīwistān *khānqāhs*. According to Bukhārī's statements in *Jāmi' al-'ulūm*, after Muḥammad b. Tughluq appointed Bukhārī *shaykh al-islām*, Shaykh Rukn al-dīn appeared to him in a dream or a vision. Rukn al-dīn told him to flee or else he would be destroyed and instructed him to go on hajj. Responsibility for the forty *khānqāhs* in Sīwistān put him in danger of becoming proud. Bukhārī took his *pīr*'s advice and left immediately, despite having no provisions for the journey, not even a horse or donkey.[77] In the end, then, while royal patronage of Sufi institutions might have been preferable to other forms of state interference in religious life, to accept such patronage and to take up a position of economic and political influence carried grave moral dangers for a Sufi aspirant. In his own self-estimation and in his visionary perception of Rukn al-dīn's opinion, Bukhārī had not yet achieved the spiritual perfection and discipline that might protect him from these dangers. Though the political and spiritual authorities of Delhi may have decided that Bukhārī was ready to be *shaykh al-islām*, his own *pīr* Rukn al-dīn had died before giving him permission to do so.

The various versions in Bukhārī's *malfūẓāt* of his meeting with the Sultan and his subsequent departure for Arabia make different points—that Bukhārī had a Chishtī *khirqa* and *ijāzat* from Naṣīr al-dīn Maḥmūd, that a certain invocation is effective, that one's *pīr* continues to guide one after death—but they all agree in their condemnation of Muḥammad b. Tughluq. Even his appointment of Bukhārī to a religious post was a threat to be fled. Bukhārī never lost his negative attitude towards Muḥammad b. Tughluq; four decades later, in 781/1379–1380, he refused to visit the Sultan's tomb while he was in Delhi. Nor would he visit the tomb built by Muḥammad b. Tughluq for Rukn al-dīn in Multan.[78] As a venerable and venerated Sufi master Bukhārī could afford to show his disapproval of a deceased monarch, but as a junior figure in the Sufi hierarchy, faced with the demands of a living and rather tyrannical ruler, he had few options other than flight.

Some time around 742/1341–1342, at the age of thirty-five, Bukhārī set out for Arabia. He spent the next seven years in the holy cities of Mecca and Medina before returning to his native Uch by 749/1348. This is the voyage that gave Bukhārī his title of Jahāngasht, world-wanderer, and set him apart from many of his contemporaries as one who had performed the hajj and studied with the scholars and saints at the sacred center of the Muslim world.

With Bukhārī's departure from India the first section of his career came to an end. He had been initiated into the Sufi order with which his father and grandfather were affiliated and had received a traditional education in the normative texts of Ḥanafī Sunni Islam. His contacts with the two great shaykhs of the 730s/1330s, Rukn al-dīn Multānī and Naṣīr al-dīn Maḥmūd Chirāgh-i Delhi, had enhanced his spiritual pedigree and given him legitimacy within both the Suhrawardī and Chishtī lineages, providing a life-long source of prestige and anecdote. Bukhārī had achieved a stature within the local religious hierarchy sufficient to warrant the attention of the state; the Sultan's appointment of him to a semi-official position was at once a recognition and confirmation of his religious authority and an attempt to co-opt it.

The narrative I have developed thus far from Bukhārī's reminiscences in the *malfūẓāt* texts is a rather predictable trajectory for the scion of a saintly family in fourteenth-century South Asia: initiation, education, and a gradual rise in stature. What is missing is a sense of Bukhārī's individuality as a person and as a Sufi. This absence is partly a result of the silences in the texts which focus so exclusively on his attainment of the markers of religious authority—*khirqa*s, texts, and contact with saints—that they make no mention even of the large scale events that must have impacted Bukhārī's life. For example, the Mongols invaded the region and laid siege to Uch several times in the first few decades of the 700s/1300s and the global Black Death pandemic struck northern India between 736/1335 and 739/1338,[79] but these disasters play no role in Bukhārī's reminiscences about his youth, as recorded by his disciples. On a more personal level, Bukhārī was married and possibly a father before he left for Arabia but neither wives nor children are mentioned until much later in his life.

Some of the generic quality of Bukhārī's early career, however, arises from the fact that many of his particular characteristics as a Sufi master and as a religious scholar were developed during his time in Arabia. In the *taẕkira* tradition of hagiographic dictionaries, Bukhārī is distinguished from other pious and learned saints of his time by a) his travels and b) his investiture with numerous *khirqa*s at the hands of shaykhs whom he met during those travels. Bukhārī's travels were fairly limited, as will be discussed in the next chapter, but they inspired fictitious travelogues (*safar-nāma*) as well as giving him his title of Jahāngasht. Bukhārī's *malfūẓāt* stand out from similar contemporary works by the emphasis they place on legal material, quoting extensively from *fatāwā* compilations and citing legally relevant hadith. Rukn al-dīn Multānī and, to an even greater extent, Naṣīr al-dīn Maḥmūd are both known as *bā-shar*ʿ Sufis ("with the Shariʿa," as opposed to *bī-shar*ʿ, "without the Shariʿa" or heterodox). Yet their careers and personas were clearly those of spiritual guides instructing their disciples in Sufi thought, practice, and ethics, and of publicly acknowledged saints providing their devotees with blessings, protection, and intercession. Bukhārī, in contrast, came much closer to blurring the boundary between a Sufi *pīr* and an *ʿālim*, a scholar of law and hadith. In this, he resembled more closely the scholars and Sufis with whom he associated in Mecca and Medina than his early masters.

TWO

Pilgrimage and Travel

According to the various travelogues ascribed to Jalāl al-dīn Bukhārī, he truly deserved the title Jahāngasht (world-wanderer). In these tales, besides performing the hajj, Bukhārī roamed from one end of the Muslim world to the other, from Egypt to Kashmir, from Mount Sarandīb (Adam's Peak in Sri Lanka) to Mount Sinai to Mount Qāf, the mythical mountain range that encircles the earth.[1] Somewhat more soberly, the *tazkira* texts limit his destination to the holy cities of Mecca and Medina and assert that he traveled there and back several times. On some of these voyages he is said to have been accompanied by his disciples, up to 12,000 of them, whom he fed by causing fish to leap into the ship or cauldrons of food to appear.[2] In comparison to such tales, Bukhārī's own account of his travels, though starting dramatically with such a hasty departure on foot from Sīwistān that the blisters on his feet received no relief until he arrived at the spring in Medina,[3] is rather tame. According to my reconstruction from the *malfūẓāt* texts, his most significant and perhaps only travels were a single voyage that lasted seven years, from 742/1341–1342 to 749/1348, during which he visited Mecca, Medina, Aden, Shiraz, and Kāzarūn.

As the *malfūẓāt* texts record comments made during teaching sessions, the information on Bukhārī's travels is limited to anecdotes illustrative of some moral or spiritual point or describing his acquisition of knowledge, *ijāzat*s, and *khirqa*s. Teachers, books, and *khirqa*s are highlighted while there are rarely any descriptions of places or everyday life. Sometimes Bukhārī mentions the religious practices of different regions but only to correct practices prevalent in South Asia. A much more vivid description of places, customs, and the means of travel is provided by Bukhārī's close contemporary, the great Moroccan traveler Ibn Baṭṭūṭa (703–770/1304–1369) whose itineraries in Arabia, Iran, and India overlapped significantly with Bukhārī's route. Ibn Baṭṭūṭa's account of his travels is exceptional; the vast majority of the numerous travelers within the medieval Islamic world, be they merchants, pilgrims, or "seekers of knowledge," made little attempt at recording their observations. Ibn Baṭṭūṭa left his home in Tangiers in 725/1325 and spent the next thirty years traveling through Asia and Africa. For our purposes here, it is not Ibn Baṭṭūṭa's famous expeditions to the far reaches of Muslim settlement in Southeast Asia and Sub-Saharan Africa, nor his embassy to

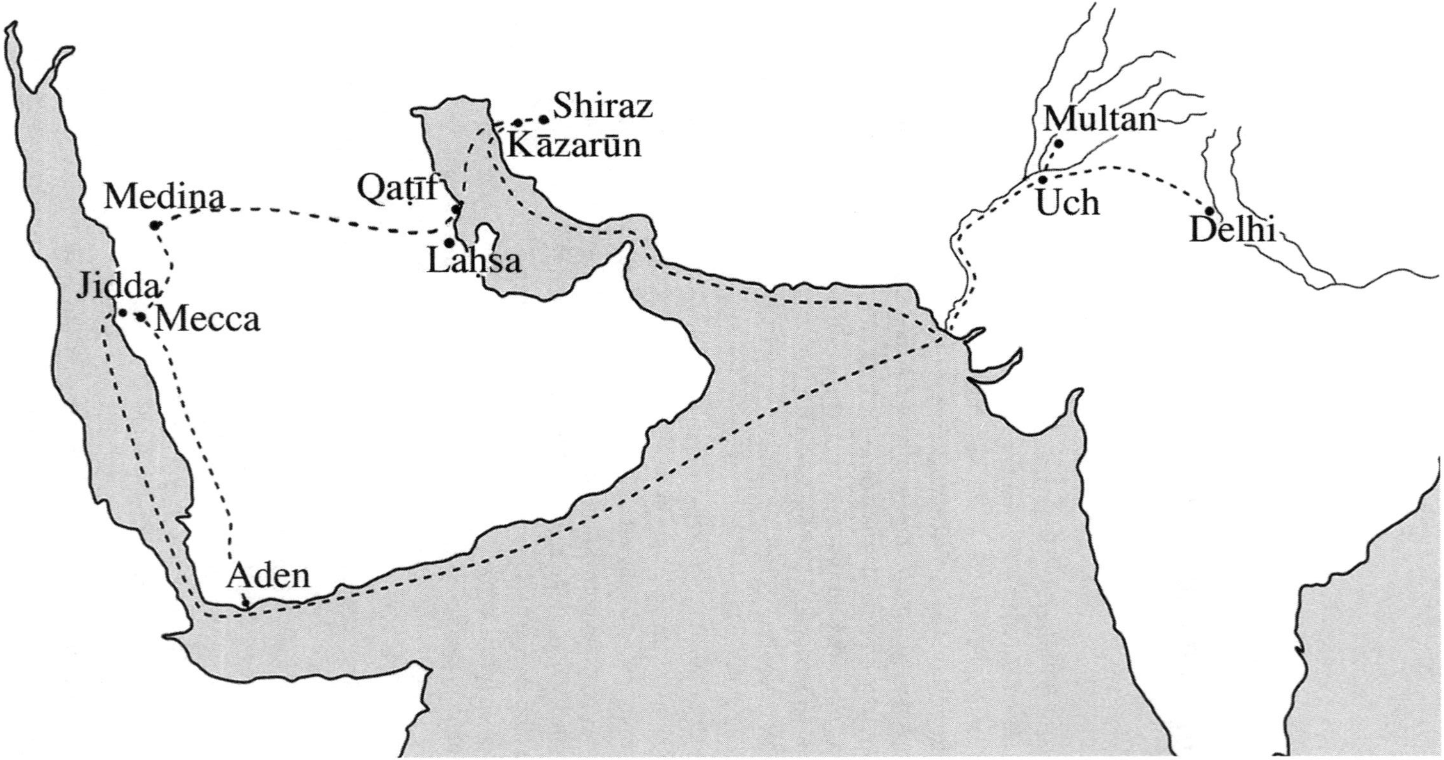

Jalāl al-dīn Bukhārī's Travels

China, nor even his travels in India, where he passed through Uch and spent some years in Delhi in service to Muḥammad b. Tughluq, that are of greatest relevance. Rather it is his descriptions of Mecca and Medina, of his travels in southern Iran, and of his routes by land and sea between these places and Sind that are of value in fleshing out the sparse anecdotes provided by Bukhārī's *malfūẓāt*.[4]

From Ibn Baṭṭūṭa's narrative it is possible to reconstruct Bukhārī's probable route to Mecca. Since Bukhārī mentions no places between Sīwistān and the Hejaz, I assume he went by sea, probably setting sail at Lahārī, a port city in the Indus Delta frequented by Yemeni merchants. From here he would have sailed to Aden and then perhaps up the Red Sea to Jeddah (which is where Ibn Baṭṭūṭa tried to find a ship to take him in the other direction to India).[5] The primary destinations of Bukhārī's travels were the holy cities of Mecca and Medina, often collectively referred to in the *malfūẓāt* texts as *ān ṭaraf-hā* (those places; over there). He remained in the Hejaz for six years and seems to have traveled several times, sometimes by foot, between the two holy cities.

The Arabian Context

In the *malfūẓāt* texts, Bukhārī's autobiographical remarks and the anecdotes with which he illustrated his teachings give a prominent place to these few years spent in Arabia. When criticizing or correcting the religious practices of Muslims in South Asia, he would contrast them with reference to the model of Meccan and Medinan practice (and sometimes to the practices of Yemen and the Persian cities he visited). When explaining a textual or doctrinal point he often commented on the enhanced value of this particular teaching (and that his disciples should write it down) because it was little known in India and he had learned it "over there." The *malfūẓāt* also emphasize the fact that his personal interactions in Arabia and his studies there were all carried out in Arabic; in recounting his conversations with the shaykhs of Mecca and Medina, Bukhārī usually quoted their statements (and his own) in Arabic and then translated them into Persian for the benefit of his disciples and students. The use of Arabic in such cases creates a linguistic bridge between these anecdotes and the extensive discussions and explanations of Arabic texts, hadith, Quran verses, and prayer formulas, within which these anecdotes are embedded. In other words, the religious prestige of Arabic as the language of scripture, prayer, and religious scholarship is thus carried over to Bukhārī's relationships in Arabia. Bukhārī (and the authors of his *malfūẓāt*) are also reminding the audience of his greater learning; *he* could converse easily in Arabic while many of his disciples and the readers of his *malfūẓāt* need Persian glosses.

Bukhārī's stay in the holy cities is also highlighted in the biographical entries on him in the *taẕkiras*. In the *malfūẓāt* and the *taẕkira* texts, Bukhārī's personal experience of life in Mecca and Medina, his association with the scholars and Sufi shaykhs of the cities, and his observation of Islamic practice there serve as a source for his own teachings and religious practice and as legitimation for his authority to instruct and guide others. Such a use of Arab models (and, to a lesser extent, of Iranian ones) of true Islamic practice might not strike us as noteworthy, given our current assumption, both popular and academic, of the centrality of the "Middle East" to the world of Islam. However, this was not necessarily the obvious attitude to take at the time. As the fundamental shrines of Islam, Mecca and Medina were immensely important to Muslims everywhere. As a meeting point for pilgrims, many of whom were religious scholars, the cities were the locale for significant exchanges of information, ideas, and texts. Furthermore, they were the stage on which the Prophet, his Companions, and the early generations of Islam performed the exemplary actions that later Muslims were supposed to imitate. But none of this necessarily made the habits of the *contemporary* residents of Mecca and Medina an authoritative guide to "true" Islam. The dominant expressions of Islam in medieval South Asia, Ḥanafī law and Sufism, both relied upon authoritative examples from the *past*: a textual tradition traced back through Central Asian and Iranian models to earlier centuries, the teaching and practices of earlier saints and scholars, and, of course, ultimately the example of the Prophet, his family, and his Companions.

I do not wish to overemphasize Bukhārī's appeals to contemporary Arab and Persian models; they are relatively infrequent in comparison to his use of past authorities. He also limits his references to the ʿulama, the Sufis, and other religious functionaries, such as muezzins, rather than the populace at large. But I suspect that such references were part of a developing construction of Islamic religious geography and India's place in it. Ibn Baṭṭūṭa's experience in India attests to the welcome given by the Sultans of Delhi to traveling scholars and Sufis, valuable sources of religious expertise and bearers of the latest intellectual developments in the rest of the Muslim world. By correcting local practice through comparison with Arab practice and by quoting the shaykhs and ʿulama of Mecca and Medina to answer questions posed by his disciples, Bukhārī's teachings suggest a contrast between the ignorance of South Asian Muslims and the knowledge of the religious authorities of West Asia.

The Sharifs of Mecca and Medina

The use of Mecca and Medina, in particular, as models of Islamic practice was made complicated by the fact that the dominant elements in their native populations were adherents of Shiʿism or at least Shiʿa sympathizers. Throughout the medieval period the two cities were ruled by local dynasties of *sharifs*, or sayyids in South Asian parlance, Ḥasanid in the case of Mecca and Ḥusaynid in Medina. Both the Ḥasanid Sharifs of Mecca and the Ḥusaynid Sharifs of Medina were mostly Shiʿa, Zaydī (Fiver) Shiʿa in the former case and Imāmī (Twelver) in the latter. Weakened by internal power struggles and ongoing rivalries with each other, neither emirate was strong enough to maintain independence from its more powerful neighbors. Richard Mortel describes Medina under the Ḥusaynid Sharifs as "a bedouin state, with an unstable political structure and a primitive economy."[6] In the eighth/fourteenth century, it was the Mamlūk empire of Egypt that dominated the region, challenged from the south by the Rasūlids of Yemen.[7]

Like other contemporary witnesses, Bukhārī remarked on the prevalence of Shi'ism in Mecca and Medina, especially amongst the sharifs, except for residents whose origins lay elsewhere. He contrasted the Shi'a affiliation of the sharifs of Arabia and Yemen with the Sunnism of most sayyids of Khurāsān and Hindūstān. Bukhārī seemed particularly struck by the possibility of difference in sectarian affiliation between a ruler and his subjects, mentioning that though the king (*pādshāh*) of Mecca and Medina was Shi'a, he was under the authority of the Sunni caliph of Egypt (that is, the 'Abbāsid caliph under the protection of the Mamlūk sultan).[8] Another example of this phenomenon given by Bukhārī was the Sunni king of Hormuz who appointed Sunni governors to rule over his Shi'a subjects in the eastern Arabian oases of Laḥsā and Qaṭīf and the islands of Bahrain.[9] The Shi'a communities in these areas belonged in part to the Ismā'īlī Qarmaṭī sect and in part to the Imāmīs[10] but Bukhārī does not remark on their sectarian specificities, nor on those of the Zaydīs of Mecca or the Imāmīs of Medina. Instead he uses the derogatory label of *rawāfiż* (turncoats, heretics) for all of them, indiscriminately.

Bukhārī's description of the "*rawāfiż*" communities of Arabia is interesting given the suspicion that he himself may have been Shi'a and concealing this allegiance from his disciples and audience. The obvious way to read these statements is as evidence of his staunch Sunnism and of his indifference to the sectarian particularities of the Shi'a. In that case, he was regaling his disciples with the oddity of distant and exotic lands where descendants of the Prophet are heretics, Sunni rulers have Shi'a subjects, and Shi'a rulers accept Sunni caliphs. On the other hand, if his repudiation of the "*rawāfiż*" was disingenuous, then perhaps he was drawn to the possibility represented by Sunni rulers who seemed more tolerant, though still disapproving, of their Shi'a subjects than his own sovereign, Fīrōz Shāh Tughluq.

Bukhārī described his contacts with the sharifs in the context of doing *ziyārat* (pilgrimage other than the hajj) to the Prophet's garments in their possession. He also went to their madrasa in Medina where he observed that they adhered strongly to the Quran and hadith. He introduced himself as a kinsman and upon being questioned about his *maẕhab* (legal school) identified himself as a follower of Abū Ḥanīfa. He then proceeded to puzzle them with a legal problem to which they had no response, although neither did the (Sunni) 'ulama and *fuqahā'* of Mecca.[11] (Such anecdotes of intellectual triumph, especially upon entering a new environment, are a recurrent motif in the biographies and hagiographies of medieval scholars and Sufis.) This account is in many ways typical of Bukhārī's activities while in the Hejaz: visitation of holy sites and relics, including the Ka'ba and the tombs of Muḥammad and his son Ibrāhīm, combined with engagement with scholars and scholarly pursuits.[12]

Shāfi'ī Scholars and Sufis

Bukhārī's interaction with the sharīf community was fairly limited. Instead, the figures with whom Bukhārī associated most closely were a number of Shāfi'ī scholars and Sufi shaykhs, particularly ʿAbdallāh b. Asad al-Yāfiʿī (ca. 698–768/ca. 1298–1367) and ʿAfīf al-dīn ʿAbdallāh al-Maṭarī (698–765/1299–1364). Maṭarī was the muezzin of the Prophet's mosque in Medina and appears in the biographical dictionaries primarily as a transmitter of hadith and a hafiz (one who knows the Quran by heart).[13] Yāfiʿī, a native of Aden in Yemen, was probably the most famous person with whom Bukhārī associated during his travels.[14] He was a prolific writer and a well-rounded scholar, his books covering a range of Islamic religious topics, including Sufism, Quran recitation, theology, and sectarian differences. Much of his most important work dealt with the lives of scholars and Sufis of the past. His *Mirʾāt al-jinān*, an annalistic biographical dictionary focused on Shāfiʿī scholars and Sufis, continues to serve as a valuable source for historians.

Yāfiʿī and Maṭarī, as well as many of the other figures with whom Bukhārī associated in Arabia, belonged to an identifiable circle of scholarly Sufis, none of them native to the Hejaz. Other members of this circle, each of whom invested Bukhārī with a *khirqa*, were Najm al-dīn ʿAbd al-Raḥmān al-Iṣfahānī (677–750/1278–1349) and two of Yāfiʿī's teachers and shaykhs, Jamāl al-dīn Abū ʿAbdallāh Muḥammad b. Aḥmad al-Dhuhaybī "Faqīh Baṣṣāl" (d. 748/1347) and Nūr al-dīn ʿAlī b. ʿAbdallāh al-Ṭawāshī "Ṣāḥib Ḥālī" (d. 748/1347), both of Yemen. Each of these figures combined the role of a Sufi shaykh with that of an *ʿālim*—a teacher and scholar of the core religious sciences: hadith, law, Quran, and so on. As mentioned before, Maṭarī was known as a transmitter of hadith and a hafiz; Iṣfahānī is described by Yāfiʿī as a *muftī* and a *mudarris* (teacher) whose areas of scholarship included law, the seven readings of the Quran, mathematics, and Arabic; and Dhuhaybī's nickname of Faqīh Baṣṣāl indicates legal expertise (as well as the profession of selling onions). Ṭawāshī was perhaps the one figure identified *primarily* as a Sufi; Yāfiʿī's biographical notice on him focuses on his asceticism, his mystical experiences, and his many *khirqas*. But he too is described as being extremely learned in many disciplines, including medicine.[15]

Yāfiʿī, Maṭarī, Iṣfahānī, Dhuhaybī, and Ṭawāshī all belonged to the Suhrawardīya lineage. Yāfiʿī and Ṭawāshī were also affiliated with the Qādirīya, and Maṭarī with the Rifāʿīya. Association with these shaykhs and investiture by them thus deepened and confirmed Bukhārī's primary Sufi allegiance to the Suhrawardīya while at the same time allowing him to expand his affiliations beyond the two orders then dominant in South Asia. In this, there is a continuity between his earlier Sufi training in South Asia and these new spiritual relationships. In terms of legal tradition or *maẕhab*, however, there was a clear difference between Bukhārī's earlier education and practice and his new intellectual and social milieu. All of these scholars were strongly associated with the Shāfiʿī *maẕhab* in their social identification, their teaching, and their religious practice, hardly surprising given that Shāfiʿism was officially recognized as the leading *maẕhab* within the Mamlūk empire.[16] Bukhārī, however, like most South Asian Muslims, was a follower of the Ḥanafī *maẕhab*, and it is curious that he seems to have made no effort to attach himself to the Ḥanafī scholars or madrasas present in the holy cities.[17] By his own account, it was the general policy of the shaykhs of Mecca and

Medina to send novices in the Sufi path to the madrasa corresponding to their *mazhab* affiliation for preliminary education.[18] Bukhārī, however, was not a novice—he had already received instruction in both Sufism and the Ḥanafī legal tradition long before his arrival in the Hejaz. We might conclude, therefore, that while commitment to a single *mazhab* was necessary for the development of an individual's religious identity and knowledge, past a certain point in his education there was less expectation of exclusive association with one's own *mazhab*. Of course, by this time period the major Sunni *mazhab*s had come to accept each other's validity. Furthermore, the legal tradition of medieval South Asian Islam had its roots in Central Asia where Shāfi'ism and Ḥanafism had long coexisted as the two dominant Sunni *mazhab*s.[19]

As a teacher and a religious guide, Bukhārī displayed a mastery of at least the basic positions of the four major Sunni *mazhab*s. Though the bibliography of texts cited in his *malfūẓāt* is heavily weighted towards Ḥanafī sources, it does include some Shāfi'ī authorities, such as al-Nawawī and Qaffāl al-Shāshī. In his own practice, Bukhārī seems to have followed the Ḥanafī rules and referred to Ḥanafism as *mazhab-i mā* (our *mazhab*), but there were occasions when he was amenable to adopting the practices of the other Sunni *mazhab*s, especially Shāfi'ism. For example, when Naṣīr al-dīn Maḥmūd Chirāgh-i Dihlī died in 757/1356, Bukhārī and his companions, who were undertaking a forty-day retreat in Uch, performed the funeral prayer for him in absentia under the rules of the Shāfi'ī *mazhab*.[20] On another occasion he asked his disciples whether he should lead them in prayer according to the Ḥanafī *mazhab* or the Shāfi'ī one.[21]

The hagiographic tradition highlights Bukhārī's relationships with Rukn al-dīn Multānī and Naṣīr al-dīn Maḥmūd Chirāgh-i Dihlī, probably because they are widely known and revered in the South Asian Sufi context. However, in Bukhārī's emphasis on combining Sufi practice with scholarship in all the traditional religious sciences, and on strictly and *knowledgeably* abiding by the dictates of the Shari'a, we see a greater reflection of his Arabian masters than of his South Asian ones. But the perception that Yāfi'ī and Maṭarī were more scholarly or more legalistic than their South Asian counterparts may be a result less of genuine difference than of the different kinds of sources available on pre-modern South Asian and Arab religious figures, arising from a different posthumous legacy. We know, after all, that Rukn al-dīn Multānī and Naṣīr al-dīn Maḥmūd were both most definitely *bā-shar'* Sufis and, at least in Naṣīr al-dīn's case, well-versed in traditional Islamic scholarship. Yet, they are invariably described and approached as Sufi saints above all other characteristics. The power of the Sufi tradition in South Asia, the resultant abundance and availability of hagiographical material, and the ongoing cults devoted to medieval South Asian saints may have produced a skewed or one-sided image of these figures. For later generations, the saints' miraculous powers, pietistic and poetical sayings, ties to earlier saints, and *barakat*-filled tombs were of greater interest than the extent of their learning.

A further factor in shaping the different images of medieval South Asian and Middle Eastern religious authorities is that scholarship on Islam in these two cultural contexts has also taken very different trajectories, influenced no doubt by the internal dynamics of the two cultural zones. Historians of South Asian Islam have focused largely on the Sufi tradition or on the religious policies and proclivities of rulers. Much less attention has been paid to the history of the 'ulama, the madrasas, and the scholarly traditions on law, theology, hadith, and Quran of pre-modern South Asia. By contrast, the balance of scholarship on Middle Eastern Islam tips the other way. Yāfi'ī and his comrades are therefore more easily approached in the context of a somewhat detailed vision of the 'ulama of their time, while Rukn al-dīn and his fellow South Asian saints appear to us in the context of their Sufi networks. In a way, the difference in the background picture can be exemplified by the most accessible biographical reference works for the two regions: for the medieval Middle East we reach immediately for the *ṭabaqāt* genre of biographical compendia of hadith transmitters and other 'ulamah; for South Asia we turn to the *tazkira* genre of hagiographical compendia. Yāfi'ī's own *Mir'āt al-jinān*, however, brings together the features and subject matter of both genres.

Study and Discipleship in Medina and Mecca

'Afīf al-dīn Maṭarī

Before settling in Mecca for any extended time, Bukhārī studied in Medina with 'Afīf al-dīn Maṭarī, the muezzin at the Prophet's mosque. Maṭarī served as both a teacher and a Sufi guide for Bukhārī. Bukhārī read the six Sunni compilations of hadith under his supervision and later transmitted hadith on his authority.[22] Bukhārī also, in his own words, "took the Sufi order (or Sufi way of life) from him" (*akhẕ-i ṭarīqa az ū kard*) and received a *khirqa-yi tabarruk* (robe of blessing) traced back to Shihāb al-dīn Suhrawardī, with permission (*ijāzat*) to pass it on.[23] The permission that he received from Maṭarī covered not only the bestowal of *khirqa*s but a range of Sufi initiation practices as well: cutting the disciple's hair (*miqrāż rāndan*), receiving repentance (*tawba dādan*), and implanting the *ẕikr* formula. Despite the permission to cut other people's hair, Bukhārī's own hair was not clipped at this point; Maṭarī informed him that that ritual awaited him in Kāzarūn.[24]

Bukhārī's investiture and permission by Maṭarī were important in the development of Bukhārī's authority as a shaykh in his own right, as highlighted by *Khizānat al-fawā'id*'s listing of the *khirqa*s from Maṭarī immediately after Bukhārī's *khirqa*s from his paternal relatives. As discussed in the previous chapter, although Bukhārī had been initiated into Sufism by his father and had received a *khirqa* from the Chishtī shaykh Naṣīr al-dīn Maḥmūd Chirāgh-i Dihlī, he had not received an *ijāzat* from a significant Suhrawardī shaykh. Bukhārī's *ijāzat* from Naṣīr al-dīn had arisen from the peculiar circumstances of his royal appointment as *shaykh al-islām* and was not given in writing until 752/1351.[25] Maṭarī's *ijāzat*, especially since it covered the whole ritual process of investiture and initiation, was a valuable acquisition.

Besides this all-important Suhrawardī *khirqa*, Maṭarī also invested Bukhārī with a *khirqa* whose lineage was derived from Sayyid Aḥmad al-Rifā'ī (d. 1182 CE), eponymous founder of the Rifā'ī order. The Rifā'ī order had a reputation for eccentric behavior and dramatic forms of *zikr* (leading to their being labeled "howling dervishes" in English). Such behavior was unacceptable to a man of Bukhārī's religious beliefs and temperament. Later in life, when a few Rifā'ī *darwēsh*es came to him seeking *khirqa*s he gave them a lecture on the misguided Rifā'ī habit of not washing one's hair. According to Bukhārī, Sayyid Aḥmad al-Rifā'ī was not *muwallah* (enraptured, the excuse for asocial conduct) but was a good Sufi. It was Sayyid Aḥmad al-Rifā'ī's grandson of the same name who started these practices because he was insane.[26] Ibn Baṭṭūṭa met Aḥmad Kūchak, whom he describes as Aḥmad al-Rifā'ī's grandson, at his grandfather's tomb in Iraq and observed the drumming, dancing, fire-walking, and snake-handling of his followers.[27]

According to Bukhārī's grandson, who compiled and traced the lineages of all of his grandfather's investitures, Maṭarī also bestowed two further *khirqa*s on Bukhārī. One had an extremely short chain of transmission (*silsila*), reaching Muḥammad in a single step via Isa b. Maryam (that is, Jesus). Obviously this ahistorical and anachronistic *silsila* indicates a *khirqa* received by Maṭarī in the realm of dreams, visions, and apparitions. Bukhārī himself received several *khirqa*s in this direct manner from Muḥammad, Khwāja Khiżr, and Jesus.[28]

Bukhārī's memories of Maṭarī focus on his learning and on his care and consideration for his disciple from South Asia. Maṭarī was impressed with Bukhārī's manners and piety. With his typical combination of humility and pride, Bukhārī recounts that once he led the prayers at the Prophet's mosque but stood one row back from where the Prophet used to stand. Maṭarī had never seen such a practice and applauded him for it.[29] In contrast, when Bukhārī raised his voice in the Prophet's mosque during a debate with a teacher, Maṭarī grabbed him by the ear and scolded him for his improper behavior.[30] These examples of Maṭarī's responses to Bukhārī's behavior highlight the importance of manners and courtesy (*adab*) in Sufi teaching.[31] The shared theme is one of respect: respect towards the Prophet, the Prophet's mosque, Maṭarī, and Maṭarī's authority.

One of the reasons for Maṭarī's attention to Bukhārī was his status as a sayyid, a descendant of the Prophet. That Bukhārī was a sayyid and that this status requires respect is a point constantly reiterated in the *malfūẓāt* through the ubiquitous use of his title *sayyid al-sādāt* (master of the sayyids). However, it seems that Bukhārī was either too humble or lacked confidence in this genealogical claim to proclaim it widely, since Maṭarī knew of it only by the miraculous intervention of the Prophet.[32] The following account, from *Jāmi' al-'ulūm*, of Maṭarī's discovery of Bukhārī's descent is typical of the anecdotes told by Bukhārī in his *malfūẓāt*, at once affirming his own claims and showing him to be aware of his own errors.

> [Bukhārī said:] "He [Maṭarī] had heard at the Prophet's tomb that I am a sayyid. He used to say: 'You are a sayyid' because he had heard that the Prophet (peace be upon him) had said to me: 'Oh, my son, do not stand in

> front of my visitors.' His belief was increased by that. That was the day I was giving my greetings [to the Prophet] in front of the wall of the Prophet's holy tomb. I was absorbed in devotions there so that the pilgrims were forced to pass behind me. I heard a voice answering me: 'Oh my son, do not stand in front of my visitors.' I determined that this was the voice of the Prophet (peace be upon him). I moved back from there.
>
> "A friend asked: 'At the time that the Shaykh of Medina [i.e., Maṭarī] heard this voice, was he with you?'
>
> "He said: 'He was not present. He received this truth in an unveiling.'"[33]

This Prophetic confirmation of Bukhārī's sayyid identity turns up, in a more dramatic and contentious form, in the hagiographic *tażkira* tradition and in some of the apocryphal travelogues.[34] In these accounts, Bukhārī had become so sun-tanned during his voyage to Arabia that the people of Medina refused to believe that he was a sayyid.[35] To prove his claim, Bukhārī challenged all those who identified as sayyids or sharifs to meet at the Prophet's tomb and test whether the Prophet would respond to their greetings. Of course, it was only Bukhārī's greeting that received a response from the Prophet.

The miraculous visits of Indian shaykhs to Medina and Mecca

The passage from *Jāmiʿ al-ʿulūm* quoted above continues:

> [Bukhārī said:] "Then he [Maṭarī] came and took my hand and lead me to a place. 'Meditate here and give your greetings here since this is where Shaykh Rukn al-dīn gave his greetings and meditated. He was here every Thursday night, and Sunday night too.' He also showed me the place of Shaykh Naṣīr al-dīn Dihlawī (may God be pleased with him) to the left of Shaykh Rukn al-dīn (may the mercy of God be upon him) and I meditated behind the place of the two shaykhs and gave my greetings.
>
> "A friend asked: 'Did Shaykh Naṣīr al-dīn used to be there too?'
>
> "He said: 'Yes. He went at midnight. As it says in *Qūt al-qulūb*, "Everyone whose sainthood (*walāyat*) is genuine is present in Mecca and Medina on Thursday night and the two ʿĪds."'"[36]

I have quoted the whole of the above passage as an example of the way in which Bukhārī's experiences in Medina and Mecca are connected, by miraculous events, to the leading shaykhs of South Asia. In another version of this story, focused not on the Prophetic recognition of Bukhārī's descent but on the greatness of Rukn al-dīn Multānī and Naṣīr al-dīn Maḥmūd, Maṭarī intervened when Bukhārī gave his greetings to the Prophet while facing the part of the tomb where the Prophet's chest would be. Maṭarī directed him, instead, to where Rukn al-dīn and Naṣīr al-dīn used to stand facing the Prophet's feet. Similarly, when Bukhārī arrived in Mecca, Yāfiʿī showed him their habitual positions of prayer at the Ka'ba and instructed him to perform his devotions there, likewise. Aware of his own inadequacy, Bukhārī did not set foot in those saintly spots and instead took up a position behind them, impressing the shaykhs of Mecca with his humility just as he had impressed the shaykhs of Medina earlier. One night, Bukhārī met Naṣīr al-dīn Maḥmūd during one of his miraculous excursions to Mecca. Naṣīr al-dīn told him not to reveal this encounter during his (Naṣīr al-dīn's) lifetime. When they later met in Uch, under more mundane circumstances, the shaykh repeated his command for discretion.[37]

Bukhārī repeatedly quotes the shaykhs of Mecca and Medina praising his South Asian masters: Jamāl al-dīn Uchchī, Rukn al-dīn Multānī and Naṣīr al-dīn Maḥmūd Chirāgh-i Dihlī.[38] We have no evidence that any of these three ever traveled, in a mundane mode, beyond the confines of the Delhi Sultanate. Presumably Maṭarī and Yāfi'ī were acquainted with them from the reports brought by South Asian pilgrims and by the shaykhs' miraculous Thursday and Sunday night excursions to the holy cities of Arabia.

> [Bukhārī said:] "One day in Medina, the chief of shaykhs 'Abdallāh Maṭarī (may his blessings remain) asked me, 'What is the name of your shaykh?'
>
> "I answered, 'Abū al-Fatḥ.'
>
> "The shaykh said, 'This is a *kunya* (filionymic).'
>
> "I again said, 'All I know is Rukn al-dīn Abū al-Fatḥ.'
>
> "Shaykh 'Abdallāh said, 'The name of your shaykh is Fayżallāh.'
>
> "I asked, 'Master, whom did you hear this from?'
>
> "He said, 'From his blessed mouth.'
>
> "Then I again asked, 'Master, have you been to Multan at some time?'
>
> "He said, 'No, but every Thursday night I met the shaykh after his visits to the Ka'ba and the Prophet.'"[39]

The shaykhs of the Hejaz also knew of the earlier generations of Indian saints and told Bukhārī the extents of the *wilāyat*s (spiritual territories) of Bahā' al-dīn Zakarīyā and of Farīd al-dīn Mas'ūd Ganj-i shakar. Naṣīr al-dīn was so popular in the region that the turban and shirt which Bukhārī had from him were torn up by overzealous fans.[40]

The purpose of linking the major South Asian Sufi figures with Bukhārī's teachers in Mecca and Medina is multifaceted. Bukhārī's position as a respected religious figure is based partially on his personal knowledge and experience of the holy cities of Mecca and Medina, something quite rare for a medieval South Asian shaykh. By assigning that experience to his predecessors as well, Bukhārī avoids the appearance of innovation and instead seems to be following their example, as a good disciple should. Bukhārī's authority—and that of his *malfūẓāt*—depends on the spiritual authority of his teachers and shaykhs. The supposed acquaintance between the South Asian shaykhs and their counterparts in the Hejaz glorifies both parties and ultimately enhances Bukhārī's status. Rukn al-dīn and Naṣīr al-dīn were well-known and highly respected by his Indian audience. By showing that they were also known and respected by the shaykhs of Mecca and Medina, Bukhārī proves their international fame and undisputed spiritual status. The fact that Yāfiʿī and Maṭarī, famous in their own contexts but presumably less known in South Asia, recognized the importance of Rukn al-dīn and Naṣīr al-dīn would also demonstrate the Hejazi shaykhs' perspicacity and virtue to a South Asian audience. If there were any hint of disloyalty to the Suhrawardī and Chishtī saints of South Asia in Bukhārī's need to seek an education elsewhere, it is dispelled by the image of mutual respect and admiration between the South Asian and Arabian shaykhs. What the shaykhs in Mecca and Medina said also supported Bukhārī's primary allegiance to Rukn al-dīn and the Multan Suhrawardīs over Naṣīr al-dīn and the Chishtīya. He was told that Rukn al-dīn was a *quṭb al-ʿālam* (a *quṭb* of the whole world) while Naṣīr al-dīn was simply a *quṭb*, and when Yāfiʿī showed him their habitual places at the Kaʿba, Rukn al-dīn's was closer to it.[41]

Shaykh ʿAbdallāh Yāfiʿī

In Mecca, Bukhārī attached himself to ʿAbdallāh b. Asad al-Yāfiʿī, who was, like Maṭarī, both a Sufi and a Shāfiʿī *ʿālim*. From Yāfiʿī, Bukhārī received further spiritual training (*tarbīyat*) and two *khirqa*s, one for the Suhrawardī lineage and the other for the Qādirī lineage.[42] Though Bukhārī is not as specific about Yāfiʿī's textual instruction as he is about Maṭarī's, it is clear that he read several works while in Yāfiʿī's circle in Mecca. From Yāfiʿī's oeuvre, Bukhārī seems to have been most familiar with his poetry and with his popular anthology of hagiographical anecdotes, *Rawḍ al-rayāḥīn fī hikāyāt al-ṣāliḥīn* (also known as *Rawḍat al-rayāḥīn*)—both are quoted extensively in the *malfūẓāt* texts. *Khulāṣat al-mafākhir*, devoted to the miracles of the twelfth-century saint ʿAbd al-Qādir Gīlānī and sometimes considered a *takmila* or supplement to *Rawḍat al-riyāḥīn*, was translated into Persian by one of Bukhārī's disciples, suggesting that Bukhārī may have read and taught this text as well.[43]

Besides these works by Yāfiʿī himself, Bukhārī was introduced to other texts while in his circle, one of which was *al-Risāla al-Makkīya*, a Sufi handbook by Quṭb al-dīn Dimashqī.[44] Though we know little about Quṭb al-dīn Dimashqī, he appears to have been closely associated with Yāfiʿī and Maṭarī and of a similar religious and intellectual bent; on their deathbeds, the latter two figures each instructed their younger relatives to complete their spiritual training under Dimashqī's care.[45] Bukhārī received a copy of *al-Risāla al-Makkīya* from the author and taught it to his own disciples later in life.[46] Like *Khulāṣat al-mafākhir*, mentioned above, it was translated into Persian by one of Bukhārī's disciples.[47] Another text for which Bukhārī received an *isnād* (chain of transmission) while in Mecca was Shāṭibī's *Qaṣīda* on the seven Quran readings.[48] Most of the numerous texts quoted and taught by Bukhārī were probably already familiar and available to South Asian audiences. These examples, however, show that his travels and scholarship were instrumental in introducing or encouraging the transmission of specific Arabic texts from the Middle East to South Asia.

Rawḍat al-rayāḥīn bears witness to Yāfiʿī's interest in the miracles and wonders performed by the prophets and saints. This is the same aspect of his personality most apparent in Bukhārī's reminiscences about their time together. On several occasions mysterious strangers approached Bukhārī at the Kaʿba and gave him food or a piece of paper. When he showed these gifts to Yāfiʿī, the shaykh told him that they were from the *abdāl*.[49] Bukhārī took the piece of paper given him by one of the *abdāl* back to Uch with him, but after it had been seen by some of his disciples it mysteriously disappeared.[50] Jinns were also present in Mecca; some of them studied with Yāfiʿī, who taught jinns at night after teaching humans during the day. Once, while circumambulating the Kaʿba, Bukhārī met and shook hands with a jinn who was also a saint (*walī*).[51]

The basic reason for the presence of such supernatural beings at the Kaʿba was that such miraculous attendance there was a primary sign and requirement of sainthood. As discussed above, both Naṣīr al-dīn Maḥmūd and Rukn al-dīn Multānī regularly teleported themselves to Arabia from India. But it was not just famous shaykhs and supernatural beings who participated in this weekly or bi-weekly attendance at the Kaʿba; Bukhārī also described a number of "common" people he knew later whose saintliness was manifested by such teleportation. As will be discussed in Chapter 5, several of his female disciples and acquaintances in India would visit the Kaʿba on a weekly basis. Another instance of such supernatural visitation was that of a young man whom Yāfiʿī and Bukhārī met while praying at the Kaʿba. Yāfiʿī noticed that the youth's hands were dirty and reprimanded him for his lack of cleanliness. But it was later revealed that the youth had been tending to his sick mother in Damascus when he heard the call to prayer and had arrived instantaneously at the Kaʿba without an opportunity to wash.[52]

Yāfiʿī's reprimand to the dirty youth is one of several examples of his strict adherence to the requirements of the Shariʿa, in this case of its ritual stipulations. The opposition sometimes implied between legalistic learned Islam and a "superstitious" and ignorant Sufism simply did not exist for Yāfiʿī. He gave Bukhārī a *taʿwīẕ* (an amulet containing a prayer) to cure an ailment in his eyes and he interpreted his dreams.[53] At the same time he would correct the pronunciation of the imam in the mosque. This is the same combination of legalistic and scholarly accuracy with a belief in the constant occurrence of miraculous events and in the efficacy of amulets and invocations that Bukhārī practiced in his own career.

As part of "his lifelong effort to vindicate Sufism as a legitimate trend within Islam" Yāfiʿī was also a defender of that most famous of Sufis, Ibn al-ʿArabī (d. 638/1240).[54] It is interesting that the debate raging in the Middle East on the legitimacy of Ibn al-ʿArabī's work left no trace in Bukhārī's reminiscences or teachings. Neither Ibn al-ʿArabī nor his most famous critic Ibn Taymīya (d. 728/1328) nor any of their writings are mentioned in the *malfūẓāt*. This is surprising given the interest raised by Ibn al-ʿArabī's thought in Sufi circles and the great influence his ideas had on later Indian Sufism. It was only later in the eighth/fourteenth century that figures such as Ashraf

Jahāngīr Simnānī (d. 808/1405) brought Ibn al-ʿArabī's theories to India, mostly as interpreted and explained by Persian commentators. Perhaps Bukhārī's teachers in Arabia sheltered their student from such potentially dangerous and misunderstood theories. Or perhaps Bukhārī's personal predilection for "orthodox" practical Sufism, on the model of Shihāb al-dīn ʿUmar al-Suhrawardī, meant that he was uninterested in speculative or theoretical Sufism. Certainly his *malfūẓāt* are devoid of any metaphysical or theosophical content other than very basic accepted theological positions. The only hint of works tending towards suspect doctrines was an Arabic commentary on the forty names of God which Bukhārī read with Maṭarī. Although Bukhārī brought this text back to Uch with him, where it was held in safe-keeping by his wife, he felt it to be too dangerous to allow anyone else to see it. According to Bukhārī, a Persian abridgment of this commentary was made by Yaḥyā Suhrawardī Maqtūl, whose philosophical ideas had lead to his execution in 587/1191.[55]

Yāfiʿī took a personal interest in his South Asian student's welfare. Once during Ramadan, Bukhārī had nothing but water with which to break his fast. He resigned himself to fasting again but was surprised by the appearance of Yāfiʿī bringing him food and money. In general while in Mecca, Bukhārī supported himself by working as a copyist. After studying all day he would copy texts in the evening by moonlight (which he claimed was as bright as day in Arabia). For his usual product of two quires a night he received one silver coin, worth half a *tanka* (the coin in use in the Delhi Sultanate). This silver coin would buy him two pieces of barley bread, or one of wheat, demonstrating the high price of grain in Arabia at the time and Bukhārī's relative poverty.[56]

Yāfiʿī's interest in Bukhārī extended to curiosity about his life back home. He asked him what people ate in India and Bukhārī gave him a recipe for *yak'hnī*, a meat dish still popular in the sub-continent. Yāfiʿī's respect for his disciple was evidently passed on to his son who told an Indian pilgrim some decades later that Bukhārī was made by God to be an object of visitation in India, like the Kaʿba in Mecca and the Prophet's tomb in Medina.[57] Such reports from later pilgrims, as well as Bukhārī's encounters in Arabia with traders, pilgrims, and even slaves from India attest to the continuous traffic between the holy cities and the South Asian Muslim community, despite the geographical distance and the difficulties of travel.[58] In the century after Bukhārī's time in Arabia, South Asian Muslims began establishing and endowing religious institutions, particularly madrasas, in Mecca.[59]

As mentioned above, Yāfiʿī was not the only scholar/shaykh with whom Bukhārī associated while in Mecca. Najm al-dīn ʿAbd al-Raḥmān al-Iṣfahānī (d. 750/1349) invested him with another Suhrawardī *khirqa*, gave him an *ijāzat* for it, made him a *khalīfa*, and taught him a prayer that Iṣfahānī had learned from the Prophet Muḥammad himself (in a dream or vision, of course). Another Meccan shaykh from whom he received a *khirqa* and *ijāzat* was Shihāb al-dīn Abū Saʿīd Ẓafar b. Maḥmūd b. Muḥammad al-Kirmānī al-Shāfiʿī. Kirmānī had received the *khirqa* from the immortal Khiżr who had received it from the Prophet.[60]

Yemen and Medina in 748/1347

The year 748/1347 was a busy time for Bukhārī. After six years in Mecca and Medina, he went to Aden in Yemen. There he visited Yāfi'ī's teacher al-Dhuhaybī, commonly known as Faqīh Baṣṣāl (the onion-selling jurist), who invested him with yet another Suhrawardī *khirqa*. It seems that Bukhārī was planning to take ship from Yemen back to Sind, since Faqīh Baṣṣāl immediately instructed him to stay in Mecca until he who sent him (that is, Rukn al-dīn Multānī) permitted him to return home. Faqīh Baṣṣāl died a few days after their meeting without appointing an heir to his *sajjāda* (prayer rug), that is, a primary successor to his position as a Sufi shaykh. This seems to have caused some confusion among his sons but was resolved by Rukn al-dīn Multānī's appearance in Bukhārī's dream. Rukn al-dīn gave Bukhārī a *khirqa* and told him to give it to Faqīh Baṣṣāl's younger son along with the *sajjāda*. Bukhārī did so, despite the intention of other local shaykhs and imams to place the older son on the *sajjāda*. A few nights later, Rukn al-dīn appeared with a *khirqa* just for Bukhārī and informed him that he, Jalāl al-dīn Bukhārī, was a *quṭb-i 'ālam*, that is, an axis of the world and one of the great saints.[61] This is Bukhārī's only account of investiture by Rukn al-dīn Multānī, supposedly one of his primary Sufi *pīrs*.

Bukhārī's visit to Yemen did not go unnoticed by local chroniclers. Abū Makhrama lists him in his biographical dictionary of Aden and mentions several people who received *ijāzat*s to transmit Ibn al-Ḥājib's *Kāfiya* (on Arabic grammar) and several of Shihāb al-dīn Suhrawardī's works from him.[62] This external source confirms Bukhārī's memories of being in Aden in 748/1347. This is also where he may have met Yāfi'ī's shaykh, Nūr al-dīn 'Alī b. 'Abdallāh al-Ṭawāshī, known as Ṣāḥib Ḥālī (d. 748/1347). Bukhārī includes a *khirqa* from him in his list of investitures but does not mention when or where they met.[63] Another *khirqa* probably received in Aden was a Qādirī one from Muḥammad b. 'Ubayd al-Ghaythī.[64] The Ghaythī family controlled a *ribāṭ* in Aden built for Abū al-Ghayth b. Jamīl (d. 651).[65]

In obedience to Faqīh Baṣṣāl's instructions, Bukhārī returned to the Hejaz. He spent another year with Maṭarī completing his study of *'Awārif al-ma'ārif*. Maṭarī's copy of *'Awārif al-ma'ārif* was a valuable and extremely accurate one, having been inspected by Shihāb al-dīn al-Suhrawardī himself. After Maṭarī's death this manuscript was given to Yāfi'ī, who eventually sent it to Bukhārī in Uch, where it was entrusted to Bukhārī's son for safekeeping.[66] It was during this period of tutelage that Maṭarī expressed his particular respect for his student-disciple. One example of this was Maṭarī's refusal to allow another scholar (*dānishmand*) to participate in their *'Awārif al-ma'ārif* study sessions because he knew that the *dānishmand* would be incapable of acting on its teachings.[67] The unstated implication, of course, is that he also knew that Bukhārī was capable of following the path laid out in *'Awārif al-ma'ārif*.

When Bukhārī was doing a forty-day retreat in the Prophet's mosque, Maṭarī would come to his cell at dawn with bread in one hand and a lamp in the other. Bukhārī protested that one should eat little in the Prophet's mosque, but Maṭarī responded that

Bukhārī had a wife, a father, and a family to whom he intended to return. If he wanted to be capable of the voyage back to them he should eat.[68] Or, Maṭarī would come to instruct him (and bring him food) after the late-night *tahajjud* prayers, knowing through mystical insight when Bukhārī had completed them. When Bukhārī protested the inappropriateness of the teacher coming to the student, rather than the other way around, Maṭarī responded that it was his duty since Bukhārī was a sayyid.[69] The record of these anecdotes in *Jāmi' al-'ulūm* emphasizes the extraordinary role reversal in a teacher coming to a student and bringing him food by his own hand by including the question always asked by a disciple upon hearing these stories: "Did Maṭarī not have a servant to carry things for him?"

Bukhārī seems to have been particularly moved by the generosity of his teachers and masters in matters of food. These anecdotes about Maṭarī fit into a pattern of reminiscences about his primary teachers—Rukn al-dīn Multānī had the women of his own family cook for Bukhārī and Yāfi'ī gave him food and money when he was in need. Perhaps this speaks simply to the ever-present threat of scarcity and hunger in a medieval world beset by famine and plague. Perhaps from the vantage point of his old age, telling these tales in the comfort of his establishment in Uch or while being generously supported by the Sultan in Delhi, hunger and relief from hunger were a primary feature of his memory of life as a student and a pilgrim. Besides this, however, to feed someone is to enact a relationship of care and dependence reminiscent of both a parent-child and a master-client relationship, both appropriate models for the relationship between teacher and student or shaykh and disciple. *Jāmi' al-'ulūm* bears witness to Bukhārī's generosity in feeding his own disciples—made possible, it must be said, by Fīrōz Shāh Tughluq's generosity in sending him food and presents every day.

Travel through Iraq and Persia

Finally, after seven years in the Hejaz, Bukhārī was given permission to go home by Rukn al-dīn Multānī, who told him, in a vision of course, that his father missed him.[70] Though he had departed Sind in a rush, fleeing a threat to his soul, his voyage home was more leisurely. As he was leaving Arabia he was told by his friends there to go overland via Iraq and Persia in order to meet a number of shaykhs and receive *khirqa*s and *ijāzat*s from them. The sources are not very clear on the extent of Bukhārī's travels or on what route he followed. In *Jāmi' al-'ulūm* and *Khizānat al-fawā'id al-Jalālīya*, Bukhārī only recalls visits to a few more places in southern Iran. Combined with his comments on the Shi'a of Laḥsa, Qaṭīf, and Bahrain, this suggests that Bukhārī traveled overland across the Arabian Peninsula and then across the Persian Gulf to Iran.[71]

It was still 748/1347 when Bukhārī arrived in "Shawakārah," where he met Mu'ammar Sharaf al-dīn Maḥmūd Shāh Tustarī, a *khalīfa* of Shihāb al-dīn al-Suhrawardī. According to Bukhārī, "Shawakārah" was a city in Iraq in the vicinity of Shiraz. The reference here is probably to the capital of the region of Shabānkāreh, a province of Iran under the Ilkhānids and at other times a part of the province of Fars.[72] (Since the disintegration of the Ilkhānid empire a decade earlier, various successor states and minor kingdoms had established themselves in the region.) Sharaf al-dīn Tustarī was a very aged man, allegedly 132 years old. The *khirqas*, and the *ijāzat* for *'Awārif al-ma'ārif*, that Bukhārī received from this shaykh thus had only one intermediary between him and Shihāb al-dīn al-Suhrawardī. He also received permission to pass on this *khirqa*, to implant the *ẕikr*, and to cut the disciple's hair. Bukhārī stayed long enough in Shabānkāreh to read all of *'Awārif al-ma'ārif* with Tustarī before moving on to Shiraz.[73]

In Shiraz, large numbers came to study with Bukhārī and he supervised a reading of *Maṣābīḥ al-sunna* by al-Baghawī (d. 516/1122). Bukhārī was visited by the famous *qāżī* (judge) of the city, Majd al-dīn Ismā'īl b. Yaḥyā (d. 756/1355), and he even attracted the attention of the ruler, presumably Abū Isḥāq b. Muḥammad Shāh Īnjū. Bukhārī's experience closely matches and might even have overlapped with Ibn Baṭṭūṭa's, who was also in Shiraz in (Rabī' II) 748/1347, also observed Majd al-dīn supervising a reading of *Maṣābīḥ* at his madrasa, and also met the Sultan.[74] Abū Isḥāq was so impressed by Bukhārī's teaching that he gave him three basins full of gold and silver coins. Bukhārī passed on this wealth to a certain Sayyid Ḥamīd al-dīn, whose son Shams al-dīn Mas'ūd 'Irāqī became one of Bukhārī's closer disciples (and troubled his master with his chronic impoverishment and indebtedness).[75]

This Sayyid Ḥamīd al-dīn, recipient of Bukhārī's generosity, is perhaps identical to a Sayyid Ḥamīd al-dīn Abū al-Waqt Maḥmūd b. Najīb al-Ḥusaynī al-Samarqandī who invested Bukhārī with a number of *khirqas*. Sayyid Ḥamīd al-dīn Samarqandī was a distant relative of Bukhārī living in Shiraz.[76] He invested Bukhārī with a *khirqa* from Abū Sa'īd Ẓafar al-Kirmānī, which Bukhārī had already received directly from Kirmānī in Mecca. The two other *khirqas* bestowed by Ḥamīd al-dīn were from the Kubrawī and Chishtī lineages. This Chishtī *silsila* is particularly interesting as it does not include Mu'īn al-dīn Sijzī (founder of the Indian Chishtīya) but branches off several generations before with Quṭb al-dīn Mawdūd b. Yūsuf Chishtī (d. 520/1126). One of the links in this genealogy, Muḥyi al-dīn 'Alī b. Aḥmad Chishtī, was buried in Delhi so this line cannot be completely independent of the South Asian Chishtīya.[77]

Like Ibn Baṭṭūṭa before him, Bukhārī proceeded from Shiraz to Kāzarūn, where he was finally invested in the waking world with a *khirqa* deriving from Rukn al-dīn Multānī. This was bestowed by Rukn al-dīn's *khalīfa* Qiwām al-dīn. Qiwām al-dīn also gave him written permission to pass on this *khirqa*, thus laying to rest any doubts as to Bukhārī's authority to carry on and propagate the Multan Suhrawardī tradition.[78] While in Kāzarūn, Bukhārī stayed at the *khānqāh* of Shaykh Amīn al-dīn Balyānī (d. 745/1345). Balyānī was a strict upholder of the Sharī'a, like most of Bukhārī's shaykhs, and a practitioner of severe asceticism.[79] Despite being affiliated with a branch of the Suhrawardī lineage and the head of several independent *khānqāhs*, he has come to be known as a reviver of the Kāzarūnī (or Murshidī) order descended from Shaykh Abū Isḥāq Kāzarūnī (d. 426/1035).[80]

According to Bukhārī, before his death Amīn al-dīn Balyānī had predicted the arrival of a Sayyid Bukhārī from Uch, and Multan and had left instructions for his brother and heir, Imām al-dīn Maḥmūd, to invest him with his *khirqa*.[81] In this instance, Bukhārī underwent a full initiation process—his hair was cut, the *ẕikr* formula was implanted in him, he was invested with a *khirqa* (bearing a Suhrawardī genealogy), and he was given a prayer rug, scissors, a staff (*'aṣā*), and a *ḥilya* (ornament, perhaps *ḥulla*, robe). Furthermore, he was given permission (*ijāzat*) to pass all of these on, that is, to perform the same process on others.[82]

The prediction of the arrival of a worthy disciple or spiritual heir and the designation of a *khirqa* or other relic for such a person is a not infrequent trope in the Sufi hagiographical tradition. Hagiographical attempts to link Amīn al-dīn Balyānī to the Kāzarūnī/Murshidī lineage cite statements from Abū Iṣḥāq foretelling Balyānī's appearance and designating him as his spiritual heir.[83] Bukhārī's *khirqa* from Balyānī turns up in similar stories in later *taẕkira* texts as ultimately intended for Bukhārī's great-grandson Muḥammad Shāh-i 'ālam (d. 880/1476) and reaching its goal through the intermediary of the Gujarati saint Aḥmad K'haṯṯū Sarkhēzī (d. 849/1446).[84]

Bukhārī was invested with the *khirqa* of the Kāzarūnīya by another figure, Rukn al-dīn Hangī (or Hanjī), probably also in Kāzarūn.[85] Abū Isḥāq himself gave Bukhārī a *khirqa*, presumably in a dream or vision.[86] Ibn Baṭṭūṭa remarks on the popularity of Abū Isḥāq Kāzarūnī among Indians and especially among seafarers, who viewed him as a protector against dangers at sea.[87] If, as I suspect, Bukhārī travelled from Kāzarūn to the coast and then by sea back to Sind, it would be fitting that he had first acquired the *khirqa* of Abū Isḥāq to protect him on his voyage home.

Bukhārī most probably embarked in the vicinity of the modern port city of Bushehr for a sea voyage down the Persian Gulf, through the straits of Hormuz, and along the Makran coast to Sind. This presumes that there is little merit to the claims in *Sirāj al-hidāya* that Bukhārī traveled to Khurāsān, Samarkand, and Ghazni; the other *malfūẓāt* texts mention only a stop at Bhakkar on the Indus on his way back to Uch, which suggests arrival in lower Sind by sea and a subsequent voyage up the river.[88] A voyage by land from Shiraz, whether through Khurāsān and the Bolan Pass or through Sīstān, would have been extremely arduous and lengthy.[89]

Whatever his route home, whether by land or by sea, Bukhārī carried with him much that he had not had when he left Uch. I do not know if all the *khirqa*s he received were actual items of clothing—he claimed that the one received from Rukn al-dīn in a dream was a real object—but if so that would have added to his luggage. Similarly he may or may not have carried away copies of the texts he had studied while in Arabia. For both books and *khirqa*s, the possession of the physical objects was less important than the event of investiture by a shaykh and the process of reading (or hearing someone else read) in the presence of a teacher. What Bukhārī had gained were not physical possessions but immaterial ones, more links in his spiritual genealogy, more learning, and, most important, more *ijāzat*s authorizing him to transmit these *khirqa*s and this learning. Certainly the mental and spiritual baggage was considerable.

Over the course of his life, at unspecified dates, Bukhārī received *khirqa*s from only six more shaykhs: two disciples of Niẓām al-dīn Awliyā,' Shams al-dīn Muḥammad b. Yaḥyā Awadhī and Quṭb al-dīn Munawwar Hansawī;[90] another disciple of Rukn al-dīn Multānī, Jalāl al-dīn al-Barakī; and three deceased shaykhs who invested him in dreams or visions, Najm al-dīn Kubrā (d. ca. 617/1221), Aḥmad al-Rifāʿī, and Niẓām al-dīn Awliyā.' Altogether Bukhārī had collected a significant number of *khirqas*; the total ranges from sixteen to forty depending on the source and what counts as a separate *khirqa*. Most of the important Sufi lineages of this period are represented in the genealogies of his *khirqas*: Suhrawardī, Chishtī, Rifāʿī, Kubrawī, Qādirī, and Kāzarūnī. In addition, his own family tree, traced back to ʿAlī b. Abī Ṭālib, served as the *silsila* of the Bukhārī family *khirqa*. (See Appendix A for all of Bukhārī's *khirqas*.)

Most of Bukhārī's predecessors and contemporaries were content with one or two *khirqas*, usually within a single order. Bukhārī himself states that his primary goal was always the *ṭarīq-i pīrān-i khud*, the path of his own shaykhs, that is, the Suhrawardī lineage.[91] This implies that he was not purposefully seeking initiation into the other orders and that these other *khirqas* were given to him solely on the initiative of their owners. Thus, his numerous *khirqas* are a tribute to his own spiritual worthiness, as recognized by so many shaykhs. Whether or not we believe Bukhārī's disavowal of an active quest of these *khirqas*, they were certainly an item of pride for him and his disciples. Bukhārī's acquaintance with a large number of shaykhs, his initiation into many Sufi lineages, and his numerous *khirqas* are often the focus of biographical entries on him. This acquisition of multiple *khirqas* may have been a developing trend within Sufism at this period. Later in life Bukhārī stated that there was a ten to one ratio between the Suhrawardī and Chishtī *khirqas* that he had bestowed on others, presumably the two orders most in demand.[92] But he was also happy, and even eager, to exercise his authority to bestow the *khirqas* of other orders. In his old age, people came to ask Bukhārī for *khirqas* with specific pedigrees, perhaps to fill out their own collections. Bukhārī's grandson, Burhān al-dīn ʿAbdallāh Quṭb-i ʿālam, followed his example and added another eighteen *khirqas* to those he had received from his grandfather's disciples. Some of Burhān al-dīn's shaykhs had up to seven *khirqas*, though the numbers include *khirqas* received directly from the Prophet as well as those with a traditional genealogy.[93]

After his seven years of travel, Jalāl al-dīn Bukhārī came home to Uch, to his family and to his father's *khānqāh*, sometime around 749/1348. Despite his reputation as a great traveler, Bukhārī seems to have spent most of the rest of his life settled in Uch. Besides his single voyage to Arabia and back, his only other reliably documented travels were occasional trips to Delhi, especially frequent during the later decades of his life.

Bukhārī as a Traveler

The South Asian hagiographic traditions recount numerous tales of holy figures who traveled far and wide seeking the company of saints and sages, often to best them in displays of piety or spiritual power. Many are said to have performed the pilgrimage to Mecca, including Mu'īn al-dīn Chishtī, Farīd al-dīn Mas'ūd, and the great proponents of the bhakti movement, Guru Nanak and Kabir.[94] In most such cases, however, we have few reliable biographical sources and in many instances must presume that such travels, especially the stereotypical pilgrimage to Mecca, are at least highly exaggerated if not altogether legendary. At the same time, we also know that though travel in pre-modern Asia may have been arduous and slow, there was a steady stream of traffic between the territory of the Delhi Sultanate and the Muslim realms of Central and Western Asia. Trade was of course the primary motive for regular travel, but pilgrimage, quests for patronage, knowledge, and opportunity, and flight from danger or hardship brought more than merchants onto the ships that plied the Arabian Sea and the caravans that traversed the passes of the Hindu Kush.

Jalāl al-dīn Bukhārī is a rare example of a pre-Mughal saint whose travels outside India can be reliably documented and detailed. The narrative that we have here is neither the generic and often anachronistic list of places visited, saints encountered, and wonders performed found in the more legendary tales of saints, nor the minimalist information of birth here, initiation and education there, and death and burial somewhere else provided by less fanciful sources. Instead, the anecdotes in Bukhārī's *malfūẓāt* allow us to reconstruct a specific and historically plausible travel itinerary to Mecca and back and identify the particular figures he encountered, as well as the textual and spiritual instruction that he received from them.

I have made repeated reference to Ibn Baṭṭūṭa's *Travels* in this chapter, partly because they provide a useful witness to the times and places under discussion, but also because of their significant overlap with Bukhārī's itinerary. Every place visited by Bukhārī had been visited by Ibn Baṭṭūṭa a decade or so earlier. Even many of the personalities encountered were the same; Ibn Baṭṭūṭa mentions Yāfi'ī, Maṭarī, and Majd al-dīn Baghdādī (the *qāżī* of Shiraz). This similarity in their experiences is not coincidental. Though Ibn Baṭṭūṭa was an Arabic speaker from Morocco in the far west and Bukhārī a Persian speaker from India, their shared ability to move through a variety of Muslim societies was based on a common characteristic: they were each fully enculturated into a social order that spanned the Muslim world. It is not merely that they were Muslims traveling among their co-religionists; rather they were Sunni Muslims, educated in Arabic in the religious and legal tradition, and participants in the Sufi path. If, despite the lack of imperial or political unity in the late middle period of Islamic history, there existed an Islamicate civilization shared by Muslims in disparate parts of the globe, it was made possible in large part by the tradition of Sunni religious learning with its normative standards of religious and legal practice, the privileged position of Arabic as the language of that learning, and the Sufi lineages that created networks of shaykhs and disciples, and saints and devotees, spanning generations as well as distances.

These three elements of medieval Muslim culture (Sunni scholarship, Arabic, and Sufism) were what enabled both Ibn Baṭṭūṭa and Bukhārī to participate in otherwise alien societies. Ibn Baṭṭūṭa found a welcome and a livelihood throughout the Muslim world because of his scholarly and judicial credentials. Bukhārī was able to participate in the religio-academic life of Yemen, the Hejaz, and Iran as both a student and a transmitter of religious texts and hadith. In this context, it is also not insignificant that he supported himself as a copyist, a career requiring more than minimal literacy. For both, religious learning was the coin with which they traded and, at least in Bukhārī's case, the wealth that he sought to gain.

Ibn Baṭṭūṭa, an Arabic speaker from North Africa, was able to occupy judicial positions in the eastern non-Arabophone Islamic lands because of the primacy of Arabic in the Islamic legal tradition, no matter the language used by the local Muslim population. In the reverse direction, Bukhārī, a Persian speaker from India, was able to participate in the Sufi and scholarly circles of Arabia because his religious education had perforce required an early training in Arabic. At the same time, it is clear from the experiences of both figures that while knowledge of Arabic made the transversal of regional and cultural boundaries possible, it did not erase linguistic divisions and difficulties. Ibn Baṭṭūṭa required interpreters to carry out his judicial duties in Delhi while Bukhārī's emphasis on his use of Arabic while in Arabia and his translations of verbatim conversations for his disciples betray a constant awareness of the linguistic distance between South and West Asia.

Although Ibn Baṭṭūṭa's Sufi affiliations have not received much attention, his *Travels* make frequent mention of his visitations to Sufi shrines, his stays at Sufi hospices, and his reception of *khirqa*s from Sufi shaykhs. The institutions of Sufism thus often provided Ibn Baṭṭūṭa with an immediate destination, lodging, and another mechanism for creating a bond with local figures. As someone whose primary activity was participation in the Sufi path, Bukhārī had an involvement with Sufi institutions that was, of course, deeper and more focused. Rather than replicating Ibn Baṭṭūṭa's brief but catholic interactions with any locally prominent Sufi personalities, Bukhārī's interactions followed the network of Sufi lineages. All of his contacts in Arabia and Iran belonged to the Suhrawardī *ṭarīqa*, though most of them were also part of other Sufi lineages. However, the Suhrawardīya were one of the most widespread and popular Sufi lineages—if that were the only basis of one's social network it would be a very large and heterogeneous category. Bukhārī's networking followed a narrower track, tracing Yāfi'ī and Maṭarī's initiatory and educational links to their masters in Yemen, and obeying their instructions in visiting the shaykhs of Kāzarūn and Shabānkāreh.

Ibn Baṭṭūṭa's *Riḥla* was a carefully constructed narrative whose purpose was to enlighten and entertain his readers with accounts of the peculiar or amazing things he had encountered during his travels. Bukhārī's accounts of his travels, in contrast, like all his autobiographical anecdotes, are brief and episodic, interspersed in his teaching sessions according to their association with the topic at hand or illustration of his point. Bukhārī's fondness for retelling anecdotes about this period of his life demonstrates its importance in his understanding of himself and his own biography. However, it does not seem to be travel in itself that he valued, since the mechanics of travel, his itineraries, and descriptions of place are all left vague or unspecified. Instead, his experiences in West Asia were valuable to him and to his audience for the specific examples of pious behavior observed by him and for the status, learning, and Sufi affiliations that he acquired from Sufis and scholars.

The End of an Era

The Accession of Fīrōz Shāh Tughluq

Jalāl al-dīn Bukhārī's departure from India had been instigated by his encounter with Sultan Muḥammad b. Tughluq and the Sultan's appointment of him to the post of *shaykh al-islām*. When Bukhārī returned to Uch, in 749/1348, Muḥammad b. Tughluq was still reigning but was embroiled in the struggle that would eventually cost him his life. During the 740s/1340s, revolts by military commanders and local rulers had broken out in various parts of the empire, most dangerously in Gujarat. One of the prime leaders of the Gujarat rebellion was given shelter by the Sumras of Thatta, the ruling family of lower Sind, a region whose submission to the Delhi Sultanate was often merely nominal if not altogether nonexistent. Muḥammad b. Tughluq's attempt to regain control of the region came to an ignominious end when he succumbed to food poisoning on his way from Gujarat to Thatta and died on 21 Muḥarram 752/ 20 March 1351.[95]

According to Bukhārī's *malfūẓāt*, the Sultan's fatal campaign in Sind was the occasion for another meeting between himself and the Chishtī shaykh Naṣīr al-dīn Maḥmūd Chirāgh-i Dihlī. During his military campaigns in the provinces, Muḥammad b. Tughluq would sometimes require leading figures from his court and capital to attend him at his temporary encampments. Naṣīr al-dīn Maḥmūd, obliged to follow his sovereign to Sind, passed through Uch where he visited the *khānqāh* of Bukhārī's father, Aḥmad Kabīr, and requested assistance in getting to Thatta. Halfway to Thatta, Naṣīr al-dīn learned that the Sultan had died and so returned to Uch where he was again a guest of Aḥmad Kabīr. It was during these meetings that Bukhārī received the written version of the *ijāzat* for the Chishtī *khirqa* he had been given nearly a decade ago in Delhi—an important moment in Bukhārī's narration of his authorization as a Sufi shaykh. As well as this *ijāzat-nāma*, he was given orders not to reveal Naṣīr al-dīn's weekly trips to Mecca during his lifetime.[96] It is interesting that both of Bukhārī's significant encounters with the Chishtī saint took place in the context of Muḥammad b. Tughluq's activities, revealing the close, though not necessarily amicable, relationship between the Chishtī order and the royal court. K. A. Nizami doubts this account of Naṣīr al-dīn's movements, arguing that the shaykh followed the Sultan to Gujarat rather than taking the western route to Sind via Uch.[97]

Muḥammad b. Tughluq was succeeded to the throne of Delhi by his cousin Fīrōz Shāh (d. 790/1388). Fīrōz Shāh Tughluq is not remembered by historians as a very dynamic ruler nor as an effective military commander.[98] In certain respects, Fīrōz's mode of ruling provides a marked contrast to that of his predecessor. For one thing, Fīrōz did not imitate Muḥammad b. Tughluq's innovative hands-on approach to governance. Furthermore, Fīrōz had a much better relationship with the religious classes and acquired a reputation as an especially pious and orthodox ruler. He made a point of patronizing and supporting Sufi institutions, such as shrines and *khānqāhs*, as well as the ʿulama, their madrasas, and their scholarship. It also seems that he attempted to rule in an orthodox fashion, especially after 778/1376 when he banned all policies prohibited by the Shariʿa, including customary taxes.[99]

The similarity between Fīrōz's variety of piety and Jalāl al-dīn Bukhārī's Shariʿa-minded Sufism is obvious and, in fact, the two developed a mutually respectful and perhaps even close relationship over the course of the next three decades. Sirāj ʿAfīf, the primary chronicler of Fīrōz's reign, described the relationship between the Sultan and the saint as one of love and friendship and claimed that Bukhārī visited Fīrōz every few years.[100] In the biographies of each figure, the relationship is viewed as an indication of the subject's praiseworthiness—Bukhārī was such a great saint that even the king was his disciple while Fīrōz was such a pious king that even a saint would visit him regularly. ʿAfīf's *Tārīkh-i Fīrōz Shāhī*, which is written largely as a panegyric on Fīrōz, concludes its praises of him with an account of his relations with Bukhārī as the final example of his piety.

It is tempting to speculate on the possible influence each man might have had on the other's career. Was Fīrōz's penchant for orthodoxy developed under the tutelage of his *pīr*? Was Bukhārī's success and popularity as a Sufi shaykh dependent on the patronage and support of the Sultan? Or was this a mutually beneficial alliance between like-minded individuals? *Jāmiʿ al-ʿulūm* provides a detailed account of the interactions between Fīrōz and Bukhārī during the latter's visit to Delhi in 781/1379–1380, near the end of their lives. That will be discussed and analyzed in Chapter 6. For the early years of Fīrōz's reign, however, we have only limited information as to the nature of their developing relationship.

The Death of Naṣīr al-dīn Maḥmūd Chirāgh-i Dihlī

Naṣīr al-dīn Maḥmūd Awadhī, Jalāl al-dīn Bukhārī's initiator into the Chishtī lineage and one of the foremost Sufi shaykhs of his time, died on 18 Ramażān 757/14 September 1356. Though Naṣīr al-dīn died in Delhi, far from Bukhārī's home in Uch, Bukhārī claimed to have received immediate news of his death. As was his custom during Ramażān, Bukhārī was undertaking a forty-day retreat (*iʿtikāf*) in the main mosque in Uch. On the day of Naṣīr al-dīn's death, the Medinan shaykh ʿAfīf al-dīn Maṭarī appeared to Bukhārī and informed him that the *quṭb-i Hind*, the axial saint of Hind, had died.[101]

According to Bukhārī, Maṭarī was traveling in the *ʿālam-i ṭayr* (the realm of flight)—that is, he was flying through the air—to attend Naṣīr al-dīn's funeral prayers. He would have carried Bukhārī along with him to the prayers if Bukhārī were not engaged in a retreat. This being the case, Maṭarī instructed Bukhārī to stay where he was and complete his retreat. Bukhārī informed his companions in the mosque, including the author of *Khizānat al-fawāʾid al-Jalālīya*, that a master of religion had died in Delhi and they should say the funeral prayer for him. Since such a prayer at a distance is allowed by the Shāfiʿī school but not by the Ḥanafīs, who predominated in India, the doors of the mosque were closed so that no one could see them praying. Some days later the news arrived from Delhi that the Chishtī shaykh had died on that very day, thus confirming for his disciples the veracity of Bukhārī's visitation by Maṭarī.[102] When Bukhārī recounted this event later in life, some of his more nit-picking companions tried to find the weaknesses in the story. If Maṭarī came for Naṣīr al-dīn's funeral why did not Yāfiʿī? Because he was engaged in a forty day retreat, just like Bukhārī, otherwise he would have been there too. In that case, why was Maṭarī not engaged in the same practice? Because he did his retreat only during the last ten days of Ramażān.[103]

Naṣīr al-dīn Maḥmūd's death marked the passing of the generation of Bukhārī's *pīr*s. Over twenty years had passed since Rukn al-dīn Multānī's death. Though we have no firm dates for their deaths, presumably Bukhārī's early teacher Jamāl al-dīn Uchchī Khandān-rū and his father Aḥmad Kabīr had either died or were quite aged by this time. Though Yāfiʿī and Maṭarī still lived, within India there was no longer a living guide or master for Bukhārī in either the Suhrawardī or the Chishtī orders. Bukhārī quotes Maṭarī as saying, on the occasion of Naṣīr al-dīn's death: "There no longer remains a shaykh in Hind and in Sind."[104] Literally, of course, this was not true. India in the second half of the fourteenth century saw the rise of a number of important Sufi shaykhs: Naṣīr al-dīn's disciple Gīsūdarāz in the Deccan, Sharaf al-dīn Manērī in Bihar, and, of course, Jalāl al-dīn Bukhārī in Sind. Furthermore, important Sufi figures from elsewhere continued to immigrate to the sub-continent, such as Ashraf Jahāngīr Simnānī, ʿAlī Hamadānī, and Abū Isḥāq Maghribī. But there is a sense in the tradition that with the passing of Naṣīr al-dīn Chirāgh-i Dihlī and Rukn al-dīn Multānī the heroic foundational period of Indian Sufism had come to a close.[105]

Now over forty, Bukhārī was at the end of his years of apprenticeship as a student and a disciple, though he continued until the end of life to consider himself merely a representative (*wakīl*) for his shaykhs. Over the course of the next decade, Bukhārī came into his own as a Sufi master sought by disciples and respected by the political powers. Having established himself as the head of his family's *khānqāh* in Uch and as the leading heir to the Suhrawardī lineage in India, Bukhārī spent the decades of the 750s/1350s–760s/1360s largely occupied in teaching and training his disciples in Uch.[106] All the books he had studied and *khirqa*s he had collected were a spiritual legacy to be passed on to disciples and students who sought him out in Uch or during his trips to Delhi. Though Bukhārī always denied that he was a shaykh, preferring to be merely an agent for his masters, it was as a shaykh, a sayyid, and ultimately as a living saint that he was seen by his contemporaries in the later years of his life.

PART TWO

Teaching and Practice

THREE

Book-Learning and Islamic Law

The twin concepts underlying Bukhārī's teachings were *ʿilm* (knowledge) and *ʿamal* (action). *ʿIlm* is an inescapable term in Islamic religious discourse and one with a rich semantic field.[1] For Bukhārī, knowledge precedes action. While both knowledge and action are indispensable for his conception of the good Muslim and Sufi, knowledge has priority: "*awwal ʿilm, baʿdahu ʿamal, agar ʿilm nabāshad, ʿamal nadānad*" (First knowledge, then action. If there is no knowledge, one does not know [right] action).[2] Knowledge can mean many things. In religious contexts, *ʿilm* came to mean religious knowledge, while the plural, *ʿulūm*, denoted the various "sciences" of religious scholarship, such as study of the Quran, hadith, law, theology, and so on. An *ʿālim* (pl. *ʿulamāʾ*) was a religious expert, not a generally knowledgeable person. An examination of Bukhārī's understanding of *ʿilm* illuminates the relationship between Sufism and the rest of the Islamic religious tradition, and between the Sufi shaykhs and the ʿulama.

Knowledge Before Action

> Over there, in Kāzarūn, Mecca, Medina, and other places, madrasas have been built for each of the four *maẕḥhabs*. No one is told the *awrād* (litanies) until he has acquired *ʿilm* and if he is ignorant, he is asked, "Which *maẕhab* do you belong to?" Whichever of the four *maẕhabs* he says, he is sent to that madrasa and told: "Study *ʿilm*." When he has become a *faqīh*, then he is told the *awrād*. *Awrād* are in the category of *ʿamal* and as long as one has no *ʿilm* how can one know *ʿamal*? How can one recognize differences in opinion, agreement, and unanimity?[3]

The Definition of ʿIlm

In Bukhārī's usage, *ʿilm* is what is taught in a madrasa and distinguished according to *maẕhab*. By studying it one becomes a *faqīh*, a master of jurisprudence (*fiqh*).[4] *ʿIlm* is thus primarily knowledge of Islamic law. According to Bukhārī, "To approach God there is nothing better than being occupied with *ʿilm-i fiqh*."[5] Because the law is rooted in the Quran and hadith, the acquisition of *ʿilm* also requires the study of these texts, their exegesis and analysis, and of Arabic language and grammar. Such knowledge is necessary for the performance of *awrād* and all other ritual and devotional practice: without it one might deviate from the precise requirements of a ritual obligation, thus making it void and fruitless. Even worse, one might take up a practice whose legality is in doubt. In Bukhārī's teaching, religious practice is highly regimented and precise; any deviation from the prescribed words and actions invalidates the performance. In order for any ritual or devotional activity to be acceptable to God it needed to be done according to the rules derived from hadith and Quran and available only from authoritative texts or the oral teachings of a reputable scholar. Bukhārī directed much scorn, combined with pity, towards the ignorant who waste their time on the incorrect performance of ritual or are unwittingly led astray by the devil.

But did one really need to enroll in a madrasa and become a *faqīh* before participating in Sufi practices? True, as I recounted in Chapter 1, Shaykh Rukn al-dīn did turn Bukhārī away from the *khānqāh* in Multan when Bukhārī arrived as a *ṭālib-i ʿilm*. However, Bukhārī himself was willing to take on fairly uneducated disciples, invest them with the *khirqa*, and give them a litany to recite. Bukhārī was being somewhat hyperbolic in the passage above, as well as making the rhetorical move of ascribing this policy to cities "over there," in order to emphasize the importance of knowledge and learning. I have no idea whether Bukhārī ever sent would-be disciples to the madrasa for preliminary education—what he did do was spend much of his time teaching them the various branches of *ʿilm*. When asked, "Is it better to be occupied with learning and teaching or with supererogatory devotions?" he said, "If possible, do both. Otherwise, if learning is with the intention of freeing oneself of ignorance, performing *ʿamal*, and benefiting others, then it is better to be occupied with learning."[6]

Books and Book-Learning

What did Bukhārī teach? His disciple Ḥusaynī, author of *Jāmiʿ al-ʿulūm*, lists 89 *ʿulūm* mastered and taught by Bukhārī.[7] More useful, perhaps, for getting an immediate sense of Bukhārī's range of subjects are the topics covered in *Khizānat al-fawāʾid al-Jalālīya*. This text addresses all the basic requirements of being a Shariʿa-abiding practicing Muslim—the obligatory rituals, legitimate sources of income and nourishment, family life, and correct belief with regard to the Prophet and his family. The final chapter, which describes supererogatory prayers, litanies, and invocations, accounts for nearly a quarter of the whole text, indicating Bukhārī's ultimate focus on instructing his disciples in devotional activities.[8] The text itself recapitulates Bukhārī's principle that *ʿilm* precedes *ʿamal*, since none of the prayers in the final chapter would be valid if any of the rules on the previous topics were disregarded.

Bukhārī's interest in studying and teaching the full range of Islamic "sciences" (*ʿulūm*) is demonstrated by his and his disciples' copious references to books on each of them—every page of his *malfūẓāt* texts is dotted with references to works on hadith, law, Quranic exegesis, theology, and Sufism, intermingled with anecdotes about his own life and those of exemplary saints. I have compiled a combined bibliography of all titles and authors mentioned in Bukhārī's *malfūẓāt* in Appendix E.[9]

A quarter of the texts cited by Bukhārī fall into the broad category of Sufism, including pietistic and ethical works, *awrād* collections, *malfūẓāt*, and hagiographies. Bukhārī referenced many of the standard handbooks of Sufi practice by well-known and widely respected authorities such as al-Ghazālī, Shihāb al-dīn al-Suhrawardī, al-Kalābādhī, and al-Qushayrī. Some later and less known texts in the list, such as *ʿAyn al-ʿilm* and *al-Risāla al-Makkīya*, also belong to the same genre of Sufi handbook. Collections of litanies (*awrād*) used by the great shaykhs are also numerous, fitting in with Bukhārī's emphasis on prayer and *wird* as the primary religious practices. Related to these are the commentaries on the Divine Names and on the names of the Prophet Muḥammad, both used in litanies and prayers. A noticeable absence in the list of Sufi texts are any of a speculative, theosophical, or visionary nature. The aspects of Sufism highlighted here are ethics, practice, and devotion.

Bukhārī's position on the centrality of *ʿilm-i fiqh* is borne out by the pride of place given to works on law and jurisprudence in his bibliography. Approximately one third of the texts are legal compendia and compilations of *fatāwā* (plural of *fatwā*; legal responsa), plus commentaries and super-commentaries. Nearly all of these are standard Ḥanafī texts, with a few Shāfiʿī additions. The numerous *fatāwā* compilations listed are evidence not only of Bukhārī's interest in the correct application of Islamic law but also of the popularity of this genre during the reign of Fīrōz Shāh Tughluq.[10] Hadith collections, including the six authoritative Sunni collections and various more specific or limited ones, *tafsīrs* (Quran commentaries), and theological or creedal works make up the rest of the bibliography.

In all of these topics, Bukhārī largely limited his references to the authoritative products of the various religious "sciences," the compilations that served as standard textbooks or reference works, rather than to works that address methodological or critical issues. In other words, he preferred hadith collections to works on the methods of hadith criticism, *fatāwā* compilations to works on jurisprudential theory, and creedal or doctrinal statements (*ʿaqīda*) to works employing the dialectical methodology of *kalām*. This suggests that Bukhārī was not interested in teaching the disciplinary methods nor the modes of reasoning employed in the various fields. Instead he presented, in as comprehensive a fashion as possible, views that had already been developed and had become normative within the Sunni Ḥanafī world. Such an emphasis suggests that Bukhārī's goal was not, in fact, to train *faqīhs*, *mufassirs* (exegetes), or any other variety of specialized ʿulama, but rather to make sure that his disciples knew the range of received positions on doctrinal and legal issues.

Besides Bukhārī's individual pedagogic agenda, however, the emphasis in his bibliography on compilations and manuals is also typical of this moment in the history of Islamic religious scholarship. The individual disciplines or "sciences" had arisen, developed their methodologies, and staked their claims to religious authority at different moments in the preceding centuries. In a trend that has led to the characterization of the post-Mongol period as a decline or a stagnation, "medieval scholars did not write what we would consider today to be 'original' works, but focused instead on the organization, classification and analysis of what earlier authors had presented before."[11] Although the dismissal of the intellectual content of such works as unoriginal is perhaps unwarranted, Bukhārī's bibliography attests to the vast number of texts available during this period that were either synthetic manuals and textbooks, collections of *awrād*, hadith, and *fatāwā* organized according to various schemes, or commentaries and super-commentaries. Bukhārī's *malfūẓāt* texts also participate in a trend of anthologizing extracts from earlier works.

Bukhārī's explicit use of books as the source for the "knowledge" that he was transmitting to his students and disciples is also indicative of the nature of religious education during this period. Despite the prolific production of books as repositories of knowledge, the written book had an uneasy and ambiguous position in the traditional structure of Islamic education. For knowledge of hadith, in particular, oral transmission from a reliable individual scholar was long considered indispensable.[12] However, despite an early suspicion of written books as authoritative, generated by the model of hadith transmission and influencing scholarship in other fields as well, by the eighth/fourteenth century books had become indispensable to the process of training religious experts. Madrasa education and the expertise of the 'ulama had begun to be understood in terms of the mastery of specific books. Although K. A. Nizami points out that there was "hardly any fixed syllabus"[13] for the medieval madrasas, he also provides a list of standard texts, which has significant overlap with Bukhārī's bibliography.[14] Attempts at reconstructing medieval syllabi from other parts of the Islamic world also show some overlap, though understandably less so.[15]

The distrust of written books as authoritative stand-alone sources of knowledge and the need for verification of learning transmitted from a teacher to a student gave rise to the process of oral transmission of books characteristic of Islamic education. Though mastery of particular books was indispensable for any claim to scholarly religious authority, individual and isolated study of a text did not qualify a scholar to claim expertise on its content. To make such a claim, one had to be instructed in that text by a recognized authority. The process of such instruction required the oral recitation of the text, whether by the teacher, or by the student, or by a third party under the teacher's supervision, and its oral explication by the teacher. Thus, to be educated required a combination of personal contact with a recognized teacher and the acquisition of book-learning from that teacher. The authenticity of a text, a student's mastery of that text, and the authority of the teacher to transmit it, all needed certification. This certification might take the combined form of an *ijāzat*, stating that the student had permission to transmit the text on the authority of the teacher under whose supervision he or she had read or heard the text, the teacher having previously received such an *ijāzat* in a chain of transmission reaching back to the author of the text.

As I have described earlier, Bukhārī had participated as a student in this formal process of textual transmission under the supervision of his teachers and shaykhs in Uch, Multan, the Hejaz, and Iran. He had also transmitted texts, giving *ijāzat*s for several books while he was in Aden and supervising a reading in Shiraz. The *malfūẓāt* texts refer to the readings done under a shaykh's supervision as *sabaq khwāndan* or *guftan* (reading a lesson) and mention this as a regular part of Bukhārī's daily activities. A disciple would read an assigned text and Bukhārī would provide any necessary explanations, commentary, or translation. Most of Bukhārī's shaykhs and teachers had also held formal teaching sessions; Shaykh Jamāl al-dīn Uchchī considered *sabaq guftan* so important that he did it until his dying days.[16]

Ḥusaynī, author of *Jāmiʿ al-ʿulūm*, records twenty-three texts, mostly in Arabic, that he heard read (*samaʿ kardam*), at least partially, during nearly a year that he spent with Bukhārī in Delhi in 781/1379–1380. He classifies these texts according to subject: hadith, law, theology, exegesis, the Sufi path (*sulūk*), and litanies.

Table 2: Books Read under Bukhārī's Supervision
Rabi II 781–Muharram 782 / July 1379–April 1380

The Quran

On Hadith:
Mashāriq al-anwār by Raḍī al-dīn al-Ṣaghānī (d. 650/1252).
Maṣābīḥ al-sunna by Abū Muḥammad al-Baghawī (d. 516/1122).
Arbaʿīn-i ṣūfīya compiled by Jalāl al-dīn Bukhārī in Mecca and Medina.

On *Fiqh* (jurisprudence):
Kitāb al-muttafiq wa al-muftariq by al-Khaṭīb al-Baghdādī (d. 463/1071).
Majmaʿ al-baḥrayn by Aḥmad b. ʿAlī Ibn al-Sāʿātī (d. 696/1296).
A portion of *al-Hidāya al-burhānīya* by Burhān al-dīn al-Marghinānī (d. 593/1197).
A portion of *Mukhtaṣar al-Qudūrī* by Qudūrī (d.428/1037).

On *Uṣūl-i fiqh* (roots of the law):
A portion of *Uṣūl-i Pazdawī* by Abū al-Ḥasan ʿAlī b. Muḥammad Pazdawī, (d. 482/1089).
A portion of *Ḥusāmī* by Ḥusām al-dīn Muḥammad al-Akhsīkatī (d. 644/1247).

On *Kalām* (theology):
ʿAqīdat al-Nasafī by Ḥāfiẓ al-dīn Abū al-Barakāt ʿAbdallāh al-Nasafī (d. 710/1310).
Qaṣīda al-lāmiya by Sirāj al-dīn al-Ūshī al-Farghānī Imām (ca. 569/1173). With a commentary.

On *Tafsīr* (Quran commentary):
Madārik al-tanzīl by Ḥāfiẓ al-dīn Abū al-Barakāt ʿAbdallāh al-Nasafī (d. 710/1310).

On *Sulūk* (traveling the path, that is, Sufism):
ʿAwārif al-maʿārif by Abū Ḥafs ʿUmar Shihāb al-dīn al-Suhrawardī (d. 632/1234).
al-Taʿarruf li madhhab ahl al-taṣawwuf by Muḥammad b. Isḥāq al-Kalābādhī (d. 380/990).
al-Risālat al-Makkīya by Quṭb al-dīn al-Dimashqī (d. 780/1378).

Other unnamed *risālas*.

On the Divine Names:
Sharḥ-i chihl o yak asmā'-i a'ẓam.
Sharḥ-i kabīr-i nawad-o-nuh nām-i bārī-yi ta'ālā.
Sharḥ-i saghīr-i nawad-o-nuh nām-i bārī-yi ta'ālā.

On *Awrād* (litanies):
Awrād shaykh al-shuyūkh by Abū Ḥafs 'Umar Shihāb al-dīn al-Suhrawardī (d. 632/1234).
Awrād-i shaykh kabīr by Bahā' al-dīn Zakarīyā (d. 666/1267).
Awrād-i khwājagān-i Chisht.
Awrād-i makhdūm-i jahāniyān by Jalāl al-dīn Bukhārī.

This list includes the standard texts on these topics, studied and cited by anyone claiming authoritative Islamic religious knowledge in medieval South Asia.[17] Al-Marghīnānī's *Hidāya*, al-Nasafī's *Madārik*, al-Baghawī's *Maṣābīḥ*, *Uṣūl-i Pazdawī*, and Shihāb al-dīn Suhrawardī's *'Awārif al-ma'ārif* were part of the standard syllabus of Islamic learning at the time.[18] The centrality of some of these texts in Bukhārī's own education is demonstrated by the fact that he specified exactly where and with whom he studied them: *Pazdawī*, *Hidāya*, and *Maṣābīḥ* with the scholars of Uch and Multan, and *'Awārif al-ma'ārif* and *al-Risāla al-Makkīya* in Mecca and Medina with Yāfi'ī and Maṭarī, with whom he also read the six canonical hadith collections. That Bukhārī and his disciples, like many participants in the Sufi path, studied the basic religious texts of Sunni Islam is unsurprising. What is striking is the degree to which the formal transmission of texts, a practice more commonly associated with the madrasa-based education of the 'ulama, was integrated into the spiritual training that Bukhārī received and that he offered his disciples.

In Bukhārī's career as both disciple and master, book-learning, as described above, was thoroughly interwoven with the process of investiture that marked a Sufi aspirant's initiation into the Sufi path. Bukhārī was invested with his first *khirqas* from his father and other paternal relatives and received his early textual instruction on Sufism, hadith, and Arabic from his father and other scholars at his father's *khānqāh*. He then proceeded to Multan where he studied more of the fundamental religious texts. Shaykh Rukn al-dīn Multānī, who appears as Bukhārī's most important *pīr* in many *tazkira* sources, enabled this period of study and assigned Bukhārī to particular teachers. During Bukhārī's time in Mecca and Medina, Yāfi'ī and Maṭarī both invested him with *khirqas*, supervised his textual education, and gave him *ijāzats* for both. Finally, in Shabānkāreh, Maḥmūd Tustarī's *ijāzats* for the Suhrawardī *khirqa* and for *'Awārif al-ma'ārif* are almost a single package of religious authorization, particularly valuable because of their short chain of transmission from Shihāb al-dīn Suhrawardī himself.

The instructions (*waṣīyat*) given by Bukhārī to one of his disciples, a judge, on the occasion of his investiture are also indicative of the way in which he embedded Sufi practice in the structures of legal orthodoxy and vice-versa.

> I invest the most dear and noble brother, the judge, the scholar, the doer [of good deeds], Shihāb al-dīn ʿAbd al-Rashīd b. Zayn al-dīn Ibrāhīm al-Farajī with the *khirqa* of the Sufi shaykhs. I was invested with it by my father, and he by his father, and he by his shaykh, the radiant pole of the world, Bahā' al-Ḥaqq waal-dīn Abū Muḥammad Zakarīyā al-Qurayshī al-Asadī etc. Each master was invested with the blessed *khirqa* by one with whom he had associated.
>
> His [i.e., the disciple's] instructions are to: make his deeds correspond to his learning; fill his moment and his life with varieties of worship, maintain the litanies (*awrād*) of the aforementioned great shaykh . . .; fulfill the rights of his parents, his teachers, his people, his kin, his neighbors, his companions, and his servants, bear ill-treatment from them, give generously to them of what he possesses, and not covet what they possess . . .; teach what he knows to those who seek to learn from him; give legal decisions on what falls within his jurisdiction, according to the respected legal texts and the cases in them which he has studied . . .; observe the manners of the judges in government which are told in *Kitāb adab al-qāżī al-Khaṣṣāf* (The book of the judge's etiquette by al-Khaṣṣāf); and bestow the aforementioned blessed *khirqa* on whoever seeks it from him and is worthy of it. Instruct him properly, accept his repentance, teach him who repents to ask for forgiveness just as he learned it from me, and run the shears over his head just as he saw me [do], thus authorized by me.
>
> I was also invested with the *khirqa* of blessing from his [Bahā' al-dīn Zakarīyā's] shaykh, Shaykh al-shuyūkh Shihāb al-dīn al-Suhrawardī from his uncle Żiyā' al-dīn from Muḥyi al-dīn ʿAbd al-Qādir al-Gīlānī. I was also invested by Sayyid Ḥamīd al-dīn Abū al-Waqt Maḥmūd al-Samarqandī from Abū Saʿīd Ẓafar al-Kirmānī from Abū al-ʿAbbās Khiżr from the Master of Messengers, Muḥammad, Seal of the Prophets.
>
> I, the servant of the *faqīrs*, the aforementioned Ḥusayn b. Aḥmad b. Ḥusayn al-Ḥusaynī al-Bukhārī, wrote this on 19 Shawwāl in the year 770 [27 May 1369], in the town of Uch, may it be preserved from all calamities and disasters.[19]

In this document, besides briefly indicating the genealogies of the *khirqa* and advising him to be generally pious, to practice the litanies, and to invest others with the *khirqa*, Bukhārī instructs his disciple to teach, to give correct legal decisions, and to follow al-Khaṣṣāf's manual for judges, *Kitāb adab al-qāżī*. In other words, rather than this individual's affiliation with Bukhārī as a disciple and his career as a judge and scholar being two separate facets of his persona, they are instead presented here as a single religious identity.

Bukhārī's Malfūẓāt Compilations and Legal Texts

Malfūẓāt as Religious Compendia

Thus far, I have been approaching the relationship between Sufism and Islamic law in terms of the place of legal teaching in the practice of a Sufi shaykh, the boundary between the categories of *ʿālim* and shaykh, and the distinction between a madrasa and a Sufi *khānqāh*. However, besides such distinctions of personnel and institution, Sufism and the law can also be viewed as two distinct textual or discursive traditions. Some of Bukhārī's *malfūẓāt* compilations lend themselves to an exploration of the intertextual relationships between Sufi works and legal ones. For this purpose, I compare these *malfūẓāt* compilations to similar contemporary texts from both the Sufi and legal traditions.

Bukhārī's two *malfūẓāt* collections that rely most heavily on quotation from and reference to legal texts—*Khizānat al-fawāʾid* and *Sirāj al-hidāya*—are also the two that are organized into topical chapters, rather than the daily diary structure usually associated with the *malfūẓāt* genre. This topical structure removes much of the conversational context of Bukhārī's teachings, although there are occasional mentions of his interlocutors and their questions or responses. Without the details of time, place, and scene, Bukhārī's teachings appear more as discrete statements about different topics and, given his dependence on textual authorities, very often as a string of quotations from relevant books. As a result, both *Khizānat al-fawāʾid* and *Sirāj al-hidāya* read like encyclopedic anthologies of Islamic religious material, interspersed with Bukhārī's commentary and definitive statements.

Khizānat al-fawāʾid and *Sirāj al-hidāya* are not unique in this regard—similar texts, some classified as *malfūẓāt*, had been produced in the circles of other South Asian Sufi shaykhs of the eighth/fourteenth century. One such is *Shamāʾil al-atqiyāʾ* by Rukn al-dīn Kāshānī, a disciple of the Chishtī shaykh Burhān al-dīn Gharīb (d. 738/1337).[20] Ernst aptly describes this work as "an enormous collection of excerpts from Sufi writings and oral traditions, covering a full range of topics related to mystical thought and practice."[21] Another is *Miftāḥ al-jinān*, composed circa 770/1368 by Muḥammad Mujīr b. Wajīh al-dīn, a disciple of Naṣīr al-dīn Maḥmūd Chirāgh-i Dihlī. *Miftāḥ al-jinān* explains essential religious practices, their spiritual benefits, supererogatory devotions, and various types of piety and sinfulness.[22] In all four of these works, every page is dotted with the titles of books quoted, often Arabic texts, with or without Persian explication, sometimes Persian translations of Arabic texts, and more infrequently Persian texts.[23]

The authors of these religious compendia draw explicit attention to their comprehensive coverage of religious topics and to their compilation of extracts from a large number of earlier works from the different Islamic sciences. In one of the prefaces to

Sirāj al-hidāya, the compiler states his intention to record what he learned from Bukhārī "about hadith, Quranic exegesis, legal problems, stories of the great shaykhs, secrets of this life and the next, from verse and prose sources."[24] He goes on to state that for every explanation of a Quran verse, every hadith, every example from the teachings of the jurists, he would ask Bukhārī for the full title of the books quoted. One of Bukhārī's disciples reprimanded him for the distrust of the shaykh's teachings implied in such a request. He responded that it was for the sake of a reader who might need further guidance from texts. Since he himself did not have access to many books while Bukhārī did, this seemed the most useful approach.[25] *Shamā'il al-atqiyā'* is prefaced by a comprehensive bibliography of all the sources used in its composition. This bibliography runs to about one hundred eighty texts plus the oral teachings of nearly seventy individuals.[26] In the preface to *Miftāḥ al-jinān*, the author states that he compiled his material from books on *tafsīr*, hadith, *fiqh*, and Sufism as a response to the inability of many "common people" to read or understand Arabic. "He copied exactly what was in Persian and translated anything that was in Arabic so that common people and children might take a liking to it and be benefited by it."[27]

Clearly these texts aspired to make available some portion of Islamic religious scholarship to an audience with limited knowledge of Arabic and limited access to books. The immediate antecedents of the South Asian Islamic tradition, and thus the sources for many of the works used in Indo-Islamic scholarship, lay in Central Asia. Though Islamic elite culture in Central Asia was Persianate, the texts taught and produced by the religious scholars there were mostly composed in the Arabic language. This traditional reliance on a syllabus of Arabic texts, and the production of further scholarship in Arabic, continued in the madrasas of South Asia. The authors/compilers of the four Sufi texts under discussion are responding to the problem posed by the inaccessibility of what they see as necessary religious knowledge dispersed in numerous hard-to-come-by books, in a language foreign even to most of the Indian Muslim elite. Despite the teaching of Arabic as the language of Islam in the context of religious education, there was no guarantee that even a moderately educated, literate, and pious South Asian Muslim would have a strong grasp of the language.

The two topical collections of Bukhārī's teachings, *Khizānat al-fawā'id* and *Sirāj al-hidāya*, as well as Muḥammad Mujīr's *Miftāḥ al-jinān*, were all composed in the 760s/1360s and 770s/1370s. All three, despite their authors' explicit self-identification as Sufi disciples, share a striking dependence on non-Sufi material, that is, material from the other branches of Islamic religious scholarship. *Khizānat al-fawā'id* cites one hundred thirty-six sources, including works of poetry. Of the books quoted, only about thirty would be classified as Sufi texts, including the standard handbooks, earlier *malfūẓāt*, and devotional manuals. Half as many texts are devoted to hadith and lesser numbers to theology and scriptural commentary. The single largest category of works cited, approximately fifty texts, is that concerned with Islamic law (*fiqh*). While *Sirāj al-hidāya*'s quotes from fewer texts, less than sixty altogether, *fiqh* is given an even more prominent place with about two-thirds of works cited concerning themselves with the law. More than eighty texts are cited or quoted by *Miftāḥ al-jinān*, of which only a dozen or so are on specifically Sufi topics. The rest are mostly legal texts, plus some works on hadith and Quran. *Shamāʾil al-atqiyā*, composed some decades earlier, is much more clearly embedded in the Sufi tradition. Less than a third of the bibliography provided by the author is devoted to Quran commentary, hadith, and law. Furthermore, in the text itself, independent of the bibliography, the vast majority of quotes are taken from a much smaller selection of texts, around twenty, all of which are closely identified with Sufism. The difference between *Shamāʾil al-atqiyāʾ* and the other three books may indicate a change in the place of law in Indian Sufism over the course of the eighth/fourteenth century. Or it may be a result of the different interests of the authors and their spiritual mentors.

The overwhelming presence of legal material in *Khizānat al-fawāʾid*, *Sirāj al-hidāya*, and *Miftāḥ al-jinān* muddles the clear distinction one might expect between Sufi texts and legal ones. This is not just a matter of the inclusion of a concern for the law—the principle that knowledge of and adherence to the Shariʿa is a prerequisite for progress on the Sufi path is a commonplace in Sufi thought. What is taking place in these texts is the intermingling of two usually distinct textual or discursive traditions. We take for granted that Sufism is not *fiqh*, and *fiqh* is not Sufism, despite their often common concerns, shared dependence on the Quran and hadith, and frequently shared practitioners. One of the ways the distinction and relationship between the two is made most apparent is when they are viewed as bodies of text, discursive traditions, rather than sets of ideas, practices, or personnel. This is in part a question of genre, though the elasticity of the Sufi tradition and its expression in different literary forms makes genre an unreliable marker of the Sufi nature of a text. A more reliable marker may be found in the intertextuality of a Sufi work.

Intertextuality

Intertextuality, a term developed by literary theorists to describe the ways in which a text is embedded in a referential network of other texts, has been fruitfully adopted for the study of religious works. In Islamic studies, intertextuality has largely been used to analyze the complex relationships between the Quran and the Biblical scriptures. Medieval Sufi texts also lend themselves to an exploration of this concept, most obviously in their reliance upon an oft-quoted set of Quran verses and hadith. William Graham has labeled as "traditionalism" "the long-standing, overt predilection in diverse strands of Islamic life for recourse to previous authorities."[28] However, Sufi texts go beyond this general reliance on past authority; they cite and comment on both earlier and nearly contemporary Sufi texts and poetry, and retell a collective body of anecdotes and dicta from earlier masters of the tradition. Thus, when reading a Sufi work from a fairly mature period in the development of the tradition, such as pre-Mughal South Asia, one is necessarily made aware of a whole discursive tradition with which that text is in dialogue. "Intertextuality is less a name for a work's relation to particular prior texts than an assertion of a work's participation in a discursive space and its relation to the codes which are the potential formalizations of that space."[29] A text may refer to prior ones in a number of ways: direct attributed quotation, unstated allusion, borrowing phrases or expressions, critique, pastiche, commentary, and so on. The reader may be expected to recognize the source of an allusion or a quotation without it being identified, as is often the case with Quranic material. Quotes may be attributed to books or to people. The particular type of intertextuality present tells us something about the relationship between this text and its referents, and about the place of the texts within the discursive tradition.

Kāshānī's *Shamā'il al-atqiyā'* is a good example of such "participation in a discursive space." Much of *Shamā'il al-atqiyā'* is built around quotes from classic Sufi handbooks such as the *Risāla* of Qushayrī (d. 465/1072), *Qūt al-qulūb* by Abū Ṭālib al-Makkī (d. 386/996), *'Awārif al-ma'ārif* by Shihāb al-dīn Suhrawardī (d. 632/1234), *Kashf al-maḥjūb* by Hujwīrī (d. 465/1072), and *Mirṣād al-'ibād* by Najm al-dīn Dāyā Rāzī (d. 654/1256), and the works of Ghazālī (d. 505/1111) and 'Ayn al-qużāt al-Hamadānī (d. 525/1131) (or translations and abridgements of these texts). (The single most quoted text is Kāshānī's own *Rumūz al-wālihīn*.) Carl Ernst has demonstrated that "Kāshānī takes a rather liberal approach to citation, picking out short phrases and longer sentences as needed, but the comments that he adds may take off in a rather different direction than that intended in the original text." Sometimes, "there is barely a verbal echo" of the original passage. For Ernst, this shows the living and mutable nature of the tradition in which new meanings are found through "personal meditation" and discipleship.[30] Sajjād Ḥusayn states that many of *Sirāj al-hidāya*'s quotations from hadith and *fiqh* texts are also inaccurate or incorrect.[31] Checking the accuracy of quotation is beyond the scope of my project, but a similar "liberal approach to citation" may be true of the other texts under discussion here.

Just as intertextuality may be used to mark out the discursive tradition of Sufism, it can also be used to investigate the relationship between Sufism and other aspects of Islam. Quran and hadith, and the scholarly texts devoted to their study and explication, are obviously discursive traditions upon which Sufism is dependent and in dialogue. Sufi texts also frequently refer to works from the philosophical tradition, to poetry, and to works on Islamic law. In all of these cases, the identity of the texts and the particular ideas, verses, or passages to which reference is made can illuminate the relationship between Sufism and these other discursive traditions. As I have discussed above, Bukhārī's *malfūẓāt* and Muḥammad Mujīr's *Miftāḥ al-jinān* are all heavily reliant on quotation from legal texts. For "orthodox" Sharī'a-minded Sufism, the teachings of the legal tradition were the foundations of correct religious practice and doctrine, a necessary first step before the subsequent exploration of Sufi devotions and ideas. However, the three texts under consideration here have a much deeper relationship to the discursive space of the law than a straightforward borrowing of essential information. And it is a particular genre of legal scholarship, the *fatāwā* compilations, with which they are in dialogue.

Fatāwā Compilations

One of the most common genres of Islamic legal writing in medieval South Asia was the compilation of *fatāwā* (plural of *fatwā*). In this context, a *fatwā* did not refer to an advisory opinion provided by a *muftī* to a questioner but rather to "an authoritative and accepted opinion of the Ḥanafī school."[32] In putting together a *fatāwā* compilation, an author would extract relevant opinions and rulings from earlier legal texts and organize them according to his own system. Highly developed in Central Asia, the genre flourished in Islamic South Asia, serving the needs of both legal scholars and judges. The eighth/fourteenth century, especially the reign of Fīrōz Shāh, was a particularly fruitful moment for legal scholarship in general, and *fatāwā* compilations specifically.[33] In compiling, re-arranging, and commenting on the legal views of earlier jurists, each new *fatāwā* collection necessarily referred to many prior texts within the tradition, with certain texts achieving a canonical and authoritative status through citation by succeeding generations. Because *fatāwā* compilations cite the textual sources from which they are quoting, each compilation allows the reader to identify the particular *fiqh* texts that had achieved a level of authority or popularity at a particular moment in time.[34]

A significant number of *fatāwā* compilations are among the texts quoted by *Khizānat al-fawā'id al-Jalālīya* and *Sirāj al-hidāya*. (The latter quotes from so many titles with the form "*Fatāwā-i* such and such," many of which I have been unable to identify, that this appears to be a formulaic label for any legal opinions ascribed to a known authority.) But *fatāwā* compilations are more than just sources of legal information for these encyclopedic *malfūẓāt*. They share a similar structure of composition and a further dependence on a similar set of texts. If we compare *Khizānat al-fawā'id* and *Sirāj al-hidāya* to the most widely known contemporary example of Indian *fatāwā* compilation, *Fiqh-i Fīrōz Shāhī* (also known as *Fatāwā-i Fīrōz Shāhī*),[35] these similarities become obvious.

Fiqh-i Fīrōz Shāhī, composed for the Sultan as a legal reference and with a focus on commercial issues, differs in its obvious intent from *malfūẓāt* meant to preserve the teachings of a Sufi shaykh. Yet, it shares the same format of compilations of extracts from past authorities, with commentary, organized into chapters covering many of the same topics of essential Islamic religious and personal practice. One aspect of *Fiqh-i Fīrōz Shāhī* is particularly striking—like Bukhārī's *malfūẓāt*, and unlike earlier *fatāwā* compilations or most other legal texts, it is composed in Persian and provides Persian translation or paraphrase for most quotations from Arabic sources. The more than forty-five sources quoted by *Fiqh-i Fīrōz-shāhī* are exclusively legal and Ḥanafī; thus it is clearly inhabiting and delineating the discursive space of the law. Many of these sources are also quoted by *Khizānat al-fawā'id* and *Sirāj al-hidāya*, including foundational texts of the Ḥanafī *maẕhab* such as Imām Muḥammad al-Shaybānī's (d. 189/804) *Jāmi' al-ṣaghīr*, later syntheses of the tradition like *al-Hidāya* by al-Marghinānī (d. 593/1197), and numerous *fatāwā* collections.[36]

Sufi Texts and Legal Texts

Comparing *Khizānat al-fawā'id* and *Sirāj al-hidāya* to similarly structured Sufi religious compendia (*Shamā'il al-atqiyā'* and *Miftāḥ al-jinān*), on the one hand, and to *Fiqh-i Fīrōz Shāhī*, on the other hand, demonstrates several points about Islamic religious writing in eighth/fourteenth century South Asia. First, the impulse to produce encyclopedic compilations of religious teachings and to make available key extracts from the preceding (mostly Arabic) textual tradition of Central and West Asia to a Persian-reading South Asian public was shared by both Sufi writers and legal scholars. Second, although *Shamā'il al-atqiyā'* and *Fiqh-i Fīrōz Shāhī* each delineate distinct discursive spaces for Sufism and *fiqh*, respectively, *Khizānat al-fawā'id*, *Sirāj al-hidāya*, and *Miftāḥ al-jinān* demonstrate that the boundary between these spaces was not inviolable.[37] Despite their authors' self-identification as disciples of Sufi shaykhs, rather than as legal scholars, and, in the case of the *malfūẓāt*, despite the identification of the contents of these books as the teaching of a Sufi shaykh, these three texts rely upon the legal tradition and present legal rulings in much the same way that the *fatāwā* compilations do.

This crossover between the legal and Sufi traditions can lead to several different conclusions about the relative status of the law and Sufism, and of legal scholars and Sufi shaykhs. To speak someone else's language can be a sign of submission to the other's power or it can be a claim to the other's authority. That is, on the one hand, the centrality of the law in these texts is an acknowledgement and a submission to the Shari'a's hegemonic claim to define correct Islamic behavior. On the other hand, it is also an appropriation of the authority of legal scholars, the authority to instruct Muslims in every aspect of their lives. Legal rulings are thus made part of the guidance provided by a Sufi master, whose authority and learning encompasses the law, rather than being limited or governed by it.

The Sufi tradition as represented by *Shamā'il al-atqiyā'* still needed the presence of legal experts to lay out the basic guidelines for Islamic behavior. Once those were fulfilled, the traveler on the Sufi path could turn his or her attention to the deeper spiritual truths offered by a Sufi *pīr*. *Khizānat al-fawā'id* and *Sirāj al-hidāya*, in contrast, represent the shaykh as providing all the guidance needed to be a good Muslim. Despite the explicit respect paid to the 'ulama in these texts, they have, in some sense, been rendered redundant, since now their function has been taken over by the Sufi shaykh. If this is the case, then the textual and human authorities of the Sufi tradition are claiming a certain totalizing religious authority.

Sufism and the 'Ulama

Bukhārī's attention to textual scholarship and to the full range of the religious sciences raises the same question as the careers of his teachers Yāfi'ī and Maṭarī: to what extent should we consider him to be an *'ālim* as well as a Sufi shaykh? In fact, how do we distinguish between the categories of ʿulama and Sufis? The compiler of *Khizānat al-fawā'id* introduces Bukhārī with the labels of *faqīh* (jurist), *muḥaddis̱* (hadith scholar), *mufassir* (commentator on the Quran), and *ʿālim*,[38] all of these titles fully justified by the range of his education and the subject matter of his teaching. Similarly the Yemeni chronicler Abū Makhrama's brief entry on Bukhārī mentions him only as a transmitter of texts (on Sufism and Arabic grammar).[39] The accounts of Bukhārī's political engagements and his relations with the Sultan in Sirāj Afīf's *Tārīkh-i Fīrōz Shāhī* never give him the label of shaykh, referring to him instead as the master of sayyids (*sayyid al-sādāt*) and as a saint (*quṭb al-ʿālam*).[40]

ʿĀlim and Shaykh

There is a tendency in both popular and academic discourse to describe the ʿulama and the Sufis as two separate social groups with distinct and often conflictual religious ideologies. Yet, the examples of Bukhārī and his teachers demonstrate that this was not necessarily the case: the activities of a Sufi shaykh could be and often were combined with those of the ʿulama. This is not to say, however, that the two categories can be collapsed—the authority of scholars to teach and, in particular, of *faqīh*s to give judicial opinions is distinct from the authority of the Sufi shaykhs to take on disciples, invest them with *khirqa*s, and guide them in devotional activities. Furthermore, the institutional bases for the two groups, the madrasa and the *khānqāh*, and the economies that supported them were quite distinct. As we saw in the example of Rukn al-dīn Multānī not receiving Bukhārī into his *khānqāh* nor feeding him from its kitchens because he was there as a *ṭālib-i ʿilm* and not as a *darwēsh*, these distinctions were taken quite seriously. In this regard, Bukhārī's home base at the family tomb and *khānqāh* complex in Uch clearly marks him as mostly inhabiting the role of a Sufi shaykh. However, outside of Uch, we often find him inhabiting rather undefined religious spaces, neither enrolling as a student nor holding a professorial chair in a madrasa nor staying in a *khānqāh* as a *darwēsh*. In Multan, Rukn al-dīn housed Bukhārī in a room over the city gate; in Medina, Bukhārī stayed in a cell at the Prophet's mosque; and during his visits to Delhi (discussed in Chapter 6), he stayed at a princely tomb complex.

Bukhārī's inclusion of madrasa-style teaching in his daily practice, despite not having any regular relationship to such an institution, should not be taken as an indication of a lack of madrasas in medieval South Asia. In fact, the Tughluq period saw the establishment of numerous madrasas, many built with the patronage of the state, including "a thousand" in Delhi alone.[41] Furthermore, illustrating the crossover between the lives of the ʿulama and that of the Sufis, many of these madrasas had space set aside for resident or visiting *darwēsh*es.[42] Some madrasas were part of what could be called a mixed-use religious complex, like the Madrasa-yi shāhzāda-yi buzurg (The Madrasa of the Prince) at the tomb of Fīrōz Shāh's son Fatḥ Khān, where Bukhārī resided when in Delhi.

Bukhārī's explicit statements on the topic of the 'ulama also emphasize the intertwining between their roles and those of the Sufi shaykhs. On the one hand, memorization of numerous books and legal points is insufficient to be a true *'ālim* or *faqīh* (jurist). One also needs to be ascetic and pure.[43] On the other hand, the true shaykh is one who has the 'ulama of his time as disciples and adherents.[44] This last qualification creates an interdependency between the shaykhs, whose authority is validated by the 'ulama, and the 'ulama who accept the shaykhs as guides. From the disciple or student's position, an identical attitude of respect is required towards both one's teacher and one's shaykh. Thus when Bukhārī was disrespectful and spoke loudly to a teacher in Medina, Maṭarī grabbed him by the ear and scolded him, a single gesture reinforcing the authority of both teacher and shaykh.[45]

Sufi Denigration of the 'Ulama and Their 'Ilm

Bukhārī's attitude towards *'ilm*, primarily identified as legal knowledge, is in striking contrast to many more well-known formulations of the Sufi path. The oft-mentioned trio of *sharī'a*, *ṭarīqa*, and *ḥaqīqa* is frequently understood as representing both the chronological order and the hierarchical relationship between three distinct terms. The first step, one obligatory for all Muslims, is acknowledgement of and regulation by the law, *sharī'a*. For the Sufi aspirant, however, this step is followed and superseded by adherence to the Sufi path, *ṭarīqa*. The ultimate goal is Divine Reality, *ḥaqīqa*. For Bukhārī, as we have seen, the Shari'a, as a regulatory scheme and as a topic of study, is never superseded.

An extreme contrast to Bukhārī's views on *'ilm* and the 'ulama can be found in the writings of his contemporary, Sharaf al-dīn Aḥmad b. Yaḥyā Manērī (ca. 690–782/ca. 1290–1381), like Bukhārī one of the most well-respected Sufi shaykhs of eighth-/fourteenth-century South Asia. In his collection of two hundred letters, *Maktūbāt-i dō ṣadī*, Manērī interprets the traditional description of the 'ulama as the heirs to the Prophet, the injunction to seek *'ilm* as far away as China, and the principle that *'ilm* precedes action as not referring to the 'ulama in the everyday sense of the word nor to the knowledge that they possess. Rather, in his view, these are references to the 'ulama and *'ilm* of reality, the afterlife, and the esoteric—that is, to the Sufi masters and their teachings. These are distinct from the worldly and exoteric 'ulama and their *'ilm* is also distinct. Manērī repeatedly enjoins his reader not to confuse the two kinds of 'ulama and the two kinds of *'ilm*.[46]

Manērī's descriptions of the 'ulama (in the usual sense of the word) range from patronizing—stuck at the first level of knowledge, like nursing babies or even unborn fetuses[47]—to insulting—like donkeys laden with books[48]—to absolute denunciation—like Satan whom the believer should shun. He recounts a tale of someone who meets Satan sitting idle and forlorn and asks him the cause of his condition. Satan responds that now that the worldly 'ulama have appeared there is no work left for him to do.[49]

The ʿulama have little knowledge of value and cannot guide the believer to salvation.[50] In their hands the quest for knowledge has become a mere profession, a path to worldly gain and the patronage of the rich and powerful.[51] True *ʿilm* is not what they teach nor what can be studied in books but rather what is born in the breast, as revelation (*waḥy*) for prophets, as inspiration (*ilhām*) for saints, and as transmitted to disciples from their *pīrs*.[52]

Manērī's condemnation of the ʿulama is accompanied by a somewhat mixed attitude towards the Shariʿa. While acknowledging its obligatory nature, he also repeatedly rejects any criticism of apparent illicit behavior by Sufis. In particular, Manērī demands that a disciple accept without question any command from his *pīr* even if it goes against the rulings of the Shariʿa.[53] He justifies himself through an analogy to medicine in which particular ailments require treatments that would otherwise be considered unwholesome or forbidden.[54] On this point, Bukhārī asserts the exact contrary—anyone who performs or enjoins actions contrary to the Shariʿa is thus revealed as a charlatan or an unbeliever rather than a true *pīr* or shaykh.

Disregard of the Shariʿa and False Claims of Sanctity

In his *malfūẓāt*, Bukhārī recounts several occasions in which the refusal to perform the rituals required by the Shariʿa exposed a supposed holy man as a fake. When Bukhārī was in Bhakkar, on his way back from his travels in West Asia, he was told of a supposed holy man who lived in a cave near Alor. This individual claimed that Gabriel had come to him, bringing him food and exempting him from saying his prayers. Such a claim was clearly delusional since Gabriel only appears to prophets and no one, not even the Prophet, is exempt from prayer. On Bukhārī's instructions, the deluded man pronounced the *shahāda* and the apparition was exposed as the devil and the food he brought as excrement.[55] Bukhārī had no patience or pity for such phony saints. Once an "ignorant" man in Uch claimed to have God with him and collected a large number of followers among the local population. When Bukhārī demanded that he recite the *shahāda*, he refused, thus proving that he was an unbeliever (*kāfir*). Bukhārī took the matter to the *qāżī* and called for his execution, but the *qāżī* protested that the governor and many others believed in this saint. So Bukhārī went to the governor and told him that if something was not done he would write to the Sultan. Finally, the fake holy man was expelled from the area.[56] In a similar case, when Bukhārī was in Delhi in 776/1375, he was consulted by Sultan Fīrōz about another "ignorant" *darwēsh* who claimed to have repeatedly seen the angel Gabriel. Bukhārī declared that the man had been led astray by the devil and suggested that the ʿulama be assembled to pass judgment on him. The ʿulama sentenced the unfortunate man to death unless he repented and, after three days, he was executed.[57] In this case, the king's solicitation of his opinion demonstrates a recognition of Bukhārī's authority on the topic, though judgment was left up to the ʿulama.

Bukhārī recounts these interactions as exposures of false claims or of the wiles of the devil, based on the axiom that all Muslims are governed by the same obligations (prayer, recitation of the *shahāda*, and so on) from which no exemptions are granted by a supposed level of sanctity. His relish in such exposures may also indicate a lack of sympathy with two sometimes related aspects of medieval Sufism: uncontrolled ecstasy and anti-nomian behavior. In the first case, extraordinary mystical experience might result in statements and claims (*shath*) that, on their surface, contradict normative Islamic beliefs and practices.[58] As I described in Chapter 1, Bukhārī does not seem to have approved of his own father's overly emotional reaction to prayer. He taught his disciples that the *sālik* (the wayfarer on the Sufi path) must be the master of his or her mystical state (*ḥāl*), not its slave. Though he quotes the dicta of such famous early ecstatics as Bāyazīd Bisṭāmī and Manṣūr Ḥallāj, he also accepts the latter's execution as the legally correct response to his problematic utterances.[59] The second aspect of medieval Sufism objectionable to Bukhārī was the purposeful defiance of the obligations of Islamic law by certain groups as expressions of asceticism and world rejection.[60] Again, as a stickler for the ritual standards laid down by the Shari'a, Bukhārī did not condone such behavior, nor did he approve even of more mild social deviance like the matted hair of the Rifā'ī's and the removal of all head hair by certain Sufi initiates.[61]

One anecdote in *Manāqib al-aṣfiyā*,' a hagiography of Manērī, brings Bukhārī into direct engagement with Manērī and his disciples and places him in the position of inquisitor of religious doctrine. Two of Manērī's disciples, Aḥmad Bihārī and 'Izz Kākawī, made public and extravagant claims of unity with the Divine resulting in their execution by Sultan Fīrōz Shāh on charges of heresy. Upon hearing of the execution of his disciples, Manērī criticized the king's action and expressed his astonishment that a city in which such blood had been shed (that is, Delhi) could still be standing. Fīrōz was infuriated by such seditious comments and he issued a *farmān* (edict) to have Manērī brought before him. At this point, after having carefully studied Manērī's *maktūbāt* (letters) to determine his orthodoxy, Bukhārī interceded on behalf of his fellow Sufi and used his influence with the Sultan to have the *farmān* rescinded. In his study of Manērī's life and teachings, Paul Jackson argues that this story is highly unlikely, given Manērī's stated disapproval of public claims to divine unity. Furthermore, since collections of Manērī's letters had been in circulation for decades and were both popular and influential, it is unlikely that Bukhārī would not have had an earlier opportunity to examine their contents.[62] Given the divergence described above between the views expressed in Bukhārī's *malfūẓāt* and those in Manērī's *maktūbāt*, it also seems unlikely that reading the latter would have convinced Bukhārī of the soundness of Manērī's doctrines.

Interestingly there is a single brief text attributed to Bukhārī's authorship, *Muqarrar-nāma*, that contains opinions similar to Manērī's and contrary to the evidence of the *malfūẓāt*.[63] This text is largely devoted to a diatribe against useless learning, reversing the principle that action without knowledge is ineffective and arguing instead that knowledge without action will not get one into heaven. Certain varieties of learning are singled out for condemnation in *Muqarrar-nāma*. These include polemic, astronomy (or astrology), medicine, poetry, horoscopes, and literature. Even grammar is regarded as useless since it does not help one get into heaven.[64] In contrast, in *Khizānat al-fawā'id al-Jalālīya*, Bukhārī said that teaching Arabic is a pious deed. He had also demonstrated how astronomy could fall into each of the five categories of Islamic law and was necessary for calculating prayer times and directions.[65] In the same text, the story of Shaykh Maṭarī grabbing his ear to punish him for speaking loudly to an *'ālim* was used to illustrate the respect owed to teachers.[66] In *Muqarrar-nāma*, this story is used to condemn intellectual debate; Bukhārī was being punished for getting involved in a debate over hadith, not for disrespect.[67] Similarly, while the *malfūẓāt* stories about ignorant people who fancy themselves to be ascetics, mystics, or saints invariably end with their exposure as deluded or unbelievers, in *Muqarrar-nāma* Bukhārī tells a story of an ignorant ascetic who is more pious than his learned brother.[68]

It is difficult to know what to make of *Muqarrar-nāma* given the mutual consistency of all of Bukhārī's *malfūẓāt* compilations in making the exact opposite points. If it is an authentic composition by Bukhārī, then we must conclude that for a specific readership he was willing to contradict the teachings he presented to his usual aural audience. However, apart from its anomalous doctrines, there are other reasons to doubt its authenticity, the first of which is that Bukhārī's full name, Ḥusayn b. Aḥmad b. Ḥusayn, is never mentioned in the text and the reference to *makhdūm-i jahāniyān* is the only formal indication that he is the author. Second, while the authorities and texts quoted in the *malfūẓāt* are fairly consistent with each other, the same is not true of texts quoted in *Muqarrar-nāma*.

Sufism, especially in South Asia, has often been perceived as ambivalent, if not hostile, towards Islamic law, the 'ulama, and their traditional areas of scholarship. The examples given above from Manērī's letters demonstrate that this stereotype has a genuine basis—many medieval Sufi thinkers denigrated traditional religious knowledge in favor of mystical insight, and textual study in favor of spiritual practice. They viewed the 'ulama as worldly or corrupt and their religious authority as a threat to that of the Sufi shaykhs. However, the evidence of Bukhārī's *malfūẓāt* requires us to acknowledge the limits of this commonplace understanding of Sufism. Bukhārī insists not only on obedience to the requirements of the Shari'a, but also on the value of studying the law and the other religious sciences, and the full incorporation of such study into the daily regimen of both master and disciple. Compilations of his *malfūẓāt* share much with the legal genre of *fatāwā* collections. Was Bukhārī's approach to the intertwining of the Sufi path with the teachings of the 'ulama typical? Probably not. But it was successful. That is to say, it was successful in attracting disciples and patrons, and in establishing his stature as a religious authority. The evidence of Bukhārī's teachings, career, and *malfūẓāt* are a useful reminder of the pitfalls of easy generalizations about the nature of Sufism and its relationship to other strands of Islamic religiosity.

FOUR

Ritual and Practice

In the previous chapter, I discussed the place of *ʿilm*, knowledge of Islamic law and the related religious sciences, in Bukhārī's teaching. *ʿIlm*, according to Bukhārī, is the prerequisite for *ʿamal*, the devotional and contemplative practices of a *darwēsh*, while the *khirqa* is a sign of the *darwēsh*'s commitment to such practices. In this chapter, I discuss the types of *ʿamal* carried out by Bukhārī, and taught by him to his disciples, as well as the ritual of investiture with the Sufi *khirqa*.

Devotional Practices

While Bukhārī's focus on *ʿilm* may have been idiosyncratic, the devotional practices he undertook and enjoined are fairly typical of mainstream institutional Sufism—*ẕikr*, retreats, fasting, and, most important, prayer. Each of these activities had its own rules and conditions, many of them explained in detail in the Sufi handbooks. From Bukhārī's teachings, several general points about these practices emerge. First, although they might appear as intrinsically valuable activities, in fact, they have the potential to be invalid and unacceptable if their conditions are not met. Second, apart from the rules specific to each activity, there are two pre-conditions that apply to all devotional and ritual practices. The practitioner must be uncontaminated by anything illegal (haram), such as food, clothing, or shelter derived from illicit sources. I discuss this issue in greater detail in chapter 5. The other general condition is "presence of the heart" (*ḥużūr-i dil*).

Ḥużūr-i dil means complete concentration on God and the banishment of, and detachment from, any distracting thoughts. Bukhārī repeatedly enjoined *ḥużūr-i dil*, especially during prayer, *ẕikr*, and Quran recitation. The compiler of *Jāmiʿ al-ʿulūm* also instructs his readers to read that work with *ḥużūr-i dil*, as it is a prerequisite for gaining real benefit from the study of religious texts.[1] Thus, beyond the concern for external formal accuracy in religious action, the need for concentration and detachment demonstrates that prayer and study are also internal meditative and contemplative practices. *Ḥużūr-i dil* is not only a prerequisite for worship; it is also the result of acts of devotion. In fact, the purpose of *ẕikr*, wearing a *khirqa*, living in a *khānqāh*, in other words of living the life of a *darwēsh*, is to have *ḥużūr-i dil*.[2] Meditative and contemplative practices require concentration and clarity of mind but are also ways of achieving them.

Ẕikr

The religious practice most characteristic of the Sufi tradition is *ẕikr*—remembrance of God through the rhythmic repetition of one of His names. Many Sufi orders and lineages practiced particular forms of *ẕikr* which, if distinctive enough, became their distinguishing feature. *Ẕikr* might be performed in solitude or in groups, aloud or silently, in particular postures and motions, and with specific breathing patterns. *Talqīn*, the implantation of *ẕikr*, was, like investiture, an initiatory event in which the disciple was taught the master's method of *ẕikr* and the formula to be recited was implanted in the disciple's heart. The *ẕikr* formula and method also had a chain of transmission (*isnād*), just like a *khirqa* or a hadith. Bukhārī stated that the *isnād* for his *ẕikr* reached back to the Prophet, and it connected to Shihāb al-dīn Suhrawardī by a single link, Sharaf al-dīn Maḥmūd Shāh Tustarī who had implanted the *ẕikr* in Bukhārī in 748/1347.[3]

The method of *ẕikr* imparted by Bukhārī to his disciples is a fairly common one, using the creedal statement *lā ilāha ilā allāh* (there is no god but God). Sitting cross-legged with hands on thighs, one should begin the first, negative portion of the creed towards the left, moving one's face or head so that the negation is completed towards the right. Then, one swings back again so that the affirmation of God is completed towards the left, since the heart is located on the left side of the body.[4] One should direct the *ẕikr* with intensity towards the left side in order to purify, polish, and soften the heart.[5] It is also in the heart that one says the silent *ẕikr* (*ẕikr-i khafī*), though Bukhārī also prescribed *ẕikr* said aloud, slowly.[6] Besides the form of *ẕikr* described above, Bukhārī stated that *ẕikr* could be done while standing, sitting, or lying down. He quoted Amīn al-dīn Balyānī that *ẕikr* should be done loud enough for others to hear and preferably in a group, and quoted Shaykh Hamza Khurāsānī that while saying the *ẕikr* one's whole body should tremble uncontrollably and visibly.[7]

Remembrance of God is a permanent duty for all Muslims, though *ẕikr* has no set times the way other religious duties do, such as *namāz* (ritual prayer), hajj, *zakāt*, and the fast.[8] Bukhārī advised his disciples to practice *ẕikr* two or three times a day. Constancy in *ẕikr* is a sign of love for God; it is also the only way to reach God.[9] In performing *ẕikr*, one must be sincere in proclaiming and attesting to the truth of the creedal statement, and one must be filled with praise, delight, and reverence. *Ẕikr* produces purity of heart, and thus, according to Bukhārī, was recommended by the shaykhs of Arabia as a preliminary practice to prepare the disciple for further disciplines, such as the recital of litanies (*awrād*).[10] However, it also requires purity: the practitioner must be pure in body and heart, his clothes must be pure, and the place in which he is performing *ẕikr* must be pure.[11] For *ẕikr* in seclusion, especially, one must have a cell and be supplied from resources that are indubitably halal. These last requirements were not always easy to fulfill; when teaching in Delhi, Bukhārī remarked that in Uch he was able to supply these for his disciples, but here it simply was not feasible. This may have been why he was unable to follow the recommendation of his teachers in Arabia to have his disciples practice *ẕikr* until they were ready for the *awrād*—he assigned *awrād* to his disciples at an early stage so that they would not be left idle.[12]

Retreats and Seclusion

Retreats (*chilla* or *iʿtikāf*), forty- or ten-day periods of seclusion (*khalwat*), were one of the primary contexts for the performance of *ẕikr*, as well as being, in themselves, a significant part of the regimen of devotion prescribed and carried out by Bukhārī. The purpose of a retreat was to detach oneself from everyday cares and worldly concerns and to devote oneself wholly to worship—prayer, *ẕikr*, and reading the Quran. Ideally the *darwēsh* should completely remove himself from society and take up his abode in a cave or in the wilderness. Such a life, subsisting on gathered fruit and so on, was also recommended to avoid any contact with ill-gotten wealth. However, this ideal was not practiced by Bukhārī nor by most of his associates. As he said, anyone with dependents or family is legally obliged to support them and therefore cannot abandon them for a life in the wilderness.

For those remaining in society, retreats scheduled for certain times of the year are the appropriate method to cultivate detachment and devotion. While in seclusion the *darwēsh* is supposed to spend all of his time in prayer, *ẕikr*, and reading the Quran. Both food and sleep are supposed to be reduced to a minimum—in fact, Bukhārī advises the *darwēsh* in seclusion to never lie down unless he is overwhelmed by sleep.[13] Though going into seclusion is necessary, one should only do so under instruction from a shaykh. Every *darwēsh* should undertake a retreat at least three times a year: the last ten days of Jumādā II and all of Rajab; the last ten days of Shaʿbān and all of Ramażān (called the *iʿtikāf* of Abraham); and all of Ẕu al-Qaʿda and the first ten days of Ẕu al-Ḥijja (the *iʿtikāf* of Moses).[14] An additional fourth *iʿtikāf* is from 15 Ẕu al-Ḥijja to 25 Muḥarram. If all four forty-day retreats are undertaken, this adds up to more than a third of the year spent in seclusion and full-time concentration on worship. However, Bukhārī also stated that it was permissible to undertake seclusion for ten-day periods, such as the last ten days of Shaʿbān or the last ten days of Ramażān.[15]

The best place to do a retreat is in the congregational mosque. In fact, if the retreat is not carried out in a mosque, then it cannot be called an *iʿtikāf* but is instead just an *arbaʿīn-i khalwat* (forty-day seclusion).[16] Once one has entered seclusion it is not permissible to leave except for the performance of the five obligatory (*farż*) daily prayers, the Friday prayer, and the ablutions. The attitude of detachment and seclusion is supposed to be maintained while going to and from the place of seclusion by not speaking to anyone and looking only at one's feet. It is, of course, also permissible to come out of seclusion for any pressing physical needs, and if one is forced out by the place burning down (or otherwise being destroyed) or by the command of a king (that is, by coercion).[17] Bukhārī would renew his intention (*niyyat*) for the retreat each day so that the exercise would not be invalidated if there was an urgent need to come out of seclusion.[18]

Samā'

One distinction usually drawn between the Suhrawardī and Chishtī lineages is the place of *samā'*, listening to music and song, in their repertoire of religious activities. For the Chishtīya, *samā'* was a core practice, an indispensable method for achieving mystical ecstasy and experience of the divine.[19] However, the propriety of listening to music was questioned and sometimes rejected by the scholars of the Shari'a.[20] The Suhrawardīya, having a greater identification with and commitment to the legalistic definition of orthodoxy, were therefore somewhat more restrained in their embrace of *samā'*. Thus, Shihāb al-dīn Suhrawardī's *'Awārif al-ma'ārif* contains both a defense of the practice and a demand for self-control and sobriety among its practitioners.[21] Bahā' al-dīn Zakarīyā, whose personality and activities have been held up as a contrast to those of the shaykhs of the Chishtīya, is described as "not inclined to listen to *samā'*."[22]

Bukhārī's attitude to *samā'* follows this Suhrawardī pattern; he allowed and approved its performance in his circle but did not himself appear to have a strong emotional response to it. One instance recorded in *Jāmi' al-'ulūm* demonstrates the power of *samā'* as well as Bukhārī's detachment from it. A band of musicians and Quran reciters from Shiraz performed in Bukhārī's presence, first reciting some Quran verses and then some poetry. When they began to play the *nāy* flute, the company began to dance and weep. One person present, Mawlānā Tāj al-dīn Muḥammad, was overcome—he cried out, fell on the ground, crawled and rolled about, foaming at the mouth, while the others attempted to hold him still. Bukhārī, meanwhile, was in a state of meditation (*murāqaba*). Disturbed by the hubbub, he asked what was going on. When informed of the situation, he lead the group in praying for God to give Tāj al-dīn strength until the *mawlānā* had regained consciousness. The band was applauded for its performance.[23]

Mystical Experience

According to al-Ghazālī, the distinguishing feature of Sufism is the role played by mystical experience, especially that of annihilation (*fanā'*) and an ultimate "closeness to God."[24] The focus on such mystical experiences, usually expressed as states (*aḥwāl*), is what has led to the characterization of Sufism as a mystical movement. Thus, when I first began to read Bukhārī's *malfūẓāt* I was struck by the paucity of references to mystic or ecstatic states, neither theoretical discussions nor anecdotes about such experiences. *Ḥużūr-i dil* (presence of the heart), discussed at the beginning of this chapter as both the result and the prerequisite for devotional and contemplative practices, is one of the only mental or emotional states discussed in any detail by Bukhārī. Bukhārī also asserted that the *awliyā'* may see the essence (*ẕāt*) of God and that his wife, for one, had done so.[25] The scene described above, in which one of Bukhārī's disciples has an overwhelming response to music, is a rare example of an ecstatic experience to be found in Bukhārī's *malfūẓāt*.

The only account of Bukhārī experiencing extraordinary states comes from *Laṭā'if-i Ashrafī*, a hagiographical work devoted to Ashraf Jahāngīr Simnānī (d. 808/1405). In this text, Simnānī describes visiting Bukhārī three times in his *khalwat*. The first time, he found Bukhārī's body separated into seven parts, each praising God in a different language. The second time Simnānī went to the *khalwat*, he saw Bukhārī's body expanded under the influence of the Divine Name *Baṣīt* (The Expander), so much so that his flesh was pushing out of the chinks in the room. The third time, Simnānī found that Bukhārī's body had become transparent, like glass.[26] It is difficult to know how to read this account, since no description by Bukhārī of such experiences was preserved by his disciples. To some extent, Simnānī is describing his own experience—what he saw in the *khalwat*—rather than whatever Bukhārī was experiencing.[27] In his own *malfūẓāt*, Bukhārī recounted that once while undertaking the Ramadan retreat in the mosque, he saw the walls of the mosque prostrating themselves while the roof remained in place.[28]

Bukhārī's reticence on the issue of mystical or ecstatic experience (bearing in mind that he was willing to explain all kinds of minutiae and his disciples were willing to write them down) demonstrates either an absence of such experience or a lack of interest in it or a belief that the topic was irrelevant to the education of his disciples. It is possible that Bukhārī was reacting to a period in the history of Sufism when both the theory supporting mystical experience and the public spectacle of ecstasy had reached new heights. On the one hand, the controversial ideas of Ibn al-'Arabī and his followers on the possibility of union with God were becoming popular among many Sufi groups. On the other hand, groups of *bī-shar' qalandars* and *ḥaydurīs* were wandering South and West Asia displaying mystical ecstasy as a justification for breaking social and legal norms.[29] Though in different ways and for different reasons, both Ibn al-'Arabī's legacy and the *bī-shar'* orders were suspect in the eyes of the Sharī'a. Bukhārī's desire for his disciples to lead legally correct lives, and to have theologically sound opinions, may have led him to avoid potentially controversial and confusing issues. The *malfūẓāt*, despite their richness, contain only what Bukhārī wanted his disciples to learn from him, not necessarily the full range of his opinions and experiences. Protecting one's followers from confusing (and therefore faith-weakening) ideas was an acceptable part of Bukhārī's role as a shaykh. He had books that he considered unsafe for his disciples to read, and he tells of Bahā' al-dīn Zakarīyā instructing his son not to expose the secret meanings of the Quran revealed to him by God because they would confuse people.[30]

What we do find in the *malfūẓāt* with some frequency are mentions of (a) strong emotional responses, such as weeping or crying out, and (b) visionary and auditory encounters with distant, dead, or supernatural beings. An example of the first type of experience can be found in the above-mentioned scene of a musical performance. Though only one member of the audience had an extreme reaction and a total loss of self-control, the rest of the company was moved to weeping. On another occasion, when Bukhārī was explaining a Prophetic hadith which mentioned weeping, he himself was overcome with tears and had to stop speaking. His companions were thrown into an uproar and, for quite a while, all were absorbed in weeping.[31] Bukhārī's father, Aḥmad Kabīr, is described by his son as prone to weeping and crying, sometimes during prayer.[32]

The second category of experience, improbable encounters or communications, is an ongoing theme in Bukhārī's autobiographical anecdotes. The most celebrated of these events was the greeting that Bukhārī received from the spirit of the Prophet at his tomb in Medina.[33] Other examples include Rukn al-dīn Multānī's posthumous advice and investiture, encounters with jinns and abdāl, and meetings with Naṣīr al-dīn Chirāgh-i Dihlī in Mecca and with ʿAfīf al-dīn Maṭarī in Uch.[34] Though Bukhārī marks out these encounters with saints as extraordinary and wondrous he also depicts them as events external to himself. For example, the first time he meets Naṣīr al-dīn Maḥmūd Chirāgh-i Dihlī is when Bukhārī visits him in Delhi, the second time they meet is in Mecca where the Chishtī saint spends every Thursday night, and the third time is in Uch when Naṣīr al-dīn was accompanying Muḥammad b. Tughluq on the Thatta campaign. The first and last meetings are "real" events, but the meeting in Mecca is made possible by Naṣīr al-dīn's saintly ability to transport himself there. But though it is a miraculous event it is also simply another conversation between Bukhārī and Naṣīr al-dīn. It is not an inward transformation of the self nor an encounter with the Divine.

Namāz

For Bukhārī and his disciples the day was structured around the performance of *namāz* (Pers., ritual prayer; Ar. *ṣalāt*). Though the performance of prayer is often taken for granted in the lives of pious Muslims and therefore rarely discussed, its importance for Bukhārī, and for his disciples, cannot be overemphasized. *Namāz*, more than any other devotional activity was the focus of Bukhārī's teaching and practice. *Khizāna-yi jawāhir-i Jalālīya* is almost wholly devoted to Bukhārī's habits of prayer and his discourses about them.

Namāz, in its standard form, consists of a required number of prostrations (*rakʿat*) and recitations at five prescribed times of day: two *rakʿat*s of Fajr at daybreak, four of Ẓuhr at noon, four of ʿAṣr in the afternoon, three of Maghrib at dusk, and four of ʿIshāʾ at nightfall for a total of seventeen *rakʿat*s. These obligatory (*farż*) prayers made up a very small portion of Bukhārī's practice. First of all, traditionally each of these prayer times is more or less doubled by the inclusion of extra *sunnat rakʿats*, which must be done in imitation of the Prophet's example. Besides these *farż* and *sunnat rakʿat*s, required by the Shariʿa of any Muslim, Bukhārī performed a number of other, supererogatory prayers.

> The *sālik* (traveler on the Sufi path) should perform four thousand *rakʿat*s a day. If he cannot, then he should perform one thousand *rakʿat*s a day and if he

> cannot do this, then he should perform two hundred *rak'ats* a day. If he cannot do this either, he should perform one hundred *rak'ats* a day, no less because this is the minimum. If he does not then he is not a *sālik*. In my old age I perform one hundred *rak'ats* a day, apart from the *sunnat* [and the *farż* prayers] and the prayers to greet the mosque, in thanks for purity, and in thanks for food.[35]

Included in these one hundred *rak'at* were prayers at five additional times—*ishrāq* (dawn), *chāsht* (mid-morning), *zawāl* (after noon), *awābīn* (twilight), and *tahajjud* (in the night after waking from sleep)—as well as *namāz-i witr* at night and prayers for preservation of faith (*ḥifẓ-i īmān*), to repent (*tawba*), for refuge (*ḥirz*), to enliven the heart (*iḥyā'-i qalb*), for blessings, and for the health of one's children.[36]

What is the purpose of all this praying? Fulfilling one's obligations under the Shari'a by performing the *farż* and *sunnat* prayers was, of course, of paramount importance to Bukhārī. The additional daily prayers created a regimen of devotion and kept the *darwēsh* concentrated on praise and gratitude to God. Beyond this, however, *namāz* could also be used to produce particular benefits, and Bukhārī prescribed different prayers for different purposes. Preservation from sin, God's forgiveness, preservation from torment in the grave and in hell, and the attainment of heaven were the object of most prayers described by Bukhārī. This-worldly benefits, such as health, wealth, good eyesight, relief from debt, and rain could also be gained through the performance of a particular *namāz*.[37]

In order to produce the desired results, a prayer must be said at a particular time, on a particular day of the week, with a certain number of *rak'ats*, and the repetition of one *sūra* of the Quran and several *du'ā*'s (supplications). For example, the prayer to meet Khiżr, the hidden guide who will fulfill a petitioner's needs, is as follows. On a Thursday one should say four *rak'ats* at mid-morning (*chāsht*). In the first *rak'at*, after reciting the *Fātiḥa* (Quran 1), recite *Sūra Ikhlāṣ* (Quran 112) fourteen times. In the second *rak'at* recite *Sūra Ikhlāṣ* thirteen times, in the third *rak'at* twelve times, and in the fourth eleven times. Then recite seven particular *du'ā*'s, seven times each. And finally, while prostrated with one's head on the prayer carpet, say particular blessings on Muḥammad.[38] *Namāz* for other purposes are structured similarly with different *sūra*s and *du'ā*'s recited particular numbers of times.

But a prayer is not efficacious simply because it contains the right words said at the right time. In order for God to answer one's prayers, there are some basic conditions, the most important of which is the condition of the supplicant. One must be firm in faith and sincerity, absolutely focused on God and detached from all else. One must also be fed and clothed from legitimate sources. This means that the prayers of someone who is not a good Muslim, for example, a tyrant who extorts illegal revenue from his subjects, will not be answered. In contrast, the more saintly one is, the greater the likelihood that God will give one what one asks for. Certain categories of supplicants are also insured an answer to their prayers: travelers, participants in jihad, the oppressed, the sick, parents praying for their children and siblings praying for each other. Prayers uttered at dawn, in the middle of the night, and on Friday are most likely to be answered. The period between the call to prayer and actually standing in prayer is also a fortuitous moment for supplication. Only prayers for proper or good things will be fulfilled. Thus, if one is being oppressed by the aforementioned tyrant, one should not pray for his death but rather for God to make him repent of his wicked ways. Though Bukhārī suggests that prayers for evil ends will not work, he also says that even if they do they will not bring the supplicant closer to God which is, after all, the ultimate goal of the Sufi.[39]

This brings us to a more problematic issue: how valid is it for Sufis to be praying for particular benefits? There is a long tradition within Sufism, represented most vividly by Rābiʿa al-ʿAdawīya (d. 185/801), that the Sufi's only motivation in prayer and other devotions should be love of God and the desire to be closer to him. Rābiʿa condemned even the attempt to insure oneself a place in heaven, declaring that she would burn down heaven and quench the fires of hell so that people would pray only for God's sake and not their own.[40] Manērī provides a more contemporary version of this position, speaking of the true seekers of God as a rare category, distinct from those who merely seek heaven through prayer, fasting, retreats, and so on.[41] Bukhārī acknowledges that this is the position of some of the greatest Sufis and says that it is best to pray without expectation of reward.[42] However, this point does not seem to concern him much since all of the particular prayers he prescribes are aimed at least at getting into heaven, if not receiving tangible benefits on earth.

Given the emphasis in the Quran on sin, repentance, heaven, and hell, Bukhārī's understanding of prayer is much more common than that of Rābiʿa and Manērī. Heaven is offered as the reward for good deeds, including prayer, and therefore it makes sense to pray for forgiveness of sins and preservation from hell. Furthermore, since God is not only judge but also creator and bestower of all things in life, there is reason to ask him for other benefits as well. But Bukhārī is careful to point out that God is under no compulsion to fulfill any prayer; it is simply part of his generosity that he does so.[43]

Quran, Duʿā', and Wird

Namāz was not the only devotional exercise that could produce desired results. Apart from its use in prayer, Quran recitation was also independently effective. Thus, according to his disciples, Bukhārī used readings from the Quran to ward off the Mongols and other invaders from Uch and to end the cholera epidemic of 755/1354.[44] *Sūra Yāsīn* was a particularly useful chapter; it could make one's spouse love one and could be used to find lost objects. Bukhārī also explained how to practice divination using the Quran.[45]

Prayer in the form of *duʿā'* (supplication) or *wird* (pl. *awrād*, litanies), both in the context of *namāz* and as separate practices, was another way to achieve certain ends.

Bukhārī provided the words for numerous *du'ā*'s for different purposes. One of the interesting points here is that although theoretically a *du'ā'* is a free-form personal prayer, the *du'ā*'s explained by Bukhārī consist of very specific formulas handed down from previous generations and frequently traced back to the Prophet or his Companions. They are also all in Arabic, requiring the same ability to correctly recite Arabic as proper performance of *namāz* and Quranic recitation, though perhaps to a lesser extent.

The *du'ā'* formulas may contain a direct statement of request but this is usually the last and most minor element in the *du'ā*.' Praise of God, particularly through some or all of his traditional ninety-nine names, or a statement of belief in his unity and other major tenets of Islam, make up the bulk of *du'ā*'s. Praise of Muḥammad and blessings upon him are also particularly effective components of a *du'ā*.' Other figures may also come in for blessings, such as the family of the Prophet, the first four caliphs, the founders of the four Sunni law schools, and the founders of Sufi orders. Again, as in the case of *namāz*, particular formulas recited a certain number of times produce particular effects, although many *du'ā'* are multi-purpose—whatever one's need is, it will be fulfilled.

Bukhārī used collections of *awrād* made by earlier saints, particularly the one by Bahā' al-dīn Zakarīyā. According to 'Alā' al-dīn Ḥusaynī, author of *Jāmi' al-'ulūm*, he also compiled an *awrād* collection himself. Bukhārī taught different *wird* formulas to be said seventy times after each obligatory prayer time, or a hundred, or a thousand times on the different days of the week. These *awrād* consist of the profession of faith, names of God, blessings on Muḥammad, and statements of repentance.[46]

Some interesting prayers described in Bukhārī's *malfūẓāt* may be of non-Islamic origin. One of these is a lengthy hymn, said to be translated from Syriac from the Book of Psalms. Another is a prayer used by Moses' mother and invoking God through a series of names which appear to be neither Arabic nor Persian. Another peculiar prayer consists of the statements "Jesus was born," " Jesus was raised," " Jesus was taken out," with each statement followed by the word *aryakarya*. This is reminiscent, in a crude form, of the statements in Christian creeds of Jesus Christ's incarnation, life, death, resurrection, and ascension to heaven. Another prayer invokes the Greek names of the Companions of the Cave (Quran 18:7–18:22), the figures known in Christian tradition as the Seven Sleepers.[47]

Given the South Asian context of Bukhārī's life we might expect to see some Hindu influence on these prayer practices. However, all of these examples of prayer which may have extra-Islamic sources are related to the Jewish and Christian traditions of the Near East and probably entered into Islamic practice much earlier in the history of the religion. This highlights the fact that prayer formulas, like other aspects of the Islamic tradition, were very carefully handed down in their Middle Eastern form in the new Islamic territory of India and were not developed anew with the materials at hand.

Ta'wīẕ

Extended prayers which need to be said accurately in Arabic posed a problem for a Muslim population which was largely ignorant of that language, and was mostly illiterate. In the case of recitations of chapters from the Quran, it was usually advisable to find someone who knew the relevant passage to say it for one. Shorter prayers, such as single verses from the Quran or short *du'ā*'s, could be written down on pieces of paper and carried with one as an amulet, or *ta'wīẕ*. Such *ta'wīẕ* could also be placed under one's pillow, or in a copy of the Quran. There are also other ways to use the written prayer: one could eat the piece of paper on which it was written, or one could wash off the ink in a cup of water and drink that. (Water was also used to transmit the power of a prayer by saying the formula and blowing over the cup and then having the supplicant drink it. Similarly a prayer said over a sacrificed sheep would benefit all who ate from it.) Or the prayer might be written on clay pots. Or one might write prayers or phrases from the Quran, or powerful names on one's hands or other body parts.[48] Since the efficacy of a prayer is related to the holiness of the supplicant, a *ta'wīẕ* written by someone widely recognized as saintly, such as a Sufi shaykh, is more useful than a prayer written or uttered by the average individual. The writing of *ta'wīẕ* was, and continues to be, one of the main income-generating practices for Sufis who accepted gifts in return for a *ta'wīẕ*.[49]

It is in the written *ta'wīẕ* that we find the most mysterious prayers. A number of *ta'wīẕ* involve writing lists of letters which are not joined together to make a word and, even if they were, would not make an intelligible word. Thus to cure epilepsy, one writes down the letters *kāf, hā, kāf, 'ayn, żād, ḥa, mīm, 'ayn, sīn*, and *qāf*.[50] Moving further away from intelligible language, some *ta'wīẕ* are in the numerical form known as a magic square.[51] It seems that for a prayer to work it is unnecessary for the supplicant to understand it, whether it is in Arabic, disjointed letters, or numbers. Another step away from intelligibility is taken by *ta'wīẕ* which simply involve a symbol or drawing.[52] Finally, some *ta'wīẕ* move from the symbolic to the concrete and involve actual holy objects. Thus the clothes or hair of a sayyid, a descendant of the Prophet, may be used. For example, while Bukhārī was in Arabia he gave a lock of his hair to an old man as a cure for his pain.[53]

The belief in the efficacy of prayers and *ta'wīẕ* is closely connected to the belief in the miraculous powers of the saints, the *awliyā*.' As mentioned earlier, the more pious a person is the more likely it is that his or her prayers will be answered. Therefore, logically, the prayers of the *awliyā'* are efficacious. Many of the miracles and wonders ascribed to the saints involve God answering their prayers. It is also true that supplications addressed to saints (or to prophets) requesting their intercession or invoking their names are very effective. Bukhārī prescribed the use of the names of Bahā' al-dīn Zakarīyā, Ṣadr al-dīn 'Ārif, Rukn al-dīn, and Jamāl al-dīn Uchchī to rid a home of jinns. Many of his prayers request the assistance of 'Abd al-Qādir Gīlānī. Some prayers ask God to make one a member of the *awliyā'* and to make one capable of performing miracles.[54] Thus a saint's supplications are effective, supplications to a saint are effective, and one can even pray to become a saint.

The intimate connection between the power of saints and the power of prayer can be seen in the different accounts of Bukhārī's encounter with Muḥammad b. Tughluq (see Chapter 1). In *Khizānat al-fawā'id al-Jalālīya*, the Sultan's decision to make Bukhārī a *shaykh al-islām* is credited to the protective virtue of initiatory robes given to Bukhārī by Naṣīr al-dīn Maḥmūd.[55] In other words, the robes of a saint acted as a *ta'wīz̤*. In *Tuḥfat al-sarā'ir*, Bukhārī was spared the Sultan's wrath because he spent the previous night calling upon all the *awliyā'* by their various titles, leading up through their ranks to Muḥammad.[56] So despite the different stories, in both of these accounts it is the power of saints, prayer, and *ta'wīz̤* that save Bukhārī.

Magic or Religion?

Explanations of how to use particular forms of prayer—*namāz, du'ā,' ta'wīz̤*, and Quran verses—for achieving specific results, both spiritual and practical, are in no way unique to Bukhārī's *malfūẓāt*. Examples can be found among Bukhārī's own *pīrs*: Bahā' al-dīn Zakarīyā produced a collection of *awrād* suitable for different occasions,[57] and Yāfi'ī's *al-Durr al-naẓīm fī khawāṣṣ al-Qur'ān al-'aẓīm* described the effects of Quranic verses, spoken and written, including their uses as protective amulets.[58] The distribution of *ta'wīz̤* was one of the major activities of *khānqāh* life in medieval South Asia.[59] *Jawāhir al-awliyā,'* by Bukhārī's descendant Sayyid Muḥammad Bāqir b. 'Us̱mān Bukhārī, consists almost wholly of prayer formulas ascribed to various saints, along with instructions on how to transform such prayers into magic squares.[60] Constance Padwick's important study of mid-twentieth-century prayer manuals demonstrates the continuity and longevity of many of these forms of prayer.[61]

Despite the prevalence of this understanding of prayer, in its different forms, as an effective method for achieving the petitioner's goals, it has received limited scholarly attention, particularly within the study of medieval Sufism. Some of the practices described above, especially the construction of *ta'wīz̤*, have been understood as magical rather than religious, or as popular, "low culture," practices and have therefore been relegated to folkloric studies. Padwick, for example, labels all practical uses of prayer as "magical," "semi-magical," "cabbalistic," and "essentially irreligious," contrasting them with "real devotions."[62] A serious examination of the history of such prayers, or of the distinction drawn between magic and religion, is clearly beyond the scope of my project. The relegation of *ta'wīz̤* and related prayers to the category of magic, as distinct from religion, is unhelpful to the task at hand.

The category of magic, as it is deployed to include *ta'wīz̤*, is both value-laden and culturally specific. Padwick, who writes from an avowedly Christian point of view and with the agenda of demonstrating the piety of Muslims to a Christian audience, is clearly discomfited by practical prayers that are motivated by "self-interest," are "mechanical and meaningless," and apparently reduce what should be sacred to "a tiny coin of supernatural value that may be spent for one's own profit."[63] Underlying such a judgment is a particularly post-Reformation Christian understanding of religion (and prayer), compounded by a need to defend that category from the modern disdain for what is irrational and unscientific, and therefore, when applied to the material world, superstitious.

The Islamic tradition also has a category of forbidden sorcery and magic: *siḥr*, used in the Quran to refer to the magic of Pharaoh's sorcerers (Q 7:116, 10:75–81, 20:56–71). What seems to characterize *siḥr*, and distinguish it from miracles, wonders, and divine blessings, is its falsehood—it is magic in the sense of illusions and tricks—and its denial of divine power. Calling upon divine aid, and believing that certain formulas are more effective for particular requests, does not fit that category. Carrying around, or eating, a piece of paper marked with obscure symbols in the hope of curing one's migraine may look like magic. However, I have tried to show how such a *ta'wīẕ* is derived from and part of the overall structure of prayer in Islam. It seems to me that there is a continuity of belief underlying the five *namāz* a day required of every Muslim, the *du'ā'* for health and success, and the *ta'wīẕ* to keep away jinn. Few would categorize the performance of *namāz* with the hope of going to heaven as a magical practice, but where do we draw the line between a purely religious or devotional exercise and a magical one?

The negative valuation of *ta'wīẕ* and related prayers, combined with the absence of much research on the topic, also leads to some confusion about their historical development and its relationship to the history of Sufism. On the one hand, amulets, talismanic prayers, magical bowls, and so on are extremely ancient Near Eastern practices. The Quran itself concludes with two brief *sūra*s in the form of talismanic prayers, each beginning with "I take refuge," *a'ūdhu*, from the same verbal root as *ta'wīẕ* (Ar. *ta'wīdh*). On the other hand, to view practical prayers as "fallen from grace," a "degradation," and a degeneration, as Padwick does,[64] is to suggest a chronological development from pure, spiritually motivated devotion to "magic." A. J. Arberry, whose opinion on *ta'wīẕ* is similar to Padwick's, describes precisely this process taking place in later Sufism: "Magic assumed an increasing importance in [the Sufis'] repertory. Early Sufism had been refreshingly free of this most mischievious variety of mystification and obscurantism; in this age of decline, charms and amulets came to acquire a special value in the eyes of men no longer confident against the vicissitudes of fortune; cabbalism and witchcraft provided an attractive substitute for defeated reason."[65] If Arberry is right that early Sufism was free of such practices, despite their antiquity, then perhaps we are looking less at a decline or a degeneration than the absorption into Sufism of an ongoing and ancient tradition. Richard Bulliet suggests that it was in the thirteenth century that the Sufi shaykhs gained a monopoly in the production of written amulets.[66] This would certainly fit with the growth and institutionalization of Sufism during that period and its ability to absorb a wide range of Islamic practices and traditions.

The relegation of *taʿwīẕ* to the category of popular or folk practice, as a sweeping generalization, is also problematic, though it may be true in certain times and places. The commitment of highly educated religious elites, like Bukhārī and Yāfiʿī, to describing in detail the powers of various phrases, or the construction of magic squares, demonstrates that these were not beliefs and practices confined to an uneducated underclass. One might argue that figures like Bukhārī were merely producing a product (prayers and *taʿwīẕ*), in which they had no strong belief, for the consumption of the ignorant masses—but that would require imputing a cynicism and hypocrisy for which there is little evidence. Finally, to label *taʿwīẕ* as either folk-practice or magic is to implicitly place them outside the bounds of normative, Shariʿa-minded, Sunnism—a polemical and historically untenable position given the evidence of Bukhārī and his contemporaries.

The Sufi *Khirqa*

Investiture with a Sufi robe (*khirqa*) was a transformative moment in the life of any individual Sufi aspirant: the moment at which he or she was accepted into a particular stream of the Sufi path by a recognized and authorized master. When accompanied by the permission to invest others, it was the moment of authorization to act as a Sufi master and take on disciples. For the individual, then, investiture with a *khirqa* could be both matriculation and graduation (moments in which medieval robing practices are preserved to this day). Investiture was also the formal mechanism by which individuals were bound together—in the hierarchical and dyadic master-disciple relationship, as links in a transgenerational lineage (*silsila*) stretching back in time to the Prophet Muḥammad or other early figures, and to a contemporary peer group of fellow disciples of the same master or in the same order. This function of creating social bonds is made explicit by the interchangeable usage of *taʿalluq dādan* and *paywand kardan* (both meaning to join) and *khirqa pōshānīdan* (investiture).

These social ties were not always of the same intensity; a *khirqa* of discipleship (*irādat*) created a singular bond between a disciple (*murīd*) and a master (*pīr*), requiring obedience from one party and guidance from the other. Such a *khirqa* could only be received by a committed aspirant from his or her primary *pīr*. *Khirqa*s of blessing (*tabarruk*), in contrast, created a much looser bond of affiliation and devotion. They could be bestowed on aspirants who were not yet spiritually ready and who might later be accepted as serious disciples. Or they could be given to those who were unlikely to ever seriously pursue the Sufi path—that is, the secular devotees of a particular Sufi master. Finally, they could be bestowed on a Sufi who had already received the *khirqa-yi irādat* from his or her primary master. This last category is what accounts for the large numbers of *khirqa*s collected by figures like Bukhārī.

The importance of investiture is borne out by the space devoted to *khirqa*s in Bukhārī's *malfūẓāt*. Bukhārī recounted, and his disciples carefully recorded, the chains of transmission for each his *khirqa*s, the names of the masters from whom he had received them, and in some cases the circumstances in which they had been given to him. The authors of the *malfūẓāt* also observed the many devotees who sought *khirqa*s from Bukhārī, described his investiture ritual, and copied the instructional texts (*waṣīyat*) which he gave to his initiates. The inclusion of all this information about Bukhārī's *khirqa*s speaks to the particular nature of Sufi authority embodied in the *khirqa*s and in the *malfūẓāt*. In a sense Bukhārī's *khirqa*s are his Sufism—they symbolize his relationship to his masters, to the Sufi orders, and to the path as a whole—a relationship formalized through the ritual of investiture. The permission (*ijāzat*) that Bukhārī received to invest others is what makes him a Sufi master, a *pīr* worthy of collecting disciples around him. Without *khirqa* and *ijāzat*, Bukhārī would have no formally sanctioned and externally recognizable Sufi authority. As proof of Bukhārī's qualifications, the *khirqa*s, or rather their names and lineages, also serve as evidence of the authority of his teachings as they are preserved in the *malfūẓāt*.

The Investiture Ritual

*Khirqa*s, and related objects, were formally bestowed in the course of a ritual variously called *ta'alluq dādan* and *paywand kardan* (creating a link), *khirqa pōshānīdan* (investiture), *irādat* (discipleship), and *bay'at* (oath of allegiance). These terms are not fully interchangeable and refer, as I discuss shortly, to different moments within a composite ritual. As mentioned earlier, this ritual process can be seen as an initiation when it involved a novice disciple (*murīd*), but it could also function not as initiation but as the creation of a looser bond between the shaykh (and his lineage) and a devotee. And, when accompanied by an *ijāzat*, the ritual was also the moment of authorization for the disciple to now be able to invest others or take on further disciples. *Khizānat al-fawā'id* provides the following description of the ritual of investiture as performed by Bukhārī. Bukhārī's version is very similar to investiture and initiation rituals described and performed by other medieval Sufi shaykhs, though it is rare to find such a complete script for the ceremony.[67]

> If someone came to [him] with the intention of becoming a disciple the *makhdūm* would say, "I am not one of them that I could make someone a disciple. But I will make the bond of brotherhood by command of the Prophetic hadith: Increase the good brothers, for God is noble and refrains from punishing man in front of his brothers."[68]
>
> The *makhdūm* would take his hand and speak to this effect: "Do you accept this poor individual as a brother?" He would say: "I accept him."
>
> Then he would say: "Both of us brothers repent." And he would say [in Arabic]: "I ask forgiveness of God, there is no god but Him, the Living, the Eternal, and I turn in repentance to Him." The two of them would recite this three times.

> Then he would say [in Arabic]: "Oh God, lay open his breast," and place his blessed hand on his [the disciple's] chest.
>
> Then with the scissors he would first cut the hair over the [disciple's] forehead and then the hair on the right and the left. Sometimes he would be content [to stop] with the hair on the forehead. While cutting the hair the *makhdūm* would recite [in Arabic]: "Oh God, shorten his expectations and protect him from sin."
>
> After the hair cut he would say [in Arabic]: "Oh God, bless Muḥammad and the family of Muḥammad and bless them and grant them salvation. Oh God, strengthen us in our repentance and preserve us from sin with preservation from you for the sake of Muḥammad (may God bless him and grant him salvation) and of the people of the house of Muḥammad (peace be upon them) and of al-Shaykh al-kabīr Bahā' al-dīn and of al-Shaykh al-'Ārif Ṣadr al-dīn and of Quṭb al-'ālam Rukn al- dīn (may God sanctify their souls). May He preserve you from sin."
>
> If someone requested to be shaved he would say there is no need, *tawba* (repentance) is preferred. If he [the initiate] insisted he would give permission for shaving.[69]
>
> Then, if there was a hat (*kulāh*) available he would put it on him at this time. While investing him with the *kulāh*, the *makhdūm* would recite [in Arabic]: "My God, crown him with the crown of nobility and happiness and preserve him from sin and strengthen him in the religion of Islam."
>
> Sometimes he would place sugar in [the disciple's] mouth with his own blessed hand and recite this prayer (*du'ā'*) [in Arabic]: "Oh God, grant him the sweetness of faith."
>
> After the hair cut and the *du'ā'* he would enjoin some to study law and Quranic recitation, and some to occupy themselves with the *ẕikr: Lā ilāha ilā allāh*, and others to concern themselves with the *awrād* of Shaykh-i kabīr Bahā' al-dīn (may God sanctify his soul). He gave each one instructions (*waṣīyat*) to the extent of his capabilities and with respect to his condition.[70]

The ceremony described above is a composite ritual in which investiture is only one of several separate events. The first of these is the handclasp and pact of brotherhood, a form of the *bay'at* oath of allegiance used in numerous political and social contexts. *Bay'at* is traced back to the practice of the Prophet and mentioned in the Quran (48:10, 48:18, 60:12).[71] The handclasp is followed by the request for forgiveness (*istighfār*) and statement of repentance (*tawba*), both Quranic concepts central to the Sufi tradition. The shaykh's placement of his hand on the aspirant's chest or his gesture in that direction is often associated with the implantation of the *ẕikr* formula in the aspirant's heart. Bukhārī's accompanying words, however, do not mention *ẕikr* at this point and, instead, request God's opening or dilation (*sharḥ*) of the disciple's breast, again referencing a Quranic expression (94:1, 39:22, 6:125, 20:25). The haircut and the feeding of something to the disciple do not have explicit roots in the Quran or in Prophetic example but were both common elements in initiation rituals of *futuwwa* organizations and Sufi orders.[72] The ritual closes with the disciple receiving the new tasks upon which he must now embark. These instructions are represented by the *waṣīyat-nāma* (testament) composed by Bukhārī and given to each disciple.

The physical gestures of this ritual, considered independently from the words that accompany them, are a performance—and thus the creation—of intimacy between master and disciple. To clasp someone's hand, touch his chest, clip his hair, dress him, and place something in his mouth is to engage physically with the other. That this is a breach of the boundaries of normal intercourse between two individuals is demonstrated by the need to adapt the ritual, and limit the physical contact, if there is a gender difference between the master and the disciple. Thus, when Naṣīr al-dīn Maḥmūd Chirāgh-i Dihlī created the bond of discipleship (*paywand*) with a woman he did it at a distance by sending her a cup of water over which he had read a prayer and into which he had dunked his finger.[73] Other mechanisms of demonstrating intimacy without coming into physical contact might include holding two ends of a piece of cloth (rather than clasping hands) and gesturing towards the disciple's heart rather than touching her chest. Furthermore, female disciples were not, as far as I know, dressed by the shaykh in any garment or headgear. Despite the problems created for norms of sexual propriety, the particular variety of intimacy created between master and disciple by these gestures is not obviously sexual but rather parental or nurturing. Like an infant, the disciple is passive in the hands of his master who grooms, clothes, and feeds him. These final steps also transform the disciple's physical appearance and condition, making manifest the spiritual transformation invoked by the accompanying prayers.

In terms of the physical actions in this ritual, the disciple is almost wholly passive. When we turn to the verbal component, however, the disciple participates, at least in the first few steps. Prompted by the shaykh, the disciple speaks the oath of allegiance and the statements of repentance and asking for forgiveness. Each of these statements can be considered a speech act, in the mode described by J. L. Austin, where saying something makes it so.[74] The rest of the verbalizations are spoken by the shaykh as prayers addressed to God. Apart from the initial oath of allegiance, all the statements are made in Arabic and in a style that we might call liturgical, drawing upon Quranic language and concepts. These statements provide a meaning for the actions that they accompany: the touch on the chest is equated with the opening of the disciple's heart, the sugar with the sweetness of faith. They firmly place the ritual in the context of Islamic tradition, Prophetic example, and Quranic concepts. The relationship created by the words, unlike that performed by the gestures, includes more than the shaykh and his disciple. The disciple repents towards God and God is called upon to act, to transform the inner condition of the disciple just as the shaykh is transforming him externally. On a secondary level, Muḥammad, his family, and the shaykhs of Multan are also involved as the objects of blessing. The initial handclasp might seem to be limited to a human bond, especially since the pact is spoken in Persian. But even here, the divine presence is implicitly invoked since the Quranic allusion to Muḥammad receiving the people's pledge states that the pledge was made to God and God's hand was present too (Quran 48:10). Other versions of the Sufi *bay'at* explicitly equate the shaykh's hand with the hand of the founder of the lineage, the Prophet's hand, and God's hand.

Ritual Language

The way in which Persian and Arabic are used in this ritual highlights the position of Arabic as the liturgical language, the one with which God is addressed, while Persian is the language with which the shaykh and disciple communicate with each other. As will be discussed further in Chapter 5, the use of Arabic could pose a problem for South Asian Muslims, whether Persian speakers or recent converts. Was the disciple expected to fully understand everything that was being said and, therefore, to understand the ritual in the terms laid out by its verbal component? The use of a ritual language different from the vernacular and incomprehensible to at least some of the participants and the community at large is a phenomenon familiar in many different cultural contexts. In the Islamic context, discussion of this issue focuses on Quran recitation and the performance of the canonical obligatory rituals, especially ritual prayer. The Ḥanafī *maẕhab* is the only one to permit (sometimes) the performance of *namāz* in vernacular languages rather than Arabic.

Some of the most extreme examples of the incomprehensibility of ritual language are the Vedic mantras that have led Frits Staal to propose the essential meaninglessness of ritual. Staal links this incomprehensibility to the invariance of ritual.[75] In the case of Sufi investiture and initiation rituals, there is, in fact, great variation. Not all of the steps described appear in every initiation and, most important, the words of the ritual vary greatly, even if the gestures and the gist of the statements remain more or less similar. Does this mean that the words are expendable? Or, that it does not matter if the participant does not understand them?

One anecdote, recorded in *Jāmi' al-'ulūm*, suggests that Bukhārī valued the words and their comprehension by the aspirant: "A friend from Sind came for *paywand*. He was extremely common. He knew nothing to the extent that he could not say the *istighfār* and the *tawba*. With a thousand difficulties [Bukhārī] did the *talqīn* (instruction or the implantation of *ẕikr*) in the Sindī language."[76] This example singles out the disciple's statements of repentance and the shaykh's instruction of him as the two crucial moments that are indispensable and need to be performed in a comprehensible manner. It is significant that the *istighfār* and the *tawba* are, as mentioned above, moments when the disciple is doing something rather than just being the object of the master's prayers. Similarly the only portion of Bukhārī's ritual script performed in Persian is the bond of brotherhood whose mutuality requires the disciple's knowledgeable participation. The effectiveness of prayers uttered in Arabic by the shaykh, on behalf of the disciple, presumably depends more on the condition of the shaykh, his knowledge, virtue, purity, and sanctity, than on the linguistic capability of the disciple.

The validity, legitimacy, and effectiveness of canonical and obligatory rituals (*'ibādāt*) are defined by the Shari'a, where the fundamental question is whether they have been performed according to the stipulations derived from the Quran and the Prophet's example.[77] Investiture and initiation do not belong to that category of *'ibādāt*; they are informal and variable rituals that are focused as much on human social bonds as they are on the human-divine relationship. Bukhārī's contemporaries who take up the question of which elements of these rituals of affiliation are indispensable focus on the bond between shaykh and devotee and whether the devotee can legitimately claim the status of disciple and affiliation to the Sufi order. Most of these authorities, interestingly, do not highlight the verbal element as key to the process. Although Manērī taught that only one who has attached himself to saintly people and submitted himself to their discipline can be called a disciple (*murīd*), he also admitted the alternate view that anyone whose hair has been clipped by a shaykh is his disciple.[78] Ashraf Jahāngīr Simnānī, who was invested with a *khirqa* by Bukhārī, taught that the *bay'at* is invalid without the handclasp, the haircut, and a *khirqa*.[79] These two views see the ritual actions as the crucial component.

Simnānī lists the *khirqa* as an indispensable element for the creation of a bond between aspirant and shaykh, and for the affiliation of an aspirant to a Sufi lineage. The *khirqa*, in fact, is viewed by other authorities as the object capable of standing in for the whole ritual and for the relationship of discipleship. Shihāb al-dīn Suhrawardī writes that not only is the *khirqa* the sign of discipleship but it is in fact synonymous with *bay'at*, that is, with the ritual that creates the relationship.[80] Similarly the passage from *Jāmi' al-'ulūm* quoted above continues: "Apropos of this situation, [Bukhārī] recounted the following anecdote: 'I heard Shaykh Rukn al-dīn say, "For people such as these, what is the point of instruction and the formulas of repentance and forgiveness? There is no need. Just give them the *kulāh* because just receiving the *kulāh* is understood as repentance."'"[81] Along the same vein, Simnānī recounts an anecdote about a certain Shaykh Aḥmad Kanbu who had received a *ṭāqiya* (skullcap) from Niẓām al-dīn Awliyā' but had not done the *bay'at*. After Niẓām al-dīn's death, Shaykh Aḥmad approached Naṣīr al-dīn Maḥmūd and asked for *bay'at*, but Naṣīr al-dīn told him that the *ṭāqiya* he had already received was sufficient.[82]

However, sole reliance upon the object of investiture, whether hat, robe, or cap, seems to lead to a relationship of less significance, or to apply to people of lesser social status. Rukn al-dīn's view quoted above creates a hierarchy between knowledgeable disciples, from whom one can expect full ritual repentance and who will receive genuine instruction, and "people such these," common people, for whom a hat is sufficient. Simnānī concludes his discussion of Shaykh Aḥmad's *ṭāqiya* by stating that though this was sufficient for the purpose of blessing (*tabarruk*), true discipleship was invalid without the *bay'at*. (In contrast, as mentioned above, female disciples did not receive hats or robes and, therefore, the metonymic replacement of the ritual with a garment did not apply to them.)

The Parallel between Khirqas *and Books*

When accompanied by an *ijāzat* (permission) to bestow that *khirqa* on another, investiture was the mechanism of giving an individual the authority of a shaykh. The supervised reading of texts played much the same role for the 'ulama, whose status as authorities on religious knowledge and normative practice was certified by *ijāzat*s for books, hadith, or whole branches of knowledge. The structure of transmission and the vocabulary of *ijāzat* are obviously shared with the process by which the genealogy of a *khirqa*, its reception by a disciple, and the shaykh's authority to bestow it were authenticated in the Sufi tradition. This combination of authorization to transmit something, with a genealogy of the authority and of the object of transmission, was modeled on the process of hadith transmission.

Najm al-dīn Kubrā, one of the leading theorizers of the *khirqa* in Persianate Sufism, explicitly compares it to hadith in his treatise *Jawāb-i nuh su'āl*. Like a hadith, the *khirqa* is ultimately derived from the Prophet, who covered the People of the House (that is, Ḥasan, Ḥusayn, Fāṭima, and 'Alī) with a cloak, bestowed a garment on Umm Khālid, and invested a man with a robe.[83] Kubrā also points out some important differences between the transmission of hadith and *khirqa*s. In the case of a hadith, in order to be sure of its authenticity, it is advisable to receive it from numerous transmitters, with a shorter chain of transmission, or from a more authoritative, widely respected teacher, and to critique and evaluate its chain of transmission. None of this is recommended for a *khirqa*, since the important point about investiture is the personal relationship created with one's spiritual master, and any such quest for authenticity undermines the confidence that is necessary for that relationship.[84]

While it makes sense that a process for the authentication and transmission of hadith be applied to other texts, its extension to a non-textual object like a *khirqa* bears further examination. This application is made possible by an understanding of the *khirqa* as reproducible in the same manner as a text, maintaining a singular identity despite multiplication. We are familiar, especially in a post-print culture, with the idea that every copy of a text is, in some important sense, identical to its original. In the medieval Islamic mode of transmission described above, it is not only the text itself that is multiplied without losing its identity but also the authority to transmit it. In fact, in many cases the reproduction of such authority was more central to the process than the transmission of the text itself—thus certificates were bestowed on children, even infants, present at a reading, even though such children might only learn or acquire the text at a much later date. In the case of a *khirqa*, though the garment bestowed in an investiture ceremony was usually not the same physical object, and might not even be of the same type, as the one that the bestower had received from his own master, the two were understood as somehow identical. The *khirqa* of the Suhrawardī lineage, for example, is singular, though Bukhārī had received it embodied in different physical garments from different shaykhs, and though he bestowed it, again variously embodied, on numerous disciples. Kubrā defends the permissibility of bestowing a *khirqa* in a form different from that of the shaykh's by again using the parallel case of hadith, which one is allowed to transmit according to its meaning in slightly different words.[85]

This is not to suggest, however, that the particular physical embodiment of a text or of a *khirqa* was unimportant. Autograph copies of books, or ones that had been owned and approved by their authors, were of obvious value for their greater reliability. Thus, Bukhārī had taken pains to point out that he had received a copy of *al-Risāla al-Makkīya* directly from its author, Quṭb al-dīn Dimashqī, and possessed a copy of *'Awārif al-ma'ārif* that had been inspected by Shihāb al-dīn Suhrawardī. In the case of *khirqa*s, garments that had been worn by a particular shaykh were valued for being imbued with the *barakat* of a saintly figure or simply by the close association with him. The compiler of *Jāmi' al-'ulūm* proudly mentions the fact that Bukhārī gave him the *dastār* (turban cloth) off his own head.[86] Similarly Naṣīr al-dīn Maḥmūd favored Bukhārī by giving him his own *bārānī* (cloak) and thus protected him from the machinations of Muḥammad b. Tughluq.[87] (On the other hand, the *barakat* of some saints was present in *khirqa*s that were theirs only in the sense that the genealogy of the *khirqa* was traced back to them. Thus, according to Bukhārī, the *khirqa*s of 'Abd al-Qādir Gīlānī and Khiżr would keep away all kinds of harm and difficulties.[88] The *khirqa*s of 'Abd al-Qādir and Khiżr which Bukhārī bestowed were presumably objects never worn by either saint and thus their protective virtue had been passed down through a chain of shaykhs and *khirqa*s rather than adhering to one physical thing.) The personal property of the shaykh was also free from any suspicion of being derived from an illegal source. When Bukhārī gave one of his visitors a *bārānī*, he made sure to tell him that it was from his own property and not from offerings (*futūḥ*), whose origins might not be fully known.[89]

Types of Khirqas

Theoretically the color and construction of garments bestowed as *khirqa*s were supposed to correspond to the condition and needs of the disciple. Bukhārī's *malfūẓāt* give two separate lists of varieties of Sufi garments, in different colors and materials, which were supposed to be bestowed on different individuals according to their particular spiritual states and virtues.[90] These lists included robes made of wool and camel hair, blue, red, white, green, and black robes, and particular forms, such as *sawzanī* (quilted), *mulamma'* (parti-colored), *hazār-khaṭṭī* (a thousand lines, perhaps seams), *jawz-girih* (buttoned), *muraqqa'* (patched), and *khirqa* (ragged). The *hazār-mēkhī* (a thousand nails) is mentioned in an anecdote about a talkative *darwēsh* and Shaykh Shihāb al-dīn Suhrawardī who wishes the *darwēsh* had one nail to shut his mouth instead of the robe of a thousand nails.[91] Ibn Baṭṭūṭa describes the *hazār-mēkhī* as "a white tunic with a lining" and makes no mention of any actual nails in its construction.[92]

Such lists of different styles and schemes of correspondence with different spiritual conditions do not, however, appear to have played much part in Bukhārī's actual bestowal of *khirqas*. When someone was made a disciple or a bond of affiliation was created, Bukhārī had his servant fetch a *khirqa* or a *kulāh* (hat) and gave it to the disciple without specifying any particular form or trying to identify the disciple's spiritual characteristics. Whatever garment a *darwēsh* received, it should be worn with attention to its meaning; for example, if it is white the recipient should try to be pure inside and out. Certain restrictive rules, such as those against wearing silk, gold thread, and colorful red and yellow clothes, and limiting open (*farajī*) garments to shaykhs, were applied, but, in general, initiatory robes and hats seem to have been bestowed fairly randomly.[93] Bukhārī asked visiting Chishtī *darwēsh*es why they wore *khirqa*s with a *tukmah* (button)—that is, *jawz-girih khirqa*s—which suggests that he did not bestow such garments (or that he was quizzing his guests).[94]

The actual object bestowed at the investiture ceremony might be a robe but was most frequently a *kulāh*, a hat or cap. According to Bukhārī, the Prophet wore a small, close cap rather than a high one. A *kulāh* could be decorated with a button but in that case it should be worn with the button turned away.[95] Bukhārī sometimes wore a *kulāh* while praying and mentions that Yāfiʿī always did so rather than wearing the more common turban (*dastār* or *ʿimāma*). Yāfiʿī's justification for this was that a turban is peculiar to men (*mardān*), and he was not a man.[96] Bukhārī did not always follow his master's example in this; we know he sometimes wore a turban since he gave the author of *Jāmiʿ al-ʿulūm* the *dastār* off his own head. A *ṭāqiya* (skullcap) was another piece of headdress that Bukhārī sometimes bestowed. Besides headgear other items of clothing given by Bukhārī or by his shaykhs are mostly varieties of cloaks and robes: *bārānī* (cloak for rain), *khilʿat* (robe), and *khirqa*.[97] Again, although there may be theoretical distinctions between the significance of these different articles of clothing, such concerns do not appear to have affected the choice of what to give to whom.

Not all objects bestowed by a shaykh were things to wear. When Bukhārī received a *khirqa* from Imām al-dīn Kāzarūnī, he was also given a staff (*ʿaṣā*), scissors (*miqrāż*), and a prayer rug (*sajjāda*).[98] Prayer beads (*tasbīḥ*) were another item that could be given. Prayer beads and prayer rugs are objects used in devotional practice, therefore these are, in a sense, the material necessities for a life of devotion bestowed on a disciple who is embarking on just such a life. Scissors were used during the investiture ritual and their bestowal is thus part of the bestowal of the authority to invest and initiate disciples. In Chapter 1, I discussed the connections between Sufi investiture and the courtly bestowal of robes of honor. Many of the objects bestowed on a disciples were symbolically related to secular or political power. *ʿAṣā* can mean scepter and mace, as well as staff, and is an embodiment of authority, even the authority to use coercive physical power—Bukhārī once appeared in a disciple's dream and used his *'aṣā* to punish him.[99] In the investiture ritual described above, the hat bestowed is equated with a crown (*tāj*). The prayer rug, especially as it was understood as representing the specific position of the investing shaykh—his authority over a shrine, a *khānqāh*, and a community of disciples—was comparable to a throne.

Bukhārī and his disciples used the term *khirqa* to refer to any garment bestowed by a shaykh and as shorthand for the fact of being affiliated to a Sufi order. Thus, it is best to understand *khirqa* not as an actual type of clothing but as Sufi affiliation in itself. In this sense, a *khirqa* may be characterized by the two categories of function and affiliation. On the level of affiliation a *khirqa* is referred to in terms of the individual who bestowed it or the Sufi order that it represents, for example, *khirqa-i khwājagān-i Chisht* (*khirqa* of the Chishtī masters) or *khirqa-i siyādat panāhī* (*khirqa* that is the refuge of sayyids). Many of the people who came to Bukhārī seeking investiture wanted a connection to a specific order, sometimes to a specific saint. The Suhrawardī and Chishtī orders were, of course, most in demand and, according to Bukhārī, there was a ten to one ratio between the number of Suhrawardī investitures carried out by him to the number of Chishtī ones.[100]

On the level of function, Bukhārī listed four kinds of *khirqa*s: *khirqa-i irādat* (discipleship), *khirqa-i taḥkīm* (control), *khirqa-i tabarruk* (blessing), and *khirqa-i karāhat* (aversion). The *khirqa-i taḥkīm* is a particular form of the *khirqa* of discipleship, and both of these can only be received once and only from one's primary *pīr*. The *khirqa-i taḥkīm* indicates that the disciple has wholly abandoned his will and put himself under his *pīr*'s control. The *khirqa-i tabarruk* resembles the *khirqa-i irādat*, but there is no limit on the number of *pīr*s who can bestow it on one. (We have already seen how Bukhārī was given numerous *khirqa*s of this kind).[101] The *khirqa-i karāhat* is one that the disciple demands of the *pīr*; it is presumably the *pīr*'s unwillingness and its bestowal under duress that makes it an object of hatred.[102] Another type of *khirqa* mentioned is the *khirqa-i tajdīd* (renewal), but Bukhārī provides no explanation for it.[103]

Conclusion

The contemplative and ritual practices undertaken and taught by Bukhārī were standard elements of mainstream Sufism. Bukhārī's *malfūẓāt* do not reveal any unknown or rare activities. What they do provide, however, is a glimpse into how these practices were actually carried out on a day to day level. Sufi handbooks and theoretical treatises tend to focus on the meaning of these practices and on their spiritual or mystical goals—what experiences of the divine might be expected from *ẕikr*, *samā'*, or seclusion and how the Sufi robe corresponds to an inner spiritual state. In the *malfūẓāt*, however, we see how a devotee's day is organized around prayer times, how prayer and *ta'wīẕ* are used for solutions to everyday problems, how an aspirant might be invested with whatever garment came most easily to hand, and how age, infirmity, and language barriers might impede one's participation in such practices.

FIVE

Money, Non-Muslims, Women, and Saints

The Economic Foundation of Sufi Life

The primary means of support for Bukhārī, his *khānqāh*, and his disciples were unsought donations (*futūḥ*) from the community at large, especially its wealthiest members, the king and the nobility. Whether or not it was appropriate to accept such donations was a topic of some disagreement among Sufis at this time. According to K. A. Nizami, one of the primary differences between the Chishtī and Suhrawardī orders lay in their attitudes towards the acceptance and accumulation of donations; the Chishtīs were reluctant to take *futūḥ*, and if they did they gave it away immediately, while the Suhrawardīs accepted gifts'and hoarded wealth.[1] This distinction was most pronounced in the lifetimes of Bahā' al-dīn Zakarīyā, who owned sixty-seven villages from grants and purchase, and Farīd al-dīn Mas'ūd, who owned none. Bukhārī's defensive explanation of Bahā' al-dīn's accumulation of property is that God and his friends are served by the world. The world, by way of rulers and the wealthy, served Bahā' al-dīn by giving him property. Furthermore, a saint is like a beautiful woman whose friends protect her from the evil eye by marking her face with black dots. The property given to the saint is the disfigurement meant to protect him from jealousy.[2] (Though I would think it would be a greater source of jealousy than his saintliness.)

Later generations of both orders deviated from the pattern of extremes set up by Bahā' al-dīn Zakarīyā and Farīd al-dīn Mas'ūd. Bukhārī's position lay somewhere between the two. According to Bukhārī, the Prophet said that one should not refuse *futūḥ* unless one knows that it comes from a haram (illegitimate or illegal) source.[3] The latter question, whether the *futūḥ* was haram or halal, was of the greatest importance for Bukhārī. Distinguishing between halal and haram was a basic requirement for Bukhārī's conception of correct action. However, besides applying the terms to the legality or illegality of action, he used them most frequently to refer to material objects, usually food, clothing, and buildings. If any of these objects is haram, the ritual action of the person who has eaten such food, or is wearing such clothing, or is praying in such a building is invalid. "If there is one thread in one's clothes that is haram or from a haram source, or one mouthful of food that is haram, no act [of devotion] of his will be accepted."[4] So the *darwēsh* who is given any donation must ascertain its legitimacy before accepting it. When is an object haram? The most familiar answer is that certain objects are simply forbidden, such as wine, pork, silk clothing on men, and so on. But things can also be haram in less obvious ways. If wealth is derived from illegal sources, then anything, such as food bought with such wealth, is also haram. Given that the Sufi community attracted significant donations from the wealthy and was frequently dependent on them, the suspicion that these donations might be haram was an ongoing problem.

In Bukhārī's anecdotes, great saints were able to discover the illegitimacy of offered food through mystical insight. Bahā' al-dīn Zakarīyā, Jalāl Surkh-posh, and Jamāl al-dīn Uchchī were once offered food from which each of them instinctively recoiled; as it turned out the dish was made from a sheep that had been sacrificed *after* it had died of natural causes.[5] In Jamāl al-dīn Uchchī's case, God would even transform donations (*futūḥ*) from illegitimate sources into something halal. Bukhārī himself once heard a voice telling him that his turban, made from clothing donated by a government official, was haram.[6] But most people could not rely on such methods, and Bukhārī constantly advised his disciples to be wary of all food, clothing, and shelter that they used.

The most likely sources of illegitimate gifts were rulers and others in authority—precisely the group upon which the Sufi establishments were most dependent. Bukhārī quotes *Fatāwā al-khānīya* (by Imām Fakhr al-dīn Ḥusayn b. Manṣūr Awzjandī, d. 592/1196) to the effect that one should not eat the food of kings since most of their income is derived from illegal taxes and extortion.[7] This is no doubt why Bukhārī refused to eat food from the *khānqāh* built for him in Uch by Malik Mardān, the governor of Multan during the 770s/1370s. (On Malik Mardān and his relationship with Bukhārī, see Chapter 6.) Bukhārī was willing to let others be less stringent, since the *khānqāh* must have housed and fed a number of his disciples. Given the suspicion placed on the wealth of rulers, it is a sign of the perceived piety of Fīrōz Shāh, or of Bukhārī's hypocrisy, that Bukhārī willingly accepted considerable gifts from the Sultan. The Sultan provided Bukhārī with funds and land grants for his *khānqāh* which Bukhārī accepted, not, according to him, in his own name or that of his family but rather for the benefit of the worshippers in general.[8] In 781–782/1379–1380, when Bukhārī spent a year in Delhi, he received a monthly allowance and food for himself and his disciples from the Sultan. The Sultan also presented him with numerous robes which Bukhārī accepted but agreed to wear only after determining that they conformed to Islamic law (that is, not containing much silk or gold thread). Somewhat apologetically, he justified his decision to wear the robes by the principle that it is obligatory to obey one's ruler.[9] Bukhārī's brother Ṣadr al-dīn Rājū-qattāl was given a village, robes, and two thousand *tanka*s by Fīrōz. Though Bukhārī expresses pity for foolish people who go on hajj funded by kings (thus invalidating their pilgrimage), he wrote a note to Fīrōz asking for provisions for the pilgrimage of one of his disciples.[10]

A less problematic source of funds than the aristocracy was the merchant community. In Mecca, a *khānqāh* was endowed in Bukhārī's name, funded by merchants with offerings from halal sources. This *khānqāh* was more acceptable to Bukhārī than the one in Uch endowed by Malik Mardān. According to Bukhārī, the endowment of *khānqāhs* by merchants was unknown in India but a common practice in other lands. Such *khānqāhs* were supposedly superior to those built by kings and nobles since there was less likelihood of being dependent on illicit funds.[11]

Besides the legitimacy of the source of *futūḥ*, the intention of the giver and what he wanted in return also affected its acceptability:

> There are different types of *futūḥ*.
> 1. For blessing.
> 2. As a votive offering.
> 3. For the removal of problems.
> 4. For assistance.
> To accept [*futūḥ*] for blessing is legally indifferent if one knows that the person making the offering wants to bestow a gift. It is permissible to accept what is given as a votive offering if it is unconditional. If it is dedicated to someone then that person, or someone who has received [his] permission, can accept it. It is permissible to accept [*futūḥ*] for the removal of problems if one is of the people of love and one has the ability to remove the problem. Otherwise it is not [permitted]. That which is given for assistance is bribery; it is not permitted. But if, before taking it, one assists in his [the donor's] work and his request is fulfilled then one can accept something as a thanks offering.[12]

Once *futūḥ* was accepted it should be spent or given away immediately. Bukhārī compares the *darwēsh* who receives *futūḥ* to a bricklayer; just as the bricklayer must place the brick in his hand before taking up the next one, so the *darwēsh* must spend the *futūḥ* he has been given before accepting anymore.[13] The immediate expenditure of *futūḥ* was the policy of the Chishtī order, and they interpreted it to imply that any gifts of land or other immovable property should be rejected. However, since Bukhārī did not object to his brother receiving a village from the Sultan, he either did not have the same objection to fixed property or did not put always into practice his own precepts.

Receiving donations, re-distributing them to beggars, guests, and resident *darwēsh*es, and keeping account of them were significant tasks in the management of a *khānqāh*. Bukhārī's *malfūẓāt* mention a *khāzin-i sufra* (treasurer or guardian of provisions) employed at Ṣadr al-dīn 'Ārif's *khānqāh* in Multan; presumably every *khānqāh* must have had someone in charge of its economic and financial activities.[14] *Khizānat al-fawā'id al-Jalālīya* records Bukhārī's instructions on the processing of gifts:

> In the year 765 (1363–1364), the *makhdūm* instructed his servant about accepting votive offerings (*naẕr*): "If someone brings something, first ask him

> what work it comes from and then put it in separate categories. Spend all votive offerings from merchants, farmers, and artisans on living expenses and personal clothing and on some of [my?] children and the *darwēsh*es of the *khānqāh*. Spend all *futūḥ* from kings and officials to pay off debts and for feeding the *darwēsh*es of the *khānqāh* and guests. Put aside anything from someone who has no apparent source of income. When a solitary beggar or mendicant or someone of that type comes, give it to him. If anyone comes [and gives something in exchange] for assistance refuse it because that is bribery."[15]

It is worth noting that donations of unknown origin are given to the beggars and mendicants—perhaps an indication of a lack of concern for the spiritual purity of the lower segments of society. *Darwēsh*es belonging to the *khānqāh*, that is, living there as full-time participants in its activities, were supported by its wealth. Only people actively engaged in devotion, or those employed there, are allowed to live off the income of a *khānqāh*, especially one supported by a *waqf* (endowment). As discussed in Chapter 1, when Bukhārī was in Multan for his studies he was not fed from the kitchens of Rukn al-dīn Multānī's *khānqāh* because he was there as a student of *fiqh* and hadith, not as a disciple or a *darwēsh*.[16]

For his own disciples, Bukhārī did not recommend reliance on donations. For those with no dependents, the best option (for reasons of detachment as well as independence from potentially illegal sustenance) is to remove oneself to the hills or the wilderness and live off gathered fruits and the like. This advice, however, seems to be purely theoretical. More concretely Bukhārī instructed his disciples to live, not on charity, but on their own earnings or on loans. Thus, despite the condemnation of earning a living as a sign of lack of trust in God found in early Sufi writers,[17] for Bukhārī the concern for the legality of one's sustenance meant that legal work was not only permissible but encouraged. He declared *kasb* (earning a living) to be legal and also said that the verses of the Quran (8:28, 64:14–15) notwithstanding, not all wealth (nor every woman and child) is an enemy.[18]

In this support for *kasb* Bukhārī followed the example of his immediate predecessors. Naṣīr al-dīn Maḥmūd Chirāgh-i Dihlī, unlike earlier Chishtīs, had a positive view of *kasb*.[19] Bukhārī cited the example of the Yemeni Faqīh Baṣṣāl who, as his name indicates, supported himself, his family, and his disciples by selling onions. In a conversation recorded in *Jāmiʿ al-ʿulūm*, Bukhārī asked the assembled disciples how they earned their livings; the answers, received with approval, were prayer leader, teacher, grave-digger, and artisan.[20] Trade was also an acceptable career and Bukhārī suggested that travel as a merchant was one good way of making the pilgrimage to Mecca. The best types of *kasb* were holy war (*ghazā'*), trade, and agriculture.[21] The acceptability of these careers is also why donations from merchants, artisans, and farmers could be spent on the immediate personal expenses of a Sufi without fear of invalidating his devotions.

Despite the permissibility of work and its advantages over doubtful charity, the *darwēsh* with an occupation could not maintain the ideal detachment and separation from the world. This is particularly true of any employment with the government. Thus Bukhārī declared that though one can give a *ṣāḥib-i shughl* (holder of a post or occupation) a turban or a prayer mat, one should not give him a *tasbīḥ* (prayer beads) as these are only for hermits who have no ties to the world. A *darwēsh* once came to Bukhārī wanting to be freed from his occupation. Bukhārī gave him a *tasbīḥ* and he subsequently lost his position.[22]

Bukhārī supported himself, his family, and his disciples on a combination of personal property, *futūḥ*, and loans.[23] Loans played a significant and problematic role in the lives of Bukhārī's companions. He frequently suggested borrowing as a way to avoid dependency on charity but was also concerned by the indebtedness of his son, Nāṣir al-dīn Maḥmūd. Bukhārī was also in debt, at least during his visit to Delhi in 781/1379–1380. He said: "I swear, after this I will not borrow. I have become old and debt remains hanging around my neck."[24] As a disciple pointed out, borrowing and lending can also involve illegal wealth—since interest is forbidden and who will lend money to a poor *darwēsh* without charging interest? Bukhārī's response to this problem was an explanation of the legal loophole by which a lender can charge a fixed fee without it counting as interest.[25]

The responsibility of a shaykh to provide for his disciples was taken quite seriously. As mentioned before, a significant portion of donations to a *khānqāh* went to the maintenance of the resident *darwēsh*es. Bukhārī tells of a Sindī *darwēsh* who was used to receiving four pieces of bread from Bahā' al-dīn Zakarīyā's *khānqāh*. When the Sindī went on hajj he complained that no one gave him anything to eat there. He was told to ask his shaykh who came from Multan every Thursday night. He did so and bread from the Multan *khānqāh* was miraculously sent to him in Mecca.[26]

Bukhārī's disciples could be similarly demanding. Sayyid Shams al-dīn Mas'ūd from Iraq seems to have been a particularly improvident individual. Bukhārī said that the motivation for his 781/1379–1380 trip to Delhi was to assist Shams al-dīn and to give him a share of any *futūḥ* received.[27] The record of Bukhārī's stay in Delhi is regularly punctuated by Shams al-dīn's requests for money, once accompanied by the threat that if he did not receive anything he would put on the *zunnār* (the belt of Christians or Zoroastrians, or the sacred thread of Brahmins) and practice fraud. He complained if he did not receive a daily allowance (*waẓīfa*)[28] and nagged Bukhārī to produce gold by alchemy, which Bukhārī refused to do. Bukhārī had previously done alchemy but he was now forbidden to do so, presumably by God.[29] Bukhārī gave Shams al-dīn funds, asked the *khān-i jahān* for money for him, tried to interest the *shaykh al-islām* in his case, and advised him to borrow from the grocer. Sayyid Shams al-dīn protested that he did not borrow from Muslims and one is not supposed to borrow from non-Muslims—but these are dubious excuses since he was already in debt. He came to India with debts, had borrowed more, and now did not have the funds to go home. The origin of his monetary problems was the acquisition of a dancing girl.[30]

Indic Languages and Religions

I have been referring to Uch as Bukhārī's home and to Bukhārī himself as an Indian, but would he have seen things in this light himself? Would he, or indeed any member of the Turco-Persian Muslim elite of South Asia, have thought of this as their homeland? There are some indications that Bukhārī and his contemporaries would not have agreed with my characterization of him as Indian. As the *shaykh al-islām* said to him in Delhi in 782/1380, in the context of a conversation about the virtues of India: *shumā ō mā az īn zamīn na-īm* (you and I are not from this land).[31]

Though Bukhārī's family had been living in Uch for over a century, neither in his *malfūẓāt* nor in the early South Asian biographical dictionaries of saints is he referred to as Uchchī.[32] Perhaps this retention of the *nisba* Bukhārī indicated the family's strong attachment to their Central Asian origins.[33] Bukhārī was a sayyid from both his paternal and maternal sides, yet, though descent from the Prophet was very important, there seems to be no real sense of an Arab ethnicity attached to this lineage. When explaining his Ḥanafī affiliation to the sayyids of Mecca, he referred to his forefathers in Bukhara, an indication that these were his real roots, though it would have been equally reasonable to refer to the dominance of Ḥanafism in South Asia.

Despite the barriers between the Muslim elite and the rest of the population and despite Bukhārī's identification with Bukhara, it was in South Asia that he spent most of his life and it was the South Asian Muslim community that he served as a teacher and guide. He was bound to this community by family ties, by master-disciple relationships, by attachment to the shrines of the saints of Multan and Uch, and by his numerous disciples throughout South Asia. Though Bukhārī frequently contrasted the misguided practices of Muslims in India with practices elsewhere, his goal does not seem to have been to denigrate his own community but rather to bring it up to perceived international Islamic standards. Even the above mentioned comment by the *shaykh al-islām* about their foreign origins took place in the context of a conversation on the virtues of India in which Bukhārī pointed out that this was the land where Adam first set foot (on Mount Sarandīb) and where there were many *abdāl* (one of the ranks of saints).[34]

Outside of India, Bukhārī could not help being seen as a representative of South Asian Muslims. Unlike Bukhārī's disciples in South Asia, the Yemeni historian Abū Makhrama calls him *Bukhārī thumma Ujjī*, showing that in Aden he was identified with his birthplace of Uch.[35] In Mecca, other South Asian pilgrims turned to him for advice, and he was called on to intervene in a dispute between an Indian slave and a merchant from Uch.[36] Even Yāfiʿī's question about what he ate at home reveals the teacher's view of his student as a visitor from a very different and distant land.

Relations with Non-Muslims

As is the case for most famous medieval Sufi saints, legend ascribes a significant missionizing role to Bukhārī. Much ink has been spilled on the question of the involvement of the Sufi orders in the conversion of large sections of the Indian population to Islam. Many popular depictions of South Asian Sufism present the Sufi saints as missionaries who converted the "masses" through the example of their piety, love, and humanitarian qualities. This narrative is presented as an alternative to one in which non-Muslim populations were forcibly converted by the conquering Muslim armies. Both of these narratives, along with others, have been masterfully taken apart by Richard Eaton.[37] Religious conversion on a mass scale is, in general, a murky topic in which it is difficult, if not impossible, to pin down motivations, agents, dates, or even what we mean by conversion. The question is even more fraught for the spread of Islam in South Asia where any narrative of conversion has potential politically charged implications for communal identity. Furthermore, given the uneven growth of Muslim populations in different parts of the sub-continent, it is unlikely that any single explanation would suffice. Finally, most Islamic textual sources of the period represent only the views of an elite that was linguistically and culturally divided from the general population and usually uninterested in its religious identity, unless this became a cause of social upheaval or public disturbance. This is as true for the Sufi texts as it is for the historical and literary compositions.

One of the sources for the widespread narrative of mass conversion at the hands of the medieval Sufi saints is the collection of oral traditions, local histories, and census information undertaken by the British administration in the nineteenth century. H. A. Rose's endlessly fascinating three-volume *Glossary of the Tribes and Castes of the Punjab and the North-West Frontier Province* ascribes the Islamization of almost every Muslim group in the region to the conversion of an ancestor at the hands of some particular saint or another.[38] Bukhārī, under the title Makhdūm-i jahāniyān, is credited with the conversion of several Rajput and Jatt clans.[39] Other clans are said to have been converted by Shēr Shāh Sayyid Jalāl of Uch, that is, Bukhārī's grandfather, and by Sayyid Jalāl, who could be either grandfather or grandson.[40] It is difficult to know what to make of these accounts, given the lack of contemporary evidence for mass conversion (though not for the conversion of individuals).[41] The British administrators and ethnographers who compiled such information operated with notions of religious identity and its formation that presumed that conversion takes place through missionary activity and results in a radical change in both individual and group identity (on the model of nineteenth-century Protestantism). To what extent would such an understanding of religion be shared by Bukhārī? Or by his putative converts? In fact, would Bukhārī and his ilk (the Muslim religious classes) have had the same conception of religion as the population at large?

In his *malfūẓāt*, Bukhārī does mention several individual converts whom he knew or whom he had converted. One such individual conversion did lead to the adoption of Islam by the convert's family as a whole. Unlike the cases listed in Rose's *Glossary* of the conversion of male heads of tribes or clans, who presumably used their leadership positions to bring their kin groups into Islam, this convert was a woman whose family's conversion was ascribed to the power of her saintliness and blessings (*barakāt*).[42]

Though Bukhārī remarked with apparent pride on those whom he had converted to Islam, conversion is generally presented as a voluntary activity brought about by the grace of God and the piety of the individual. He quotes an Indian slave girl on hajj who, when mocked for asking God to love her, responded that if God did not love her, he would not have brought her out of the darkness of unbelief.[43] Those who do not convert of their own accord should not be forced, only prayed for. When in Delhi in 781/1379–1380, Bukhārī presented a number of individuals to Sultan Fīrōz Shāh, recommending them for royal appointments or for other forms of patronage. Among those presented was a young Hindu boy, and Fīrōz demanded to know why the child had not become a Muslim. Bukhārī responded that when the boy came to him he had asked Bukhārī (in Hindawī) to pray that someday God would make him a Muslim. God willing, he would be made a Muslim some day.[44] In other words, conversion to Islam, though clearly desirable, was not something that could be brought about simply by the will and actions of either Sultan or saint. It had to wait for divine action.

Along with a missionary impulse, other qualities popularly ascribed to the medieval Sufi saints are religious tolerance, openness to the truth of other traditions, and a tendency towards syncretism. Bukhārī's religiosity, in its commitment to the mainstream, Shariʿa-centered, text-based Sunni tradition shared with the Muslim lands to the west, would likely have little space for such attitudes. At the same time, however, Bukhārī does not come across in the *malfūẓāt* texts as particularly bigoted—for his historical context. He even went so far as to say that the punishments of the afterlife would be alleviated for those *kāfir*s who did good in the world. Bukhārī had little interest in correcting the beliefs and practices of non-Muslims nor, in his conversations with the Sultan and other holders of power, did he express any opinion on state policies towards the non-Muslim subjects of the Sultanate. Bukhārī reserved his chastisement for the errors of his fellow Muslims, for their sins of ignorance or depravity. On a personal level, too, Bukhārī seems to have interacted amicably enough with non-Muslims. When Bukhārī was ill, for example, he was attended by a Persian-speaking Hindu doctor, accepted his ministrations, and prayed that God would show him the true path.[45]

Vernacular Languages

The attention of the author of *Jāmiʿ al-ʿulūm* to the languages spoken by the Hindu doctor and by the Hindu child presented to Fīrōz highlights one of the significant social barriers dividing the Turco-Persian Muslim elite from the population at large. It is unclear whether Bukhārī was able to speak any of the Indian vernaculars with ease, an ability which would have greatly facilitated his interaction with non-Muslims and recent converts. In the case of the Hindu doctor mentioned above, the text specifies that he spoke Persian, making it easier for Bukhārī to converse with him. In contrast, the Hindu boy presented by Bukhārī to the Sultan is described as speaking Hindawī, that is, the North Indian vernacular that ultimately developed into modern Hindi and Urdu.

It has been suggested that if the Sufi shaykhs played a significant role in the spread of Islam in South Asia, one factor must have been the use of vernacular languages and literatures in the dissemination of their teaching.[46] Although the source material is meager and not always reliable, there is sufficient evidence to demonstrate that Hindawī and other "New Indo-Aryan" languages were being used for Sufi poetry from the thirteenth century onward.[47] In Bukhārī's case, as for most of the Sufi shaykhs of his period, the primary records of his life and teaching are in Persian. These texts present Persian as the language of religious teaching and of ordinary conversation between Bukhārī, his close disciples, and most of his visitors. The reading, quoting, and explication of Arabic texts was also a central feature of Bukhārī's teaching, usually present in a manner that makes clear the foreignness of Arabic within this linguistic context. We have only passing hints about Bukhārī's facility with any vernacular language.

Sirāj al-hidāya contains a few examples of Bukhārī's use of vernacular language. He warns against applying to humans any names that are used for God, such as *ṯ'hakur* (lord), *d'hanī* (owner), and *kartār* (creator).[48] And he recites the following verse in Hindawī:

جس کهنه راکهه دي تون مار نسکي کوئي
بال نه بيکا کر سکي جي جگ بيري هوي

No one can hurt someone whom you protect
Not a hair on his head can be harmed though the world be his enemy.[49]

As I have mentioned earlier, the recension of *Sirāj al-hidāya* is complicated and its authenticity as a direct record of Bukhārī's teachings somewhat doubtful. We should, therefore, be wary of accepting this verse as a genuine example of his use of Hindawī. One of the complications in trying to determine the likelihood of Bukhārī's reciting verses in Hindawī is that Uch falls outside of the North Indian region in which Hindawī was emerging and becoming dominant. The linguistic history of the area is quite unclear, but it would seem likely that the language spoken in the region of Uch and Multan would have been an early form of Siraiki or Punjabi, which belong to a slightly different linguistic group than Hindawī.[50]

The linguistic challenges inherent in the inclusion of Indian converts into Bukhārī's Sufi path are exemplified by the "extremely common" (*bighāyat 'āmī*) man from Sind, discussed in Chapter 4, who sought initiation and investiture from Bukhārī, despite his ignorance of even the basic formulaic prayers of repentance and for forgiveness. It was with great difficulty that Bukhārī performed the ritual of *talqīn* (implantation of the *ẕikr* formula) in "Sindī."[51] Sind at this time indicated not only the territory covered by the modern Pakistani province of that name, but might also often include the Indus Valley all the way north to Multan. Within this region, a number of languages and dialects, early forms of modern Sindhi and Siraiki, were presumably in use. There is no way to know which of these was the language of the aspiring disciple in this anecdote;

the author of *Jāmiʿ al-ʿulūm*, being a resident of Delhi, was unfamiliar with the languages and linguistic geography of Sind. The central problem for the initiation of this disciple went further than whether Bukhārī could communicate with him in "Sindī," Hindawī, or Persian—the verbal elements in the ritual were a set of prayer formulas in Arabic. We can imagine the difficulty of teaching and learning such wholly foreign phrases if shaykh and aspirant had no shared language.

Apropos of this situation, Bukhārī quoted Rukn al-dīn Multānī to the effect that for people like these—presumably those who were "common" and spoke only a vernacular language—the rites can be waived since investiture with the Sufi hat (*kulāh*) is equivalent to receiving their repentance. Rukn al-dīn's statement appears to be dismissive of the possibility of full inclusion into the Sufi path for such "common" people. If "common" people could not be expected to learn the proper prayer formulas, could they be expected to be truly pious Muslims? Bukhārī himself seems to have had no trouble believing in the virtue and piety of Indian converts and other "common" people. As will be discussed below, some of Bukhārī's favorite examples of saintliness included servants, slaves, converts, and women. This was surprising to some of his contemporaries—when he told Sultan Fīrōz Shāh about an Indian woman who converted to Islam, became his disciple, achieved the status of a saint (*walīya*), and converted her whole family, the Sultan remarked: "That there is such a *walīya* among such evil-doers (*mufsidān*) is an astonishing thing."[52]

The Story of Nawāhūn

In some secondary literature, Bukhārī is presented as a missionary for Islam whose zeal for conversion reached the point of persecution of non-Muslims. This reputation is largely based on a single anecdote that is found in the *tażkira* tradition but is never mentioned by the extant *malfūẓāt*. One of the earliest *tażkiras* to provide a biography of Bukhārī is *Siyar al-ʿārifīn* by Jamālī (d. 942/1536), whose *pīr* Shaykh Samāʿ al-dīn was a disciple of Bukhārī's younger brother Ṣadr al-dīn Rājū-qattāl. According to Jamālī, near the end of his life Bukhārī was visited on his sickbed by a Hindu official by the name of Nawāhūn. Nawāhūn prayed for Bukhārī's health and praised him, saying that he was "the seal of the saints just as Muḥammad was the seal of the prophets." Bukhārī and his younger brother, Ṣadr al-dīn, understood this as a sign of conversion to Islam since Nawāhūn had acknowledged the prophecy of Muḥammad, as well as the finality of that prophecy. They were, therefore, most perturbed when Nawāhūn did not immediately adopt proper Islamic behavior, especially the obligatory ritual prayer. Jalāl al-dīn Bukhārī died shortly thereafter but Ṣadr al-dīn took up the case and pursued Nawāhūn all the way to Delhi, hoping to get him to acknowledge and perform his new religious affiliation or be executed for apostasy. Nawāhūn sought refuge in the Sultan's court where the Sultan tried, but failed, to trick Ṣadr al-dīn into referring to Nawāhūn as "that Hindu," which would have contradicted his accusation of apostasy. Eventually Ṣadr al-dīn exerted enough public pressure, as well as magically causing the death of a *qāżī*'s son, that Nawāhūn had to be executed. This gave Ṣadr al-dīn his nickname of *Rājū-qattāl* (king killer).[53]

This tale is fascinating for its depiction of conversion as an irrevocable transformation of identity brought about *unintentionally* by well-meaning platitudes. In this story, religious identities are absolutely mutually exclusive and they are created through speech. Having said that Muḥammad was the last prophet, Nawāhūn was no longer a Hindu. From that point onward he was either a Muslim or an apostate. Similarly, if Ṣadr al-dīn had referred to Nawāhūn as a Hindu, then he would have verbally acknowledged that as Nawāhūn's real identity and could no longer accuse him of apostasy.

The story of Nawāhūn was the starting point for my own interest in the life and personality of Bukhārī. However, I very soon came to doubt its representation of Bukhārī's character. The entry on Bukhārī in Jamālī's *Siyar al-'ārifīn* is largely made up of anecdotes that conform to certain frequent hagiographic motifs. One such motif represented here is a saint's conflict with and victory over the representatives of secular power—in this case, the saintly brothers defeat Nawāhūn, the Sultan, and the *qāżī*. Another trope is a saint's miraculous power to bring death, insanity, or other calamity upon anyone who opposes him—Rājū-qattāl causes the *qāżī*'s son to die. Third, many hagiographic anecdotes hinge on a play on the literal meaning of words—the Sultan attempts to trick Rājū-qattāl into calling Nawāhūn a Hindu.

Other examples of these motifs in the *taẕkira*s include anecdotes in which Bukhārī causes a ruler of Uch to go mad as punishment for his disrespect towards the Sufis,[54] accidentally/miraculously kills his own four-year-old grandson when the child interrupts him at prayer,[55] and turns away the famous Kubrawī shaykh Sayyid 'Alī Hamadānī on the grounds that only God is *hama-dān* (all-knowing).[56] All of these incidents seem highly unlikely from the perspective of Bukhārī's biography and personality as documented by the *malfūẓāt*. His relations with secular powers, though sometimes conflictual, were complex, nuanced, and not directly confrontational. Similarly, the miracles and wonders described in the *malfūẓāt* are never of the fearsome variety found in the *taẕkira*s (where Bukhārī's own little grandson falls victim to his wrath). And although Bukhārī was very concerned with words, his concern was focused on the correct pronunciation, orthography, and understanding of Arabic words for the purpose of ritual performance, legal accuracy, and textual interpretation.

Jamālī's tale of Nawāhūn is part of a portrayal of the Sufi saint as a fearsome being whose supernatural powers cannot be withstood by secular authority. Recent scholars, sifting through the meager evidence on pre-Mughal Sufi involvement in conversion, have read it as a sign of Bukhārī's missionary zeal and religious bigotry—in contrast to the popular vision of Sufi saints spreading Islam through universal love and tolerance.[57] The evidence of the *malfūẓāt*, however, shows us that Bukhārī fits neither model of Islamic proselytizer. Bukhārī was intolerant. But his intolerance was of any deviance *by Muslims* from the norms of the Shari'a, making him, on the one hand, less interested in the religious identities and practices of non-Muslims and, on the other hand, unlikely to support any process of conversion that depended on making Islamic practice more accessible or less stringent in its requirements.

Women and Other Saints

Married Life

Uch was also the center of Bukhārī's family life. In Chapter 1 we saw the importance of Bukhārī's father, grandfather, and uncles in shaping his early education. Similarly, Bukhārī's younger male relatives constituted the inner core of his circle of disciples and were among the most important conduits of his spiritual legacy. Bukhārī's younger brother, Sayyid Ṣadr al-dīn Rājū-qattāl, is described in the hagiographic tradition as his *khalīfa*, though Bukhārī himself never alludes to this designation. After Rājū-qattāl, Bukhārī's sons, especially Nāṣir al-dīn Maḥmūd (d. 800/1397–1398) and his numerous descendants, went on to become some of the major inheritors of this Sufi lineage. Nāṣir al-dīn Maḥmūd's son Burhān al-dīn ʿAbdallāh Quṭb-i ʿālam (790–858/1388–1454), who migrated to Gujarat, and grandson Sirāj al-dīn Muḥammad Shāh-ī ʿālam (817–880/1414–1475) were Bukhārī's only descendants to achieve a stature comparable to their famous ancestor.[58]

While the female members of Bukhārī's household could not play quite the same role in the continuation of Bukhārī's lineage, his wives (and perhaps his daughters) also participated in the family's practice of Sufism and Sufi instruction. Bukhārī had married, at least once, sometime before his departure for Mecca and Medina. He mentions his wife repeatedly in *Jāmiʿ al-ʿulūm* as *mādar-i farzandān* (mother of [my] children), usually to say that he has left some important or valuable item in her care, but never tells us her name. These comments, made in 781/1379–1380, suggest that he had only one wife still living at that time. According to Lak'hnawī, Bukhārī had three wives, one a daughter of his uncle Sayyid Muḥammad b. Jalāl Surkh, another from among the sayyids of Delhi, and the third from Rūm (Anatolia). By each wife he had one son, Nāṣir al-dīn Maḥmūd, ʿAbdallāh, and ʿAlī al-Akbar, respectively.[59]

Despite the norm of marriage and reproduction established by the Prophet's example and enjoined by the Shariʿa, the Sufi tradition has often produced expressions of ambivalence, disdain, or even rejection towards active heterosexuality. Celibacy was sometimes adopted as an ascetic practice, misogynist arguments identified women and, therefore, wives with this world that is to be rejected in favor of the next, and marriage and procreative sex were irrelevant to the anti-nomian *qalandar*s and *malang*s, who lived in opposition to all of society's strictures and structures. Furthermore, the practice of gazing at beardless youth as signs (*shāhid*) of divine beauty, and the use of the terminology of romantic desire for the love of a (usually male) devotee for his shaykh, for the Prophet, and for God, both led to the recurrence of male homoerotic desire as a discursive trope in Sufism—though homosexual activity was forbidden by the Shariʿa.

Bukhārī, at any rate, was unabashedly heterosexual. Besides his marriages, which would have sufficed to fulfill the requirements of the Shariʿa and the expectations of his family and society, Bukhārī probably possessed concubines throughout his life. He approvingly described the custom of *khānqāh*s, endowed by merchants in Arabia, of providing women to travelers, who took them as wives or concubines for the duration of their stay. In Hindustan, sadly, this model was not followed—"when travelers were in need, what were they to do?"[60] In 781/1380, at the age of 71, he was given five hundred *tanka*s (coins) and two slave girls as concubines. He had the money distributed to his son and disciples but reserved the concubines for himself, saying, with a smile at his own off-color pun, "I have become weak, perhaps they will learn something, I will raise them up or else perhaps they will make me rise."[61] Similarly, he jokingly offered to take a slave girl off the hands of an elderly (120-year-old) Arab who had come to visit him, since the girl was young and the Arab was old and weak.[62] When telling his disciples that only those who have fallen in love can understand how lover, beloved, and love can be one, he recounted his own youthful passion for the beautiful child of his father's concubine (*kanīzak-zādeh-i wālid*). Though the lack of grammatical gender in Persian makes it unclear whether this person was male or female, she was most likely a girl—Bukhārī refrained from acting on his desires because she was his father's property (*mamlūk*, masc., but glossed by the editor as *mamlūka*, fem.), not because of the impermissibility of homosexual conduct.[63]

Although we do not know the name of his wife or wives, Bukhārī tells us enough to form some idea of the religious personality of one of them (the one still living in 781/1379). That she was pious and religiously observant, saying her morning prayers before waking up Bukhārī, is only to be expected. But she was also a participant in the Sufi path of scholarship and contemplation. She recited the forty greatest names of God every day. Once while praying she appeared to have fainted but on reviving she claimed to have seen God with the eye of her heart. She supervised the reading of *'Awārif al-ma'ārif* by a local woman, and another woman came to talk and meditate with her.[64] This suggests that there may have been a circle of women who came to practice their devotions and study with her.

Female Sufis and Saints

The information provided by Bukhārī's *malfūẓāt* is typical of the difficulties in determining women's participation and role in medieval Sufism. Enough is said to show that women were participating but few names or personalities are provided. During Bukhārī's visit to Delhi in 781/1379–1380, when numerous members of the nobility and the religious classes came to receive his teachings, blessings, and *khirqa*s, women were also amongst his devotees. One day he visited a friend's family and allowed twenty-one women to be spiritually affiliated with him (*ta'alluq dād*). He made the oldest of these women a "sister," that is, a full-fledged disciple. (In Bukhārī's *ijāzat-nāma*s he invariably uses the vocabulary of brotherhood or sisterhood for disciples receiving *khirqa*s and *ijāzat*s). These women, like Bukhārī's wife, are examples of the female members of a family associated with Sufism participating with their husbands in that tradition. A different segment of society is represented by a Hindu woman who converted to Islam and became Bukhārī's disciple. She was a saint (*walīya*) and by her blessing (*barakat*) her whole family converted to Islam.[65] Bukhārī mentions a number of women from Uch, Thatta, Sīwistān, and Delhi whom he knew to be saints (*awliyā'*). But he leaves their identities obscure.

Anonymous female contemporaries were some of Bukhārī's most frequently cited examples of saintliness. In *Jāmi' al-'ulūm*, he describes one of the women who studied *'Awārif al-ma'ārif* with his wife as an *'ālima* (scholar) and a *walīya* (saint). Signs of her greatness were her smelling like attar, being at the Ka'ba every Thursday night, and experiencing the graces of *laylat al-qadr* (the night in Ramażān when the Quran was revealed). Despite her sanctity, this holy woman seems to have treated Bukhārī as a spiritual mentor—she would bring food from Mecca for him, she came to him for confirmation of her identification of *laylat al-qadr*, and she sought his permission to carry out retreats.[66] In *Tuḥfat al-sarā'ir*, Bukhārī mentions a very similar woman from Sīwistān who also traveled on Thursday nights to Mecca and Medina and then to Multan and Uch.[67] Another woman, a servant of a follower of Bukhārī's wife, flew to Damascus on 27 Rajab every year to pray with all the other *awliyā'* of the world behind Quṭb al-dīn Dimashqī. Finally, there was a holy woman in Thatta whose prayers prevented Fīrōz Shāh from conquering that city in his campaign of the 760s/1360s.[68]

Sainthood

By Bukhārī's time, sainthood, like many aspects of the Sufi tradition, had already been extensively theorized by earlier Sufi writers.[69] Rather than an original or highly systematic doctrine, what we find in Bukhārī's *malfūẓāt* is a presentation of mainstream Sufi thought on sainthood and its application to individuals, living and dead, with whom Bukhārī was familiar. Bukhārī very rarely labeled any of his living male contemporaries as *awliyā'.* Instead, the people whom Bukhārī mentions as *awliyā'* fall into three groups: 1) the well-known early heroes of Sufism, such as Bāyazīd Bisṭāmī and 'Abd al-Qādir Gīlānī; 2) Bukhārī's shaykhs and their predecessors, Maṭarī, Yāfi'ī, Jamāl al-dīn Uchchī, his own grandfather, the Suhrawardī shaykhs of Multan and the Chishtī ones of Delhi and Ajūdhān; and 3) contemporary women, mostly anonymous and humble, as discussed above.

In the chapter on the *awliyā'* in *Khizānat al-fawā'id al-Jalālīya*, as well as in other discussions by Bukhārī, the most apparent feature of the saints is their ability to perform supernatural feats (*karāmāt*). Yet, if such feats are performed without visible evidence of piety and correct knowledge, they do not prove sainthood but rather its opposite: the action of the devil.

> The first thing necessary for a student is the Shari'a and by this is meant everything commanded by God and his Prophet, like ablution, prayer, fasting, alms, pilgrimage, seeking what is licit, rejecting what is illicit and the rest of whatever is enjoined or forbidden. So if you see someone fly through the air, walk on water, or swallow fire, or do anything else that looks like *karāmat*

> (wonder performed by saints) but he has neglected any duty to God or any tradition of the Prophet, then know that he is a devil, whether jinn or man. His action is not a wonder but is magic (*siḥr*) or deception (*istidrāj*).[70]

The variety of *karāmāt* ascribed to the *awliyā'* are typical of the Sufi tradition: knowledge of hidden things, divine inspiration, the ability to transport oneself great distances, to produce water in a desert, to turn stones into gold, to save others from harm, and so on.[71] These wonders are not supposed to be made public by the saint nor, during his lifetime, by his audience, except for practical purposes, such as the instruction of disciples and warding off of harm, or with permission from God, or when overcome by ecstasy.[72]

In the case of the shaykhs of the Sufi orders, being able to perform wonders seems to be a necessary part of their role as shaykhs. Thus the perfect shaykh is endowed with power over life and death and has the ability to guide his disciples even when absent or dead.[73] In Bukhārī's conversation there is often little distinction made between the shaykhs and the *awliyā'*—the two groups frequently seem interchangeable. For example:

> He said: "One hour in the gaze of the *awliyā'* has such value. One must associate with a shaykh and read and hear *'ilm* and in this one will find value and happiness."
>
> Then his blessed face turned to this *faqīr* and he said: "As you find in association with me, and the *'ilm* you hear from me, and that you read, and the actions you acquire—what happiness it is!"
>
> [We] all kissed his feet.[74]

Inasmuch as the perfect master-disciple relationship requires that the shaykh be able to guide and help his disciple under *all* circumstances and to understand what is in the disciple's heart, he must have at least some of the capabilities of a saint.[75] Such qualities are ascribed only to the perfect (*kāmil*) shaykh, who is therefore also a perfect human, that is, a fully realized mystic who has reached God and is therefore a *walī*. Though a shaykh could be less than perfect, it seems nearly impossible (at least for Bukhārī) to think of one's shaykh as imperfect—that would go against the disciple's requisite attitude of respect and trust. Despite this exaltation of the role and capacities of the shaykh, there is no hint in Bukhārī's teaching of the practice of *fanā' fī 'l-shaykh* (annihilation in the shaykh) developed and popularized by the Naqshbandīya order. Bukhārī forbade his disciples from contemplative exercises focusing on the shaykh, such as repeating the shaykh's name a thousand times. Even Muḥammad's name should not be used in this way.[76]

Besides the great mystics of the past and major shaykhs of the previous generation there are only one or two other men whom Bukhārī considered as belonging to the *awliyā*.' The most notable of these was his disciple Turābī. After several years in Bukhārī's company, Turābī went on hajj and stayed at the Ka'ba. He then became one of the *abdāl* with the ability to fly around the world.[77] No further name, geographic origin, profession, or other social identifier is provided for Turābī, making him a rather mysterious figure who flies in and out of Bukhārī's life. Another male *walī* was the servant of an Indian merchant whom Bukhārī met in Mecca.[78] Notwithstanding these two figures, the typical saint from a lowly background in Bukhārī's anecdotes is female. However, his examples of ignorant fools deluded by the devil into thinking they are saints are all men.

It should be borne in mind that the belief of Bukhārī and his contemporaries in the extraordinary abilities of the *awliyā'* and the presence of angels, *abdāl*, jinns, and Khiżr was not an all-accepting credulousness towards the supernatural. Physical evidence was often demanded and produced to back up stories of miraculous events. Proof of the Uch woman's overnight trips to the holy land was the food, *qurṣ-i makka ō nabāt-i miṣrī* (bread of Mecca and herbs of Egypt), which she brought back. Not only had Bukhārī eaten of it but so too had his disciple Shams al-dīn Mas'ūd, and the latter confirms this to the author of *Jāmi' al-'ulūm*.[79] Similarly, the *abdāl* Bukhārī met in Mecca gave him a piece of paper which he brought back to Uch and showed to others.[80]

Sainthood and Femininity

Why are all the *awliyā'* whose sanctity is accepted by Bukhārī either well-respected shaykhs of the previous generations or anonymous women, converts, and slaves, without any middle-ground between the elite and the humble?[81] One explanation is probably the thread of self-aggrandizement that runs throughout Bukhārī's teachings and his disciples' writings. Description of the sanctity of his own *pīr*s and of those who take him as their *pīr* only serves to reaffirm his own status. In contrast, the absence of any mention of contemporaries who were viewed as saints by their own disciples, such as Manērī, Hamadānī, Simnānī, and Gīsūdarāz, removes any competitors to his claims of religious authority.

Another factor may be the etiquette of saints not wishing their status nor their miracles publicized, thus restricting the identification of *awliyā'* to those who are dead and those who would be difficult to identify, such as anonymous female converts. In fact, the rhetoric of modesty applied to saints draws upon the model of feminine modesty. In the terms of the tradition, *karāmāt* are analogous to menstruation. Just as menstruation is *the* mark of womanhood but at the same time is intensely private, so miracles are the mark of sainthood which must be hidden, an intimate secret between the saint and God.[82] This is not the only way in which sainthood is explained in terms of the markers of femaleness or femininity. When discussing whether the possession of great wealth was appropriate in a Sufi shaykh or saint, specifically the case of Bahā' al-dīn Zakarīyā and his vast land-holdings, Bukhārī compared the saint to a beautiful woman. Just as the friends and relatives of a beautiful woman protect her from the evil eye by marking (or tattooing) her face with black dots, so does God protect his friend from jealousy by disfiguring him with wealth.[83] Finally, of course, the use of *'urs* (wedding) as the standard term for the death anniversary of a Sufi saint makes explicit the image of the saint as a bride of God.

Bukhārī's anecdotes about humble female saints also serve a rhetorical function. They demonstrate, through the juxtaposition of low social status with saintliness, the power of piety and devotion to make *anyone* into a *walī*. Sainthood is a status to which any Sufi devotee can aspire. Of a woman in Delhi, Bukhārī said: "She was a Hindu, became a Muslim, became my disciple, and has now become a *walīya*. She never sleeps."[84] Becoming a *walīya* was the final step in a process of transformation from Hindu to Muslim to Sufi disciple. That sainthood is a practical goal is also borne out by a number of prayer formulas taught by Bukhārī which help the supplicant become one of the *awliyā'* or *ahl-i karāmat*.[85]

The *awliyā'* who are not shaykhs, although they perform wonders and act to protect their companions and neighbors, do not have the same public authority as guides or social mediators as the shaykhs. This is representative of their place in the social order; in Fīrōz Shāh's Sultanate it is difficult to imagine a female convert from Hinduism achieving the same status as Shaykh Rukn al-dīn Abū al-Fatḥ, whose father and grandfather were shaykhs and saints, who claimed descent from the Quraysh, and, not of least importance, controlled an immensely wealthy *khānqāh* and tomb complex. Some women, like Bukhārī's wife, could instruct others. Whether women could act as spiritual guides on the Sufi path, investing and supervising disciples, is a point of some disagreement—Ashraf Jahāngīr Simnānī categorically stated that they could not, even as he acknowledged the important role played by older female shaykhs and saints in Ibn al-'Arabī's spiritual training.[86] They certainly could not take on the public leadership role of one of the great shaykhs, in charge of a *khānqāh* and representative of a major Sufi lineage. According to the Chishtī hagiographer Mīr Khwurd, Farīd al-dīn Mas'ūd said that he would have liked to appoint his daughter, Bībī Sharīfa, as his primary spiritual heir (*khalīfa*) and to give her his prayer rug (*sajjāda*). Despite her piety and devotion, however, it was impermissible to give a woman the shaykh's *sajjāda*, that is, to recognize her as a shaykh of that stature.[87]

While shaykh is a social label, one which indicates a relationship between the shaykh, his disciples, and his community, *walī* is not. The *awliyā'* are defined through their relationship to God, which results in their supernatural abilities. Vincent Cornell has attempted to illuminate the relationship between sainthood and socio-political power through the lens of the two possible words for sainthood: *wilāyat*, which has the sense of authority and protection, and *walāyat*, which indicates closeness and intimacy. According to him, *walāyat* referred to the "internal visage," "nature," or "metaphysical essence of sainthood as seen from the perspective of Islamic mysticism."[88] That is, sainthood as *walāyat* is internal to both the saint and the Sufi tradition. *Wilāyat*, in contrast, is the aspect of sainthood more accessible and visible to the general public. "This visible dimension of sainthood was primarily understood in terms of power. . . . [The] Moroccan saint was above all else an empowered person—empowered to perform miracles, empowered to communicate with God, empowered to help the weak or oppressed, empowered to act on behalf of others, empowered to mediate the course of destiny, and empowered to affect the behavior of other holders of power."[89] In this description, Cornell identifies both supernatural power and social or political status with *wilāyat*.

The evidence from Bukhārī's *malfūẓāt* does not, however, fully support Cornell's analysis. Bukhārī's defines *walāyat* as *maḥbūbiyat* (being beloved) and *wilāyat* as *taṣarruf fī al-aqālīm* (power over regions). Other expressions used for this spatial authority or power are *wilāyat-i ruknī* and *taṣarruf-i ruknī*. We have already noted the division of India into the *wilāyat* of Bahā' al-dīn Zakarīyā' and his descendants and the *wilāyat* of Mu'īn al-dīn Chishtī and his successors. In these cases, Cornell's argument that *wilāyat* encompasses both supernatural and socio-political power holds true, suggesting that this kind of sainthood is limited to the great shaykhs. However, Bukhārī also describes the female saint of Sīwistān as possessing *taṣarruf-i ruknī*, just like Rukn al-dīn and Naṣīr al-dīn, though it is unclear how much territory she controlled.[90] Furthermore, the ability of the female saint of Thatta to hold off the Sultan's army was a demonstration of power in the political realm, even if it was not power based on any visible political or social role.

Since both *wilāyat* (in Bukhārī's usage) and the ability to perform wonders are characteristics of saintly women, while political power and authority are not, the social authority of the great shaykhs cannot be fully identified with their *wilāyat*. In other words, by virtue of *wilāyat* a *walīya* has the power to hold off an army; but she does not have a well-known shaykh's public authority to advise or influence a ruler. Cornell's analysis, collapsing the supernatural capabilities of a saint into the social and political power of a public religious authority, reduces the great saintly shaykhs to bishops and erases the existence of saints who were female, otherwise socially disempowered, or simply hermetic. He argues that sainthood is a social phenomena and that therefore there can be no really "hidden" (*majhūl*) saints; either they are known to someone or they are "doctrinal topoi."[91] It seems to me that the female saint is a clear example of someone whose very piety would render her invisible to anyone but her family and her shaykh. Those who know her can bear witness to her miracles, but she cannot be a public figure.

The relative status of shaykhs and saints is also illustrated by Bukhārī's attitude towards being given these labels. Whenever the topic of being a shaykh came up in discussion with his disciples, he denied that he was one, claiming to be only a *wakīl* (representative or agent) of his masters. Of course, this disavowal of the status of shaykh should not be taken too seriously since he acted as a shaykh and was treated as such by his disciples. It was part of the purposeful rhetoric of self-deprecation in which he couched most of his obvious claims to status and authority. It was also an expression of his respect for Bahā' al-dīn Zakarīyā and his son and grandson.

It seems, however, that he was less reticent about being described as a saint. Bukhārī made no definite claims to miraculous abilities of his own but did recount various wonderful events that had happened to him. When his circle of disciples referred to various acts of his as *karāmāt*, Bukhārī did not protest, saying only "*man kīstam* (who am I)?"[92] For one thing, his hair made an effective *ta'wīẕ* since he was a sayyid. Often during Ramażān he would know when *laylat al-qadr* had arrived by various signs and visions. He had spoken with the angel who came to his friend Khiżr in Sīwistān.[93] Once in a whispered aside to some disciples, including the author of *Jāmi' al-'ulūm*, Bukhārī mentioned that he had heard the Prophet respond to his greeting.[94] An anecdote reported in *Sirāj al-hidāya* ascribed to Bukhārī the typical saintly characteristic of presence at the Ka'ba on Thursday nights:

> One day several *darwēsh*es came to Quṭb-i 'ālam's [Bukhārī's] *khānqāh*. With one voice they said: "Sayyid Jalāl al-dīn, we met you every Thursday night at the Holy Ka'ba as long as we were there. We were there six months ago." Quṭb-i 'ālam had been at home for the last fifteen years. Quṭb-i 'ālam said: "Do you remember your promise to me?" "We remember. The promise was that we would never tell anyone. But we could not contain your greatness within our narrow breasts, so we spoke."[95]

Shaykh Rukn al-dīn Abū al-Fatḥ had told him in a dream that he was a *quṭb al-'ālam*, so he must have thought of himself as a saint with a saint's abilities. Bukhārī even clarified for his disciples that he was a *quṭb-i aqālīm*, a *quṭb* of multiple regions rather than of only one region.[96] However, though Bukhārī might have viewed himself as a *quṭb* but not a shaykh, his disciples saw these as interdependent roles. Their response to his recounting of how he came to be a *quṭb* was to declare that the people, both elite and common, believe in him because thousands had repented at his hands and become his disciples.[97] For them, it was his widely recognized status as an initiatory master, a shaykh, that proved that he was a saint.

PART THREE

Served by the Inhabitants of the World

SIX

A Public Figure

Sayyid Jalāl al-dīn Bukhārī, having established himself as the head of his family's *khānqāh* in Uch and as the leading heir to the Suhrawardī lineage in India, spent the last few decades of his life as an increasingly well-known public figure. From the mid-750s/1350s onward, he was sought out, not only by would-be disciples and students, but also by prominent visiting Sufi shaykhs, by members of the nobility, and by government officials.

His interaction with the latter two groups sometimes involved him in the political affairs of the state and is revelatory of the interdependent relationships between the state, the Sufi shaykhs, and the state-appointed religious functionaries. So far in this study of Bukhārī's life, we have been mostly absorbed in the professionally religious segment of medieval Indo-Muslim society, that is, the world of saints, shrines, the 'ulama, and so on. But though this was a highly important and influential segment of society, it was not the only one. The circle of the court, and the "secular" poets, writers, and scholars patronized by it, was another pole of Muslim culture and learning. Now Bukhārī's growing prominence and his good relations with the new Sultan Fīrōz Shāh began to attract the attention of this secular world of rulers, governors, and courtiers.

Interactions with Courtiers, Rebels, and Governors

Żiyā' al-dīn Baranī

An example of this new attention paid to Bukhārī is a letter from Żiyā' al-dīn Baranī preserved in one of Bukhārī's *malfūẓāt* collections. Baranī is one of the most interesting and well-known personalities of eighth-/fourteenth-century South Asia. His fame rests largely on his historical work, *Tārīkh-i Fīrōz Shāhī*, the most significant source of information on the reigns of Muḥammad b. Tughluq and his predecessors. As Peter Hardy writes: "Baranī's *Tārīkh-i Fīrūz Shāhī*, completed in 758/1357, is the vigorous and trenchant expression of a conscious philosophy of history which lifts Baranī right out of the ranks of mere compilers of chronicles and annals."[1] Since Baranī's historical, ethical, and political theories played a significant role in shaping his depiction of events, the study of his personality and thought has been necessary for historians of the period, particularly of the reign of Muḥammad b. Tughluq. Baranī, though for a while a disciple of Niẓām al-dīn Awliyā,' belonged more to the milieu of the court and secular Muslim culture than to the professionally religious classes. He had been a courtier and boon companion of Muḥammad b. Tughluq, but after the Sultan's death in 752/1351 he fell from royal favor. He was implicated in a plan to place a putative son of the deceased king on the Delhi throne while Fīrōz Shāh had already been acclaimed Sultan by the army.[2] As a result, Baranī was banished from court by Fīrōz, imprisoned in the town or fort of Bhatnēr for five or six months, and spent the last years of his life in poverty and exile.

It was only after his exile from court that Baranī began his writing career, and it seems that one of the first things he wrote was a treatise entitled *Ma'āṣir-i Jalālī* containing hadith about the obligation to love the Prophet and his descendants, which he sent to Bukhārī. The letter that accompanied this text was copied by the author of *Khizānat al-fawā'id al-Jalālīya*, and this appears to be the only record of its existence since it does not appear in the list of Baranī's works compiled by Mohammad Habib.[3] This letter, sent from Bhatnēr after nearly half a year there (in other words, close to the end of his confinement), complains of Baranī's wretched situation, which he describes as confining his life, comfort, and society. Most of the letter consists of hyperbolic praise, sometimes in verse form, of Bukhārī and of the family of the Prophet, especially 'Alī and Fāṭima. It claims that Bukhārī is an ideal sayyid, like 'Alī in wisdom and Zayn al-'ābidīn (the fourth Imam) in piety. To seek refuge in such a descendant of the Prophet is equivalent to seeking refuge with the Prophet, Fāṭima, and 'Alī, and leads to salvation in the afterlife.

It is worth noting that Baranī's praises of Bukhārī are only marginally based on Bukhārī's position as a Sufi shaykh. Rather it is his descent from the Prophet, his identity as a sayyid through the line of 'Alī and Fāṭima, that is highlighted. In praising the family of the Prophet, Baranī focuses on 'Alī, Fāṭima, Ḥasan, and Ḥusayn, that is, on the *ahl-i bayt* (people of the house) whose veneration is particularly associated with the Shi'a. From Baranī's other writings it is clear that he was not Shi'a, and this praise of the *ahl-i bayt* shows the degree to which respect for the family of 'Alī was not an exclusively Shi'a phenomena. At this moment in his life, Baranī appears to have been focused on praise of the Prophet; his other work from this period was *Ṣaḥīfa-yi na't-i Muḥammadī* (Pages in Praise of Muḥammad). In both of these works, Baranī's sufferings and sense of the approach of death led him to write something in hope of achieving salvation.[4] Because of Baranī's flowery and figurative style it is unclear what he hopes from Bukhārī—he writes of wanting to be his bondsman and to rub the dust of Bukhārī's alley in his eyes. If only Bukhārī will reach out his hand to him he will be saved. It is possible that this letter is an attempt at generating some interest in his case; perhaps Baranī hoped that Bukhārī would put in a word for him with the royal court.

Bukhārī responded to this letter by sending him a Meccan turban cloth and some funds and by praying for his swift release.[5]

Though this letter does not contain much of historical or intellectual interest, it is important for a number of reasons. First, it confirms and elaborates the dismal picture of Baranī's situation after his fall from royal favor which has already been pieced together from brief remarks in his other works. This moment in his life has been seen as a potential key to fully understanding Baranī's changing political opinions and the relationship between his different works, particularly the two versions he wrote of his *Tārīkh-i Fīrōz Shāhī*.[6] Furthermore, in terms of Jalāl al-dīn Bukhārī's life, the letter demonstrates that he was no longer merely a provincial religious teacher. His reputation as an important, politically well-connected figure had reached Baranī's ear. That Baranī wrote to him while in trouble with the Sultan suggests, though it does not prove, that Bukhārī may have had some measure of political influence. The question raised by this letter is whether Bukhārī would have been willing to intercede with the Sultan on Baranī's behalf and whether he had sufficient influence to affect the Sultan's decisions.

The Sultan and his authority were locally represented by the governor of Multan, who had responsibility for what is today southern Punjab and upper Sind, including Uch. During the mid 750s/1350s and 760s/1360s the governor of Multan was ʿAyn al-mulk ibn Māhrū, the son of an Indian convert to Islam.[7] A collection of Ibn Māhrū's letters has been preserved under the title *Inshā'-i Māhrū* and provides an intimate view into some of the political events of the period. Ibn Māhrū wrote to many of the religious dignitaries of the region—to sayyids, shaykhs, and *qāżīs* (judges)—and therefore it is not surprising that he wrote at least one letter to Bukhārī. The single letter to Bukhārī included in the *Inshā'-i Māhrū* is, like many of Ibn Māhrū's letters, mostly taken up with formalities, rhetorical flourishes, and compliments—in this case to the religious classes and particularly to the sayyids. However, the ultimate purpose of the letter is practical; he writes to complain of the laxity of the sayyids (it is unclear which ones are meant) in paying their *kharāj* (land tax). A notice had been sent to the shrine of Shaykh Kabīr (perhaps meaning Bahā' al-dīn Zakarīyā or Bukhārī's father Aḥmad Kabīr) the previous year, but there had been no result. Ibn Māhrū appears to want Bukhārī's advice on this problem and professes his desire to deal gently with the descendants of the Prophet while simultaneously implying various veiled threats.[8]

Mediation and Diplomacy

One of the most well-documented instances of Bukhārī's involvement in politics was his role as a mediator between Sultan Fīrōz Shāh and the rebellious leaders of Sind. The region of southern Sind had long been a source of disquiet and rebellion for the Sultans of Delhi. Fīrōz Shāh had come to power at the death of his cousin Muḥammad b. Tughluq during the latter's pursuit of the rebel Taghī to Sind. During the early years of his reign, Fīrōz struggled to quell the rising power of the chiefs of the Samma tribe of Sind. The letters of 'Ayn al-mulk ibn Māhrū, Sirāj al-dīn 'Afīf's *Tārīkh-i Fīrōz Shāhī*, and several of Bukhārī's *malfūẓāt* all mention Bukhārī's participation in this conflict, but the extent and nature of his role are somewhat unclear. Riazul Islam's article "The Rise of the Sammas in Sind" is the clearest and most extensive reconstruction of these events.[9]

According to Riazul Islam, the Sammas achieved supremacy in lower Sind some time soon after 752/1351–1352. By 760/1359, two Samma chiefs, Jām Jūnā (or Jawnā) and his nephew Bānhbīna, jointly ruled lower Sind, basing themselves in the city of Thatta on the Indus River. Throughout the next decade, various diplomatic and military attempts were made by Fīrōz and by his governor in Multan, Ibn Māhrū, to bring Thatta and its rulers under the authority of the Sultanate. On their side, Jām Jūnā and Bānhbīna alternated between conciliation and open rebellion, sometimes in alliance with the Mongol forces which had been harassing the western edges of the Sultanate throughout the century.

The earliest mention of Bukhārī's involvement in this affair is in a *parwāna* (official order) from Ibn Māhrū addressed to Jām Jūnā and Bānhbīna. Riazul Islam dates this letter and the events it describes to the period between 761/1360 and 766/1365.[10] In this *parwāna*, Ibn Māhrū mentions that the Jām and Bānhbīna had brought Bukhārī and the *shaykh al-islām* Ṣadr al-dīn (a grandson of Bahā' al-dīn Zakarīyā)[11] to intercede for them. Based on the esteemed character of the two mediators, the Sultan had accepted a pledge of obedience and support from the two Sammas. Since then, the Jām and Bānhbīna had reneged on their pledge, causing Ibn Māhrū to admonish them.

In order to effectively intercede on behalf of the Sammas, Bukhārī and the *shaykh al-islām* must have been able to command the trust and respect of both parties. As religious dignitaries, they would have been a logical choice for Jām Jūnā and Bānhbīna to choose as mediators. Having a connection to the local population and its interests, while also being part of the dominant religious structures recognized by the Sultan, allowed Bukhārī to mediate between regional and imperial forces. The *shaykh al-islām*, in contrast, was a royal appointee as the leading Sufi shaykh of the Sultanate. He had accompanied the royal army from Delhi, just as Naṣīr al-dīn Maḥmūd Chirāgh-i Dihlī had accompanied Muḥammad b. Tughluq during his campaign in Sind. But he too had local ties, as the grandson of Bahā' al-dīn Zakarīyā of Multan.

The willingness of Suhrawardī shaykhs to enter into political events or associate with rulers has sometimes been interpreted as general support for the authority of the Delhi Sultanate. Such favoring of the Sultan, over local rulers, cannot definitely be inferred from this instance of Bukhārī's mediation. That Jām Jūnā and Bānhbīna sought his intercession and received some recognition from the Sultan as a result could suggest that Bukhārī was viewed as sympathetic to their anti-imperial interests. Riazul Islam's interpretation is that Bukhārī "generally put his weight on the side of the central authority and exercised a stabilizing and moderating influence on the Sind politics."[12] It should also be borne in mind that information about the events described above comes from the governor of Multan, 'Ayn al-mulk ibn Māhrū, and therefore represents the imperial point of view, which might assume the shaykhs' support for the Sultan and his army.

In any case, this deal between the Sammas and the Sultan did not last long and Fīrōz Shāh eventually felt the need to engage them in battle. Riazul Islam places Fīrōz Shāh's campaign against Thatta in the "last months of 1365, the whole of 1366 and about the first half of 1367."[13] After various set-backs the imperial army finally gained the upper hand and was in a position to decisively defeat the rebels. At this point Bukhārī was once more called upon to act as mediator between the two parties. According to 'Afīf's *Tārīkh-i Fīrōz Shāhī*: "Then the Jām and Bānhbīna after much thought and consultation found a solution. They sent wise and skillful individuals to Sayyid Jalāl al-dīn Ḥusayn Bukhārī (may God sanctify his soul) in Uch and they explained their situation [to him], 'Unless the sayyid should come from Uch, we will be under the feet of Sultan Fīrōz.'"[14]

So Bukhārī came to the camp of the Sultan's army. "When the sayyid arrived in the encampment all the people there endeavored to kiss his feet. And whoever of the people in the court kissed the sayyid's feet, the sayyid said [to him]: Baba, God willing, with the grace of God there will be peace in a few days. When the sayyid came closer, Sultan Fīrōz, like the devotees, wished with heart and soul to meet the sayyid. As a friend he welcomed him."[15] Bukhārī then explained that the reason Fīrōz Shāh had previously been unable to take Thatta was the presence of a virtuous and holy woman in that city. Her prayers for her hometown had preserved Thatta from the imperial army. However, she had died three days earlier and therefore Bukhārī expected Thatta to be defeated soon. "When the people of Thatta heard that Sayyid Jalāl al-dīn had arrived at the army camp they continued to send him messages explaining their difficulties."[16] He conveyed their wishes to the Sultan and the Sultan was merciful.

This account by 'Afīf, like Ibn Māhrū's letter, represents Bukhārī as the mediator chosen by the Jām and Bānhbīna but also as the object of Fīrōz's respect and devotion. It is worth noting that in this account there is no suggestion that Bukhārī's saintly powers played any role in intimidating either the rebels or the Sultan. Rather, it is his position as a figure respected and trusted by both parties that enables his diplomacy. 'Afīf records Bukhārī's opinion that the presence of a holy woman had protected Thatta, but the historian himself does not corroborate this information nor does he otherwise include it in his detailed description of the changing fortunes of Fīrōz Shāh's campaign.

Bukhārī's involvement in the surrender of the Sammas is also mentioned in two of his *malfūẓāt*: *Sirāj al-hidāya* and *Malfūẓāt-i Makhdūm-i jahāniyān*. Unfortunately I have been unable to access the latter text. Riazul Islam translates the relevant passage from the *Malfūẓāt-i Makhdūm-i jahāniyān* as follows: ". . . for the second time the late Sulṭān Fīrūz Shāh went to Thatta with the intention of attacking Bānhbīna and Jām, and Ḥaḍrat Makhdūm Quṭb 'Ālam (Makhdūm-i-Jahāniyān Sayyid Jalāluddīn Bukhārī) also arrived at Thatta in order to bring Jām and Bānhbīna (to obedience), so as to establish peace, for in the first invasion of Thatta by the above-mentioned late Sulṭān, the Mussalmans (the imperial army?) had suffered considerably."[17] Riazul Islam's understanding of this passage is that Bukhārī's "efforts were directed at not only rescuing Jām Jūnā and Bānhbīna from a difficult situation but also at saving the military the political prestige of the imperialists."[18] I am not wholly convinced of this interpretation since it depends on Riazul Islam's inference that Bukhārī wanted the rebels brought to *obedience* and that the Muslims for whom he was concerned were the army.

The account given in *Sirāj al-hidāya* is quite different. This text gives no explanation of how Bukhārī became involved in the conflict but says that the people on both sides welcomed his intervention, expecting peace to be brought about by a descendant of the Prophet. As in the other accounts, Bukhārī brought about the surrender of Jām Jūnā and Bānhbīna. In this version, however, peace is achieved not through diplomacy but through spiritual power. In the middle of the night, Bukhārī put on Shaykh Rukn al-dīn Multānī's turban and prayed to God to bring the two rebels to the Sultan. A voice from the unseen responded that his prayer had been accepted. The next day, Jām Jūnā arrived at the camp. Bānhbīna's continued absence was a source of concern, so, the next night Bukhārī prayed once more. This time, he had Sayyid Qāsim, one of his disciples, call out seven times: "Come, Bānhbīna." As a result Bānhbīna arrived.[19]

Sirāj al-hidāya represents a more mystically inclined understanding of events. While a historian like 'Afīf, focused as he was on the military and political career of Sultan Fīrōz Shāh, would describe the sequence of events in mundane terms, Bukhārī's disciples and hagiographers, in contrast, can be expected to focus on the miraculous powers of the saint. To them, Bukhārī's ability to bring about a peaceful resolution to the conflict would logically arise from his spiritual capabilities, rather than from his abilities as a politician or diplomat. Bukhārī himself certainly believed in the efficacy of prayer and the power of holy objects, like Rukn al-dīn's turban. Therefore, it is not unlikely that while acting as a diplomat Bukhārī would also have used spiritual mechanisms in attempting to resolve the situation.

After the submission of Jām Jūnā and his nephew, they were taken back to Delhi by the Sultan, and two of their relatives were left to rule Thatta. Bukhārī may also have accompanied the king and his captives to Delhi. According to the *Malfūẓāt-i Makhdūm-i jahāniyān*, Bukhārī was later sent back from Delhi with Jām Jūnā to suppress a rebellion by one of the new rulers of Thatta and to bring him back as a captive.[20]

Malik Mardān

Malik Naṣīr al-mulk Mardān Dawlat, Ibn Māhrū's successor as governor of Multan in the 770s/1370s, also patronized Bukhārī and gave him several significant grants and endowments, including a *khānqāh*.[21] This may have been recompense for some spiritual help or advice sought from him. Malik Mardān's son once came to Bukhārī to request a prayer for the *malik* who was said to have incurred the king's wrath. One of Bukhārī's companions saw in a vision that Fīrōz Shāh had been merciful to Malik

Mardān and bestowed robes of honor on him and Bukhārī was able to reassure his son.[22] Histories of the Sultanate period are filled with accounts of the frequently perilous and fragile relationships between the nobles and the Sultans. In this case, we see Bukhārī's spiritual, not political, intervention sought in such a case.

Malik Mardān was not a particularly pious individual and Bukhārī seems to have had some reservations about accepting his donations. Bukhārī would not eat any food from the *khānqāh* endowed by him. In a conversation in 782/1380, Fīrōz Shāh wonders at Bukhārī even going to Malik Mardān's *khānqāh*, given the *malik*'s lack of religious observance. Malik Mardān had died by that time and Bukhārī was asked several times about his current condition—that is, whether he was in heaven or hell. The first time the question was raised Bukhārī was incapable of answering, but the second time he responded that Malik Mardān had been in torment because he had angered his *pīr*, Naṣīr al-dīn Maḥmūd. However, Bukhārī interceded on his behalf with Naṣīr al-dīn (or rather with his spirit since he had died in 757/1356), and Malik Mardān was forgiven and was in a better situation in the afterlife.[23]

According to later hagiographers, Bukhārī's relationship with Malik Mardān had far-reaching historical effects. Malik Mardān's adopted son Sulaymān was the father of Khiżr Khān (d. 825/1421), founder of the Sayyid dynasty (817–855/1414–1451) after the fall of the Tughluqids. Sulaymān's claim to being a sayyid was supposedly established in his boyhood by Bukhārī when the saint was a guest at Malik Mardān's home. Sulaymān had been assigned the duty of washing the guests' hands and Bukhārī remarked that this task was unbecoming a descendant of the Prophet, thus revealing Sulaymān's identity as a sayyid.[24] This story is reminiscent of the anecdote about the confirmation of Bukhārī's status as a sayyid by the voice of the Prophet at his tomb in Medina.

Further Travels

Possible Returns to Arabia

Most *tazkira* entries on Bukhārī assert that he went on hajj several times, by land and by sea, sometimes accompanied by disciples. The various travelogues ascribed to Bukhārī expand the theme of his travels to fantastical lengths. The voyage described by the travelogues with the most realistic details is one that is said to have taken place soon after the death of Muḥammad b. Tughluq in 752/1351 and the acclamation of Fīrōz Shāh. Upon ascending the throne, the new Sultan sent Bukhārī to acquire a robe of honor from the ʿAbbāsid caliph in Cairo. Several elements found elsewhere in Bukhārī's *malfūẓāt* and in the *tazkira* sources are also present here: he performed the hajj seven times, the sun turned him green so that the keepers of the Prophet's tomb in Medina doubted his claims to being a sayyid, and the Prophet responded to his greeting at the tomb.

Bukhārī returned to Delhi with the robe of honor and a footprint (*qadam*) of the Prophet Muḥammad. Fīrōz Shāh decided that the footprint would be placed on his own grave after his death. However, sometime later the Sultan offered his orphaned grandson Fatḥ Khān any boon from his treasury and the prince chose the *qadam-i sharīf.* Fīrōz did not want to give it up but finally agreed that whichever of the two should die first, the footprint would be put on his grave. Thus, when the prince died the *qadam-i sharīf* was placed on his grave and a tomb with a mosque, a madrasa, a well, and fortifications was built. A *waqf-nāma* (deed of endowment) was written by Fīrōz for the complex in Ṣafar 767/October–November 1365.[25] *Jawāhir al-awliyā',* written by a descendant of Bukhārī in the eleventh/seventeenth century, also tells of Bukhārī bringing the *qadam-i rasūl* from Medina to Delhi, along with a *kachkūl* (begging bowl) belonging to 'Alī b. Abī Ṭālib.[26]

Although Fīrōz Shāh did receive titles and mandates from two successive caliphs,[27] there are a number of reasons to doubt the truth of this account. First, nowhere in *Khizānat al-fawā'id al-Jalālīya* nor in *Jāmi' al-'ulūm*, Bukhārī's two most reliable and extensive *malfūẓāt*, is there any mention of this trip to Cairo and the Hejaz. Given Bukhārī's great veneration for the Prophet and his fondness for reminiscing about his travels abroad, this silence is significant. Second, if the Ḥaẓīra-i Fīrōz Khān, where Bukhārī stayed during the period covered by *Jāmi' al-'ulūm* (781–782/1379–1380), is correctly identified with the shrine later known as Dargāh Qadam Rasūl and the holy footprint was already in place, then there should certainly be some mention of such a significant relic close at hand. Yet nowhere in *Jāmi' al-'ulūm* is there any indication of the presence of this relic. Finally, neither Baranī nor 'Afīf mentions the *qadam-i sharīf* in either of their *Tārīkh-i Fīrōz Shāhī*s and, though this does not negate the antiquity of the relic, it does make its history more obscure. To further confuse the matter, there is also a ninth-/fifteenth-century mosque in Bengal containing another Prophetic footprint, also supposedly brought from Arabia by Bukhārī.[28] There is also a footprint of 'Alī at Bukhārī's own tomb in Uch.

As stated above, there is no mention in *Khizānat al-fawā'id, Jāmi' al-'ulūm,* or *Tuḥfat al-sarā'ir* of any travels beyond the itinerary reconstructed in Chapter 2. However, in comments recorded in *Sirāj al-hidāya*, Bukhārī mentions having been in the cities of Damascus, Baghdad, Samarkand, Ghazni, and Tabriz, and the regions of Khurāsān and Arabia. These place-names appear in the context of discussions of the legitimacy of square tombs, of trees in mosques, and of eating shrimp.[29] These lists of places are presented in a somewhat formulaic manner, as in the following example:

> Khān-i a'ẓam Ẓafar Khān asked *quṭb-i 'ālam* [Jalāl al-dīn Bukhārī] whether planting a tree in a mosque was acceptable or not. He graciously answered: "When this *faqīr* reached the noble city of Ghazni, I saw a number of fruit-bearing trees in the mosque planted by Sultan Maḥmūd . . . . When I went to Khurāsān, I saw shady trees planted in every mosque. I reached the kingdom of Iraq [and saw] large fruit bearing trees in whose shade people would sit on Fridays. In Yemen, *amīr al-mu'minīn* 'Alī (may God honor him) had planted a pomegranate tree in the congregational mosque. The traces of this tree still

> remain. From its seed other trees have been planted in this mosque and reached maturity. In the Prophet's mosque in Medina, *amīr al-mu'minīn* 'Umar (may God be pleased with him) had planted a number of date trees. . . . In the mosque of Tabriz, Ka'b Aḥbār (may God be pleased with him) had also planted five pomegranate trees. . . .In the mosque of Imām-i a'ẓam Abū Ḥanīfa Kūfī (may God be pleased with him) several fig trees were planted . . . . In the mosque of Damascus there were four trees in the four corners planted by Imām-i Ḥanbal."[30]

The route suggested by such passages in *Sirāj al-hidāya* is quite different from the itinerary reconstructed in Chapter 2. For this voyage Bukhārī would have traveled by land through either the Bolan or Khyber Pass to Khurāsān and then through Iran to Iraq. As mentioned earlier, and discussed in greater detail in Appendix B, the transmission and authorship of *Sirāj al-hidāya* is somewhat obscure, and I have doubts about the reliability of its biographical details. It is also unclear when these further travels implied by *Sirāj al-hidāya* would have been undertaken.

Visits to the Imperial Capital

Much better-documented than such later voyages to West Asia are the numerous trips to Delhi made by Bukhārī during the last two decades of his life (765–785/1363–1383). During these visits, Bukhārī was in greater contact with the royal family, the military rulers, and state officials than he would be in Uch. According to 'Afīf, Bukhārī visited Sultan Fīrōz Shāh in Delhi every few years because of their mutual friendship. Bukhārī would bring with him petitions from the people of both Uch and Delhi which the Sultan granted to the best of his abilities.[31]

Though 'Afīf ascribes all of Bukhārī's journeys to Delhi to his love for the Sultan, Bukhārī's *malfūẓāt* record his statements of other reasons for these trips. In *Sirāj al-hidāya*, Bukhārī says that he did not come to Delhi (in 772/1371) for fame or wealth. Instead, the son of a teacher of his, who had taught him only one *sipāra* (a thirtieth of the Quran), came to tell him that this teacher had died leaving behind seven indigent daughters. Would Bukhārī get some provision for them from the Sultan and his nobles? It was to fulfill this request that Bukhārī came to Delhi.[32] Similarly, in *Jāmi' al-'ulūm*, Bukhārī ascribes his 781–782/1379–1380 trip to Delhi to the indebtedness of his disciple Shams al-dīn Mas'ūd and his intention to provide him with funds from any donations that might come his way.[33] In other words, these trips were essentially fundraisers, though supposedly for the sake of his disciples rather than for his own enrichment. In *Tuḥfat al-sarā'ir*, Bukhārī says he went to Delhi in 776/1374–1375 in order to intercede for, and fulfill the needs of, the Muslims, perhaps through his good relations with the Sultan.[34] Clearly, in all of these explanations, Bukhārī is attempting to deny the obvious inference that he was dependent on the Sultan's patronage and financial support.

It would have been during such a visit, perhaps the one after the conquest of Thatta (769/1367–1368), that Bukhārī allegedly came into conflict with Fīrōz Shāh's trusted *wazīr*, Khān-i jahān Maqbūl Tilangī (d. 770/1368–1369). I say allegedly because this anecdote is only recorded in Jamālī's *Siyar al-ʿārifīn*, the source for the story of Nawāhūn discussed in Chapter 5, and, in my view, one of the less reliable *taẕkira* texts. The *khān-i jahān*, an Indian convert to Islam who had risen to eminence during Muḥammad b. Tughluq's reign, was in many ways the true ruler and administrator of the empire. According to Jamālī, Bukhārī was disliked by the *khān-i jahān*. When Bukhārī came to him to intercede on behalf of an imprisoned youth, the *khān-i jahān* turned him away, despite Bukhārī's persistence in returning twenty times. On the twentieth visit, the *khān-i jahān* asked Bukhārī if he was not ashamed to keep returning with this petition. Bukhārī responded that on the contrary he was gaining merit by each attempt and only wanted the *khān-i jahān* to share in that merit by releasing the boy. The *khān-i jahān* was so moved by this answer that he came out bare-headed with a rope around his neck like a captured slave, fell at Bukhārī's feet, became his disciple, and released the young man.[35]

The editor of *Siyar al-ʿārifīn* doubts the veracity of this story, given the evidence of *Jāmiʿ al-ʿulūm* about the good relations between Bukhārī, Fīrōz Shāh, and the *khān-i jahān*. However, the *khān-i jahān* mentioned in *Jāmiʿ al-ʿulūm* is the second of that title, Jawnā (or Jawnān) Shāh, son and successor of Khān-i jahān Maqbūl Tilangī. The story is still somewhat unbelievable because of the hyperbolic details of Bukhārī's twenty visits and the *khān-i jahān* (who is known to have been both a harsh ruler and a pleasure-loving individual) actually putting a rope around his neck. In any case, Bukhārī held no grudge after the *khān-i jahān*'s death; he visited his tomb and prayed for his salvation.[36]

Bukhārī also visited Delhi in Rajab 772/January 1371 and stayed at least ten months, during which visit his conversations and discourses were recorded by the one of the authors of *Sirāj al-hidāya*. *Sirāj al-hidāya* records a number of inquiries put to Bukhārī by Khān-i aʿẓam Ẓafar Khān, who would have been more likely to come into contact with Bukhārī in Delhi than in Uch. This *khān-i aʿẓam* might be either Tāj al-dīn Muḥammad Lūr Fārsī or his son Daryā Khān, who successively held the *iqtāʿ* of Gujarat and the title of Ẓafar Khān.[37] Fīrōz Shāh's sister's son Malik ʿAlī was also sometimes in attendance at the discussions recorded in *Sirāj al-hidāya*.[38]

In 776/1374–1375 Bukhārī was again back in the capital, as mentioned in *Tuḥfat al-sarāʾir*.[39] This visit to Delhi may have lasted into early 777 since the author of *Jāmiʿ al-ʿulūm* met him there on 10 Muḥarram of that year (11 June 1375). Fīrōz Shāh's son Ẓafar Khān (not to be confused with the two governors of Gujarat mentioned above) was also present that day.[40] It was during this visit that the Sultan asked Bukhārī's opinion of a certain *darwēsh* in Delhi who claimed to have repeatedly seen the angel Gabriel. Bukhārī declared the man an ignoramus who had been lead astray by the devil, and suggested that the ʿulama be assembled to pass judgment on him. The ʿulama sentenced the unfortunate *darwēsh* to death unless he repented, and after three days he was executed.[41] As was discussed in Chapter 3, Bukhārī had a consistently harsh opinion of fools who thought that they were holy. In this case, the king's solicitation of his opinion demonstrates a recognition of Bukhārī's authority on the topic, though judgment is left up to the 'ulama. By early Ẕū 'l-qa'da 777/March 1376 Bukhārī was with the author of *Tuḥfat al-sarā'ir*.[42] No indication is given of where the conversations recorded in that work took place, though it is implied that it was not Delhi. The author was from the town or region of Kara but there is no reason to think Bukhārī spent time there.

Encounters with Various Shaykhs

In Uch, Bukhārī was sought out by a number of Sufi shaykhs and disciples, some of whom went on to become very famous in their own right. Though they are not mentioned in Bukhārī's *malfūẓāt*, two of the best-known of these visitors were Sayyid Ashraf Jahāngīr Simnānī (d. 808/1405) and Sayyid 'Alī Hamadānī (714–787/1314–1385), both of whom traveled to India from their homes in Central Asia. Sayyid Ashraf Jahāngīr Simnānī came to Bukhārī's *khānqāh* in Uch after having been a disciple of 'Alā' al-dawla al-Simnānī (659–736/1261–1336) and 'Abd al-Razzāq al-Kāshānī (d. 736/1335). Ashraf Simnānī stayed for sometime with Bukhārī, learning from him and observing his practice.[43] However, despite his praise of Bukhārī's great learning, insight, and spiritual prowess, Simnānī did not remain long with him. He traveled east to Bihar and Bengal, became a disciple of the Chishtī shaykh 'Alā' al-Ḥaqq Bangālī, and settled in Kichawcha, where he became famous for his extensive writings and his legendary ability to vanquish jinns.[44]

Sayyid 'Alī Hamadānī's contact with Bukhārī is more tenuous, both in the event and in its authenticity. *Akhbār al-akhyār*, the tenth-/sixteenth-century *taẕkira*, reports that Hamadānī came to visit Bukhārī and announced himself to Bukhārī's servant. When Bukhārī heard that someone named Hamadānī was there, he said there is no one who is *hama dān* (all-knowing) except the knower of the invisible, that is, God, and did not invite his guest to come in. Hamadānī left in a huff and wrote the *Risāla-yi Hamadānīya* to show the real meaning of the word. The author of *Akhbār al-akhyār* seems to doubt the truth of this story and considers it incongruent with Bukhārī's greatness.[45] Certainly Bukhārī usually comes across as a very courteous individual, not one to give precedence to word play (even of religious significance) over the social duty of hospitality. Bukhārī's youthful interest in meeting Sufi shaykhs from different orders and places is unlikely to have been completely erased by age. If this story originated among the devotees of the two saints, it may represent later animosities between the two groups.

Delhi is the setting for other anecdotes about Bukhārī's encounters with famous saints, recorded not in his *malfūẓāt* but in the *taẕkira*s and in works devoted to other figures. One such figure was Shaykh Sharaf al-dīn Manērī, whose views on *'ilm* I summarized in Chapter 3. Though Bukhārī never sought a *khirqa* from Manērī nor mentioned him to his own disciples, Manērī's hagiographers claim that Bukhārī held him in great esteem. In his biography of Manērī, Sayyid Muṭīʿ al-imām summarizes the accounts of the interactions between the two saints as follows. When Bukhārī came to Delhi he would face east towards Manērī's home in Bihar and say: "The smell of love comes from the direction of Bihar." When asked what he was occupied with at the end of life, Bukhārī replied that he was studying the letters of Shaykh Sharaf al-dīn Manērī since parts of them were still beyond his comprehension. Once Manērī sent Bukhārī a pair of shoes and Bukhārī responded by sending him a turban. Bukhārī's explanation of this exchange to his disciples was that the shoes from Manērī meant "I am the dirt of (or under) your feet," while the turban Bukhārī sent meant "you are my crown."[46] Given Paul Jackson's doubts about the reliability of the hagiographic accounts of Manērī's life,[47] the silence of Bukhārī's *malfūẓāt* on the topic, and the difference in their outlooks, it is likely that these are pious fictions meant to increase the stature of both saints by showing a bond of mutual respect between them.

A lesser known shaykh with whom Bukhārī is said to have come into contact during one of his visits to Delhi was Shaykh Fakhr al-dīn Ṣānī. Shaykh Fakhr al-dīn's father, Shihāb al-dīn Ḥaqq-gūy (truth-teller), had been executed by Muḥammad b. Tughluq for heterodox statements. Fakhr al-dīn was in the habit of keeping slips of paper before him with "do it" and "don't do it" written on them and would consult these before doing anything. When Bukhārī came to visit him, Fakhr al-dīn repeatedly received a negative on whether to meet him or not. After Bukhārī had left disappointed, Fakhr al-dīn tried again and this time he got a positive response. So he pursued Bukhārī's palanquin on foot until Bukhārī became aware of him and stopped to wait. Fakhr al-dīn received Bukhārī's blessing and praises for not taking a single step without God's command.[48]

Bukhārī is also said to have had some contact with Aḥmad K'haṯṯū Sarkhēzī (738–849/1337–1446), who later settled in Gujarat and counted Bukhārī's grandson Quṭb-i ʿālam as one of his primary disciples. Aḥmad K'haṯṯū belonged to the Maghribī Sufi order and was the disciple and adopted child of Bābā Isḥāq Maghribī (d. 776/1374–1375). Biographical notices on Aḥmad K'haṯṯū contain a number of different encounters with Bukhārī. In one anecdote, Aḥmad and Bābā Isḥāq passed by the tomb of Prince Fatḥ Khān in Delhi where there was a big crowd in the courtyard. Aḥmad asked his master what was going on and was told that Sayyid Jalāl al-dīn Bukhārī was there, initiating disciples. If Aḥmad wanted, he could join them and become a disciple. Aḥmad protested vehemently that he would never leave his master for anyone.[49]

Bābā Isḥāq is also said to have told Aḥmad to avoid Bukhārī, since Bukhārī had the power of giving people sainthood (*walāyat*) or barring them from it. He feared that the spiritual stature that Aḥmad had acquired might be taken away from him. As a result Aḥmad spent his time in Delhi attempting to avoid Bukhārī, ducking down alleys when he saw his palanquin approach. However, Bukhārī knew of his existence and his virtue, and sought him out. When he found him, Bukhārī told Aḥmad that he gave off the scent of the Friend. As Bukhārī got back in his litter to get on his way, Aḥmad's hair got entangled in it and Bukhārī said: "you have entered my *ḥalqa* (wheel or circle, that is, my circle of disciples)." Aḥmad became a disciple of Bukhārī and received a *khirqa-yi maḥbūbiyat*, the same that Bukhārī received in Kāzarūn from Amīn al-dīn Balyānī.[50] This event is described as taking place in 758/1357 and this *khirqa* was later given to Bukhārī's great-grandson, Muḥammad Shāhī 'ālam, in 834/1430–1431.[51]

A slightly different version of this encounter, including Bukhārī's statement that Aḥmad gave off the scent of the Friend, makes no mention of the *khirqa* and places it at the Masjid-i Khān-i jahān in Delhi. This is where Aḥmad K'haṯṯū undertook a retreat after Bābā Isḥāq's death, suggesting that Aḥmad and Bukhārī met sometime in the late 770s/1370s or early 780s/1380s.[52] Given the contradictions and overlaps between these stories and the general unreliability of much hagiographic material, it is difficult to determine the real relationship between Bukhārī and Shaykh Aḥmad K'haṯṯū. It seems that the general purpose of these anecdotes is to demonstrate either that there was such a relationship, in which two saints of different generations recognized and reinforced each other's significance, or that, if there was not, it was only due to Aḥmad's devotion and obedience to his master Bābā Isḥāq.

Bukhārī's *malfūẓāt* provide no evidence in support of his encounters with any of these figures. Simnānī's relationship with Bukhārī is recorded fairly definitively in Simnānī's *malfūẓāt* but the rest of these anecdotes are found only in later *taẕkira* texts. It seems unlikely to me that Bukhārī would have met with such well-known and highly respected shaykhs as Manērī and Hamadānī without any mention being made of them in his *malfūẓāt*. Encounters with junior not-yet-famous figures like Fakhr al-dīn and Aḥmad K'haṯṯū might, however, go unmentioned. In any case, these tales are clearly of interest to later Sufi writers trying to trace out or establish connections between the venerated saints of the fourteenth and fifteenth centuries. Some anecdotes display the rivalry between the followers of different figures; others attempt to reconcile the rival claims to authority and present more harmonious relations.

Final Visit to Delhi

Guest of the Sultan

Bukhārī spent the ten months from Rabī' II 781/July 1379 to Muḥarram 782/April 1380 in Delhi. Much of this visit is recorded in great detail in *Jāmi' al-'ulūm*, making this the period of Bukhārī's life about which we have a nearly daily account. By this time he was 72 (solar) or 74 (hijrī) years old; he came to Delhi as a widely respected senior figure. In many respects, his visit resembled a state visit by a foreign dignitary, or a tour by a popular celebrity. Nearly every day members of the royal family, or other nobles, or 'ulama came to see him, or in the words of his chronicler "to kiss his feet (*qadam būs kardan*)."[53] When Bukhārī traveled he went in a *pālkī* (palanquin); the young man who had set out on foot to Mecca now needed to be carried around the sprawling city of Delhi. Wherever he went in Delhi, Bukhārī was thronged by devotees and supplicants who, if unable to touch him, kissed his palanquin and its bearers.

Delhi, capital of the empire, was at this time a metropolis with nearly a quarter million inhabitants.[54] Throughout the eighth/fourteenth century the Sultans of the Tughluq dynasty had built citadels and settled new areas around the original city. "Delhi in the second half of the fourteenth century was a collection of walled cities and citadels, linked by roads and separated by gardens, orchards, and fields."[55] Fīrōz Shāh built the new citadel and city of Fīrōzābād beginning in 755/1354 and this is where he received Bukhārī's visits. During his visits to Delhi, Bukhārī usually stayed at the tomb of Prince Fatḥ Khān or Fīrōz Khān. Ḥusaynī, the author of *Jāmi' al-'ulūm*, identifies the site of Bukhārī's residence in the period covered by that text as Ḥaẓīra-i Fīrōz Khān but other authorities declare it to be the tomb of Fīrōz Khān's son, and Fīrōz Shāh's grandson, Fatḥ Khān.[56] This tomb complex was fortified and contained a mosque, a *langar-khāna* (soup kitchen; charity house), and one of the most important madrasas in Delhi, Madrasa-yi Shāh-zāda-yi Buzurg. It lay three kilometers north-west of Fīrōzābād and the area in between was the most heavily populated part of Delhi at that time.[57] The shrine complex is now known as Dargāh Qadam Sharīf or Qadam Rasūl because it contains a footprint (*qadam*) of the Prophet Muḥammad. As discussed above, legend credits Bukhārī with bringing this relic from Arabia to India.[58]

Though it is unclear which prince was buried in this tomb and whether or not there was a relic of the Prophet's footprint there, it is meaningful that Bukhārī stayed at a royal tomb/madrasa complex rather than at one of the various saints' shrines (mostly Chishtī) which made up such a conspicuous part of the Delhi landscape. Though Bukhārī proclaimed his investiture by the Chishtī Naṣīr al-dīn Maḥmūd Chirāgh-i Dihlī and visited and prayed at his tomb and those of Niẓām al-dīn Awliyā' and Quṭb al-dīn Bakhtiyār Kākī, it seems that he did not choose to spend his time in Delhi as a guest or pilgrim to those shrines.[59] This may suggest that ultimately, despite his multiple affiliations, Bukhārī's identity remained firmly tied to the Suhrawardīya order rather than to the rival Chishtīs. Furthermore, by staying at what was essentially a madrasa and conducting classes on law, Quran, and hadith, as well as specifically Sufi topics, Bukhārī was acting as a member of the 'ulama. Certainly it seems that access, or accessibility, to the royal court was more important to Bukhārī than contact with the Chishtī community. The tomb of the prince was both spatially and symbolically close to Fīrōz Shāh's palace in Fīrōzābād. On Fridays, Bukhārī would go to the *jāmi' masjid* at Kūshak Shikār (also known as Jahān-numā palace), a hunting lodge built by Fīrōz.[60] Kūshak Shikār lay several kilometers to the north of Fīrōzābād and therefore even further away from the older sections of Delhi.

While settled at the shrine of the prince, Bukhārī was surrounded by a considerable number of disciples. Among these was the compiler of *Jāmi' al-'ulūm*, Sayyid 'Alā' al-dīn Ḥusaynī, as well as Sayyid Mu'izz al-dīn Rasūl-dār, author of *Manāqib-i quṭbī*, also about Bukhārī.[61] Bukhārī had so many companions with him that when invited by Fīrōz to come to Fīrōzābād and stay in the palace, he wondered whether there would be space for them all. Some portion of his family was with him as well. His wife (or wives) was in Uch but both his son, Nāṣir al-dīn Maḥmūd, and his grandson, Ḥāmid, were in

Delhi. Ḥāmid regularly read a portion of the Quran aloud before Bukhārī and the assembled disciples.[62] Practical affairs were taken care of by Bukhārī's assistant Khwāja Ḥasan who was responsible for distributing food and other offerings (for example, flowers) to the assembly and for fetching robes or hats to be bestowed upon disciples.

Relations with the Official Religious Establishment

Bukhārī received a constant stream of visitors seeking *khirqa*s or offering donations. The religious classes were well represented among these visitors; numerous *mawlānās*, *khwāja*s, sayyids, shaykhs, and *shaykh-zāda*s are mentioned in *Jāmiʿ al-ʿulūm*. The two most significant religious officials in Delhi were the *shaykh al-islām*, the head of the Sufis, and the *ṣadr-i jahān*, the chief judge. Bukhārī was on friendly visiting terms with both of these dignitaries.

The *shaykh al-islām* at this time was Ṣadr al-dīn, the grandson of Bahāʾ al-dīn Zakarīyā, who had been involved, along with Bukhārī, in the Jām Jūnā and Bānhbīna affair.[63] Bukhārī expressed his respect for the shaykh by visiting him rather than the other way around. (The *shaykh al-islām* lived at the Ḥauẓ-i Khāṣṣ, a madrasa and mosque complex built by Fīrōz around a reservoir and containing his own tomb.)[64] One such visit was in honor of the beginning of the month of Shaʿbān. Bukhārī and the *shaykh al-islām* greeted and embraced each other as equals—neither is said to have kissed the other's feet. When a *darwēsh* entered and attempted to shake his hand, Bukhārī indicated that he should take the *shaykh al-islām*'s hand first. (Bukhārī still suffered from the overenthusiasm of this person; though his hand was the second to be shaken, this was done with too much force to be pleasant to a frail elderly man.)[65]

Bukhārī expressed his sense of the *shaykh al-islām*'s importance on another occasion when visited by a certain Shaykh-zāda Muʿaẓẓam. Muʿaẓẓam had come to meet Bukhārī and to receive his instruction but Bukhārī advised him to first go visit the *shaykh al-islām*. The *shaykh al-islām* was both head of all the shaykhs and a *makhdūm-zāda*, the descendant of the master, that is, of Bahāʾ al-dīn Zakarīyā. Bukhārī was careful to add that he was not sending his visitor away from any displeasure with him but only as a matter of courtesy.[66] The *shaykh al-islām* was also one of the people Bukhārī visited to say farewell before leaving Delhi in Muḥarram 782/April 1380. On this occasion the *shaykh al-islām* quizzed Bukhārī on the relative virtues of ʿĀʾisha and Fāṭima, whether only the descendants of Fāṭima, not Muḥammad's other daughters, were sayyids, and whether it was appropriate to curse Yazīd. All of these issues have a hint of Shiʿism about them—perhaps the *shaykh al-islām* suspected Bukhārī's orthodoxy. This visit took place on the 11th of Muḥarram, that is, the day after ʿĀshūra when the massacre of Karbala is commemorated, so perhaps the topic of conversation was simply appropriate to the occasion. Bukhārī's answers on ʿĀʾisha, Fāṭima, and Yazīd were equivocal but he was definite that only descendants of Fāṭima are sayyids. In any case the visit ended cordially with the *shaykh al-islām* walking Bukhārī to the door himself.[67]

While Bukhārī made his respect for the *shaykh al-islām* clear, his attitude towards the *ṣadr-i jahān*, the chief judge, was somewhat more arrogant and combative. The *ṣadr-i jahān*, Qāżī 'Alā' al-dīn, visited Bukhārī once at the beginning of Ramażān 781/ December 1379. The *ṣadr-i jahān* was responsible for correct religious observance and the supervision of various religious functionaries. Thus, when halfway through the month Bukhārī figured out that the beginning of Ramażān had been incorrectly announced, he wanted the *ṣadr-i jahān* to come to him and be informed.[68] On 'Īd al-Ażḥā, 10 Ẕū 'al-Ḥijja 781/18 March 1380, after attending the prayers at the congregational mosque, Bukhārī was invited home by the *ṣadr-i jahān* and treated with great respect. All the religious functionaries—judges, imams, *muftīs*, 'ulama—were present as well as Bukhārī's chief disciples. Surrounded by those responsible for correct religious observance, Bukhārī took the opportunity to complain to the *ṣadr-i jahān* of an error in the praises to God at the 'Īd prayers. *Akbār* had been substituted for *akbar*. Bukhārī explained the implications of this error and went on to criticize Indian muezzins as a whole for their ignorance, especially in comparison to the well educated muezzins of Arab lands. When the *ṣadr-i jahān* had a drink brought for him to break his fast, Bukhārī said that on 'Īd al-Ażḥā one should break one's fast with meat from the sacrifice. The *ṣadr-i jahān* complied and brought out kebabs.[69]

Despite the fuss Bukhārī had made about incorrect pronunciation, the same mistake, *akbār* instead of *akbar*, was made at the Friday prayers a few weeks later. This took place while he was staying at Fīrōz's palace in Fīrōzābād at the end of Ẕū al-ḥijja. Bukhārī exclaimed aloud at the error and was heard by the king, the *ṣadr-i jahān*, and all the other dignitaries present. He seems to have wanted to be as public as possible in his reproach. When Fīrōz Shāh's boon companion Sayyid Ma'rūf, the *sayyid al-ḥujjāb* (chamberlain), visited him the next day and reported that the muezzins had been punished and turned over to the *ṣadr-i jahān*, Bukhārī asked several times if the king had heard his correction. Finally the muezzins themselves turned up, fearing for their lives, or at least their livelihoods, to beg Bukhārī to ask the king to have mercy on them.[70]

In these quibbles with the *ṣadr-i jahān* over ritual technicalities we can see in action the attitudes towards the 'ulama and their *'ilm* discussed in Chapter 3. Bukhārī does not, as some Sufis might, dismiss the persnickety concerns of ritual law as external formalism. Nor, however, does he accept the final authority of the 'ulama, represented by the *ṣadr-i jahān*, despite the fact that ritual law is part of their domain. Instead, he claims the authority to determine ritual validity based upon his own learning.

Interactions with the Sultan and His Court

The issue of correct pronunciation is typical of Bukhārī's concern for formal accuracy. But this case also indicates something about his attitude towards the court and court-appointed religious functionaries. He was unafraid to use his own authority as a religious scholar and exemplar of pious behavior to call attention to the errors of others.

For example, he told Fīrōz Shāh's grandson, Mubārak Khān, that he and his sons were wearing a forbidden variety of headgear and were thus sinning. The guardians of other young princes were reproached for dressing them in gold and silk.[71] However, Bukhārī made no attempt to judge the king or his *amīrs* on the virtues or sinfulness of their policies of state, such as taxation, conduct of war, treatment of subjects, and so on. Since he was, at least publicly, reluctant to accept or use funds from the king and the *amīrs*, despite Fīrōz Shāh's famous repeal of all un-Islamic taxes,[72] he must have had some doubts on these issues. The most he does is advise Fīrōz's *wazīr*, Khān-i jahān Jawnā Shāhī, to be good and to follow and enforce the Shari'a.[73] So it seems that while he was capable of making quite rude comments to members of the royal family on their personal habits without fear of reprisals, he was incapable of or uninterested in addressing them on larger issues.

What exactly was Bukhārī's relationship to the authority of the state? Did he court its patronage or did he see himself as above its authority? One of Bukhārī's major objectives in any contact with the Sultan or his representatives was to extract favors, funds, and positions for various people. Two of his most specific requests, made to the *khān-i jahān*, were for loans for his disciple Sayyid Shams al-dīn Mas'ūd and for the assignment of Sayyid Rukn al-dīn Rājā Mānikpūrī to a particular rank in the military aristocracy. The latter request was denied, the *khān-i jahān* pleading lack of authority on the topic. Bukhārī's brother, Sayyid Ṣadr al-dīn Rājū-qattāl, visited Fīrōz Shāh in his military encampment and was given a village as well as a thousand *tānkas* (the coinage current in the Delhi Sultanate).[74] Peter Jackson suggests that such attentions on Fīrōz's side to the religious classes, as well as his orthodox policies, "might not necessarily have sprung from devotion alone."[75] The Sultan would have gained the support of a section of society which had been alienated by his predecessor, Muḥammad b. Tughluq. If we accept *Jami' al-'ulūm*'s depiction of Bukhārī's popularity with the people of Delhi, it might have been useful to the Sultan to be linked with him in popular perception.

The historian Sirāj 'Afīf claimed that the reason for Bukhārī's visits to the capital was his desire to see the Sultan, whom he loved. From the evidence of the *malfūẓāt* texts, Bukhārī's feelings are not so clear. During Ramażān 781/December 1379, the *khān-i jahān* sent his brother, Khwāja Ḥasan, to inform Bukhārī that Fīrōz Shāh had written to say that he was currently occupied (apparently on a military campaign), but would the sayyid extend his stay in Delhi until he returned? Otherwise he should present the requests and needs of his companions from Uch and they would be fulfilled, allowing them to go home satisfied. Bukhārī courteously responded that he would not leave without seeing the Sultan since such a meeting might never be possible again. He asked the *khān-i jahān* to write to the Sultan that either he would come to the royal camp himself or he would wait until the Sultan's return. Because his masters had paid their respects to the Sultans he would do the same.

However, as soon as the Sultan's emissary had left, Bukhārī turned to his companions and said: "Though I said this myself, my reason for staying in this city is completely different." After ascertaining that no one was present except his own disciples, he told them that he was waiting for several things before he returned home to Uch. One was that Khiżr, the deathless guide, had promised to bring him guidance from God, and Bukhārī was going to meet him and have some of his disciples meet him. This was going to take place on four nights in four saintly tombs.[76] In this case, Bukhārī juxtaposed a totally religious reason for being in Delhi with the mundane one of meeting the Sultan. Does this mean that he did not care whether he met with the king or not? Or, perhaps, he wanted his disciples to believe that he acted only from religious reasons and not in deference to political authorities.

On another occasion, Bukhārī seemed to relish discomfiting the agents of the state. He told his disciples how, when returning from an errand, he had met the *khān-i jahān* (II) coming to visit him. "'As soon as he saw my palanquin, he dismounted from his horse. He came a few steps on foot. I said [to myself]: "When he has come closer, I will get down, because I am weak and he is healthy."' And he [Bukhārī] smiled."[77] Such minute formalities as who is on his feet in the presence of another were significant indicators of the precise hierarchies of respect between two parties. 'Afīf emphasizes Fīrōz's great respect for Bukhārī by describing how he behaved when the sayyid visited him. As soon as Bukhārī arrived and greeted him from the entrance to the audience chamber, Fīrōz got up from his throne and remained standing. Then both would sit down together. When Bukhārī got up to leave, Fīrōz would again stand and would not resume his throne until Bukhārī was out of sight.[78] The author of *Jāmi' al-'ulūm* is also careful to point out little signs of respect on the part of the Sultan, besides the *qadambūsī* (obeisance) that Bukhārī received from everyone. One such example is of Fīrōz having Bukhārī sit on the same carpet with him during a visit from the Sultan to the saint, which is described as the greatest possible sign of respect. At the conclusion of that visit Fīrōz prevented Bukhārī from walking downstairs to see him out.[79]

When Fīrōz visited Bukhārī on the 1st of Muḥarram to celebrate the new year (782 AH), the sayyid was occupied in prayer. Fīrōz remained standing and did not enter until the prayer was over. On this occasion, Bukhārī said that he had wanted to come to the king. The king was very kind in having come to him. Bukhārī then proceeded with the next scheduled prayers and devotions, taking for granted the king's participation. Bukhārī and Fīrōz Shāh conversed on various topics and Bukhārī brought a number of his disciples and companions to the king's attention. The king, on his side, seemed to want to recommend the *ṣadr-i jahān* to Bukhārī, informing him that he was the son of Fīrōz's teacher, Sayyid Jalāl al-dīn Kirmānī. He called the *ṣadr-i jahān* a disciple of the sayyid, which Bukhārī denied, as usual, since he did not consider himself a shaykh. This visit also concluded with Bukhārī wanting to accompany the king downstairs but Fīrōz Shāh taking his hand and preventing him. Bukhārī protested that he would come down and show his respect to the king who had come so far. The king responded: "I will not allow you to come down. You are the one to be respected, do not come to show respect for me."[80]

Bukhārī's last days in Delhi were spent at Fīrōz Shāh's citadel in Fīrōzābād and in visiting various sites around the city. On 26 Ẕū al-ḥijja 781/3 April 1380, Fīrōz's grandson, Maḥmūd Khān (the future Sultan Naṣīr al-dīn Maḥmūd Shāh, r. 795–815/1394–1412), came with the king's invitation for Bukhārī to move, with his entourage, to one of the palaces. A few days later the invitation was reiterated by a delegation of nobles including Fīrōz's son Ẓafar Khān and Fīrōz's great-grandson Tughluq Shāh (who reigned as Sultan Ghiyāṡ al-dīn, 790–791/1388–1389). This time Bukhārī acquiesced, and the young prince Tughluq Shāh himself helped him into his palanquin.[81] During the next few days, Bukhārī met several times with the king as well as with other members of the royal household, including Mubārak Khān, another of Fīrōz's grandsons, Fīrōz's boon companion Sayyid Ma'rūf *sayyid al-ḥujjāb*, Fīrōz's nephew Malik 'Alī, and the *dād-beg* (military justiciar) of Jahānpanāh, who was the nephew of Dāwar Malik, himself a nephew and son-in-law of Sultan Muḥammad b. Tughluq.[82] Bukhārī presented various petitions to the king, on behalf of his disciples and the populace, usually through the *khān-i jahān* or the *sayyid al-ḥujjāb*.

Bukhārī had decided to leave Delhi after 'Āshūra 782, that is, 10 Muḥarram/16 April 1380, and spent a few days making farewell visits before his departure. He visited the *shaykh al-islām* as well as doing the round of the shrines of various saints: Niẓām al-dīn Awliyā', 'Alā' al-dīn Kirmānī, Quṭb al-dīn Bakhtiyār Kākī (d. 633/1235), Badr al-dīn Ghaznawī (d. ca. 645–715/1296–1316), Ḥamīd al-dīn Nagōrī (d. 643/1246), 'Alā' al-dīn Jīwarī, and the tombs of his granddaughter and of his disciple Jamāl al-dīn Ma'barī. Having said farewell to Fīrōz Shāh, Bukhārī left Fīrōzābād on 17 Muḥarram 782/23 April 1380, stopped one night in Kūshak Shikār, and another in Kūshak Sālūra. This was as far as Ḥusaynī, author of *Jāmi' al-'ulūm*, accompanied him. Bukhārī embraced Ḥusaynī, would not let him kiss his feet, and said a prayer for him. After the mid-day prayers, Bukhārī went on his way back to Uch.[83]

When Ḥusaynī loses sight of Bukhārī, we do so as well. There is little reliable information about his life after this. He lived only another four years, dying on 'Īd al-Aẓḥā, 10 Ẕū 'al-Ḥijja 785/3 February 1384, at the age of 78 according to the Hijrī calendar. Bukhārī was not long outlived by his patron/devotee Sultan Fīrōz Shāh, nor indeed by the Tughluq dynasty itself. Fīrōz Shāh died five Hijrī years after Bukhārī, in 790/1388. The empire had already fallen into strife during the last years of his reign with the expulsion first of the *khān-i jahān* and then of Fīrōz's only surviving son Muḥammad. The next ten years saw various royal princes struggling for the throne, each supported by various factions within the military aristocracy. Finally, the Tughluq dynasty came to an end when Tīmūr's Turco-Mongol forces swept in. Uch was of course on the frontlines, as it had always been in conflicts with the Mongols, and was taken shortly after the invaders crossed the Indus in Rabī' I 800/November–December 1397. A year later Delhi was sacked and the empire of the Delhi Sultanate was effectively brought to an end.[84]

SEVEN

Legacy

For a Christian saint, death is the real beginning of one's identification as a saint. For a Sufi saint too, though public recognition and activity as a holy person during one's lifetime is important, death is not the end of one's spiritual functions as guide, intercessor, and teacher. After death these functions are preserved and remembered in three forms: through the saint's spiritual heirs (that is, disciples and their lineages), through the saint's shrine, and through texts by and about him.[1] Seeking neither his *khirqa*s, nor his intercession and *barakat*, I have approached Jalāl al-dīn Bukhārī and his life through texts. Therefore, the Bukhārī presented in this book is the man found in a particular set of texts, not the one whose spiritual presence might be discovered at his *'urs* (death anniversary celebration) in Uch or through association with his successors. Here I briefly discuss the other two carriers of Bukhārī's legacy, his spiritual heirs and his tomb.

Spiritual Heirs

Descendants

Though Bukhārī initiated numerous disciples the main line of his influence was preserved in his own family. His brother, Sayyid Ṣadr al-dīn Muḥammad Rājū-qattāl, is described in the hagiographic tradition as Bukhārī's *khalīfa*, that is, as his primary spiritual successor. Bukhārī himself never used the term *khalīfa* either in reference to himself nor to anyone else in relation to him. After Rājū-qattāl, Bukhārī's sons and grandsons seem to have become the major inheritors of the tradition. Bukhārī had at least three sons, 'Abdallāh, Nāṣir al-dīn Maḥmūd (who was with him in Delhi in 781/1379–1380) and Jalāl al-dīn Kabīr, by three different wives. Nāṣir al-dīn Maḥmūd (d. 800/1397–1398), whose mother was Bukhārī's first cousin, had numerous children. One of his sons, Burhān al-dīn 'Abdallāh Quṭb-i 'ālam (790–858/1388–1454), and his son Sirāj al-dīn Muḥammad Shāh-ī 'ālam (817–880/1414–1475–1476), were the only descendants of Bukhārī to achieve a stature comparable to their famous ancestor.[2]

Burhān al-dīn Quṭb-i 'ālam settled in Gujarat, in Baṭwah (or Vatva, in the vicinity of Ahmadabad), where he became the spiritual advisor to the local Sultan Aḥmad

b. Tatar (d. 846/1442). Sultan Aḥmad was the grandson of Muẓaffar Shāh (Sadhāran), who had been Sultan Muḥammad b. Fīrōz's (r. 792–6/1390–4) governor in Gujarat under the title Ẓafar Khān Wajīh al-Mulk.[3] According to the *Tażkira-yi awliyā'-i Aḥmadābād*, Muẓaffar Shāh owed his rule to Bukhārī's blessing. As a devotee of Bukhārī, he had once provided food to Bukhārī's *khānqāh* and disciples in a time of shortage. His reward was the kingdom of Gujarat.[4] Burhān al-dīn Quṭb-i 'ālam had twelve sons, one of whom, Sayyid Dā'ūd, became the *wazīr* of Sulṭān Bahādur b. Muẓaffar under the name Ikhtiyār Khān.[5] Most of Quṭb-i 'ālam's sons seem to have become Sufi shaykhs, such as Nāṣir al-dīn Abū al-Ḥasan Maḥmūd (809–884/1406–1479) who was known as Daryā-nōsh (sea-drinker) and Shāh Buḏā.[6] Quṭb-i 'ālam's spiritual stature, popularity, and political influence were inherited and surpassed by his son Sirāj al-dīn Muḥammad Shāh-ī 'ālam (817–880/1414–1476).[7] (In 2002, Shāh-ī 'ālam's shrine was used as a refuge for Muslims displaced by the communal rioting in the state of Gujarat.)

Other descendants of Bukhārī's son Nāṣir al-dīn Maḥmūd moved to various parts of South Asia, including Kashmir, Lahore, and Bhopal. In Uch, the Bukhārī *khānqāh* and the shrines of Bukhārī, his brother Rājū-qattāl, his father, and his grandfather constituted a significant religious complex, control of which was sometimes a bone of contention between different sections of the extended family. Another of Nāṣir al-dīn Maḥmūd's sons, Fayżallāh (or Fażlallāh), inherited control of the *khānqāh* for some generations, although his family was ultimately displaced by a different branch of the Bukhārī family.[8]

Disciples

As we have seen, Bukhārī's instruction and initiation of disciples were not in any way limited to his family members. *Jāmi' al-ṭuruq*, a compilation of spiritual genealogies by Bukhārī's grandson Burhān al-dīn Quṭb-i 'ālam, lists four other *khalīfas* besides Rājū-qattāl: Sayyid Sharaf al-dīn al-Ḥusaynī al-Mashhadī, Sayyid Maḥmūd b. Muḥammad al-Shirāzī, Sayyid Sikandar b. Mas'ūd, and Tāj al-dīn Bhakkarī.[9] The first of these, Sayyid Sharaf al-dīn Mashhadī, was the author of a *risāla* (treatise) about Bukhārī used by some later hagiographers. *Laṭā'if-i Ashrafī* adds a few more names to this list of Bukhārī's *khalīfas*: Sayyid Ashraf Jahāngīr Simnānī, Sayyid Sharaf al-dīn Sāmī, Mawlānā 'Aṭā'allāh, and Sayyid 'Alā' al-dīn Ḥusaynī, author of *Jāmi' al-'ulūm*.[10] Others of Bukhārī's disciples who compiled his *malfūẓāt* or otherwise wrote about him—Aḥmad al-Bhaṯṯī (*Khizānat al-fawā'id al-Jalālīya*), Fakhr Muḥammad Ghaznawī (*Tuḥfat al-sarā'ir*), Fażlallāh b. Żiyā' al-'Abbāsī (*Khizāna-yi jawāhir-i Jalālīya*), and Sayyid Mu'izz al-dīn Rasūl-dār (*Manāqib-i quṭbī*)—were extremely important for the preservation of information about him but were not necessarily his chief disciples.

Given Bukhārī's long life, his fame, and his willingness to initiate new disciples, it is unsurprising that he turns up in the spiritual genealogies of numerous Sufis throughout the Indian sub-continent. The mention of a few of the more famous among these is sufficient to demonstrate the extent of Bukhārī's influence. One cluster of figures consists of some Chishtī disciples of Bukhārī: Shaykh Qiwām al-dīn Lak'hnawī and Shaykh Yusuf Bud'h Īrajī (d. 834/1430–1431), their disciple Shaykh Sārang (d. 855/1541–1542), a converted Hindu nobleman, for whom is named Sārangpūr in Bhopal, and his disciple Shaykh Mīnā, buried in Lucknow.[11] Shaykh Akhī Rāj-gīrī was given his nickname, *akhī* (brother), by Bukhārī and sent to Jawnpūr.[12] Sālār Bud'h (862–942/1457–1536), buried in Kara, was two links away from Bukhārī in his spiritual genealogy.[13] Shaykh Samā' al-dīn (d. 907/1501–1502), buried in Delhi, was a disciple of both Rājū-qattāl and Bukhārī's disciple Kabīr al-dīn Ismā'īl. His disciple Jamāl al-dīn Fażlallāh Dihlawī (d. 942/1535–1536) was the famous poet known as Jamālī, author of *Siyar al-'ārifīn.* Another famous figure was Pīr Badr-i 'ālam, the Bengali patron saint of sailors and boatmen. He too was one of Bukhārī's disciples before settling in Chittagong. According to legend, Pīr Badr floated or sailed to Chittagong on a rock and could also travel riding on a fish.[14]

The Shrine in Uch

Like his father and grandfather before him and his brother after him, Bukhārī was buried in Uch in the part of town called, after its famous residents, Uch Bukhāriyāṉ. The Bukhārī shrines, though decorated with the locally typical blue and white tiles, are not nearly as grand or beautiful as the two most famous tombs of the region, those of Rukn al-dīn Multānī in Multan and of Bībī Jāwandī in Uch. Unlike these imposing domed octagonal structures, the Bukhārī tombs are rectangular with flat roofs supported by wooden columns. (One of the columns in the tomb of Bukhārī's grandfather is said to have been sent down from heaven, along with a pulpit.) The interiors are quite bare but the ceilings are painted with intricate and colorful designs. Suspended inside the tombs are miniature models of plows and cradles, expressions of the requests that devotees bring to the Bukhārī saints. The courtyard of Bukhārī's tomb also contains a small shrine of a footprint of 'Alī. Bukhārī's tomb underwent significant repairs in 1330/1912, and most of the other Bukhārī tombs were also "restored or rebuilt during the 19th or early 20th century, most probably on the original plans."[15] In October 2007, the United States Embassy to Pakistan announced a grant of $50,000 for the restoration of the shrine of Bukhārī's grandfather, Sayyid Jalāl al-dīn Surkh.[16] That project was completed by the spring of 2009, though the floods of 2010 may have caused further damage to the site.[17]

When I visited the Bukhārī tombs, in the winter of 1998, they were almost completely deserted apart from the doorkeepers collecting *nażrāna* (offerings) from anyone who wished to enter. The current popularity of a shrine-cult is not necessarily linked to the historical importance of the saint interred there. The shrine of Farīd al-dīn Mas'ūd (Bābā Farīd Ganj-i shakar, d. 664/1266) at Pakpattan is the most striking example in Pakistan of an instance in which the saint's influence in his own lifetime is matched by the current popularity of his shrine. In contrast, the two most celebrated shrines and festivals in Pakistan are those devoted to ʿAlī Hujwīrī (Dātā Ganj Bakhsh, d. 464/1072) in Lahore, Punjab, and to ʿUsmān Marwandī (Lāʿl Shāhbāz Qalandar, d. ca. 665/1267) in Sehwan, Sind.[18] Though ʿAlī Hujwīrī wrote the famous compendium of Sufism, *Kashf al-maḥjūb*, he was not as significant an actor in the propagation of either Sufism or Islam in the Indian sub-continent as modern accounts would have us believe. About ʿUsmān Marwandī we know nearly nothing except that he was a disciple of Bahāʾ al-dīn Zakarīyā.

Though I cannot make any definitive statements on the causes for the relative popularity of different shrines, a few possible reasons may be suggested. One obvious factor is the geographical location of a shrine, its nearness to a population center, and its accessibility to pilgrims. Another reason for the popularity of a shrine can be its adoption by members of a particular trade or profession, or its reputation as a cure for a particular problem. Politics and the patronage of the state, or other power-holders, are perhaps the most important factors. In the cases of the tombs of Dātā Ganj Bakhsh and of Lāʿl Shāhbāz Qalandar, the use of shrines and saints as politically potent symbols of regional culture has led to their renovation and to increased public awareness. Thus, when Z. A. Bhutto, originally from Sind, was Prime Minister of Pakistan (1973–1977), Lāʿl Shāhbāz Qalandar's shrine in Sehwan received much attention and funding. Dātā Darbār, in Lahore, has undergone significant government-funded expansion and renovation, especially during the terms in office of the Sharif brothers of Lahore. Such patronage is not just a matter of displaying local allegiances but also often an attempt to promote particular, politically useful, constructions of Islam and Sufism.[19]

The U.S. ambassador's patronage of the shrine of Bukhārī's grandfather can also be understood in this vein—as an element, however small, of the United States' "War on Terror." "Experts" have repeatedly recommended that the global military campaign be complemented by a diplomatic and cultural offensive aimed at weakening the appeal of "extremist" Muslim groups. A frequently suggested tactic is the patronage and encouragement of Sufi forms of Islamic practice with the funding of shrine restorations given as a specific example of action that the United States could easily undertake.[20] It is important to point out that since 2009 Sufi shrines in Pakistan, including Dātā Darbār and the tomb of Bābā Farīd, have increasingly become targets of militant attacks in which hundreds of devotees have been killed. I fear that open receipt of funding from the United States might make the Bukhārī tombs a more attractive target for such attacks.

These days Uch as a whole is quite deserted; "the place, once a centre of religious and scholarly activities, is left almost ruined."[21] In Bukhārī's day, though past its seventh-/thirteenth-century peak as the capital of Qabācha's kingdom, Uch was one of the more significant towns of the Sultanate. Though geographically marginal and prone to Mongol invasions, it was on the main road down the Indus Valley to the sea or west across the Indus into Afghanistan. Today, however, Uch is a depopulated, dusty collection of villages with more tombs and graves visible than people on the street. The river G'hāg'hrā (or Hākrā), which made life possible here for thousands of years, dried up in the eighteenth century, leaving a desiccated landscape on the margins of the expanding Cholistan Desert.[22] The main city of the region is now Bahawalpur, founded 1748 C. E., and even nearby little Ahmedpur East is a much more lively and bustling town than Uch. Both the railway line and the National Highway run through Ahmedpur East while Uch is no longer on the main traffic corridor (unless one is going to Panjnad where the rivers of the Punjab meet and are dammed by the Panjnad Barrage before flowing into the Indus).

Though the Bukhārī tombs may be more lively during the annual festivals on the death anniversaries (*'urs*) of their saints, in December 1998 they were deserted even in comparison to the rest of the town. The shrine of Sayyid Muḥammad Ghawṣ (d. 923/1517) and Sayyid 'Abd al-Qādir Gīlānī (d. 939/1533), descendants of the famous Baghdādī saint for whom the latter is named, in Uch Gīlānī, had a good number of people visiting the tombs, praying at the mosque, and buying souvenirs and mementos. Though the presence of multiple saintly lineages has enhanced the spiritual reputation of a town as a whole, I suspect that in this case the two shrine complexes compete for devotees to the disadvantage of the Bukhārī tombs. Certainly the current descendants of the Bukhārī and Gīlānī families do not appear to get along, to judge by disparaging comments about his neighbors (though not, of course, about the Bukhārī saints themselves) made to me by Makhdoom Syed Zafar Husain Gillani, the brother of the current Gīlānī *sajjāda-nashīn*. Descendants of both saintly families are also political rivals involved in Pakistani electoral politics. At the time of my visit to Uch both families were campaigning for local office—which involved the frequent kidnapping of rival campaign workers.

A final reason for the relative desertion of the Uch Bukhārī tombs may lie in the fact that the branch of the Bukhārī family which remained in Uch, and in control of the tombs, belongs to the Shī'a sect. Bukhārī himself was a Ḥanafī Sunni and so, we presume, was his immediate family. But at some point after the eleventh/seventeenth century the Uch Bukhārīs came to identify as Shī'a. The Shī'a community is an increasingly embattled and marginalized minority in Pakistan, especially in southern Punjab where extreme Sunni groups have been very active. This no doubt handicaps the ability of the Uch Bukhārīs to attract pilgrims and devotees.

The Model of a Saint

Jalāl al-dīn Ḥusayn Bukhārī was a great personage of his own era: teacher and guide to many religious seekers, authority on matters of law and doctrine, respected by king and rebel, Arab and Indian alike. Under the titles of *makhdūm-i jahāniyān* (served by the inhabitants of the world) and *jahāngasht* (world-traveler) he passed into legend as one who had been to the ends of the world, seen Mount Qāf and Mount Sarandīb, been seven times to Mecca, and heard the Prophet's voice speak to him. In the land of his birth, southern Punjab and northern Sind, numerous tribes and clans credited him or his family with their conversion to Islam.

How did Bukhārī achieve this stature and what does his fame tell us about South Asian Islamic culture and its expectations for those whom it would respect and revere? Bruce Lawrence, building on the work of Annemarie Schimmel and Simon Digby, has attempted to construct an "ideal profile of a great Indo-Muslim shaikh." This profile highlights paradox and tension as the central characteristics of the great shaykh's life and personality through a series of binary oppositions.

1. Well-born into a good Muslim family, the saint must yet be motivated to seek a Sufi master in order to improve the quality of his Islamic faith.
2. Well educated in the Qur'ān, *ḥadīth*, theology and also Sufi literature as well as Persian poetry, he must yet be able to divine the deepest truths behind, and often beyond, the written word.
3. Initiated by a *shaikh* (usually after an epiphanic moment) and acknowledging his *shaikh* as the sole vehicle of divine grace for him, he must strive to attain his own level of spiritual excellence, often through severe fasting and prolonged meditation.
4. Living in isolation from the company of others, he must yet constantly attend to the needs of his fellow Muslims, or at least to those needs evidenced by his disciples and visitors to his hospice. . . .
5. Married and the father of sons, he must yet be celibate in temperament and disposition.
6. Capable of performing miracles, he must be careful to suppress them on most occasions.
7. Prone to ecstacy, whether in solitude or aided by music and verse in the company of other Sufis, he must be able to perform his obligatory duties as a Muslim.
8. Poor and unmindful of worldly possessions, he must yet be receptive to large donations of money and be able to dispense them quickly for the benefit of the needy.
9. Avoiding the company of worldly people, merchants, soldiers, and government officials, including kings, he must yet live in proximity to them (i.e., near a city) and stay in touch with them through his lay disciples.[23]

Independent of the specifics of this list, the underlying theme of Lawrence's proposed profile seems to provide a way to understand the attraction or charisma of the great shaykhs for their followers. A personality able to bring together opposing impulses and qualities and hold them in perfect balance would be riven by tension, fascinating to behold, and a challenge to imitate. "The great saint was one who lived out paradoxes, holding seemingly irreconcilable tensions in a delicate, unresolved balance."[24]

However, when we examine Bukhārī's life and character, tension and paradox do not strike one as dominant traits, or at least not ones emphasized by his disciples. In fact, as I have pointed out in my discussion of the *malfūẓāt*, those texts, through their structure and their use of quoted materials, present as coherent an image of Bukhārī as possible. The general ethos of Bukhārī's teaching and practice is one of moderation, rationality, and orthodoxy. There is little or no value placed on behavior that is extreme, shocking, or in any way surprising.

Although the first item on this list appears to apply to Bukhārī—he was well-born and he did seek Sufi masters—there is no tension between the two points. In fact, one seems a logical result of the other; as heir to a family Sufi tradition, Bukhārī is sent to various masters to be properly educated and trained. His departure for Arabia, and consequent meeting with other shaykhs, is not a result of any lack at home but a response to circumstances beyond his control. It is, furthermore, explicitly commanded (in a dream) by Shaykh Rukn al-dīn Multānī, Bukhārī's family *pīr*.

The two oppositions in Lawrence's list whose absence from Bukhārī's life is most significant are points 2 and 7: combining traditional textual knowledge with deeper mystic insight and balancing ecstatic experience with Islamic ritual requirements. In Bukhārī's life and teachings, though there is space for ecstasy and insight, the Sunna of the Prophet is paramount as an object of study and as an object of imitation. The study of hadith and law and the performance of *namāz* are not just minimum requirements fulfilled before going on to deeper levels. They are the framework for the daily life of a true *darwēsh*. Rather than going beyond these traditional pursuits, Bukhārī and his disciples seek only to intensify them. *Namāz*, in Bukhārī's practice, is not something to which one returns from other, more exciting religious practices and experiences—it is the starting point and the central component of most devotional activities. Furthermore, though Bukhārī taught and undertook the supererogatory practices of *ẕikr*, *awrād*, and seclusion, there is a marked absence of any description of ecstatic experiences resulting from them. As I have discussed earlier, much of what we think of as mysticism, including ecstatic experience and spiritual insight, is underemphasized in Bukhārī's *malfūẓāt* and writings. Rather than a mystic path, his is a path of piety and devotion.

The paradoxes in this list that do apply to Bukhārī are those most deeply a part of Sufi thought and practice. Thus the suppression of a capacity to work miracles, exemplified in Bukhārī's case by his reluctance to make gold for his disciples, is a result of the concept of a saint's miracles, as opposed to a prophet's, as private events. Similarly the tension between a saint's devotion to and humility before his shaykh and the acknowledgment of his own spiritual stature, by his followers or through his exercise of authority, is tied in to the initiatic structure of Sufism. We have seen how in Bukhārī's practice the ritual of investiture with a *khirqa* often brings together the two different aspects of initiation: the oath of allegiance to the shaykh (*bay'at*) and the permission (*ijāzat*) to invest others with the *khirqa*. Thus the moment of humility is also the moment of authorization. One cannot be a shaykh without also being a disciple. In Bukhārī's case this tension is made explicit by his refusal to call himself a shaykh and his insistence on imitating and obeying his masters while at the same time exercising his authority to initiate and instruct.

The combination of poverty, or detachment from possessions, with the reception of large gifts is perhaps not peculiar to Sufism. Any institution which disdains full participation in economic production is dependent on the patronage of others, either the productive classes or the ruling elite. The professionally religious classes, though frequently self-supporting through the sale of socially useful skills (for example, Bukhārī's work as a copyist, his disciples' employment as teachers and grave-diggers), are embarked on a materially non-productive path and make a virtue of necessity. Disdain for the production and, more important, the accumulation of wealth becomes a measure of piety. However, society at large expresses its respect and admiration, and its own piety, through material gifts. Bukhārī received assistance and patronage from Sultan Fīrōz Shāh and other members of his court despite his warnings about the dangers of wealth from such sources. Thus we have the tension between the disdain for wealth which makes a saint great and the large gifts he receives which indicate his greatness.

One of the more peculiar oppositions in Lawrence's list is that between marriage and a celibate temperate and disposition. I am not quite sure what Lawrence means by a celibate temperament. If this indicates simple chastity, that is, the limitation of sexual activity by the bounds of legal marriage and concubinage, then that is to be expected of any Shariʿa-abiding Muslim. Perhaps what is meant by a celibate temperament is an ideological (but not physical) rejection of sexual activity on the basis of asceticism, misogyny, or even respect for women. In that case, it simply does not apply to Bukhārī's life nor is it a part of his descriptions of the ideal *darwēsh* or shaykh. Apart from legal questions, marriage, sexuality, and even gender are not marked by Bukhārī as help or hindrance on the religious path. His remarks on his attraction to his father's concubine, and his approval of Meccan and Medinan *khānqāhs* providing women as wives or concubines to pilgrims, suggest an active and unselfconscious heterosexual outlook. Medieval Sufism contained a rather wide range of attitudes towards hetero- and homosexuality and eroticism; in this, as in much else, Bukhārī falls into the most socially and legally acceptable pattern of marriage and fatherhood.

Some of the contradictions that apparently exist in Bukhārī, though not included in Lawrence's list, are more a result of our own preconceptions than oppositions felt by him or his disciples. Thus, though Bukhārī's commitment to orthodox learning and to *namāz* (ritual prayer) as the central devotional activity is seemingly at odds with his use of *taʿwīẕ* (amulets and charms), these practices are presented in the *malfūẓāt* as related parts of a seamless whole. It is our concepts of orthodoxy and superstition, of high and low religion, which produce a sense of contradiction. Similarly the repeated exaltation of Bukhārī's status as a sayyid and his veneration of the *ahl al-bayt* (family of the prophet Muḥammad), combined with his firm identification with the Sunni Ḥanafī *maẕhab* and his disparagement of the *rawāfiż* (renegades, an insulting term for the Shiʿa), jar our sense of the clear sectarian distinction between Sunni and Shiʿa.

Though Lawrence's model of the great shaykh as a figure of paradox and tension does not fit Bukhārī very well, it does capture some of the characteristics and problems of South Asian Sufism in general. In the figures discussed by Bukhārī as models of piety or of ignorance, we find varying degrees of success in balancing some of the binary oppositions outlined by Lawrence. Thus, Bukhārī's revered early teacher Jamāl al-dīn Uchchī taught religious texts until his dying day but was one day interrupted in the process of instruction by the need to miraculously rescue a sinking ship off the coast of Yemen. In learning, purely through insight, of this distant tragedy and spiritually absenting himself for only a moment to deal with it before returning to his teaching, Shaykh Jamāl al-dīn exemplified the perfect combination of devotion to textual study and reliance upon insight.[25]

In contrast, Bukhārī's own father Sayyid Aḥmad Kabīr is described as needing greater guidance and supervision because of his susceptibility to *shawq* (desire) and his habit of yelling and weeping while performing his prayers. Though Sayyid Aḥmad would fit Lawrence's model in combining prayer and ecstasy, in the opinion of Bukhārī's masters, Shaykh Rukn al-dīn Multānī and Shaykh Jamāl al-dīn Uchchī, his behavior was inappropriate and a sign of weakness.[26] Those who were led into total neglect of ritual observance by their supposed mystical experiences were strongly condemned by Bukhārī as fools deluded by the devil.

Much of Lawrence's list of a great shaykh's characteristics relates to a balance between activities that are legally normative and socially mainstream (for example, traditional learning, religious observance, marriage) and activities that might be peculiar to the Sufi path (ecstasy, mystic insight, seclusion). In Bukhārī, rather than balance we find the scales tipped heavily in one direction, that of the Shari'a and the Sunna. The focus on law and hadith might suggest an erasure of the difference between the Sufi shaykhs and the 'ulama, especially since Bukhārī taught that the true shaykh is one whom the 'ulama follow. However, what distinguishes the shaykhs from the 'ulama is their place in the initiatic structure of the Sufi orders.

If the suggested "ideal profile of a great Indo-Muslim shaikh" does not fit Bukhārī's case, then how are we to explain his stature and fame, at least during his own lifetime? It is possible that it was Bukhārī's absolute mastery of multiple levels of religious authority that made him a figure of respect and veneration. His own spiritual masters had authorized him to bestow *khirqa*s from numerous Sufi orders and lineages, including the two most widespread in South Asia, the Suhrawardīya and the Chishtīya. They had also authorized him to teach and transmit both Sufi texts and the standard works of law, hadith, and Quran commentary. Besides formal permission to teach these texts, Bukhārī's own intellectual ability, learning, and knowledge of Arabic allowed him to use this textual basis to speak with authority on matters of law and ritual observance. His travels to the holy cities of Mecca and Medina were central in giving him the opportunity to receive many of his *khirqa*s, to study with well-known scholarly authorities, and to observe the practice of a community he considered a model of correct Islamic behavior. Finally, Bukhārī's scrupulous observance of the Shari'a combined with his identity as a sayyid made him an automatic object of respect.

Bukhārī's success as a Sufi shaykh on the basis of initiatic, genealogical, and textual authority tells us something significant about South Asian Islamic society in the second half of the eighth/fourteenth century. The numerous madrasas built and endowed by Fīrōz Shāh Tughluq and his nobles, and the proliferation of works on *fiqh* (jurisprudence) and hadith, point to a strong Shari'a-oriented Sunni religiosity during this period. At the same time, Sufi shaykhs had become significant figures of spiritual authority, respected by much of the Muslim population. The eighth/fourteenth century was also a period of transition for South Asian Sufism in which the Suhrawardī lineage in Multan declined in significance, the center of gravity of the Chishtī order shifted from Delhi to the Deccan, and new Sufi orders were introduced into the subcontinent. In such an environment, it makes sense that a figure who represented numerous Sufi lineages, was heir to both the Multan Suhrawardīs and the Delhi line of Chishtīs, and was an authority on the orthodox textual tradition would be revered by the widest range of devotees.

This model of Islam—a combination of adherence to the Shari'a and Sunna, and devotional, *ṭarīqa*-based, Sufism—was not only the basis for Bukhārī's prestige but also partly the product of his own activities as a teacher and educator. Through his travels to and from the Hejaz and his instruction of numerous disciples and students, he served as a link between the developing Indo-Islamic community and the larger Muslim world. In his teaching of texts and practices learned in the Holy Land, Bukhārī acted as a conduit for the normative Arab Islamic tradition and as a translator of this tradition into the cultural and linguistic context of South Asia.

Conclusion

While recent scholarship on Islam has grown increasingly nuanced, much of it continues to presume a binary opposition between legalistic orthodoxy and the mystical tradition of Sufism. There is an underlying presumption that mysticism and legalism, identified respectively with Sufis and the ʿulama, are essentially two independent and oppositional trends within Islam. In popular discourse, Sufism and Shariʿa (Islamic law) are often deployed as symbolic shorthand for two different visions of Islam: one tolerant, spiritual, and polymorphous, the other uniform, puritanical, and rigid. In this model of Islam, Sufism is closely identified with the first choice, that is, with an Islam more palatable to the tastes of secular modernity and, supposedly, more amenable to the political interests of the West. The other side of the coin is frequently associated with the jumble of isms that have become a familiar part of contemporary journalistic vocabulary: militant Islamism, extremism, fundamentalism, Salafism, and Wahhabism.[1] That this is much more than an academic question is demonstrated not only by its appearance in the popular press and public discourse but also by its place in the policy decisions of various state and non-state actors. Thus, the patronage by the U.S. ambassador to Pakistan of Bukhārī's grandfather's tomb fits into an overall suggested strategy of support for Sufi institutions—a strategy based on the idea that Sufism and "extremism" are mutually exclusive; to support one is to undermine the other.[2] The other side of that coin is the ongoing spate of attacks by militant, Taliban-related groups on Sufi shrines in Pakistan.

Discussions of Islam in South Asia, whether academic or popular, have been especially prone to use Sufism as the label for all that is spiritual, syncretic, non-violent, poetic, local, heterodox, and apolitical in the religious practices of South Asian Muslims. These elements of Muslim religiosity are thus distinguished and segregated from a putative universal and normative Islam, identified with the Middle East and characterized by a concern for legalistic orthodoxy, scriptural fidelity, scholasticism, and intolerance. Such a binary view of South Asian Islam is most vividly exemplified by stereotyped characterizations of the two seventeenth-century Mughal princely brothers Dārā Shukōh and Awrangzēb—the former a syncretically inclined devotee of Sufi saints and student of Hindu philosophy who lost the imperial throne to the latter, a puritanical and intolerant enforcer of Islamic law and Muslim dominance.[3]

There are several reasons for the potency of this binary approach in the context of South Asia. The millennial history of South Asian Muslims as a minority community identified with imperial power, the visibility of Sufism in the South Asian religious landscape, the partition of the sub-continent on communal lines, and the concomitant rise of historical writing committed to either religious (Hindu and Muslim) or secular nationalist agendas have all resulted in the overuse of Sufism as a catchall category. Sufism, as typified above, is sometimes viewed as "other than Islam," at other times as "true Islam," and the choice of labels is a political one. The current crisis of religious extremism in Pakistan and the rise of Hindu nationalism in India have both raised the political stakes in such conceptions of Islam and Sufism.

For those Muslims who wish to impose a globally homogeneous variety of Islam, restrict popular religious practices, and exclude marginal groups (especially women) from religious spaces, Sufism—or at least its current manifestation—is "other than Islam."[4] For those who wish to argue that "true Islam" is fundamentally foreign to South Asia and has no place there, Sufism as the catchall category for all Islamic practices that are locally adaptive and cross-culturally attractive is, again, "other than Islam," a product of the creativity of South Asian culture. On the other hand, for those Muslims who wish to dissociate themselves from a history of Islamic supremacy and domination and from the present vitality of Islamic extremism, Sufism is a useful alternative notion of "true Islam." Similarly, for those with a stake in furthering the possibility of religious and communal pluralism in South Asia, Sufism, understood as apolitical, tolerant, and locally adaptive, is "true Islam." The aspects of South Asian Sufism that have attracted the greatest interest from scholars have been precisely those that support the dichotomy between Sufism and Shari'a-minded Islam: theosophical speculation, poetry and music, syncretic traditions, and the cults of saints and shrines. In contrast, very little scholarship has been done on the South Asian scholarly tradition of Islamic law and ancillary disciplines, except in the context of the reform movements of the last two centuries.

In no way do I wish to deny the specificity and distinctiveness of the Sufi tradition within Islam. Many of the binary oppositions used to characterize the difference between Sufism and other strands of Islamic religiosity have their roots in long-standing intra-Islamic debates about the centrality of the Shari'a in defining orthodoxy, about the relative authority of Sufi shaykhs and the 'ulama to create and police such definitions, and about the validity of various religious practices—whether characterized as Sufi or as local tradition or as popular custom. However, I believe that my research on Sayyid Jalāl al-dīn Bukhārī demonstrates that the hard division frequently assumed between devotion to local saintly cults and participation in an orthodoxy defined as universal and enshrined in normative Arabic texts; between a "low" tradition of practical prayers, charms, and amulets and a "high" tradition focused on textual fidelity and intellectual rigor; between an openness to visions, wonders, and mystical ecstasy and a commitment to the requirements of the Sharīʿa—in sum, the line between the authority and career of the Sufi shaykh in his *khānqāh* and the ʿulama in the madrasa—cannot always be discovered. Nor can one assume a direct relationship between legalism or mysticism and societal attitudes, such as tolerance towards non-Muslims, misogyny, or cooperation with the power of the state. Neither adherence to the Sharīʿa nor commitment to the Sufi path are sufficient independent predictors for such social stances—though they may inform and justify them.[5]

APPENDIX A

Jalāl al-dīn Bukhārī's *Khirqas*

Table 3: Suhrawardī *Khirqas* from the Shaykhs of Multan and Uch

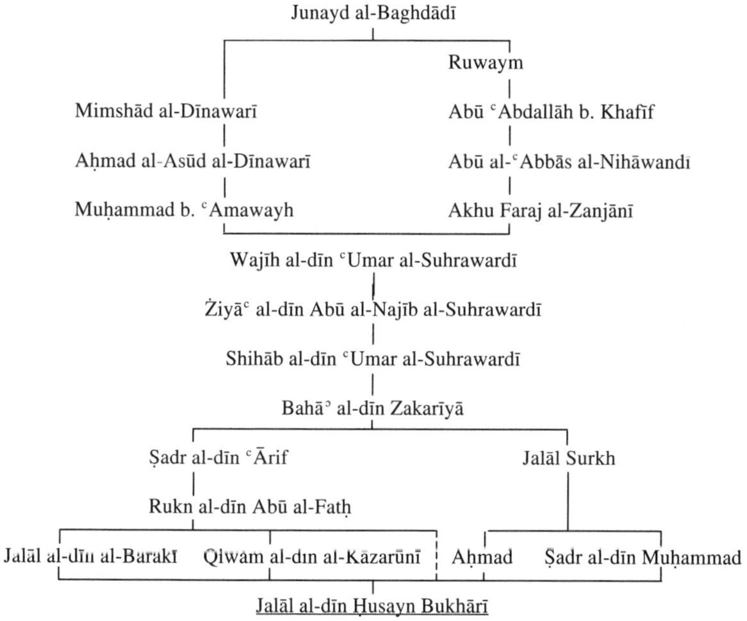

Table 4: Suhrawardī *Khirqa*s from the Shaykhs of Hejaz, Yemen, and Iran

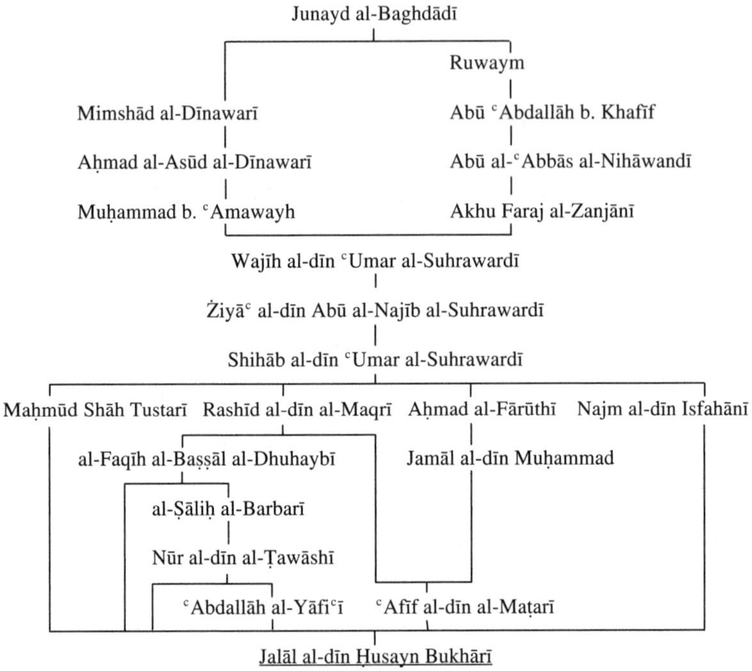

Table 5: Suhrawardī *Khirqa* from Amīn al-dīn al-Balyānī al-Kāzarūnī

Junayd al-Baghdādī

Mimshād al-Dīnawarī
Aḥmad al-Asūd al-Dīnawarī
Muḥammad b. ᶜAmawayh

Ruwaym
Abū ᶜAbdallāh b. Khafīf
Abū al-ᶜAbbās al-Nihāwandī
Akhu Faraj al-Zanjānī

Wajīh al-dīn ᶜUmar al-Suhrawardī
Żiyāᶜ al-dīn Abū al-Najīb al-Suhrawardī
Shihāb al-dīn ᶜUmar al-Suhrawardī
Abū al-Rashīd Aḥmad al-Abharī
Abū al-Ghanāᶜim al-Khaṭīb al-Sanjāsī
Abū al-Ḥasan ᶜAbdallāh al-Shirāzī
Awhād al-dīn ᶜAbdallāh al-Balyānī
Amīn al-dīn al-Balyānī al-Kāzarūnī
Imām al-dīn al-Balyānī al-Kāzarūnī
Jalāl al-dīn Ḥusayn Bukhārī

Table 6: Chishtī *Khirqa*s

- Ḥasan al-Baṣrī
- ʿAbd al-Wāḥid b. Zayd
- Fużayl b. ʿIyāż
- Ibrāhīm b. Adham
- Ḥużayqa al-Marʿashī
- Hubayra al-Baṣrī
- ʿAlū al-Dīnawarī
- Abū Isḥāq al-Shāmī
- Qudwat al-dīn Abū Aḥmad Farastāfa
- Nāṣir al-dīn Muḥammad b. Abū Aḥmad
- Nāṣir al-dīn Yūsuf b. Muḥammad
- Quṭb al-dīn Mawdūd Chishtī
  - Aḥmad b. Mawdūd Chishtī
    - Rukn al-dīn Abū Aḥmad al-Chishtī
    - Muḥyī al-dīn ʿAlī (buried near Delhi)
    - Muḥammad b. Aḥmad
    - Qudwat al-dīn Abū Aḥmad al-Chishtī
    - Ḥamīd al-dīn Maḥmūd al-Ḥusaynī al-Samarqandī
  - Ḥājjī Sharīf Zandanī
    - ʿUthmān Hārwanī
    - Muʿīn al-dīn Sijzī
    - Bakhtiyār Kākī Ūshī
    - Farīd al-dīn Masʿūd
    - Niẓām al-dīn Awliyāʾ
      - Shams al-dīn Awadhī
      - Naṣīr al-dīn Maḥmūd
      - Quṭb al-dīn Munawwar

<u>Jalāl al-dīn Ḥusayn Bukhārī</u>

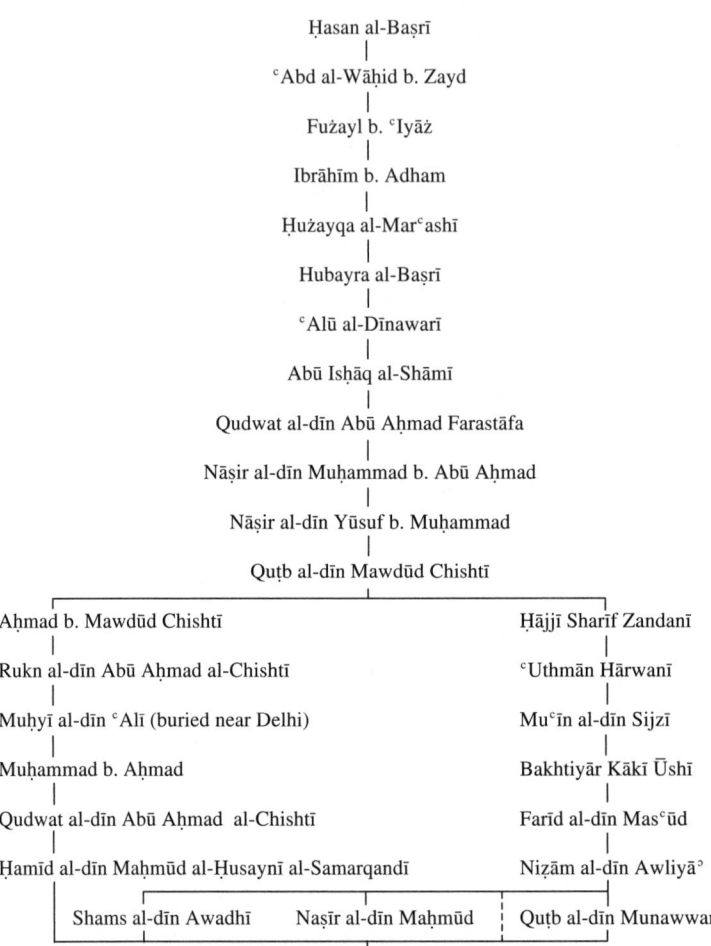

Table 7: Kubrawī *Khirqa*s

^{c}Alī b. Abī Ṭālib

	Ḥasan al-Baṣrī
	Ḥabīb al-^{c}Ajamī
	Dā^{c}ūd al-Ṭā^{c}ī
Kambīd (?) b. Ziyād	Ma^{c}rūf al-Karkhī
^{c}Abd al-Wāḥid b. Zayd	Sarī al-Saqaṭī
Abū Ya^{c}qūb al-Sūsī	Junayd al-Baghdādī
Abū Ya^{c}qūb al-Nahrajūrī	Abū ^{c}Alī Rūdbārī
Abū ^{c}Abdallāh b. ^{c}Uthmān	Abū ^{c}Alī Katīb
Abū Ya^{c}qūb al-Ṭabarī	Abū ^{c}Uthmān al-Maghribī
Abū al-Qāsim b. Ramaḍān	Abū al-Qāsim al-Gurgānī
Abū al-^{c}Abbās b. Idrīs	Abū Bakr al-Nassāj
Dā^{c}ūd b. Muḥammad	Aḥmad al-Ghazālī
Muḥammad b. Mankīl (or Malkīl)	Abū al-Najīb al-Suhrawardī
Ismā^{c}īl al-Qaṣrī al-Zarqawī	^{c}Ammār al-Bidlīsī

Najm al-dīn Kubrā$^{\supset}$

[Bābā Kamāl al-Ḥaydarī]
Aḥmad Mawlānā
Fakhr al-dīn Abū Yāḥyā al-Qaṣṣārī
Niẓām al-dīn Abū al-^{c}Aṭā$^{\supset}$ al-Khālidī
Shams al-dīn al-Nassājī al-Farghānī
Ḥamīd al-dīn Maḥmūd al-Samarqandī

Jalāl al-dīn Ḥusayn Bukhārī

Table 8: Qādirī *Khirqas*

Junayd al-Baghdādī

Left line:

- Abū Bakr b. Muḥammad al-Shiblī
- ^{c}Abd al-^{c}Azīz
- Abū al-Fażl ^{c}Abd al-Wāḥid al-Yamanī [or al-Tamīmī]
- Ibrāhīm b. Adham
- Abū al-Faraj al-Ṭurṭūshī
- Abū al-Ḥasan ^{c}Alī b. Muḥammad al-Maqdisī al-Hakārī
- Abū Sa^{c}īd ^{c}Alī b. Mubārak al-Makhzanī

Right line:

- Mimshād al-Dīnawarī
- Aḥmad al-Āsūd al-Dīnawarī

^{c}Abd al-Qādir Jīlānī

Left line:

- Shams al-dīn ^{c}Aliyān al-Ḥaddād
- Shams al-dīn ^{c}Alī b. Aflāḥ
- Quṭb al-Yaman Abū al-Ghayth b. Jamīl
- Fāżl b. ^{c}Ubayd al-Ghaythī
- Shams al-dīn ^{c}Ubayd b. Fāżl
- Muḥammad b. ^{c}Ubayd al-Ghaythī

Middle line:

- ?
- ^{c}Alī Majẕūb Qādirī

Right line:

- Sa^{c}īd al-dīn al-Baghdādī
- Kamāl al-dīn al-Kūfī
- al-Ṣāliḥ al-Barbarī
- Nūr al-dīn al-Ṭawāshī
- ^{c}Abdallāh al-Yāfi^{c}ī

Jalāl al-dīn Ḥusayn Bukhārī

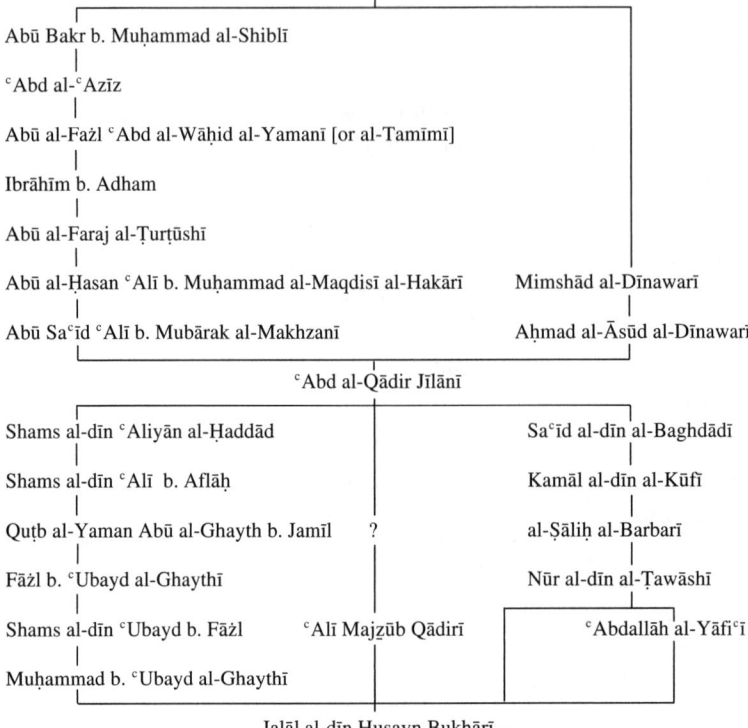

Table 9: Kāzarūnī *Khirqas*

^{c}Alī b. Abī Ṭālib
|
Uways al-Qaranī
|
Mūsā b. Zayd
|
Ibrāhīm b. Ad'ham
|
Shaqīq al-Balkhī
|
Ḥātim al-Aṣamm
|
Abū Turāb al-Nakhshī (Nakhshabī)
|
^{c}Umar al-Iṣṭakhrī
|
Muḥammad Abū Muḥammad Ja^{c}far
|
Abū ^{c}Abdallāh b. Khafīf
|
Ḥusayn al-Bāziyār
|
Abū Isḥāq al-Kāzarūnī

Dāniyāl al-Hanjī
|
Shams al-dīn al-Hanjī
|
Rukn al-dīn al-Hanjī

Jalāl al-dīn Ḥusayn Bukhārī

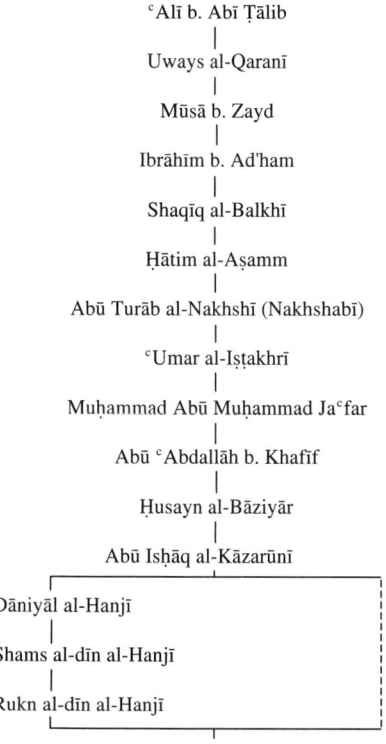

Table 10: Rifāᶜī *Khirqas*

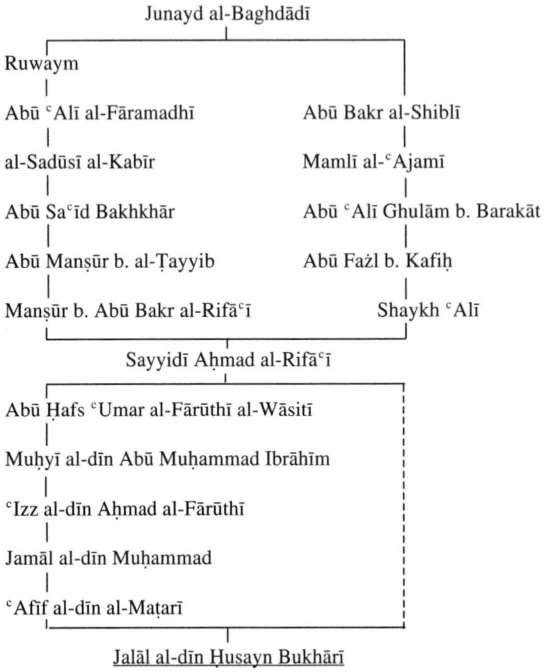

Table 11: Ahistorical or Miraculous *Khirqas*

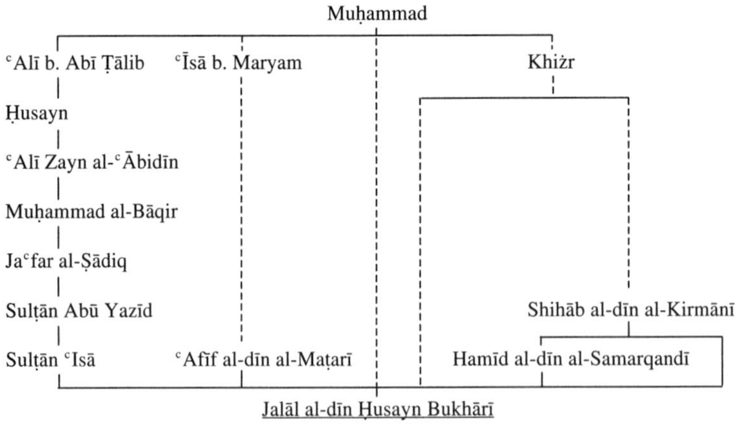

APPENDIX B

The *Malfūẓāt* of Jalāl al-dīn Bukhārī

1. Khizānat al-fawā'id al-Jalālīya

A. MS. 15427. Kitābkhāna-yi Dātā Ganj-bakhsh, Islamabad. Copied 933/1527 by Ibn Ṭāhir b. Jalāl b. Ibrāhīm. 488 folios.
B. MS. 2557. Kitābkhāna-yi Dātā Ganj-bakhsh, Islamabad. Copied eighth or ninth/fourteenth or fifteenth century, vertical format. 327 folios.
C. MS. 577. India Office. British Library, London. 276 folios.
D. MS. Del. Ar. 319 B. British Library, London. Incomplete at beginning.
E. Extract entitled *Risāla fi lubs khirqat al-mashā'ikh al-ṣūfīya*. MS. 312 (d), Arabic and Persian. Government Oriental Manuscripts Library, Madras. 9 pages.

Khizānat al-fawā'id al-Jalālīya, sometimes referred to as *Khizāna-yi Jalālī*, was compiled by Aḥmad Bahā' al-dīn b. Ya'qūb b. Ḥusayn b. Maḥmūd b. Sulaymān al-Bhaṯṯī (d. before 777/1375–1376). Judging by dates and places mentioned in the course of the text, Bhaṯṯī recorded Bukhārī's teachings in Uch over an extended period starting before 25 Rabī' II 752/21 June 1351 and ending after 767/1365–1366. The latter date is the date of a *waṣīyat-nāma* included in all manuscripts available to me. Some of the manuscripts include more *waṣīyat-nāmas* with dates extending to 770/1368–1369, suggesting that these were added by the compiler to later versions of the text.[1] *Khizānat al-fawā'id al-Jalālīya*, to my knowledge, has never been edited, printed, or translated.

Bhaṯṯī cites *Rāḥat al-qulūb*, the *malfūẓāt* of Farīd al-dīn Mas'ūd Ganj-i shakar's (d. 664/1265) teaching ascribed to Niẓām al-dīn Awliyā' (d. 725/1325), as the model for his work. His goal in producing *Khizānat al-fawā'id al Jalālīya* is to gain merit and assure himself of a place in heaven.[2] Besides Bukhārī's words, extensive quotations from hadith, legal works, and poetry are included. Arabic quotes are not translated or glossed in Persian, suggesting Bhaṯṯī's facility with the language and his assumption of a fairly educated readership. Bhaṯṯī attempts to organize Bukhārī's teachings according to different topics, producing a text with a structure similar to a handbook or encyclopedia. In doing so, he does not always reproduce the way in which Bukhārī's teaching sessions flowed from one topic to another, mingling hadith, anecdote, grammar lesson, and poetry. Since he also tries to preserve Bukhārī's words exactly and lose nothing that he taught, he has some difficulty fitting everything under the chosen chapter headings.

2. Jāmi' al-'ulūm

A. *Khulāṣat al-alfāẓ-i jāmi' al-'ulūm*. Edited by Ghulām Sarwar. Islamabad: Markaz-i Taḥqīqāt-i Fārsī-yi Īrān ō Pākistān, 1412/1992.[3]
B. *Jāmi' al-'ulūm*. Edited by Sajjād Ḥusayn. New Delhi: Indian Council of Historical Research, 1987.[4]

Khulāṣat al-alfāẓ-i jāmi' al-'ulūm, usually known as *Jāmi' al-'ulūm*, was compiled by Sayyid Abū 'Abdallāh 'Alā' al-dīn 'Alī b. Sa'd b. Ashraf b. 'Alī al-Qurayshī al-Ḥusaynī. It was compiled in Delhi, where Ḥusaynī lived, and records Bukhārī's stay there. It is a day by day memoir of the ten months between Sunday 8 Rabī' II 781/ 24 July 1379 to Tuesday 17 Muḥarram 782/24 April 1380 when

Ḥusaynī was part of Bukhārī's circle of disciples and students. Though not every day is recorded, each entry is extremely detailed, including meals and prayer times and listing all people present. According to Ḥusaynī, he sometimes took notes in the *majlis* (teaching session) and sometimes waited until later and wrote in his cell. Bukhārī was informed that Ḥusaynī was writing down his *malfūẓāt* and approved of the plan. Often after mentioning something he felt to be particularly important, or little known, he would turn to Ḥusaynī and tell him to write it down. However, there is no mention of Bukhārī's having read Ḥusaynī's text in its entirety.[5]

The diary structure of *Jāmi' al-'ulūm* makes it an engaging representation of daily life in a Sufi circle—although the sobriety and scholarly nature of Bukhārī's teachings also result in a certain dry and pious quality. Ivanow suggests that it is this very sobriety, straightforward language, and lack of dramatic wonder tales that has led to the neglect of the text over the centuries.[6] In contrast, Nizami remarks that "in the *malfuzat* of Makhdum-i-Jahanian, miraculous and the supernatural elements run throughout and thus give an otherworldly atmosphere to the conversations of the great saint."[7]

Over the last century, *Jāmi' al-'ulūm* has received a fair amount of scholarly attention. In 1891 C.E., an Urdu translation was published under the title *Durr al-manẓūm*.[8] In 1987, the Indian Council of Historical Research published an edition in Delhi by Sajjād Ḥusayn. A few years later, in 1992, another edition, this one by Ghulām Sarwar, was published in Islamabad at the Iran Pakistan Institute of Persian Studies (Markaz-i Taḥqīqāt-i Fārsī-yi Īrān ō Pākistān). Ghulām Sarwar appears not to have known of the Delhi edition; Dr. Muḥammad Taṣbīḥī, librarian at the Iran Pakistan Institute, where Dr. Sarwar had also worked until his death, was unaware that the Islamabad edition was not the first.

3. Tuḥfat al-sarā'ir

A. MS. 448 (a), Arabic and Persian. Government Oriental Manuscripts Library, Madras.
B. MS. 1090, Arabic and Persian. Government Oriental Manuscripts Library, Madras. Copied in 1957 from MS. 448. 56 pages.

This is a much shorter text compiled by Fakhr Muḥammad Ghaznawī after receiving permission to do so from Bukhārī. It was compiled as a day to day record of Bukhārī's discourses during one week from the first to the seventh of Ẕu al-Qa'da 777/23–29 March 1376. It is unclear where these conversations took place, though by implication probably not in Delhi. The compiler was from the town or region of Kara but there is no evidence that Bukhārī went there. Ghaznawī mentions *Khizānat al-fawā'id al-Jalālīya* but complains that, because that text includes many hadith and quotations from other texts in Arabic, it is beyond the comprehension of common folk. His own work is brief and contains only Bukhārī's lectures and answers to questions posed by disciples.

4. Sirāj al-hidāya

A. *Sirāj al-hidāya: malfūẓāt-i Ḥusayn al-ma'rūf bi Jalāl al-dīn Makhdūm-i jahāniyān Jahāngasht.* Edited by Qāẓī Sajjād Ḥusayn. New Delhi: Indian Council of Historical Research, 1983.[9]
B. MS. 430 (333), Arabic and Persian. Government Oriental Manuscripts Library, Madras. Copied by Shaykh Ismā'īl b. Shaykh Ḥasan Ḥakīm Nūrallāh. 298 folios.
C. MS. I. O. Isl. 1038. British Library, London.

Sirāj al-hidāya is another extensive collection of Bukhārī's *malfūẓāt* organized in a similar fashion to *Khizānat al-fawā'id al-Jalālīya* with chapters devoted to different topics. Its authorship and place of origin are somewhat obscure. It has two prefaces. In the first, Aḥmad Baranī declares that he met Bukhārī when the saint came to Delhi in Rajab 772/January–February 1371, after the conquest of Thatta by Fīrūz Shāh. Baranī studied with him for ten months and collected hadith, legal knowledge, Quran interpretations, poetry, and anecdotes from him. Having received Bukhārī's permission for the project, he worked day and night on the text he titled *Sirāj al-hidāya*. Because he did not have access to all the books quoted by Bukhārī, he asked him for complete titles of the works.

The second preface is by Aḥmad Mu'īn Siyāh-pōsh 'Alawī of Īraj. In 787/1385 he went to Delhi to visit the graves of the saints and Bukhārī came there from Uch. This is a problematic statement since, according to most sources, Bukhārī died in 785/1384. Before Bukhārī's arrival, his son 'Abdallāh was already in Delhi and Aḥmad Siyāh-pōsh received from him a manuscript of a compilation of Bukhārī's teachings. Aḥmad Siyāh-pōsh transcribed this *malfūẓāt* text and checked it against the original in ('Abdallāh?) Bukhārī's presence. It is a little unclear whether these two prefaces refer to the same work. One problem is that while Aḥmad Baranī mentions a period of ten months spent with Bukhārī in Delhi in 772/1371, the text recounts events that took place much earlier in Uch and Sind. Aḥmad Baranī's preface also turns up as part of another text, *Sayr-nāma*. On the other hand, Aḥmad Mu'īn Siyāh-pōsh 'Alawī is the recipient and transmitter of a different text attributed to Bukhārī's authorship, *Muqarrar-nāma*. (See Appendix C on both of these texts.)

Scholars familiar with *Sirāj al-hidāya* are not in agreement about its authorship nor about its authenticity. In his article on Bukhārī's *malfūẓāt*, Riazul Islam writes that the text given by 'Abdallāh to Aḥmad Mu'īn Siyāh-pōsh was a copy of a work by Aḥmad Baranī, a long-time disciple of Bukhārī who was with him during Fīrōz Shah's Thatta campaigns of the 760s/1360s. Elsewhere, Riazul Islam describes Aḥmad Mu'īn Siyāh-pōsh as the compiler and notes that he was not familiar with Sind. Maḥmūd Ḥasan Siddiqui believes the author to be Bukhārī's son 'Abdallāh.[10]

An edition of *Sirāj al-hidāya*, by Qāżī Sajjād Ḥusayn, was published in New Delhi in 1983 by the Indian Council of Historical Research. In his introduction, Ḥusayn argues that *Sirāj al-hidāya* is not an authentic *malfūẓāt* compilation of Bukhārī. For one thing, the two prefaces and the different statements of authorship obviously cast some doubt on the whole text. Furthermore, many of the quotations from hadith and *fiqh* texts are inaccurate or incorrect and therefore unlikely to have been taught by a scholar like Bukhārī. Finally, according to Ḥusayn, the organization of *Sirāj al-hidāya* by topics, rather than by daily entries, precludes its being a true collection of *malfūẓāt*.

It is certain that the text we have before us cannot be accepted on face value as an accurate collection of Bukhārī's teachings. I would suggest that *Sirāj al-hidāya* is ultimately based on Bukhārī's teachings but that these have been poorly preserved and transmitted, so that numerous errors may have crept in. It has the same focus on prayer, hadith, and legal issues as Bukhārī's other *malfūẓāt*. In terms of religious doctrine it has the same basic message as the other texts. Furthermore, there is little that is utterly fantastical, as in the *Safar-nāma* or in the *taẕkira* accounts of Bukhārī's life. But the details always seem a little off the mark, suggesting a reconstruction from memory or hearsay. There is also a formulaic character to *Sirāj al-hidāya*'s treatment of various topics, as if the author felt compelled to fill in the blanks. Despite these doubts, I have used information from *Sirāj al-hidāya* not found elsewhere but I have tried to alert the reader to its weakness.

5. Khizāna-yi jawāhir-i Jalālīya

A. MS. 5193. Kitābkhāna-yi Dātā Ganj-bakhsh, Islamabad.
B. MS. 2463. Kitābkhāna-yi Dātā Ganj-bakhsh, Islamabad. Twelfth/eighteenth century. 593 pages.
C. MS. 1749. Kitābkhāna-yi Dātā Ganj-bakhsh, Islamabad. Copied by Mullā Ḥasan b. Mullā Mūsā of Qalāt in 1208/1793–1794. 478 pages.

Khizāna-yi jawāhir-i Jalālīya was compiled by Fażlallāh b. Żiyā' al-'Abbāsī, who was invested by Bukhārī on 15 Rajab 780/7 November 1378. It is wholly devoted to prayer and prayer formulas and therefore is more of an *awrād* collection than a compilation of general teachings. It provides little information on Bukhārī's life.

6. Unavailable Malfūẓāt and Biographies

Ivanow's catalogue of the Asiatic Society of Bengal lists *Manāqib-i Makhdūm-i jahāniyān*, MS. 143. This manuscript is incomplete, covering *majlis* 46–76.[11] A partial manuscript of this text, of unknown authorship, was described (sometimes under the title *Malfūẓāt-i Makhdūm-i jahāniyān*) and utilized by Riazul Islam. It was completed sometime after Fīrōz Shāh's death in 790/1388.[12] It may be identical to *Manāqib-i quṭbī* or *Jāmi'-i quṭbī* by Sayyid Mu'izz al-dīn Rasūl-dār. This is either another *malfūẓāt* text or a biography of Bukhārī. It is mentioned in a list of Bukhārī's *malfūẓāt* given by his descendant Muḥammad b. Jalāl-shāhī Riżawī.[13] From *Jāmi' al-'ulūm* we know that Mu'izz al-dīn Rasūl-dār was with Bukhārī in Delhi in 782/1380.[14] *Jāmi'-i quṭbī* was used extensively by later hagiographers for information on Bukhārī, but I have not yet found it listed in any library catalogue.

APPENDIX C

Works Attributed to Jalāl al-dīn Bukhārī

We might expect that the best access to Bukhārī's teachings would be through his own writings. However, like many of his predecessors in the Indian Suhrawardī and Chishtī orders, Bukhārī did not produce a significant body of work. I have examined five works attributed to Bukhārī: two religious treatises, *Risāla Makkīya Jalālīya* and *Muqarrar-nāma*, and three travelogues, *Safar-nāma*, *Sayr-nāma*, and *Musāfir-nāma*. Of these, *Muqarrar-nāma* is of doubtful authenticity, and the travelogues are definitely spurious. I have not had the opportunity of examining two commentaries on hadith collections ascribed to Bukhārī, *Sharḥ-i mashāriq al-anwār* and *Sharḥ-i maṣābiḥ al-sunna*,[1] nor his collections of *awrād* and forty hadith mentioned in *Jāmi' al-'ulūm*.[2]

1. Risāla Makkīya Jalālīya

MS. Garret 12 W. Princeton University Library. 20 folios. Undated.

Only a portion of this work is extant. It is not, as often assumed, a Persian translation of Quṭb al-dīn Dimashqī's *Risāla Makkīya*. The place and date of composition are not mentioned but the author's name is clearly stated as Ḥusayn b. Aḥmad b. Ḥusayn al-Ḥusaynī al-Bukhārī, known as Jalāl al-dīn. In the preface, Bukhārī writes that he has traveled widely and met most of the 'ulama and shaykhs of his time. He performed the pilgrimage to Mecca and there met a certain Sayyid Ḥamīd al-dīn, whom he calls a second Abū Ḥanīfa.[3] Bukhārī goes on to explain that he was, as yet, no one's disciple because, although he was attached to the family of Bahā' al-dīn Zakarīyā' through his father and grandfather, he had been unable to reach any shaykh of that line. But God finally gave him the means to reach the skirt of Shaykh Rukn al-dīn, grandson of Bahā' al-dīn. The rest of the text is devoted to an explanation of repentance and its importance for the attainment of heaven.

2. Muqarrar-nāma or Naṣā'iḥ-i Makhdūm-i jahāniyān

A. MS. 1089, Arabic and Persian. Government Oriental Manuscripts Library, Madras. Copied in 1957 from MS. 448.

B. MS. 448 (b), Arabic and Persian. Government Oriental Manuscripts Library, Madras.

C. MS. 775, Taṣawwuf. Andhra Pradesh Oriental Manuscripts Library and Research Institute, Hyderabad, India. Copied Rajab 14 1159/2 August 1746.

This text is addressed to Tāj al-dīn Aḥmad Mu'īn Siyāh-pōsh 'Alawī, a resident of Sultānpūr, near Delhi. He had requested some words from "Makhdūm-i jahāniyān Jahāngīr" and received these pages on the first of Rajab 776/Wednesday 6 December 1374 through the good offices of Mawlānā 'Izz al-dīn. The work is divided into short sections, each beginning *muqarrar farzandī bād* (My son, it is certain).

As is typical of Bukhārī's teaching style, many hadith are quoted as well as anecdotes about early Sufis. Both 'Afīf al-dīn Maṭarī (d. 765/1364), Bukhārī's teacher and spiritual guide in Medina, and Rukn al-dīn Multānī (d. 735/1334), his teacher in Multan, are mentioned. These two points are evidence for this being an authentic work by Bukhārī. However, there are several reasons to doubt this authenticity, the first of which is that Bukhārī's full name is never mentioned in the text and the reference to Makhdūm-i jahāniyān is the only formal indication that he is the author. Makhdūm-i jahāniyān is the title under which Bukhārī was known to later generations but in the *malfūẓāt*, in documents such as *waṣīyat-nāmas*, he always referred to himself by his proper name, Ḥusayn b. Aḥmad b. Ḥusayn, and in speech as *īn du'ā'-gō* (this speaker of prayer). His disciples and others referred to him as Sayyid Bukhārī, Sayyid Jalāl al-dīn, Sayyid al-sādāt, and Quṭb-i 'ālam. Second, while the authorities and texts quoted in the *malfūẓāt* are fairly consistent with each other, the same is not true of texts quoted in *Muqarrar-nāma*.

As I discussed in Chapter 3, the most problematic aspect is the actual content of the work, being largely devoted to a diatribe against useless learning. In all other sources, Bukhārī repeatedly emphasized the importance of learning. Given the consensus of the *malfūẓāt* texts that learning was of central interest to Bukhārī, one wonders at the reversal of his estimation of the relative roles of *'ilm* (knowledge) and *'amal* (action). Perhaps this work was aimed at particular individuals or groups whom he felt had become so absorbed in learning that they neglected their religious duties. Certainly, the kinds of knowledge that he advocated were aimed at producing correct action; therefore it does make sense that without action knowledge is not very useful. But it is also possible that this work was put together by someone else using pieces of information from other, more genuine sources.

3. Safar-nāma-yi Makhdūm-i jahāniyān

A. MS. 429, Taṣawwuf. Andhra Pradesh Oriental Manuscripts Library and Research Institute.
B. MS. 448 (c), Arabic and Persian. Government Oriental Manuscripts Library, Madras.
C. MS. 1091, Arabic and Persian. Government Oriental Manuscripts Library, Madras. Copied in 1957 from MS. 448.
D. MS. Maj. 27/3. Salar Jung Museum and Library, Hyderabad, India. 105 folios. Copied in the thirteenth/nineteenth century by Mīr Ghulām Ḥusayn.

One of the most easily available, and yet most unreliable, texts attributed to Bukhārī is his spurious travelogue, or *Safar-nāma*. I have examined several manuscripts of this text and concur with most assessments of its inauthenticity. The *Safar-nāma* begins with an account of Bukhārī's meeting with 'Afīf al-dīn Maṭarī during his seventh hajj. Maṭarī takes Bukhārī to the Prophet's tomb, where Bukhārī's greeting to the Prophet is answered. Maṭarī then gives Bukhārī a shirt (*pīrāhan*) which had been held in trust for him. So far, this is a recognizable retelling of some events also discussed in the *malfūẓāt*, though more compressed and schematized in the *Safar-nāma* version.[4]

After this, however, Bukhārī is instructed by a voice from the unseen to visit a number of different places all over the Muslim world, from Egypt to Kashmir, from Mount Sarandīb to Mount Sinai to Mount Qāf. There is neither rhyme nor reason to his travels. Everywhere he goes, he visits the tombs of saints, prophets, and kings. The style is hyperbolic, fabulous, and, after a while, tedious. There are tens, or hundreds, or thousands of saints and prophets buried in different cities. Every *langar* (free kitchen) feeds thousands of *darwēshes*, every mountain has thousands of holy men doing *ẕikr*, every king has thousands of knights, and every building is enormous, made of precious stones and lit by thousands of candles. The narrative is interrupted by the retelling of various tales and romances, about Alexander the Great, Hārūn al-Rashīd, Nūshirwān, and Amīr Ḥamza and his love for the Sky Fairy. At the end of his travels, Bukhārī returns to Mecca. There is a last anecdote about Maṭarī being absent from prayers because he had gone to Multan for Rukn al-dīn Abū al-Fatḥ's funeral. On his return he declares that Bukhārī is now promoted to the status of *quṭb* (one of the ranks of saints). This, like the opening anecdote, is a recognizable version of events from Bukhārī's life.[5]

Altogether, the *Safar-nāma* is in no way a reliable source of information. It takes the well-known fact that Bukhārī had traveled abroad and combines it with the legends of various places and people. It would be worth determining the earliest appearance of this narrative or variations on it. We might learn a great deal about popular South Asian Muslim perceptions of different parts of the world. But we would probably not learn much about Bukhārī himself.

4. Musāfir-nāma and Sayr-nāma

Sayr-nāma. MS. 551 (a), Taṣawwuf. Folios 1–12. Andhra Pradesh Oriental Manuscripts Library, Hyderabad.

Musāfir-nāma. MS. 1826, Taṣawwuf. Andhra Pradesh Oriental Manuscripts Library, Hyderabad. 52 folios, incomplete.

These are also travelogues ascribed to Bukhārī. *Sayr-nāma* begins with the same preface as *Sirāj al-hidāya* in which the author, Aḥmad Baranī, states that he was with Bukhārī in Delhi in 772/1371. It then goes on recount how Bukhārī brought a stone bearing the mark of the Prophet's foot, *qadam-i sharīf*, to Delhi. This footprint can be found at the Dargāh Qadam Sharīf in Delhi. An abbreviated version of this tale also begins *Musāfir-nāma* which then goes on to recount the legendary voyages typical of the *Safar-nāma*.

APPENDIX D

Tazkira Entries on Jalāl al-dīn Bukhārī

Introduction

Tazkira (memorial) texts are biographical dictionaries, many devoted to Sufi saints, with one text usually focusing on a number of figures from a single order or region. An enormous number of such *tazkiras* were produced in India, especially during the Mughal period.[1] Many of them include entries on Bukhārī and his life. In this section I will examine some of these brief biographies.[2] Though each *tazkira* text could be examined as a whole to determine the viewpoint of the author and his understanding of sainthood, I will only be looking at the entries on Bukhārī. These entries, examined chronologically, show the development of Bukhārī's reputation and legend over time. They are mostly dependent on the anecdotes preserved in the *malfūẓāt* for basic biographical information, and have a tendency to embroider fantastical and wondrous tales around that core biography.

As Hermansen and Lawrence have pointed out, the South Asian *tazkira* genre is closely tied to location. A *tazkira* sanctifies and makes Islamic a particular city or region by commemorating and remembering its saints and heroes.[3] Because of their focus on regions and Sufi orders, *tazkiras* map the spread of influence of an order or of a saint, through his disciples and his political entanglements. Thus, while *malfūẓāt* texts display a single individual during a limited period of his life, *tazkiras* reveal a network of connections between holy figures, stretching back through time and ranging over space, but always leading towards the particular place and order of interest to the author.

Only one of the *tazkiras* I am examining, *Siyar al-'ārifīn*, represents either the Suhrawardīya order or the region of Uch. The rest are concerned largely with the Chishtiya, Qadiriya, and Shaṭṭārīya orders and are focused on other regions of India. Therefore, Bukhārī appears in them as a somewhat marginal, though highly respected, figure and their entries on him are largely devoted to showing his links with different shaykhs and disciples.

The *tazkiras* agree on the familiar outlines of Bukhārī's life and career. His piety, his attachment to the *sunna*, his travels, his multiple affiliations to many Sufi masters, and his descent from the Prophet Muḥammad are all common points. The most valuable information provided by the hagiographies and unavailable in the *malfūẓāt* are death dates for Bukhārī and other saints. The hagiographies are also indispensable in tracing the careers of Bukhārī's descendants and disciples. Entries on later saints whose spiritual genealogy included Bukhārī provide information on the spread of his order and influence. As for the details of Bukhārī's life, these *tazkiras* tend to contain exaggerated versions of what we already know. Thus, the number of Bukhārī's shaykhs, of his disciples, and of his journeys is increased. Though only two or three generations separate the earliest *tazkiras* from Bukhārī's life, significant distortion has already crept in.

Many of the *tazkiras* are partisan in their attitude towards the different Sufi orders and try to demonstrate the primacy of one order or saint over others. Thus, some texts highlight Bukhārī's Suhrawardī affiliation, particularly to Rukn al-dīn Abū al-Fatḥ Multānī; others emphasize the role of Naṣīr al-dīn Maḥmūd Chirāgh-i Dihlī (and thus of the Chishtī order) in his life; and still others focus on Bukhārī's devotion to 'Abd al-Qādir Gīlānī, from whom the Qādirī order takes its name.

The differences in these accounts are not ones of fact but of emphasis. Furthermore, the vocabulary used to show these affiliations is different in the *tazkiras*. In the *malfūẓāt*, Bukhārī and his disciples spoke of the *khirqa* and the *ijāzat* as the sign of becoming a *murīd*, or of *paywand dāshtan* (having a bond), to describe the relationship between a shaykh and his disciples. In the *tazkiras*, the language of *khilāfat* (succession) is used. Becoming a *khalīfa* meant that one was not just a disciple, but a designated spiritual heir.

There are two assertions made by nearly all the *tazkiras* whose authenticity I have disputed. The first such assertion is that Bukhārī received a *khirqa* from Rukn al-dīn Abū al-Fatḥ and was his *murīd* or *khalīfa*. However, the *tazkiras* are unable to fix on a date for Bukhārī's initiation or investiture by Rukn al-dīn—some placing it before his travels abroad and some placing it after. From the absence of any account of this investiture in the *malfūẓāt* texts, other than in a dream state, I have concluded that it did not happen in the waking world. I have suggested that this belief in Bukhārī's designation as Rukn al-dīn's successor arises from the close connections sustained between the Bukhārī family in Uch and the tombs of the Suhrawardī saints of Multan. The second assertion is that Bukhārī went back and forth from Uch to the Hejaz several times. However, the chronology of Bukhārī's life and travels that I pieced together from the information in the *malfūẓāt* is more suggestive of a single journey.

The component of some of the *tazkiras* which contributes most to their air of unreliability is their focus on the miraculous capabilities of saints, especially in the context of challenges presented by political or religious rivals. Since I have largely accepted the reliability of the *malfūẓāt*, despite their containing Bukhārī's statements about the wondrous abilities of contemporary saints, it is necessary to explain why similar statements about Bukhārī contained in the *tazkiras* are problematic. Most of the miraculous events mentioned in Bukhārī's *malfūẓāt*, whether experienced by himself or those around him, are private subjective events. For example, he reports having seen saints, *abdāl*, and angels and or heard the voice of the Prophet. The wonders performed by Bukhārī and reported in the *tazkiras* are of a different order. They involve bringing death to the living and life to the dead, causing insanity, and having cauldrons of food and silken pavilions enough to feed and house twelve thousand pilgrims appear from nowhere. In other words, they are dramatic and highly public events.

A final caveat on my discussion of these *tazkiras* is that I have relied exclusively upon printed editions, and frequently on Urdu translations. Therefore, particular editorial and interpretive decisions have already been made and these may result in a misrepresentation of the original works.

1. Siyar al-ʿārifīn

The earliest and most original of these texts is *Siyar al-ʿārifīn*, written by Darwēsh Jamālī (d. 10 Ẕū al-Qaʿda 942/1 May 1536) during the last five years of his life.[4] Jamālī was the disciple of Shaykh Samāʿ al-dīn (d. 11 Jumādā II 907/22 December 1501) who was a disciple of Bukhārī's brother Rājū-qattāl and his disciple Kabīr al-dīn Ismāʿīl. In his account of Bukhārī's life, Jamālī draws on stories told to him by his shaykh and by other elders. In other words, Jamālī draws on an oral tradition alive among Bukhārī's spiritual heirs to construct his narrative. He mentions the existence of *Khizānat al-fawāʾid al-Jalālīya* and gets some of his information from *Manāqib-i quṭbī*.

Siyar al-ʿārifīn provides a brief account of Bukhārī's family history beginning with the arrival of his grandfather, Sayyid Jalāl Surkh, in Multan from Bukhara. Jamālī confirms that Bukhārī studied with Shaykh Jamāl al-dīn Uchchī and was the disciple of his own father Aḥmad Kabīr. He also asserts that Bukhārī was a disciple and a *khalīfa* of Shaykh Rukn al-dīn Abū al-Fatḥ. Bukhārī's brother, Rājū-qattāl, is quoted to the effect that Bukhārī met over three hundred saints and traveled throughout the world. Bukhārī's connections to ʿAbdallāh Yāfiʿī are mentioned but only as the background for Bukhārī's meeting with Shaykh Naṣīr al-dīn Chirāgh-i Dihlī. According to Jamālī, it was Yāfi'ī's praise of Naṣīr al-dīn that motivated Bukhārī to seek him out and receive the Chishtī *khirqa* from him. The day of Bukhārī's death is quoted from *Manāqib-i quṭbī* as 'Īd al-Aẓḥā in his 77th year (10 Ẕu al-Ḥijja 785/3 February 1384).[5]

As might be expected of a hagiography, Jamālī assembles anecdotes which demonstrate Bukhārī's saintliness. Bukhārī's holiness is proved by Rukn al-dīn Multānī's declaration that Bukhārī had reached a stage of saintliness beyond which it is impossible to go, given the finality of Muḥammad's prophethood.[6] Similarly, Bukhārī receives the title of Makhdūm-i jahāniyān from a voice at Bahā' al-dīn Zakarīyā's tomb as an 'Īd present. This title is confirmed at the tombs of Ṣadr al-dīn 'Ārif and Rukn al-dīn and by everyone whom he meets that day.[7]

Other anecdotes demonstrate Bukhārī's stature by his victory over secular authorities. Jamālī tells the stories of Bukhārī's conflict with the Hindu official Nawāhūn and with Fīrōz Shāh's trusted *wazīr*, Khān-i jahān Maqbūl Tilangī.[8] In a similar case reported by Jamālī, the ruler of Uch, called Sumrāh, threw out some of the *darwēsh*es performing the Ramadan retreat with Bukhārī in the main mosque. Bukhārī asked him if he was mad, to behave in such a fashion. Sumrāh immediately went mad and only recovered after his mother intervened on his behalf with Bukhārī.[9] Bukhārī's power over others was also evidenced by the sudden death of his own little four-year-old grandson who happened to have the misfortune of attracting his attention while he prayed.[10] From the *malfūẓāt* we know that Bukhārī could be stern and demanding. But in Jamālī's stories, Bukhārī's power takes on a much more combative and terrifying quality.

A more friendly aspect of Bukhārī's might is displayed in two stories about a final pilgrimage to Mecca he supposedly took with a number of disciples. While aboard ship, the disciples wished for fried fish. Bukhārī intuited this desire and smiled. Immediately, several pounds of fish leaped into the boat, ready to be fried and eaten. When Bukhārī and his companions arrived in Jeddah, the funeral of a certain Shaykh Badr al-dīn Yamanī was under way. Bukhārī had it stopped and revived the apparently dead shaykh.[11]

Overall, Jamālī's brief biography of Bukhārī highlights key components in the legend of his life. His ties to the two most important orders in India at the time, the Suhrawardīya and the Chishtīya, and their two most famous saints, Rukn al-dīn Abu al-Fatḥ and Naṣīr al-dīn Maḥmūd, are emphasized. Yāfi'ī is briefly mentioned but Maṭarī and all the rest of Bukhārī's masters and the orders they represent are completely absent. So is any mention of Bukhārī's great learning. His contact with the secular powers of his day is represented in the stereotypical form of saintliness triumphing over despotism rather than the more nuanced and pragmatic relationship seen in the *malfūẓāt*.

Of all the *tazkira* works, Jamālī's is the closest in time to Bukhārī's life, is the most representative of the oral tradition among Bukhārī's spiritual heirs in Uch, and is the only one by a member of his *silsila*. It also contains some of the most unbelievable tales of Bukhārī's miraculous powers. We might expect that closeness in time and in Sufi affiliation would preclude exaggeration and legend. Instead the opposite is true, suggesting that it is precisely those most closely tied to Bukhārī's spiritual legacy who are most prone to believe and repeat tales of his extraordinary greatness. For Sufi biographers unaffiliated with Bukhārī and his spiritual and biological descendants, there is less incentive to stray from concrete information about his affiliations and travels. This becomes clear when we compare *Siyar al-'ārifīn* to two works written half a century later, *Gulzār-i abrār* and *Akhbār al-akhyār*.

2. Gulzār-i abrār

Gulzār-i abrār, by Muḥammad Ghawṡī Shaṭṭārī (b. 962/1554–5), was written in 998/1589–1590, over half a century after *Siyar al-'ārifīn*.[12] Shaṭṭārī's biography of Bukhārī is very brief and largely free of unbelievable events. He gives the dates of Bukhārī's birth as 15 Sha'bān 707/8 February 1308 and death as 'Īd al-Ażḥā 785/3 February 1384. Bukhārī is called a *murīd* of Rukn al-dīn Abū al-Fatḥ and a *khalīfa* of Naṣīr al-dīn Chirāgh-i Dihlī. His time with 'Abdallāh Yāfi'ī is also mentioned. Shaṭṭarī concludes with a list of Bukhārī's initiatory masters and the *silsila* represented by them. This list overlaps with but is not identical to the lists I have compiled (see Appendix A), and he remarks that different authorities mention different numbers of initiations.[13]

Shaṭṭārī does not appear to have used Jamālī's work, though he mentions a *Jāmi' al-'ulūm Jalālī* by Shaykh Jamāl which appears to be a confusion between *Jāmi' al-'ulūm* and *Siyar al-awliyā'*. He also mentions the existence of *Khizāna-yi Jalālī*, i.e., *Khizānat al-fawā'id al-Jalālīya*. One text which he does quote is a *risāla* by Sayyid Sharaf al-dīn Mashhadī.[14] According to this authority, Bukhārī received *khilāfat* from four hundred forty shaykhs. Although this number seems very high, it may be a result of counting all the different initiatic chains represented by each shaykh from whom Bukhārī received a *khirqa*.

3. Akhbār al-akhyār

Akhbār al-akhyār, by 'Abd al-Ḥaqq Muḥaddiṣ Dihlawī (958–1052/1551–1642), was completed in 996/1587–1588 and revised in 999/1590–1591.[15] According to *Akhbār al-akhyār*, Bukhārī was a *murīd* of Rukn al-dīn Multānī, a *khalīfa* of Naṣīr al-dīn Maḥmūd, and an associate of Yāfi'ī. Mention is made of Bukhārī's travels, his meetings with many saints, and of *Khizānat al-fawā'id al-Jalālīya*, from which a few points are quoted. Dihlawī dates Bukhārī's birth on Shab-i Barāt 707/8 February 1308 and his death on 'Īd al-Ażḥā 785/3 February 1384.

Another text quoted by Dihlawī is *Tārīkh-i Muḥammadī*, by Muḥammad Bihāmad Khān.[16] The quoted portion of *Tārīkh-i Muḥammadī* gives the same account of Bukhārī's reception of *khirqas* from Maṭarī in Medina and from Imām al-dīn Kāzarūnī as is found in the *malfūẓāt*. However, it goes on to say that Bukhārī became a disciple and *khalīfa* of Rukn al-dīn Multānī after his travels. He then received the title of *shaykh al-islām* and forty *khānqāhs* from Muḥammad b. Tughluq and after a few years went to the Holy Land again.[17] This chronology of events disagrees with my reconstruction in Chapter 1.

Dihlawī is the source for the anecdote discussed in Chapter 6, of 'Alī Hamadānī's abortive visit to Bukhārī.[18] Bukhārī's devotion to 'Abd al-Qādir Gīlānī is emphasized with a quote from *Khizānat al-fawā'id al-Jalālīya* about his having met Shāh Maḥmūd Tustarī (see Chapter 2), who had met Shihāb al-dīn Suhrawardī, who had met 'Abd al-Qādir Gīlānī. Furthermore, Dihlawī mentions the translation by one of Bukhārī's disciples of Yāfi'ī's *Rawżat al-riyāḥīn*, which focuses on 'Abd al-Qādir Gīlānī's miracles. The only miraculous event mentioned in this entry on Bukhārī is an anecdote about him putting out a fire by calling upon 'Abd al-Qādir Gīlānī.[19]

4. Ṣamarāt al-quds min shajarāt al-uns

One of the richest entries on Bukhārī can be found in *Ṣamarāt al-quds min shajarāt al-uns*.[20] This work, by Mirzā La'l Bēg Badakhshī (968–1022/1560–1614), was written sometime after *Akhbār al-akhyār*. Badakhshī seems to have been somewhat acquainted with Bukhārī's *malfūẓāt* texts and briefly quotes *Khizānat al-fawā'id al-Jalālīya, Sirāj al-hidāya, Jāmi' al-'ulūm*, and *Jāmi'-i quṭbī*.[21] Badakhshī quotes extensively from a work entitled *I'timād al-murīdīn* by Bukhārī's great-grandson, Shāh-i 'ālam (817–880/1415–1475). *I'timād al-murīdīn* provides Badakhshī with Bukhārī's family background—his grandfather's arrival in Multan from Bukhara and settling in Uch under Bahā' al-dīn Zakarīyā's instructions—and genealogy, as well as dates for his birth and death (Thursday, 15 Sha'bān 707/8 February 1308 and 'Īd al-Ażḥā 785/3 February 1384).[22]

The fact that the information in *I'timād al-murīdīn* was passed down through Bukhārī's family does not necessarily make it more reliable. Much of what Badakhshī quotes from it is clearly exaggerated and legendary. For example, Bukhārī had one hundred seventy thousand, two hundred eighty-six (170,286) disciples who could all fly through the air and walk on water. Some points are simply historically impossible, such as Bukhārī having received a *khirqa* from Bahā' al-dīn Zakarīyā (d. 661/1262–3).[23]

I'timād al-murīdīn also contains the tale of how Bukhārī got his title of Makhdūm-i jahāniyān at Bahā' al-dīn Zakarīyā's tomb. Another incident involving Bahā' al-dīn Zakarīyā may hint at some rivalry between the two Suhrawardī centers of Multan and Uch. Bahā' al-dīn had claimed that whoever saw his face was spared from the fires of hell. Bukhārī made a similar claim but went further to say that whoever visited his house or, after his death, his tomb or was a disciple of his companions and disciples was also spared from hell-fire. Bahā' al-dīn's adherents complained that he was claiming a greater status than his *pīr*. Bukhārī had three wise men go into the mosque, meditate, and commune with Bahā' al-dīn's soul. Each one came out with the same message from Bahā' al-dīn, and from the Prophet, that Bukhārī was correct. Whoever saw his descendants, visited their tombs, or saw the disciples of his disciples would be spared from hell and would be among the *awliyā'* on judgment day.[24]

Badakhshī quotes or paraphrases the entire entry on Bukhārī from *Akhbār al-akhyār*. As mentioned above, *Akhbār al-akhyār* highlighted Bukhārī's devotion to 'Abd al-Qādir Gīlānī. Badakhshī pursues this theme further by pointing out similarities between Bukhārī's virtues and wonders and those of 'Abd al-Qādir Gīlānī. He also quotes an anecdote from *Jāmi'-i quṭbī* in which Yāfi'ī says that Bukhārī is the only contemporary figure who can compare to 'Abd al-Qādir Gīlānī.[25]

Sayyid Shams al-dīn Mashhadī's *risāla* is quoted that Bukhārī had over four hundred forty shaykhs.[26] (The same quote is used in *Gulzār-i abrār*.) Badakhshī describes several different trips to the Hejaz, some by land and some by sea. On one voyage overland, Bukhārī became so sunburned that the people of Medina did not believe he was a sayyid. The result of exposure to the sun is described, in this story, as becoming green, an idea reminiscent of the depictions of the dark-skinned Krishna as blue in Hindu iconography. Bukhārī challenged all those who claimed to be descendants of the Prophet to meet at the Prophet's tomb and see if any of their greetings would be answered. Of course, the Prophet responded only to Bukhārī's greeting.[27]

According to Badakhshī, Bukhārī undertook two other overland trips to Mecca, each time accompanied by twelve thousand *darwēsh*es. At each stop on the journey, luxurious pavilions and cauldrons of food appeared miraculously to house and feed the pilgrims. Badakhshī also repeats the story told by Jamālī of Bukhārī's sea voyage in which fish leapt on board to be eaten, and which concludes with Bukhārī's revival of Badr al-dīn Yamanī.[28]

5. Gulshan-i Ibrāhīmī

Gulshan-i Ibrāhīmī by Firishta (d. 1032/1623) is widely known as a work of history, often under the title *Tārīkh-i Firishta*.[29] Its twelfth section consists of biographies of Chishtī and Suhrawardī saints along the model of the *tazkira* literature. One of the last figures discussed by Firishta is Sayyid Bukhārī. Firishta's account of Bukhārī's life consists entirely of material found in Jamālī's *Siyar al-'ārifīn*, though he does not mention the earlier work. Bukhārī's relationships with Jamāl al-dīn Uchchī, Rukn al-dīn Abū al-Fatḥ, 'Afīf al-dīn Maṭarī, 'Abdallāh Yāfi'ī, and Naṣīr al-dīn Maḥmūd Chirāgh-i Dihlī are all discussed with significant information about their spiritual genealogies. According to Firishta, Bukhārī sought out Naṣīr al-dīn in Delhi in 772/1370–1371. Since Naṣīr al-dīn died in 757/1356, this appears to be a misunderstanding of one of Bukhārī's later visits to Delhi. Firishta seems to be familiar with *Manāqib-i quṭbī* (i.e., *Jāmiʿ-i quṭbī*), but this reference could have been drawn from Jamālī.[30]

6. Mir'āt al-asrār

Another eleventh-/seventeenth-century hagiography with a significant entry on Bukhārī is *Mir'āt al-asrār* composed between 1045/1635–1636 and 1065/1654–1655 by ʿAbd al-Raḥmān Chishtī (1005–1094/1596–1683).[31] *Mir'āt al-asrār* quotes extensively from Jamālī's *Siyar al-ʿārifīn*, reproducing the information on Bukhārī's father and grandfather, the account of how he got the name Makhdūm-i jahāniyān, and his conflict with the *khān-i jahān*.[32] Other sources used are *Akhbār al-akhyār* and *Laṭā'if-i Ashrafī*, the *malfūẓāt*/biography of Ashraf Jahāngīr Simnānī. Mention is made of *Khizānat al-fawā'id al-Jalālīya* and *Manāqib-i quṭbī*.

According to Chishtī, Bukhārī first became a disciple and *khalīfa* of Rukn al-dīn Abū al-Fatḥ and then went to Arabia. In Medina, the Prophet's voice responded to Bukhārī's greeting and this proof of his sayyid status was witnessed by Badr al-dīn Yamanī (the individual revived by Bukhārī in Jamālī's account). The number of Bukhārī's affiliations is more reasonable in Chishtī's account than in others we have seen; he gives a total of four *silsila*s (orders) and twenty-one *guroh*s (suborders) with whose shaykhs Bukhārī was affiliated. But he also quotes Jamālī's version that Rājū-qattāl counted his brother's affiliations at over three hundred.

According to *Mir'āt al-asrār*, Bukhārī's last *khirqa* was received from Naṣīr al-dīn Maḥmūd Chishtī, after which Bukhārī had no need for any more guidance. Here we can see the author's Chishtī loyalties demonstrated in his depiction of Bukhārī's career as a disciple. It begins with Rukn al-dīn's training, which was clearly insufficient if it required the pursuit of other *khirqa*s, and concludes with Naṣīr al-dīn's *khirqa*. *Mir'āt al-asrār* also emphasizes Bukhārī's relationship to Naṣīr al-dīn by quoting the account given in *Khizānat al-fawā'id al-Jalālīya* of Bukhārī's encounter with Muḥammad b. Tughluq. In that account (see Chapter 1) it is Naṣīr al-dīn's robes that preserve Bukhārī from persecution by the Sultan and cause the Sultan to bestow upon him the title of *shaykh al-islām*.[33]

Bukhārī's influence in the eastern regions of India, particularly in Bengal is credited by *Mir'āt al-asrār* to Shaykh ʿAlā' al-Ḥaqq of Pandua (d. 800/1398). On his deathbed ʿAlā' al-Ḥaqq told his companions that Bukhārī would lead his funeral prayers. As they were wondering how this was possible, since Bukhārī was presumably in Uch, he appeared and led them in prayer. He stayed long enough to complete the spiritual training of ʿAlā' al-Ḥaqq's son Nūr Quṭb-i ʿālam (who went on to become an important local saint and play a significant role in regional dynastic conflicts, particularly through calling on the Sharqī ruler of Jawnpūr to defeat the Hindu Raja Ganesh of Bengal).[34] On his way back to Uch, Bukhārī passed through Jawnpūr and the ruler and all the local nobility became his disciples.[35] *Mir'āt al-asrār* does not specify who the ruler of Jawnpūr was at this point. The subsequent quote from *Laṭā'if-i Ashrafī* that Sultan Ibrāhīm Sharqī (r. 803–844/1401–1440) was a disciple or devotee of Bukhārī and the mention of Nūr Quṭb-i ʿālam suggests that the ruler was a member of the Sharqī dynasty. This whole narrative is historically impossible since Bukhārī died before ʿAlā' al-Ḥaqq's death, and before the Sharqī dynasty was established in Jawnpūr in 796/1394.[36]

7. Ẕikr al-aṣfiyā'

Ẕikr al-aṣfiyā', also called *Takmila-yi siyar al-awliyā'* (in reference to Mīr Khwurd's famous *Siyar al-awliyā'*), was written by Khwāja Gul Muḥammad Aḥmadpūrī sometime after 1230/1814–1815.[37] Its primary purpose is to document the lives of the saints of the author's *silsila* in Gujarat and therefore discussion of Bukhārī is focused on his relationship with two Chishtī figures, Khwāja ʿAllāma Shaykh Kamāl al-dīn (d. 756/1355 in Delhi) and his son Sirāj al-dīn (d. 817/1414–1415 in Gujarat).[38]

Aḥmadpūrī's main source of information on this relationship is *Majālis-i Ḥusaynīya*, the *malfūẓāt* of Shaykh Ḥasan Muḥammad (fl. late 900s/1500s) compiled by his son Shaykh Muḥammad.[39]

According to *Majālis-i Ḥusaynīya*, Kamāl al-dīn was a disciple of Naṣīr al-dīn Maḥmūd Chirāgh-i Dihlī. When Bukhārī was in Delhi, staying at Naṣīr al-dīn's *khānqāh*, he studied the commentary on *Mashāriq* under Kamāl al-dīn's supervision. Furthermore, the certificate of initiation (*manshūr-i khilāfat*) that Bukhārī received from Naṣīr al-dīn Maḥmūd was written by Kamāl al-dīn.[40] (Presumably this took place during the visit to Delhi when Bukhārī met with Muḥammad b. Tughluq; see Chapter 1.)

During another visit to Delhi, after Naṣīr al-dīn Maḥmūd's death, Bukhārī and Sirāj al-dīn were both present at a gathering of 'ulama. Sirāj al-dīn impressed Bukhārī (whom he had never met before) by answering some scholarly questions which he had posed to the assembled company. When informed that this learned individual was Shaykh Kamāl al-dīn's son, Bukhārī met with him and apologized for entering into a scholarly debate with him. Bukhārī told Sirāj al-dīn that he was one of his father's pupils and that it was his father who had written out his certificate from Naṣīr al-dīn Maḥmūd.[41]

Aḥmadpūrī's spiritual lineage was also connected to Bukhārī through a grandson of Shaykh Sirāj al-dīn who had received a *khirqa* traced back to Ṣadr al-dīn Rājū-qattāl (Bukhārī's brother). In this context, Aḥmadpūrī gives extensive information on the Suhrawardī saints of Multan and Uch. Aḥmadpūrī highlights Bukhārī's learning, on matters external and internal, and his piety. He does not provide any new information but relies upon *Mir'āt al-asrār*, *Tārīkh-i Muḥammadī*, *Akhbār al-akhyār*, *Jāmi' al-'ulūm*, *Khizānat al-fawā'id al-Jalālīya*, and *Khizāna-yi jawāhir-i Jalālīya*. It is worth noting that Jamālī's *Siyar al-'ārifīn* is missing from this list, along with all the miraculous anecdotes reported there. In fact, Aḥmadpūrī's account is free of supernatural events and instead focuses on Bukhārī's practices with regard to the initiation of disciples. The one peculiarity of Aḥmadpūrī's account is that he reverses the usual chronological and hierarchical order of Bukhārī's Sufi affiliations, placing the Chishtī *khirqa* first, then the Suhrawardī, and finally the family *khirqa* traced through Bukhārī's father and grandfather.[42] This is no doubt due to the primary allegiance of Aḥmadpūrī's *silsila* to the Chishtīya.

Conclusion

As these *tazkiras* show, the basic outlines of Bukhārī's life story are fixed quite early and the same material is repeated by later authors. During the ninth/fifteenth century younger associates, disciples, and descendants wrote texts containing some biographical information about Bukhārī. These were Sayyid Shams (or Sharaf) al-dīn Mashhadī's *Risāla*, *I'timād al-murīdīn* by Bukhārī's grandson Shāh-i 'ālam, and *Tārīkh-i Muḥammadī* by Muḥammad Bihāmad Khānī. The next century sees the production of Jamālī's *Siyar al-'ārifīn*, the beginning of Bukhārī's appearance in *tazkira* works. After this, most later *tazkiras* rely upon the *malfūẓāt*, the ninth-/fifteenth-century works just mentioned, and each other. Their differences are mostly confined to how much information they pull from various sources.

APPENDIX E

Jalāl al-dīn Bukhārī's Bibliography

Bukhārī's teaching relied heavily on quotation from numerous books. He also taught a number of texts to his disciples and students, mostly by having them read aloud in his presence and then commenting upon them. This appendix lists all such books quoted, mentioned, or discussed in Bukhārī's *malfūẓāt* and other texts preserving his teachings. References to the sources of this bibliography have been made parenthetically using the following abbreviations. In the case of texts cited frequently, only a few references have been supplied.

JU: Sayyid 'Alā' al-dīn 'Alī b. Sa'd al-Qurayshī al-Ḥusaynī. *Khulāṣat al-alfāẓ-i jāmi' al-'ulūm*. Edited by Ghulām Sarwar. Islamabad: Markaz-i Taḥqīqāt-i Fārsī-yi Īrān ō Pākistān, 1412/1992.

KFJ: Aḥmad Bahā' b. Ya'qūb al-Bhaṭṭī. *Khizānat al-fawā'id al-Jalālīya*. MS 15427. Kitābkhāna-yi Dātā Ganj Bakhsh, Islamabad.

KJJ: Faḍlallāh b. Ḍiyā' al-'Abbāsī. *Khizāna-yi jawāhir-i Jalālīya*. MS 5193. Kitābkhāna-yi Dātā Ganj Bakhsh, Islamabad.

SH: *Sirāj al-hidāya*. MS 430 (333). Arabic and Persian. Government Oriental Manuscripts Library, Madras.

TS: Muḥammad Ghaznawī. *Tuḥfat al-sarā'ir*. MS 1090. Arabic and Persian. Government Oriental Manuscripts Library, Madras.

Abū Makhrama: Abū Makhrama. *Arabische Texte zur Kenntnis der Stadt Aden im Mittelalter (Tārīkh taghr 'Adan)*. Edited by Oscar Lofgren. Arbeten Utgivna med Understod av Vilhelm Ekmans Universitetsfond, no. 42:2. Uppsala: Almqvist & Wiksells Boktryckeri, 1936.

Bukhārī and his disciples usually referred to books in an abbreviated fashion, using only a single word from a title phrase, or a portion of an author's name. I have attempted to provide more complete identifications of lesser known works—though these identifications are necessarily tentative—and to classify the texts into a few broad categories. I have also provided publication information for printed editions of some texts. The following works have been used for these identifications.

GAL: Carl Brockelmann. *Geschichte der arabischen Litteratur*. 2nd ed. Leiden: E. J. Brill, 1943–49.

GALS: Carl Brockelmann. *Geschichte der arabischen Litteratur. Supplementband*. 2nd ed. Leiden: E. J. Brill, 1943–49.

GAS: Fuat Sezgin. *Geschichte des arabischen Schrifttums*. Leiden: E. J. Brill, 1967.

Storey: C. A. Storey, *Persian Literature: A Bio-Bibliographical Survey*. 2 vols. London: Luzac and Co., 1927–71.

Khuda Bakhsh: *Catalogue of the Arabic and Persian manuscripts*. 36 Volumes. Patna: Khuda Bakhsh Oriental Public Library, 1962. http://www.kblibrary.org/onlinecat.html. Accessed 7 July 2011.

Ernst: Carl W. Ernst. *Eternal Garden: Mysticism, History, and Politics at a South Asian Sufi Center*. Albany: State University of New York Press, 1992.

Ḥusayn: Qāḍī Sajjād Ḥusayn. Notes to his edition of *Sirāj al-hidāya: malfūẓāt-i Ḥusayn al-macrūf bi Jalāl al-dīn Makhdūm-i jahāniyān Jahāngasht*. New Delhi: Indian Council of Historical Research, 1983.

Islam: Zafarul Islam. "Origin and Development of *Fatāwā* Compilation in Medieval India". *Studies in History*, 12.2 (1996):223–241.

Sarwar: Ghulām Sarwar. Notes to his edition of *Khulāṣat al-alfāẓ-i jāmiʿ al-ʿulūm* (Islamabad: Markaz-i taḥqīqāt-i fārsī-yi Irān ō Pākistān, 1412/1992).

Subtelny and Khalidov: Maria Eva Subtelny and Anas B. Khalidov. "The curriculum of Islamic higher learning in Timurid Iran in the light of the Sunni Revival under Shāh-Rukh." *Journal of the American Oriental Society* (1995) 115.2:211–236.

Masud et al: Muhammad Khalid Masud, Brinkley Messick, and David S. Powers, ed. *Islamic Legal Interpretation: Muftis and their Fatwas*. Cambridge, Mass.: Harvard University Press, 1996.

Khadduri: Majid Khadduri. *The Islamic Conception of Justice*. Baltimore: The Johns Hopkins University Press, 1984.

A. Sufism, Asceticism, Devotion, and Piety

1. *Asrār al-ʿārifīn* (KJJ 176a).
2. *ʿAwārif al-maʿārif* (KFJ 16a, 64a, 67b; SH 81; KJJ 127b). Abū Ḥafs ʿUmar Shihāb al-dīn al-Suhrawardī (d. 632/1234). *ʿAwārif al-maʿārif*. Arabic. Various editions and translations available.
3. *Awrād-i khwājagān-i Chisht* (JU 8).
4. *Awrād-i Makhdūm-i jahāniyān* (JU 8). Jalāl al-dīn Ḥusayn Bukhārī.
5. *Awrād-i masṭūr* (KFJ 66b, 68b).
6. *Awrād-i shaykh kabīr* (KFJ 66a, 76a; SH 80b; JU 8). Bahāʾ al-dīn Zakarīyā (d. 666/1267). *al-Awrād : ishāʿat-i awwalīn makhṭūṭah-i qadīm*. Edited by Muḥammad Miyān Ṣiddīqī. Islāmābād : Markaz-i Taḥqīqāt-i Fārsī-i Īrān ō Pākistān, 1978.
7. *Awrād shaykh al-shuyūkh* (KFJ 81a; JU 8). Abū Ḥafs ʿUmar Shihāb al-dīn al-Suhrawardī (d. 632/1234). Arabic. [GAL I, 440; GALS I, 789].
8. *ʿAyn al-ʿilm* (KFJ 223a, 251b numerous). *ʿAyn al-ʿilm wa zayn al-ḥilm*. Arabic. An abridgement of *Iḥyāʾ ʿulūm al-dīn*, no. 12. Perhaps by Muḥammad b. ʿUthmān b. ʿUmar al-Balkhī (8th/14th cent). Or by ʿAbdallāh b. ʿAbd al-Raḥmān al-Madāʾinī with alternate title of *Manāhij al-ʿārifīn*. [Khuda Bakhsh 13:25, no. 842].
9. *Bustān* by al-Nawawī (KFJ 48b). Abū Zakarīyā Muḥyi al-dīn al-Nawawī (631–676/1233–1278). *Bustān al-ʿarifīn*. Arabic. [GAL I, 397].
10. *Fawāʾid al-fuʾād* (KFJ 34b; KJJ 95b). Amīr Ḥasan ʿAlāʾ Sijzī Dihlawī (1253–1336). *Fawāʾid al-fuʾād*. *Malfūẓāt* of Niẓām al-dīn Awliyāʾ (d. 725/1325). Persian. Edited by Muḥsin Kiyānī. Tehran: Rawzanah, 1998/1377. Several translations into English and Urdu available.
11. *Fawāʾid al-sālikīn* (KFJ 253a). Apocryphal *malfūẓāt* of Quṭb al-dīn Bakhtiyār Kākī Ūshī (d. 633/1235) by Farīd al-dīn Masʿūd Ganj-i shakar. Persian. [Ernst 258]. Delhi, 1892/1310. Availiable in numerous Urdu translations.
12. *Iḥyāʾ ʿulūm al-dīn* (KFJ numerous, SH 71a). Abū Ḥāmid al-Ghazālī (d. 505/1111). *Iḥyāʾ ʿulūm al-dīn*. Arabic.
13. *Iʿlām al-hudā wa ʿaqīdat arbāb al-tuqā* (KFJ 207a). Abū Ḥafs ʿUmar Shihāb al-dīn al-Suhrawardī (d. 632/1234). *Iʿlām al-hudā wa ʿaqīdat arbāb al-tuqā*. Arabic. [GAL I, 441; GALS I, 789].
14. *Irshād al-murīdīn* (KFJ 129b). Either: Abū Ḥāmid al-Ghazālī (d. 505/1111). *Irshād al-murīdīn ilā minhāj al-ʿābidīn*. Arabic. [GALS I, 751]. Or: Abū Ḥafs ʿUmar Shihāb al-dīn al-Suhrawardī (d. 632/1234). *Irshād al-murīdīn wa majād al-ṭālibīn*. Arabic. [GALS I, 790].

15. *Kashf al-maḥjūb* (KFJ 98a). 'Alī b. 'Uthmān al-Hujwīrī al-Jullābī (d. 465/1072). *Kashf al-maḥjūb*. Persian.
16. *Kitāb-i sulūk* (KFJ 246a).
17. *Malfūẓāt-i Shaykh Burhān al-dīn* (KFJ 18b). Persian. There are a number of *malfūẓāt* of Burhān al-dīn Gharīb (d. 738/1337), a *khalīfa* of Niẓām al-dīn Awliyā' (d. 725/1325). [See Ernst 71–77].
18. *Manāqib Abū al-Khayr Sa'd Allāh b. Abī Ghālib al-Azajī* (KFJ 308b).
19. *Mirṣād al-'ibād* (SH 50a). Najm al-dīn Dāyā Rāzī (d. 654/1256). *Mirṣād al-'ibād*. Persian.
20. *Qūt al-qulūb* by Abū Ṭālib al-Makkī (SH 10a). Abū Ṭālib Muḥammad al-Makki (d. 386/996). *Qūt al-qulūb fī mu'āmalāt al-maḥbūb*. Arabic. [GAS I, 667, 936].
21. *Qūt al-qulūb min mu'āmalāt al-maḥbūb wa waṣf al-murīd ilā shifā' al-tawhīd* by Abū Ya'qūb Yusuf al-Hamadānī (KFJ 58a, 76a, 227b, 320a). Abū Ya'qūb Yusuf al-Hamadānī (d. 1140 CE). Arabic. I have not been able to trace this work; it may be a consistent misattribution of no. 20.
22. *Rawḍat al-rayāḥīn* by 'Abdallāh Yāfi'ī (KFJ 130b, 147b). Abū 'Abdallāh b. As'ad Abu al-Sa'āda 'Afīf al-dīn Yāfi'ī (d. 768/1367). *Rawḍat al-rayāḥīn fī ḥikāyāt al-ṣāliḥīn*. Arabic. [GALS II, 228].
23. *Rawḍat al-'ulamā'* by al-Zandawaysī (KFJ 20a, 30a, 43b, 46b, 76a; SH 58b). Abū al-Ḥasan 'Alī b. Yaḥyā b. Muḥammad al-Zandawaysatī al-Bukhārī (d. 382/ 922). *Rawḍat al-'ulamā' wa nuzhat al-fuḍalā'*. Arabic. [GALS I, 361].
24. *Rawnaq al-majālis* (KFJ 14b). Persian. Quote recounts a story about the early Sufi Bishr ibn al-Ḥārith al-Ḥāfī (d. 226/841).
25. *Risāla-yi Shaykh Amīn al-dīn Kāzarūnī* (KFJ 49a,b). Amīn al-dīn Balyānī Kāzarūnī (d. before 748/1347). Persian.
26. *Risāla Makkīya* by Quṭb al-dīn al-Dimashqī (JU 8). Quṭb al-dīn 'Abdallāh b. Muḥammad b. Ayman al-Aṣfahīdī al-Dimashqī (d. 780/1378). *al-Risālat al-Makkīya fī khalwat al-ṣūfīya* or *fī ṭārīq al-sāda al-ṣūfīya*. Arabic. [GAL II, 227].
27. *Risāla Qushayrī* (KFJ 49b). Abū al-Qāsim 'Abd al-Karīm al-Qushayrī (376–465/986–1072). *al-Risāla al-Qushayrīya fī al-taṣawwuf*. Arabic. [GALS I, 770–771].
28. *Risala* by Sulaymān b. Qudwat al-dīn Aḥmad b. Shaykh al-Kabīr Bahā' al-dīn (KFJ 50a-54b). Arabic.
29. *Risāla al-ṭayr* by Shihāb al-dīn al-Suhrawardī (Abū Makhrama, 234). Abū Ḥafs 'Umar Shihāb al-dīn al-Suhrawardī (d. 632/1234). Arabic.
30. *Sharḥ-i awrād* (KFJ 70a, 180a). Commentary on any of nos. 4–7.
31. *Sharḥ-i kabīr-i chihl ō yak asmā'-i a'ẓam* (JU 8, 328).
32. *Sharḥ-i kabīr-i nawad nah nām-i bārī-yi ta'ālā* by Jalāl al-dīn Tabrīzī (JU 8; KFJ 78a). Jalāl al-dīn Tabrīzī (d. 642/1244).
33. *Sharḥ-i saghīr-i nawad nah nām* (JU 8).
34. *al-Ta'arruf* (JU 8). Muḥammad b. Isḥāq al-Kalābādhī (d. 380/990). *al-Ta'arruf li madhhab ahl al-taṣawwuf*. Arabic. [GAS I, 668].
35. *Ṭahārat al-qulūb* (KFJ 200a, 291b). 'Izz al-dīn Abū Muḥammad 'Abd al-'Azīz b. Aḥmad al-Dīrīnī, (d. 697/1297). *Ṭahārat al-qulūb wa 'l khuḍū' li 'allām al-ghuyūb*. Arabic. [GAL I, 452; GALS I, 811].
36. *al-Tanbīh* by al-Faqīh al-Zāhid Abū al-Layth (KFJ 46b, 48b, 68a). Abū al-Layth Naṣr b. Muḥammad. b. Aḥmad b. Ibrāhīm al-Ḥanafī al-Samarqandī (d. 373/983). *al-Tanbīh al-ghāfilīn*. [GAL I, 196].
37. *Ta'rīkh al-ṣūfīya* by Abū 'Abdallāh al-Sulamī (KFJ 19b). Abū 'Abd al-Raḥmān al-Ṣulamī (d. 412/1021). *Ṭabaqāt al-ṣūfīya*. Arabic.

38. *Tashwīq* (KFJ 88a, 89a, 90a, 110ab, 114ab, 116a). Muḥammad b. ʿAlī b. al-Sarrāj al-Qurashī al-Dimashqī (fl. 714/1314). *Tashwīq al-arwāḥ wa al-qulūb ilā dhikr ʿallām al-ghuyūb*. Arabic. [GAL II, 119].
39. *ʿUmdat al-abrār* (KFJ 16a). Arabic.
40. *ʿUmdat al-ʿārifīn* (KJJ 116b).
41. *Kitāb ʿumdah* by Shaykh Junayd (KFJ 63a). Abū al-Qāsim Junayd al-Baghdādī (d. 298/910). [Unidentified *ʿUmda-i Junaydī*, Ernst 258].
42. *Wasīyāt Shihāb al-dīn al-Suhrawardī* (KFJ 17a). Abū Ḥafs ʿUmar Shihāb al-dīn al-Suhrawardī (d. 632/1234). Arabic.
43. *Kitāb-i zuhd* by Aḥmad b. Ḥanbal (KFJ 54a). Aḥmad Ibn Ḥanbal (d. 241/855).

B. Hadith and Other Works on the Prophet Muḥammad

44. *Arbaʿīn-i Shaykh al-ʿĀrif Ṣadr al-dīn Muḥammad* (KFJ 61a, 82b). Ṣadr al-dīn ʿĀrif Muḥammad b. Bahāʾ al-dīn Zakarīyā (d. 684/1286). Arabic.
45. *Arbaʿīn-i ṣūfīya* (JU 7). Compiled by Jalāl al-dīn Bukhārī in Mecca and Medina.
46. *Arbaʿīn Ṭāʾī* (KFJ 42b, 61a, 66a). Abū al-Futūḥ Muḥammad al-Hamadānī al-Ṭāʾī (d. 555/1160). *al-Arbaʿūna ḥadīthān al-Ṭāʾīya*. Arabic. [GALS I, 623].
47. *Kitāb āthār ṣaḥāba* (KFJ 208b).
48. Bukhārī (SH 9b). Muḥammad b. Ismaʿīl b. Ibrāhīm al-Bukhārī (d. 255/869). *al-Ṣaḥīḥ*. Arabic.
49. Abū Daʾūd Sulaymān b. al-Jārūd al-Sijistānī (d. 275/889). *al-Sunan*. Arabic.
50. Abū ʿĪsā Muḥammad b. ʿĪsā al-Tirmidhī (d. 279/892). *Jāmiʿ al-ṣahīḥ*. Arabic.
51. Abū ʿAbd al-Raḥmān al-Nasāʾī (d. 303/915). *al-Sunan*. Arabic.
52. Abū ʿAbdallāh Muḥammad b. Yazīd Ibn Māja al-Qazwīnī (d. 273/886). *al-Sunan*. Arabic.
53. *Jamʿ bayn al-ṣaḥīḥayn* (KFJ 124a). Perhaps by ʿUmar b. Badr b. Saʿīd al-Mawṣilī (d. 622/1225). [Subtelny and Khalidov 232]. Or by Abū ʿAbdallāh Muḥammad b. Abū Naṣr Futūḥ b. ʿAbdallāh b. Ḥumayd al-Azdī al-Ḥumaydī al-Andalūsī al-Miyūrqī (d. 488/1095). [Khuda Bakhsh 5:98, no. 204].
54. *Khulāṣat siyar sayyid al-bashar* (KFJ 149b). Muḥibb al-dīn Abū l-ʿAbbās Aḥmad b. ʿAlī al-Makkī al-Ṭabarī (d. 694/1294). *Khulāṣat siyar sayyid al-bashar*. Arabic. [GAL I, 361; GALS I, 615].
55. *Majmūʿa al-masāʾil* (SH 28b). Perhaps Sirāj al-dīn Abū Ḥafs ʿUmar al-Qazwīnī (d. 745/1344). *al-Masāʾil al-jāmiʿa li al-fawāʾid al-nāfiʿa*. [Subtelny and Khalidov 228].
56. *Maṣābīḥ* (KFJ 47a; JU 7; KJJ 90a). Abū Muḥammad al-Ḥusayn b. Masʿūd al-Farrāʾ al-Baghawī (d. 516/1122). *Maṣābīḥ al-sunna*. Arabic. [GAL I, 363; GALS I, 620].
57. *Mashāriq al-anwār* (KFJ 26b, 72a, 78a, 111a; JU 7; TS). Raḍī al-dīn Abū al-Faḍāʾil al-Ḥasan b. Muḥammad al-Ḥanafī al-Ṣaghānī (b. 577/1181 in Lahore, d. 650/1252). *Mashāriq al-anwār al-nabawīya min ṣiḥāḥ al-akhbār al-muṣṭafawīya*. Arabic. [GAL I, 361; GALS I, 613].
58. *Musnad* of Bahāʾ al-dīn ʿUmar b. Aḥmad b. Naṣr b. Maẓhar al-Ḥanafī al-Yamanī (KFJ 183b).
59. Muslim (SH 9b). Muslim b. Ḥajjāj al-Qushayrī al-Nīshāpūrī (d. 261/875). *al-Ṣaḥīḥ*. Arabic.
60. *Muwaṭṭāʾ* by Imām Mālik (KFJ 313b). ʿAbū ʿAbdallāh Mālik b. Anas al-Aṣbaḥī al-Madanī (d. 179/795). *Muwaṭṭāʾ*. Arabic.
61. *Risāla-yi māʾṣir-i Jalālī* by Żiyāʾ al-dīn Baranī (KFJ 193b). Żiyāʾ al-dīn Baranī (d. after 758/1357). *Risāla-yi māʾṣir-i Jalālī*.
62. *Sharḥ ṣaḥīḥ Muslim* by al-Nawawī (KFJ 35a). Abū Zakarīyā Yaḥyā Muḥyi al-dīn al-Nawawī (631–676/1233–1278). *Sharḥ ṣaḥīḥ Muslim*. Commentary on no. 59.

63. *Sharḥ mashāriq* by Mawlānā Naṣīr al-dīn (KFJ 112a). Commentary on no. 57.
64. *Sunan* by Abū Bakr Bayhaqī (KFJ 243b, 200b). Abū Bakr Aḥmad b. al-Ḥusayn al-Bayhaqī (d. 458/1066). *al-Sunan wa al-āthār* or *al-Sunan al-kabīr*. Arabic. [GAL I, 363; GALS I, 618].
65. *Sunan-i Ghaznawī* (KFJ 19b). Jamāl al-dīn Aḥmad b. Muḥammad al-Ghaznawī (d. 593/ 1197). *Sunan al-Ghaznawī*. Arabic. [GAL I, 378; GALS I, 649].
66. *Zād mawlāna Shams al-dīn fī sharḥ al-mashāriq* (KFJ 125b). Further commentary on no. 57, perhaps as addition to no. 63.

C. Law

67. *Kitāb adab al-qāḍī al-Khaṣṣāf* (KFJ MS Brit. Lib. 218b). Abū Bakr Aḥmad al-Khaṣṣāf. *Kitāb adab al-qāḍī*. [Masud et al 386].
68. *Dhakhīrat al-fiqh* (KFJ 91b). Burhān al-dīn Maḥmūd b. Aḥmad b. al-Ṣadr al-Shahīd Ḥusām al-dīn al-Bukhārī Ibn Māza (d. 573/1177). *al-Dhakhīra al-Burhanīya fi al-fatāwā*. Arabic. [GAL I, 375; GALS I, 642].
69. *Fatāwā Abū Layth* (KFJ 87b). Abū al-Layth Naṣr b. Muḥammad. b. Aḥmad b. Ibrāhīm al-Ḥanafī al-Samarqandī (d. 373/983).
70. *Fatāwā-yi asrār* (SH 91a).
71. *Fatāwā-yi 'Attābī* (KFJ 97b). Zayn al-dīn Abū Nāṣr Aḥmad b. Muḥammad b. 'Umar al-Bukhārī al-'Attābī (d. 586/1190). *Fatāwā al-'Attābīya*. Arabic. [GALS I, 643].
72. *Fatāwā al-badīya* (SH 90b).
73. *Fatāwā-yi Bākharzī* (SH 62a, 69a).
74. *Fatāwā-yi dhakhīra* (SH 103a).
75. *Fatāwā al-ghiyābīya* (SH 8b, 100a). Perhaps identical to no. 71 or no. 76.
76. *Fatāwā-yi Ghiyāthī* (KFJ 28b, 46a; SH 119b). Dā'ūd b. Yūsuf Khaṭīb. *Fatāwā-yi Ghiyāthī*. Dedicated to Sultan Ghiyāth al-dīn Yamīn Balban (r. 665–685/1266–1286). Arabic. [GALS II, 951; Islam 225].
77. *Fatāwā al-hidāya* (SH 91b). Perhaps related to no. 99.
78. *Fatāwā al-ḥujja* (KFJ 70a, 71b, 76b, 84b; SH 115b).
79. *Fatāwā wa al-kāmil* (KFJ 186a, 71b, 72a).
80. *Fatāwā al-khānīya* (KFJ 215b; SH 38a). Imām Fakhr al-dīn Ḥusayn b. Manṣūr Awzjandī (d. 592/1196). [Islam 226; Ḥusayn 547].
81. *Fatāwā-yi khulāṣa* (KFJ 171b) and *Khulāṣa* (SH 121b). Iftikhār al-dīn ṭāḥir b. Aḥmad b. 'Abd al-Rashīd al-Bukhārī (d. 542/1147). *Khulāṣat al-fatāwā*. Arabic. [Khuda Bakhsh 19:113, no. 1616].
82. *Fatāwā-yi maghrib* (KFJ 96a).
83. *Fatāwā-yi Mas'ūdī/Fatāwā al-Mas'ūdī* (KFJ 59a, 65a). Perhaps related to no. 130.
84. *Fatāwā-yi mukhtār* (SH 39b). Perhaps identical to no. 117.
85. *al-Fatāwā al-multaqaṭ* (KFJ 65b; SH 67b). Mas'ūd b. Shujā' al-Dimashqī (d. 599/1203). *Kitāb al-multaqaṭ min al-masā'il al-wāqi'āt*. Extract of *Fatāwā* of Abū al-Layth Naṣr b. Muḥammad. b. Aḥmad b. Ibrāhīm al-Ḥanafī al-Samarqandī (d. 373/983).
86. *Fatāwā-yi Naṣafī* (KFJ 214b).
87. *Fatāwā-yi Nāṣirī* (KFJ 97b) or *Fatāwā al-Nāṣirīya* (SH 115a). Perhaps identical to no. 120.
88. *Fatāwā-yi Qāḍīkhān* (SH 100b). Fakhr al-dīn Ḥasan b. Manṣūr al-Ūzjandī al-Farghānī al-Ḥanafī Qāḍīkhān (d. 592/1195). [Islam 224; Ḥusayn 553; Subtelny and Khalidov 234].
89. *Fatāwā-yi sa'īdī* (KFJ 96a).
90. *Fatāwā-yi Samarqand* (SH 120a). [Islam 226].
91. *Fatāwā-yi Shāshī* (SH 62b).

92. *Fatāwā-yi Sirājī* (KFJ 30a; SH 114a). Either: Sirāj al-dīn ʿAlī b. ʿUthmān al-Farghānī al-Awshī. *al-Fatāwā al-Sirājīya*. Completed in 569/1173. Arabic. [Khuda Bakhsh 19:159, no. 1674]. Or: Sirāj al-dīn Abū Ṭāhir Muḥammad b. Muḥammad al-Sajāwandī (sixth/twelfth century). *Fatāwā al-Sirājīya*. Arabic. [GAL I, 379 GALS I, 651; Islam 228].
93. *Fatāwā al-ṣughrā* (SH 113a). Ḥuṣām al-dīn Abū Muḥammad b. ʿUmar b. ʿAbd al-ʿAzīz al-Ḥanafī (d. 536/1141). *al-Fatāwā al-ṣughrā*. An abridgement of the same author's *al-Fatāwā al-kubrā*. Arranged by Yūsuf b. Aḥmad al-Khāṣī al-Khwārazmī. Arabic. [Khuda Bakhsh 19:106, no. 1608].
94. *Fatāwā-yi wāqiʿāt* (SH 88b).
95. *Fatāwā al-yatīma (yamīma)* (SH 116b).
96. *Fatāwā-yi Ẓahīrī* (KFJ 40b, 74a; SH 51b, 113a). Either: Ẓahīr al-dīn al-Ḥasan b. ʿAlī al-Marghīnānī (c. 600/1203). *al-Fatāwā al-Ẓahīrīya*. Arabic. [GALS I, 651]. Or: Ẓahīr al-dīn Abū Bakr Muḥammad b. Aḥmad al-Qāḍī al-Muḥtasib (d. 619/1222). *al-Fatāwā al-Ẓahīrīya*. Commentary on *Hidāya*, no. 99. Arabic. [Khuda Bakhsh 19:163, no. 1678].
97. *Fawāʾid jāmiʿ ṣaghīr-i Ḥusāmī* (KFJ 65a, 127b). al-Ṣadr al-Shahīd Ḥusām al-dīn b. ʿAbd al-ʿAzīz b. Māza al-Bukhārī (d. 536/1141). *Fawāʾid jāmiʿ al-ṣaghīr-i Ḥusāmī*. Arabic. [GAL I, 376].
98. *Ḥāshīya muntaqā* (KFJ 190b). Commentary on no. 121. Ernst lists an unidentified *Sharḥ-i mantiqī*. [Ernst 255].
99. *Hidāyat al-bidāya* (JU 7; KFJ 241b). Burhān al-dīn ʿAlī b. Abū Bakr al-Farghānī al-Marghinānī (d. 593/1197). *al-Hidāya al-burhānīya fī al-fiqh al-nuʿmānī*. [GALS I, 644; Subtelny and Khalidov 227].
100. *Ḥusāmīya* (SH 121a). Ṣadr-i shahīd Ḥusām al-dīn ʿUmar b. ʿAbd al-ʿAzīz Ibn Māza Bukhārī (d. 536/1141). *Wāqiʿāt-i Ḥusāmīya*. [Ḥusayn 554; Islam 226].
101. *Ḥusāmī* (JU 7). Ḥusām al-dīn Muḥammad al-Akhsīkatī (d. 644/1247). *Kitāb al-muntakhab fī uṣūl al-madhhab*. [GAL I, 381; GALS I, 637].
102. *al-Ikhtiyār sharḥ al-mukhtār* (KJJ 182a). Majd al-dīn ʿAbdallāh b. Maḥmūd al-Buldajī (d. 683/1284). Commentary on his *Mukhtār lil-fatwā*, no. 117. [Subtelny and Khalidov 234].
103. *Jāmiʿ al-fatāwā* (KFJ 234b; SH 52b). Nāṣir al-dīn Abū al-Qāsim Muḥammad b. Yūsuf al-Samarqandī (d. 656/1258). [Ḥusayn 545].
104. *Jāmiʿ al-fiqh* (SH 78b).
105. *Jāmiʿ al-muḍammarāt* (KFJ 161b) or *Muḍammarāt* (KFJ 76a; KJJ 203b). Ernst lists an unidentified *Muḍammarāt*. [Ernst 255].
106. *Jāmiʿ al-ṣaghīr* or *Jāmiʿ al-ṣughra* (KFJ 65a, 110b, 111a; JU 6; SH 116a). Muḥammad b. al-Ḥasan al-Shaybānī (d.189/804). *al-Jāmiʿ al-ṣaghīr fī al-furūʿ*. Arabic.
107. *Kāfī* (KFJ 29b). Either: Muḥammad b. Muḥammad b. ʿAbd al-Ḥākim al-Marwāzī (d. 334/945). *al-Kāfī fī l-fiqh*. Arabic. Or: *al-Kāfī sharḥ al-Bazdawī*. Ḥusām al-dīn Ḥusayn b. ʿAlī b. Ḥajjāj al-Saghnāqī (d. 714). Edited by Fakhr al-dīn Sayyid Muḥammad Qānat. Riyādh: Maktabat al-Rashīd, 1322/2001.
108. *Kanz al-daqāʾiq* (KFJ 18a). Abū al-Barakāt Ḥāfiẓ al-dīn ʿAbdallāh b. Aḥmad al-Nasafī (d. 710/1310). *Kanz al-daqāʾiq fī al-furūʿ*. Arabic. [GAL II, 196; GALS 11, 265].
109. *Kāshif al-asrār* (KJJ 130a). Perhaps *Kashf al-asrār* by ʿAbd al-ʿAzīz b. Aḥmad b. Muḥammad al-Bukhārī (d. 730/1329). A commentary on Pazdawī, no. 127. Arabic. [Khuda Bakhsh 19:3, no. 1491].
110. *al-Khizānat al-fiqh* (SH 15b; MN 13). Abū al-Layth Naṣr b. Muḥammad. b. Aḥmad b. Ibrāhīm al-Ḥanafī al-Samarqandī (d. 373/983). Arabic. [GAL I, 196; GALS I, 347].
111. *Kifāyat al-fuqahāʾ* (KFJ 65a; SH 7b, 43b, 90a).

112. *Mabsūṭ* (SH 43b, 89a). Muḥammad b. al-Ḥasan al-Shaybānī (d.189/804).
113. *Majma' al-baḥrayn* (KFJ 20b; JU 7). Muzaffar al-dīn Aḥmad b. 'Alī Ibn al-Sā'ātī (Ḥanafi, d. 696/1296). *Majma' al-baḥrayn wa multaqa al-nayyirayn*. [GALS I, 658].
114. *al-Manthūra sharh al-manẓūma* (SH 90b). Probably a commentary on *al-Manẓūma al-Nasafīya fī al-khilāfīyāt* by Najm al-dīn Abū Ḥafs 'Umar al-Nasafī (d. 537/1142). [GAL I, 428; GALS I, 761].
115. *Miftāḥ al-masā'il* (KJJ 203a). Ḥujjat al-dīn Balkhī. *Mafātīh al-masā'il wa maṣābīḥ al-dalā'il*. [Ḥusayn 554].
116. *Muḥīṭ* (KFJ 90ab, 96a; SH 38b, 83b; KJJ 87a). Either: Burhān al-dīn Maḥmūd Ibn Māza (d. 616/1219). *al-Muḥīṭ al-Burhānī fī al-fiqh al-Nu'mānī*. [Subtelny and Khalidov 234]. Or: Raḍī al-dīn Muḥammad b. Muḥammad al-Sarakhsī (d. 543/1149). *Kitāb al-muḥīṭ al-Raḍawī*. [Harald Motzki, "Child Marriage in Seventeenth-Century Palestine" in Masud et al 348 n. 21]. Or: Abū Muḥammad 'Abdallāh b. Yūsuf al-Juwaynī. [Sarwar 162].
117. *Mukhtār al-fatwā* (KFJ 124b, 229b). Abū l-Faḍl Majd al-dīn 'Alī b. Maḥmūd al-Buldajī al-Mawṣilī (Ḥanafī, d. 683/1282). *Mukhtār lil-fatwā*. [GAL I, 382].
118. *Mukhtaṣar nawādir al-Hishām* (SH 9a). Related to no. 125.
119. *Multaqaṭ al-fiqh* (KFJ 71a, 91a, 92a). Perhaps identical to no. 120.
120. *Multaqaṭ-i Nāṣirī* (KFJ 136b; KJJ 199a). Nāṣir al-dīn Abū al-Qāsim Muḥammad b. Yūsuf al-Samarqandī (d. 656/1258). *al-Multaqaṭ fi al-fatāwa al-Ḥanafīya*.
121. *Muntaqā* (KFJ 20a, 26b, 28a). Either: Majd al-dīn Abū al-Barakāt 'Abd al-Salām b. 'Alī Ibn Taymīya (d. 652/1245). *al-Muntaqā fī al-aḥkām*. [GALS I, 691]. Or: Ḥakim Abū al-Faḍl Muḥammad b. Muḥammad (d. 344/955–6). *al-Muntaqā fī furū' al-Ḥanafiya*. [Ḥusayn 554].
122. *Mustakhliṣ* (JU 21). Ibrahīm b. Muḥamad al-Qārī al-Ḥanafī. *Mustakhliṣ al-ḥaqā'iq sharḥ kanz al-daqā'iq*. A commentary on *Kashf al-ḥaqā'iq sharḥ kanz al-daqā'iq* by Shaykh 'Abd al-Ḥakīm Afghānī, itself a commentary on no. 108. [Sarwar 21, n. 1; Ḥusayn 547].
123. *Kitāb al-muttafiq* (KFJ 41b, 95a, 207b; JU 7) and *Naẓm kitāb muttāfiq* (JU 120, 126, 149, 150). Abū Bakr Aḥmad b. 'Alī b. Thābit al-Khaṭīb al-Baghdādī (d. 463/1071). *Kitāb al-muttafiq wa al-muftariq*. [GALS I, 564; Sarwar 7 n. 7].
124. *Nawādir al-fatāwā* (SH 29a, 43b).
125. *Nawādir al-Hishām* (SH 44a).
126. *Nawāzil al-fiqh* (KFJ 92b). Abū al-Layth Naṣr b. Muḥammad. b. Aḥmad b. Ibrāhīm al-Ḥanafī al-Samarqandī (d. 373/983). *al-Nawāzil min al-fatāwā*. [GAL I, 196].
127. Pazdawī (JU 7). Abū al-Ḥasan 'Alī b. Muḥammad Pazdawī (d. 482/1089). *Kanz al-wuṣūl ilā ma'rifat al-uṣūl*. Arabic. [GAL I, 373; GALS I 637].
128. Qudūrī (JU 7). Abū al-Ḥusayn Muḥammad b. Muḥammad Qudūrī (d.428/1037). *Mukhtaṣar al-Qudūrī*. [Subtelny and Khalidov 234].
129. *Qunya* (KFJ 147a). Ḥāfiẓ al-dīn Abū al-Barakāt 'Abdallāh b. Aḥmad al-Nasafī (d. 710/1310). *al-Qunya fi al-fiqh*.
130. *Ṣalāt-i Mas'ūdī* (SH 53b, 64b). Mas'ūd b. Maḥmūd al-Samarqandī. *Ṣalāt-i Mas'ūdī*. Completed in first half of eighth/fourteenth century. Persian. [Khuda Bakhsh 14:76–77, no. 1223; Ḥusayn 552].
131. *Salwat al-'ārifīn al-ma'rūf bī nawādir al-uṣūl* by Abū 'Abdallāh Muḥmmad b. 'Alī al-Ḥakīm al-Tirmidhī (KFJ 46b, 295a, 309a). Abū 'Abdallāh al-Ḥakīm al-Tirmidhī (ca. 286/900). *Nawādir al-uṣūl fī ma'rifat akhbār al-rasūl*. Arabic. [GALS I, 355–356].
132. *Shāhān sharḥ al-hidāya* (KJJ 201b, SH 83b, 85a). Commentary on no. 99.
133. *Sharḥ athār nayyirayn* (KFJ 28a, 77b).
134. *Sharḥ hidāya* (KFJ 90a, 111a, 96a). Commentary on no. 99. Perhaps identical to no. 132.

135. *Sharḥ majma‘ al-baḥrayn* (KFJ 69b, 80b). Commentary on no. 113.
136. *Sharḥ uṣūl shāshī* (KFJ 13b). Commentary on *Uṣūl al-shāshī* by Niẓām al-dīn al-Shāshī (seventh/thirteenth cent.). [Ernst 256].
137. *Kitāb al-shifā' fi awṣāf al-muṣṭafā* by Abu al-Faḍl 'Iyāḍ b. Mūsā b. 'Iyāḍ al-Yaḥṣubī (KFJ 176b, 89a; SH 86a). al-Qāḍī 'Iyāḍ b. Mūsā b. 'Iyāḍ al-Yaḥṣubī (d. 1149). *al-Shifā' bi-ta'rīf ḥuqūq al-muṣṭafā*.
138. *Ṭabaqāt al-fuqahā'* (KFJ 170b).
139. *Tafsīr sharā'ī' al-islām* (KFJ 303b).
140. *Tajnīs al-multaqaṭ al-Nāṣirī* (KFJ 212a). See no. 120.
141. *Targhīb al-ṣalāt* (SH 65a). Either: Muḥammad b. Aḥmad al-Zāhid. *Targhīb fī al-ṣalāt*. Persian. [Khuda Bakhsh 14:89, no. 1230; Ḥusayn 551]. Or: Aḥmad Bayhaqī. Arabic. [Ḥusayn 551].
142. *Tā'sīs al-qawā'id* (SH 241b).
143. *Zād al-fuqahā'* (KFJ 230a). Imām Abū al-Ma'ālī Bahā' al-dīn. *Zād al-fuqahā'*. [Ḥusayn 550].

D. Theological Works and Creedal Statements

144. *Kitāb al-'ālim wa al-muta'allim* (KFJ 92a). Abū Ḥanīfa al-Nu'mān b. Thābit b. Zūṭā (d. 150/767). *Kitāb al-'ālim wa al-muta'allim*.
145. *'Aqīdat Nasafī* (JU 7). Ḥāfiẓ al-dīn Abū al-Barakāt 'Abdallāh al-Nasafī (d. 710/1310). *al-'Umda fī al-'aqā'id*. [GAL I, 168; GALS I, 283].
146. *'Aqīdat al-Shaykh Abū al-Najīb al-Suhrawardī* (KFJ 48b). Abū al-Najīb al-Suhrawardī (d. 563/1168).
147. *'Aqīdat taḥāh* (SH 59b).
148. *Kitāb bayān al-firaq* (KFJ 207a). Perhaps Abū Manṣūr 'Abd al-Qāhir b. Ṭāḥir al-Baghdādī. *Kitāb al-farq bayn al-firaq*. [Khadduri 244]. Various editions.
149. *Bidāya* by Ṣābūnī (KFJ 223a). Nūr al-dīn Aḥmad b. Maḥmūd al-Bukhārī al-Ṣābūnī (d. 580/1184). *al-Bidāya min al-kifāya fī 'uṣūl al-dīn* or *Bidāyat al-'aqā'id*. Edited by Fathallah Hulayf. al-Qahira, 1969. [GAL I, 375; GALS I, 643].
150. *Fiqh-i akbar* (JU 28). Abū Ḥanīfa al-Nu'mān b. Thābit b. Zūṭā (d. 150/767). *al-Fiqh al-akbar*. [GAL 1, 168; GALS I, 283]. Various editions.
151. *Lawāmi'* by Fakhr al-dīn Rāzi (KFJ 300b). Fakhr al-dīn Muḥammad b. 'Umar al-Rāzī (d. 606/1209). *Lawāmi' al-bayyināt fī al-asmā' wa al-ṣifāt*. Various editions.
152. *Ma'rifat al-madhdhāhib* by Abū Ḥanīfa Kūfī (SH 225a). Abū Ḥanīfa al-Nu'mān b. Thābit b. Zūṭā (d. 150/767).
153. *Qaṣīda al-lāmiya* (JU 7). Sirāj al-dīn 'Alī b. 'Uthmān al-Ūshī al-Farghānī al-Ūshī (ca. 569/1173). *Qaṣīda al-lāmiya fī al-tawhīd*. [GAL I, 429].
154. *Sharḥ 'aqīda Ḥāfiẓiya* (RM 4a). Commentary on no. 145.
155. *Sharḥ qaṣīda al-lāmiya* (JU 7). Commentary on no. 153.
156. *Sharḥ al-ṭaḥāwī* (KFJ 18b; SH 53a). Ibn Abī al-'Izz, 'Alī ibn 'Alī (1330 or 1331–1389 or 1390). *Sharḥ al-ṭaḥāwīya fī al-'aqīda al-salafīya*. Commentary on the creed of Abū Ja'far Aḥmad b. Muḥammad (d. 321/933). [Khadduri 60 n. 47]. Numerous editions.
157. *Tafsīr i'timād*. Perhaps *al-I'timād fī al-i'tiqād*, a commentary on no. 145 by the author. [Subtelny and Khalidov 235].
158. *Tamhīd* by Abū Shukūr Sālimī (KFJ 195a). Abū Shukūr Muḥammad b. 'Abd al-Sayyid al-Kashshī al-Ḥanafī al-Sālimī (fl. fifth/eleventh century). *Kitāb al-tamhīd fī bayān al-tawḥīd*. [GAL I, 419; GALS I, 744].
159. *Kitāb-i uṣūl* by Imām-i Ā'ẓam (SH 65b). Abū Ḥanīfa al-Nu'mān b. Thābit b. Zūṭā (d. 150/767).

E. Quran, Quran Recital, and Tafsīr

160. *Kashshāf* by Zamakhsharī (JU 549; KFJ 198 b, 199a). Maḥmūd b. 'Umar Zamakhsharī (d. 538/1144). *al-Kashshāf 'an ḥaqā'iq al-tanzīl*. Edited by 'Ādil Aḥmad 'Abd al-Mawjūd and 'Alī Muḥammad Mu'awwaḍ. al-Riyāḍ: Maktabat al-'Ubaykān, 1998. 6 vols. Arabic. [GAL I, 289; GALS I, 507].
161. *Madārik* (JU 8; SH 40b; KFJ 132b). Ḥāfiẓ al-dīn Abū al-Barakāt 'Abdallāh al-Nasafī (d. 710/1310). *Madārik al-tanzīl wa ḥaqā'iq al-ta'wīl*. Edited by Marwān Muḥammad al-Sha''ār. Bayrūt, Lubnān: Dār al-Nafā'is, 1996. Arabic. [GALS II, 267].
162. *Qur'ān*.
163. Shāṭibī (JU 578). Abū al-Qāsim al-Qāsim b. Firruh b. Khalaf al-Shāṭibī (d. 590/1194). *al-Qaṣīda al-Shāṭibīya fī al-qirā'āt al-sab'*. Arabic. [Subtelny and Khalidov 228].
164. *Tafsīr* by Fakhr al-dīn al-Rāzī (SH 54b). Fakhr al-dīn al-Rāzī (d. 606/1209). *al-Tafsīr al-kabīr* also known as *Mafātiḥ al-ghayb*. Arabic. Numerous editions.
165. *Tafsīr* by Imām Zāhid Qaffāl al-Shāshī (SH 7a, 88a). Abū Bakr Muḥammad al-Qaffāl al-Shāshī (429/1037–507/1114).
166. *Tafsīr* by Kāshānī (KFJ 154a). Perhaps Abū Bakr Mas'ūd b. Aḥmad al-Kāshānī. *Kitāb al-ta'wīlāt*. [Subtelny and Khalidov 232].
167. *Tafsīr-i baṣā'ir* (SH 74a). Muḥammad b. Maḥmūd al-Nishābūrī (ca. 529/1125). *Tafsīr-i baṣā'ir-i yamīnī*. Edited by 'Ali Riwaqi. Tehran: Bunyad-i Farhang-i Iran, 1980. Persian. [Storey I, 5; Ernst 252].
168. *Tafsīr al-gharīb* by Ibn Jawzī (KFJ 94a, 129b). Ibn al-Jawzī Abū al-Faḍā'il Jamāl al-dīn (d. 597/1200). *Kitāb tadhkirat al-arīb fī tafsīr al-gharīb*. Edited by 'Alī Ḥusayn al-Bawwāb. al-Riyāḍ: Maktabat al-Ma'ārif, 1986. Arabic. [GAL I, 504]. Commentary on linguistic oddities in the Qur'ān.
169. *Tafsīr-i Nāṣirī* (KFJ 310a).
170. *Tafsīr al-Zāhidī* (SH 7a; KFJ 105a). Either: Abū Naṣr Aḥmad b. al-Ḥasan Sulaymānī (ca. 519/1125). *Laṭā'if al-tafsīr*. Persian. [Ernst 252; Storey I, 4 and I, 1190]. Or: Zāhid Muḥammad b. 'Abd al-Raḥmān Abū 'Abdallāh Bukhārī (d. 546/1151). *Tafsīr-i Zāhidī*. [Ḥusayn 544].

F. History

171. *Tawārīkh-i Ṭabarī* (KJJ 312b). Muḥammad b. Jarīr al-Ṭabarī (838–923). *Ta'rīkh al-rusul wa al-mulūk*. Edited by Muḥammad Abu al-Faḍl Ibrāhīm. Miṣr, Dār al-Ma'ārif [1960–69]. 10 volumes. Arabic.

G. Religious Encyclopedia

172. *Jāmi' al-'ulūm* (SH 60a). Fakhr al-Dīn Muḥammad ibn 'Umar Rāzī. *Jāmi' al-'ulūm*. Edited by 'Alī Āl-i Dāvūd. Tihrān: Bunyād-i Mawqūfāt Duktar Maḥmūd Afshār, 1382/2003. Persian.

H. Arabic Dictionaries and Grammars

173. *al-Kāfiya* by Ibn al-Ḥājib (Abū Makhrama, 12). Abū 'Amr 'Uthmān b. 'Umar Ibn al-Ḥājib (d. 646/1249). *al-Kāfiya*. Arabic grammar. [Subtelny and Khalidov 226.]
174. *Tāj a'sāmī* (KFJ 123b). *Tāj al-as'āmī fī al-lugha*. Edited by 'Alī Awsaṭ Ibrāhīmī. Tihrān: Markaz-i Nashr-i Dānishgāhī, 1988. Arabic-Persian dictionary.
175. *Tāj al-maṣādir* (SH 95a). Abū Ja'far Aḥmad b. 'Alī b. Muḥammad Bayhaqī (d. 544/1149 or 1150). *Tāj al-maṣādir*. Edited by Hādī 'Ālim-zādah. Tihrān: Mu'assasah-i Muṭāla'āt va Taḥqīqāt-i Farhangī, 1987. Arabic-Persian dictionary.

I. Miscellaneous and Unidentified Texts and Authors

176. Abū Isḥāq al-Tha'labī (KJJ 313b). Abū Isḥāq Aḥmad b. Muḥammad al-Tha'labī (d. 427/1035). Either: *'Arā'is al-majālis fī qiṣaṣ al-anbiyā'*. Or: *al-Kashf wa al-bayān 'an tafsīr al-Qur'ān*.
177. *Kitāb al-anwār* (KFJ 92a).
178. *Asrār al-da'wāt* (JU 365).
179. *Badr al-sa'ādat* (KFJ 28a, 42b, 195b; SH 43b).
180. Mawlānā Burhān al-dīn Balkhī (KFJ 300b).
181. *Fawz al-najāt* (KFJ 323b).
182. Ibn Ḥājib (KFJ 146a).
183. Ibn al-Jawzī (KFJ 94a). Abū al-Faḍā'il Jamāl al-dīn Abū al-Farraj Ibn al-Jawzī (d. 597/1200). Quoted on dates of Muḥammad's birth and death and celebrations.
184. *Khulāṣat al-adhkār* (KFJ 275a).
185. *Kifāyat al-majālis* by al-Sha'bī (KFJ 93a, 251b, KJJ 190a). Iraqi jurist d. 110/728–729.
186. *Kitāb Makkīyāt* by al-Faqīh al-Zandawaysī (KFJ 103b). Abū al-Ḥasan 'Alī b. Yaḥyā b. Muḥammad al-Bukhārī al-Zandawaysatī (d. 382/922).
187. *Kitāb-i sibṭīya* (KFJ 42a).

J. Sources of Quoted Verse

188. Imām-i Ā'ẓam Abū Ḥanīfa (KFJ 228b). Abū Ḥanīfa al-Nu'mān b. Thābit b. Zūṭā (d. 150/767). Arabic.
189. Amīn al-dīn Kāzarūnī (JU 544; KFJ 120a, 47b). Amīn al-dīn Balyānī Kāzarūnī (d. before 748/1347). Persian.
190. *Arbāb al-qulūb* (KFJ 13b).
191. Ibrāhīm b. Adham (KFJ 245a). Ibrāhīm b. Adham (d. 159/776 or 174/790). Arabic.
192. Shaykh Junayd (KFJ 40a). Abū al-Qāsim Junayd al-Baghdādī (d. 298/910). Arabic.
193. Sultan Nāṣr al-dīn (KFJ 193b). Persian.
194. *Naẓm-i Ghiyāthī* (KFJ 46a). Perhaps related to no. 76.
195. *Naẓm* by al-Zandawaysī (KFJ 46b). Abū al-Ḥasan 'Alī b. Yaḥyā b. Muḥammad al-Zandawaysatī al-Bukhārī (d. 382/ 922). Arabic.
196. Niẓāmī (KFJ 235b). Ilyās b. Yūsuf Niẓāmī (d. 606/1209). Persian.
197. al-Qushayrī (KFJ 219a). Abū al-Qāsim 'Abd al-Karīm al-Qushayrī (376–465/986–1072). Arabic.
198. Shaykh Sa'dī (KFJ 251b, MN 69). Muṣliḥ al-dīn Sa'dī Shīrāzī (d. 691/1292). Persian.
199. al-Sanā'ī (KFJ 78a). Abū al-Majd Majdūd al-Sanā'ī (d. 525/1131). Persian.
200. Shaykh Shiblī (KFJ 233b). Abū Bakr b. Jaḥdar al-Shiblī (d. 333/945).
201. Shaykh Yāfi'ī (KFJ 278b-283a). Abū 'Abdallāh b. As'ad Abu al-Sa'āda 'Afīf al-dīn Yāfi'ī (d. 768/1367). Arabic.

NOTES

Introduction

1. Andre Wink, *Al-Hind: The Making of the Indo-Islamic World*, 3 vols. (Leiden: Brill, 1990–2004).

2. For the political history of the Delhi Sultanate, see Peter Jackson, *The Delhi Sultanate: A Political and Military History* (Cambridge: Cambridge University Press, 1999); and Ishtiaq Husain Qureshi, *The Administration of the Sultanate of Dehlī*, 4th Edition (Revised) (Karachi: Pakistan Historical Society, 1958).

3. Marshall G. S. Hodgson, *The Venture of Islam: Conscience and History in a World Civilization* (Chicago: The University of Chicago Press, 1974), 2:293.

4. For an encyclopedic overview of South Asian Sufism, see Sayyid Athar Abbas Rizvi, *A History of Sufism in India*, 2 vols. (New Delhi: Munshiram Manoharlal, 1978). For more-focused studies, especially on the Sufis of the thirteenth through fifteenth centuries, see the works of K. A. Nizami, Richard Eaton, Carl Ernst, Simon Digby, Riazul Islam, Iqtidar Husain Siddiqui, Bruce Lawrence, and Paul Jackson listed in the bibliography.

5. See Zafarul Islam, "Origin and Development of *Fatāwā* Compilation in Medieval India," *Studies in History* 12, 2 (1996): 223–241 and "Works of Legal Nature in the Reign of Firuz Shah Tughluq," in *Bias in Indian Historiography*, ed. Devahuti (Delhi: Indian History and Culture Society, 1980).

6. Rizvi, *A History of Sufism in India*, 2:36.

7. Alexander D. Knysh, *Ibn ʿArabi in the Later Islamic Tradition* (Albany: State University of New York Press, 1999).

8. On Shihāb al-dīn Suhrawardī and *ʿAwārif al-maʿārif*, see Erik S. Ohlander, *Sufism in an Age of Transition: ʿUmar al-Suhrawardī and the Rise of the Islamic Mystical Brotherhoods* (Leiden: Brill, 2008); and Qamar-ul Huda, *Striving for Divine Union: Spiritual Exercises for Suhrawardī Ṣūfīs* (London: RoutledgeCurzon, 2003).

9. On Uch, see Ahmad Nabi Khan, *Uchchh, History and Architecture* (Islamabad: National Institute of Historical and Cultural Research, 1980); and Masʿūd Ḥasan Shihāb, *Khiṭṭa-yi pāk: Ūch*, 3rd Edition (Bahawalpur: Urdu Academy, 1993).

10. On the genre of *malfūẓāt*, see my article "His Master's Voice: The Genre of *Malfūẓāt* in South Asian Sufism," *History of Religions* 44, 1 (2004): 56–69; Muḥammad Aslam, *Malfūẓātī adab kī tārīkhī ahmīyat* (Lahore: Idāra-yi Taḥqīqāt-i Pākistān, Punjab University, 1995); S. H. Askari, *Maktub and Malfuz Literature as a Source of Socio-Political History* (Patna: Khuda Bakhsh Oriental Public Library, 1981); and Carl W. Ernst, *Eternal Garden: Mysticism, History and Politics at a South Asian Sufi Center* (Albany: State University of New York Press, 1992), 62–84.

11. On *tazkiras* and similar texts, see Marcia K. Hermansen, "Religious Literature and the Inscription of Identity: The Sufi Tazkira Tradition in Muslim South Asia," *The Muslim World* 87, 3–4 (1997): 315–329; Marcia K. Hermansen and Bruce B. Lawrence, "Indo-Persian Tazkiras as Memorative Communications," in *Beyond Turk and Hindu: Rethinking Religious Identities in Islamicate South Asia*, ed. David Gilmartin and Bruce Lawrence (Gainsville: University Press of

Florida, 2000); and J. A. Mojaddedi, *The Biographical Tradition in Sufism: The Ṭabaqāt Genre from al-Sulamī to Jāmī* (Richmond, Surrey: Curzon Press, 2001).

12. For full information on all of these texts, their manuscripts, and publication, see Appendix B.

13. Aḥmad Bahā' b. Ya'qūb al-Bhaṯṯī, *Khizānat al-fawā'id al-Jalālīya* (MS. 2557, Kitābkhāna-yi Dātā Ganj-bakhsh, Islamabad). Unless otherwise noted, all subsequent references are to this manuscript.

14. Sayyid 'Alā' al-dīn 'Alī b. Sa'd al-Qurayshī al-Ḥusaynī, *Khulāṣat al-alfāẓ-i jāmi' al-'ulūm*, ed. Ghulām Sarwar (Islamabad: Markaz-i Taḥqīqāt-i Fārsī-yi Īrān ō Pākistān, 1412/1992). Unless otherwise noted, all subsequent references are to this edition.

15. Muḥammad Ghaznawī, *Tuḥfat al-sarā'ir* (MS. 1090, Arabic and Persian. Government Oriental Manuscripts Library, Madras). Unless otherwise noted, all subsequent references are to this manuscript.

16. *Sirāj al-hidāya: malfūẓāt-i Ḥusayn al-ma'rūf bi Jalāl al-dīn Makhdūm-i jahāniyān Jahāngasht*, ed. Qāżī Sajjād Ḥusayn (New Delhi: Indian Council of Historical Research, 1983). Unless otherwise noted, all subsequent references are to this edition.

17. For details see Appendix B.

18. Fażlallāh b. Żiyā' al-'Abbāsī, *Khizāna-yi jawāhir-i Jalālīya* (MS. 5193, MS. 2463, and MS. 1749, Kitābkhāna-yi Dātā Ganj-bakhsh, Islamabad).

19. Ḥāmid b. Fażlallāh Jamālī, *Siyar al-'ārifīn*, Urdu trans. Muḥammad Ayyūb Qādirī (Lahore: Markazī Urdu Board, 1976).

20. Muḥammad Ayyūb Qādirī, *Makhdūm-i jahāniyān Jahāngasht: Mufaṣṣil-i ḥālāt ō sawāniḥ-yi Jalāl al-dīn Makhdūm-i jahāniyān Jahāngasht Bukhārī Uchchī* (Karachi: Idāra-yi Taḥqīq ō Taṣnīf, 1963).

21. Mirzā Sakhāwat, *Taẕkira-yi ḥażrat sayyid Jalāl al-dīn Makhdūm-i jahāniyān Jahāngasht* (Hyderabad: Institute of Individualist Cultural Studies, 1962).

22. Qādirī, *Makhdūm-i jahāniyān*, 203–210.

23. Bazmee Ansari, "Djalāl al-Dīn Ḥusayn Bukhārī," in *Encyclopaedia of Islam*, New Edition (Leiden: Brill, 1965), 2:392a–393b; Rizvi, *A History of Sufism in India*; Annemarie Schimmel, *Islam in the Indian Subcontinent* (Leiden-Koln: E. J. Brill, 1980); Bruce B. Lawrence, *Notes from a Distant Flute: The Extant Literature of Pre-Mughal Indian Sufism* (Tehran: Imperial Academy of Philosophy, 1978).

24. Riazul Islam, *Sufism in South Asia: Impact on Fourteenth Century Muslim Society* (Oxford: Oxford University Press, 2002).

One: Initiation into the Sufi Path

1. The complete form of his name is Sayyid Jalāl al-dīn Abū 'Abdallāh Ḥusayn b. Aḥmad b. Ḥusayn Bukhārī and he is most commonly known as Makhdūm-i jahāniyān Jahāngasht. I have chosen to refer to him as Bukhārī for the sake of convenience and brevity.

2 . Roy P. Mottahedeh, *Loyalty and Leadership in an Early Islamic Society* (Princeton: Princeton University Press, 1980), 101.

3. *Manba' al-sādāt* (MS. Or. 2,014, British Library, London), 17a; Shihāb, *Khiṭṭa-yi pāk*, 205. Though Shihāb does not consistently indicate his sources, he has amassed almost everything known about the history of Uch and had access to documents in local private collections. His information on the life of Jalāl Surkh is mostly taken from one such document, *Insāb-i Jalālī* by Sayyid Ṣafī al-dīn Muḥammad Shāh Bukhārī. This manuscript, found in a private collection, was copied in 1003/1594–1595 and Shihāb suggests that it was composed in the preceding century.

Insāb-i Jalālī contains many details not found elsewhere, some of which are historically impossible (Shihāb, *Khiṭṭa-yi pāk*, 215).

4. Richard Gramlich has argued that Jalāl Surkh-pōsh is the founding figure of the Khāksārs, an Iranian Shiʿa Sufi order deriving, according to him, from an order of extreme Shiʿa *qalandars*, the Jalālīs (Gramlich, *Die Schiitischen Derwischorden Persiens*, vol. 1, *Die Affiliationen*, Abhandlungen fur die Kunde des Morgenlandes: 34, 1 [Wiesbaden, 1965], 73). These Khāksārs are not to be confused with the Indian movement of the same name active in the 1930s and 40s. The presence of such a Jalālī order in Sind is mentioned in *Dabistān-i maẕāhib*, a seventeenth-century survey of Indian religious communities ([Kaykhusraw Isfandiyār], *Dabistān-i maẕāhib*, ed. Raḥīm Riżāzāda Malik, 2 vols. [Tehran: Kitābkhāna-yi Ṭāhūrī, 1983], 1:191). However, as Aditya Behl has shown, the author of the *Dabistān* was motivated by a particular polemical agenda and his descriptions of the religious beliefs and practices of different groups are highly inaccurate (Aditya Behl, "The Politics of 'Other People's Myths,'" in *Notes from a Mandala: Essays in the History of Indian Religions in Honour of Wendy Doniger*, ed. Laurie L. Patton and David L. Haberman [Newark: University of Delaware Press, 2010]). Richard Burton also mentioned Jalālī Sufis present in Sind, applying the label to all *bī-sharʿ* or anti-nomian *qalandars*. He explained the term as a reference to their imitation of God's more awesome and awful characteristics, i.e., *jalāl* (majesty) in contrast to *jamāl* (beauty) (Richard Francis Burton, *Sindh, and the Races That Inhabit the Valley of the Indus* [London: W. H. Allen, 1851], 208–212).

5. Shāh Ṣalāḥ al-dīn, *Maẓhar-i Jalālī* (MS. 2–F/8295, Punjab University, Lahore).

6. Ḥusaynī, *Jāmiʿ al-ʿulūm*, 278.

7. Ḥusaynī, *Jāmiʿ al-ʿulūm*, 284.

8. Bhaṭṭī, *Khizānat al-fawāʾid al-Jalālīya*, 196b–198b; Fīrōz Shāh, *Futūḥāt-i Fīrōz Shāhī*, ed. Shaikh Abdur Rashid (Aligarh: Aligarh Muslim University, 1954), 6.

9. Devin J. Stewart, *Islamic Legal Orthodoxy: Twelver Shiite Responses to the Sunni Legal System* (Salt Lake City: The University of Utah Press, 1998). It is suggestive, though probably coincidental, that Uch was also the seat of some of the most important leaders of the Ismāʿīlī Shiʿa mission, *dāʿīs* who practiced *taqīya* and often assumed the guise of Sufi *pīrs*. The shrines of Pīr Ṣadr al-dīn and his son Pīr Ḥasan Kabīr al-dīn are located in or near Uch. Although their lives cannot be dated definitively, the evidence of Ismāʿīlī traditions indicates the fourteenth and fifteenth centuries as the most likely period, making it possible for Bukhārī to have come in contact with them (Farhad Daftary, *A Short History of the Ismailis: Traditions of a Muslim Community* [Edinburgh: Edinburgh University Press, 1998], 179).

10. *Jawāhir al-awliyā,ʾ* by an eleventh-/seventeenth-century descendant of Bukhārī, relies largely on Sunni authorities while expressing devotion to the descendants of the Prophet, especially the Shiʿa imams (Muḥammad Bāqir b. ʿUṣmān Bukhārī, *Jawāhir al-awliyā,ʾ* ed. Ghulām Sarwar [Islamabad: Markaz-i Taḥqīqāt-i Fārsī-yi Īrān ō Pākistān, 1396/1976]).

11. *Sayyid* (plural *sādāt*) is used in South Asia for a descendant of Muḥammad, especially through his daughter Fāṭima and grandson Ḥusayn. Elsewhere such a person might be called *sharīf* (plural *ashrāf*) but in South Asia *ashrāf* means all those who claim a "foreign" origin, i.e., descent from someone other than an Indian convert to Islam.

12. Muḥammad ibn ʿAbdallāh Ibn Baṭṭūṭa, *The Travels of Ibn Battuta, A. D. 1325–1354*, trans. H. A. R. Gibb (Cambridge: Published for the Hakluyt Society at the University Press, 1958–2000), 3:670.

13. Żiyāʾ al-dīn Baranī, *Tārīkh-i Fīrōz Shāhī/Tarikh-i Feroz-Shahi of Ziaa al-Din Barni, commonly called Ziaa-i Barni*, ed. Sayyid Aḥmad Khān (Calcutta: Asiatic Society of Bengal, 1862), 558.

14. Riazul Islam, *Sufism in South Asia*, 199.

15. Shihāb, *Khiṭṭa-yi pāk*, 205. Muḥammad b. Jalāl-shāhī Riżawī, *Sawāl ō jawāb* (MS. H-125, Punjab University, Lahore), 232a. This text contains questions about the Bukhārī family answered by Sayyid Bahū in 1042/1632–1633.

16. See, for example, Pnina Werbner, "The Ranking of Brotherhoods: The Dialectics of Muslim Caste among Overseas Pakistanis," in *Muslim Communities of South Asia: Culture, Society and Power*, ed. T. N. Madan (Delhi: Institute of Economic Growth, 2001), 111–147 and 117.

17. Riżawī, *Sawāl ō jawāb*, 232a. Jalāl al-dīn Bukhārī received a *khirqa* from his uncle Awḥād al-dīn; therefore, if this is the same man, he was still in Uch in the first quarter of the eighth/fourteenth century.

18. *Majma' al-awliyā' wa maḥfil al-aṣfiyā'* (MS. I.O. 1647, British Library, London), 2: 623a.

19. Shihāb, *Khiṭṭa-yi pāk*, 207; Riżawī, *Sawāl ō jawāb*, 232b; 'Abd al-Ḥayy b. Fakhr al-dīn al-Ḥasanī al-Lak'hnawī, *Nuzhat al-khawāṭir wa bahjat al masāmi' wa al-nawāzir* (Hyderabad: Maṭba'at Dā'irat al-Ma'ārif al-'Uṣmānīya, 1366/1947), 1:143.

20. *Majma' al-awliyā,'* 2: 623b. Riżawī and Lak'hnawī mention only the first two, bringing Jalāl Surkh's sons to a total of four (*Sawāl ō jawāb*, 233a–b; *Nuzhat al-khawāṭir*, 1:143). Both Shihāb and Ghulām Sarwar mention Bahā' al-dīn, whose descendants had control of Jalāl Surkh's tomb in the ninth/fifteenth century (*Khiṭṭa-yi pāk*, 210; Sarwar, editor's introduction to *Jawāhir al-awliyā,'* by Muḥammad Bukhārī, 20.)

21. Lak'hnawī, *Nuzhat al-khawāṭir*, 1:143; 'Abd al-Qādir b. Malūk Shāh al-Badā'unī, *Muntakhab al-tawārīkh*, 2 vols., trans. George S. A. Ranking, Bibliotheca Indica: 97 (Calcutta: Asiatic Society of Bengal, 1898), 1:129–130; Yaḥyā Sirhindī, *The Tārīkh-i Mubārakshāhī*, trans. K. K. Basu, Gaekwad's Oriental Series: 63 (Baroda: Oriental Institute, 1932), 34.

22. Ḥusaynī, *Jāmi' al-'ulūm*, 29.

23. On Bahā' ud-dīn Zakarīyā and the Suhrawardī lineage in Multan, see Huda, *Striving for Divine Union*. On Shihāb ud-dīn Suhrawardī, see Ohlander, *Sufism in an Age of Transition*.

24. Ḥusaynī, *Jāmi' al-'ulūm*, 182.

25. Bhaṯṯī, *Khizānat al-fawā'id al-Jalālīya*, 338a–b; Ḥusaynī, *Jāmi' al-'ulūm*, 280.

26. Peter Jackson remarks that "The term 'Khurāsān' is itself ambiguous. For the inhabitants of India during the Sultanate period, and even as late as Bābur's era, it denoted loosely the territories west of the Indus. . . . But 'Khurāsān' also designated the regions that today comprise northern Afghanistan and were at this time subject to the Chaghadayid khans." (Jackson, *Delhi Sultanate*, 263.)

27. Ḥusaynī, *Jāmi' al-'ulūm*, 182 and 559.

28. Wāriṣ Shāh, *Hīr Wāriṣ Shāh: matn wa urdū tarjuma*, ed. and Urdu trans. Hamīd-allāh Shāh Hāshmī (Lahore: Dāniyāl Press, 2000), 66; Wāriṣ Shāh, *Hīr Vāriṣ Śāh: Poème panjabi du XVIIIe siecle*, ed. and French trans. Denis Matringe (Pondichéry: Institut Français, 1988), 1:329.

29. Shihāb, *Khiṭṭa-yi pāk*, 223.

30. Bhaṯṯī, *Khizānat al-fawā'id al-Jalālīya*, 262a and 256b; Burhān al-dīn 'Abdallāh Quṭb-i 'ālam, *Jāmi' al-ṭuruq* (MS. Sufism 1549, Andhra Pradesh Government Oriental Manuscripts Library, Hyderabad, India), *khirqas* no. 7.4 and 7.5.

31. For an overview of Sufi robes, see Jamal Elias, "The Sufi Robe (*Khirqa*) as a Vehicle of Spiritual Authority," in *Robes of Honor: The Medieval World of Investiture*, ed. Stewart Gordon (New York: Palgrave, 2001), 275–290.

32. Abū Makhrama, *Arabische Texte zur Kenntnis der Stadt Aden im Mittelalter (Tārīkh taghr 'Adan)*, ed. Oscar Lofgren, Arbeten Utgivna med Understod av Vilhelm Ekmans Universitetsfond, 42: 2 (Uppsala: Almqvist & Wiksells Boktryckeri: 1936), 58.

33. Ḥusaynī, *Jāmiʿ al-ʿulūm*, 397. The aural reception of a text by a student was the standard mechanism for the transmission of a written work.

34. Ḥusaynī, *Jāmiʿ al-ʿulūm*, 281 and 385.

35. Ḥusaynī, *Jāmiʿ al-ʿulūm*, 576. Little is known about the Kāzarūnī establishment in Uch. Bukhārī's links with the Kāzarūnī order were forged in Kāzarūn itself and he does not say much about the Uch Kāzarūnīs. The *khānqāh* was founded by, or grew up around the tomb of, Sayyid Ṣafī al-dīn Kāzarūnī. Shihāb summarizes the various conjectures as to when this individual lived, when he came to Uch, and how he was related, if at all, to the order named for Abū Isḥāq Kāzarūnī (d. 426/1035). Suggested dates for his life range from the fourth/tenth to the seventh/thirteenth century and Shihāb settles on the fifth/eleventh century as the most likely period (Shihāb, *Khiṭṭa-yi pāk*, 172–181).

36. Bhaṯṯī, *Khizānat al-fawāʾid al-Jalālīya*, 240a.

37. Jamālī, *Siyar al-ʿārifīn*, 225.

38. Ḥusaynī, *Jāmiʿ al-ʿulūm*, 377 and 373.

39. Qādirī, *Makhdūm-i jahāniyān Jahāngasht*, 88–101.

40. Ḥusaynī, *Jāmiʿ al-ʿulūm*, 373, 420, and 180–181.

41. Ḥusaynī, *Jāmiʿ al-ʿulūm*, 29, 436, and 97.

42. Ḥusaynī, *Jāmiʿ al-ʿulūm*, 420 and 559.

43. For example, see ʿAbd al-Raḥmān Chishtī, *Mirʾāt al-asrār*, Urdu trans. Waḥīd Bakhsh Siyāl (Lahore: Sufi Foundation, 1402/1982), 411.

44. Ḥusaynī, *Jāmiʿ al-ʿulūm*, 385, 420, and 566. Bukhārī seems to have taken it as a personal compliment that he was fed from Rukn al-dīn's family property.

45. Ḥusaynī, *Jāmiʿ al-ʿulūm*, 420.

46. Ḥusaynī, *Jāmiʿ al-ʿulūm*, 385–386.

47. Ḥusaynī, *Jāmiʿ al-ʿulūm*, 360.

48. Ḥusaynī, *Jāmiʿ al-ʿulūm*, 21–22; Bhaṯṯī, *Khizānat al-fawāʾid al-Jalālīya*, 257b–262a.

49. ʿAbd al-Raḥmān Chishtī, *Mirʾāt al-asrār*, 409; Jamālī, *Siyar al-ʿārifīn*, 201.

50. Burhān al-dīn ʿAbdallāh, *Jāmiʿ al-ṭuruq*, *khirqa* no. 7.6.

51. Ḥusaynī, *Jāmiʿ al-ʿulūm*, 420, 191, and 193.

52. Ḥusaynī, *Jāmiʿ al-ʿulūm*, 386.

53. Ḥusaynī, *Jāmiʿ al-ʿulūm*, 336.

54. Peter Jackson, *Delhi Sultanate*, 164. For an overview of Muhammad b. Tughluq's reign, see Jackson, *Delhi Sultanate*, 255–277.

55. Anthony Welch and Howard Crane, "The Tughluqs: Master Builders of the Delhi Sultanate," *Muqarnas* 1 (1983): 125.

56. Ibn Battuta, *Travels of Ibn Battuta*, 3:657.

57. Welch and Crane, "The Tughluqs," 125; S. M. Ikram, *Muslim Rule in India and Pakistan (711–1858 A. C.)* (Lahore: Star Book Depot, 1961), 97–8. For examples of Muḥammad's harsh unsparing punishments of Sufi shaykhs, see Ibn Battuta, *Travels of Ibn Battuta*, 3:697–706.

58. Simon Digby, "The Sufi *Shaykh* and the Sultan: A Conflict of Claims to Authority in Medieval India," *Iran* 28 (1990).

59. Digby, "The Sufi *Shaykh* and the Sultan," 71.

60. Ikram, *Muslim Rule in India and Pakistan*, 97–98.

61. *Darwēsh*, *faqīr*, and *sālik* were the usual terms for an individual committed to the Sufi path, unless he or she were specified as a disciple (*murīd*) or a master (*shaykh*, *pīr*, and *murshid*). For an overview of labels used within the Sufi tradition, see Carl W. Ernst, *The Shambala Guide to Sufism* (Boston: Shambala, 1997), 1–31.

62. Bhaṯṯī, *Khizānat al-fawā'id al-Jalālīya*, 260a–b.

63. Muḥammad Ghaznawī, *Tuḥfat al-sarā'ir* (MS. 1090, Arabic and Persian. Governmental Oriental Manuscripts Library, Madras), 10.

64. According to *Jāmi' al-'ulūm*, the garments were a turban and a shirt (*darā'*) (Ḥusaynī, *Jāmi' al-'ulūm*, 335).

65. Ghaznawī, *Tuḥfat al-sarā'ir*, 10. For further discussion of amulets and prayers, see Chapter 4.

66. Riżawī, *Sawāl ō jawāb*, 233b.

67. On Chishtī *samā*,' and the Chishtīya as a whole, see Carl W. Ernst and Bruce B. Lawrence, *Sufi Martyrs of Love: The Chishti Order in South Asia and Beyond* (New York: Palgrave Macmillan, 2002), 34–46.

68. Aziz Ahmed, "The Sufi and Sultan in Pre-Mughal Muslim India," *Der Islam* 38 (1962): 147. See also Khaliq Ahmad Nizami, "Early Indo-Muslim Mystics and Their Attitude towards the State," *Islamic Culture* 22 (1948): 387–398; 23 (1949):13–21, 162–170, 312–321; 24 (1950): 60–71.

69. Nizami, "Early Indo-Muslim Mystics"; Nizami, "Some Aspects of Khānqāh Life in Medieval India," *Studia Islamica* 8 (1957): 51–60.

70. Richard M. Eaton highlights the existence of this discrepancy in his review of Ernst's *Eternal Garden* in *The Journal of Asian Studies* 53, 1 (February, 1994): 249–251.

71. On Naṣīr al-dīn Maḥmūd, see K. A. Nizami, *The Life and Times of Shaikh Nasir-u'd-din Chiragh-i-Dehli* (Delhi: Idarah-i Adabiyat-i Dilli, 1991) and Ḥamīd Qalandar, *Khayr al-majālis: Malfūẓāt-i ḥażrat shaykh Naṣīr al-dīn Maḥmūd Chirāgh-i Dihlī*, ed. K. A. Nizami (Aligarh: Aligarh Muslim University, 1959). On Burhān al-dīn Gharīb see Ernst, *Eternal Garden*, 118–154.

72. Paul Jackson, *The Way of a Sufi: Sharafuddin Maneri* (Delhi: Idarah-i Adabiyat-i Delli, 1987); Sayyid Muṭī' al-Imām, *Shaykh Sharaf al-dīn ibn Yaḥyā Manērī wa sahm-i ū dar mutaṣṣawafāna-yi fārsī* (Islamabad: Markaz-i Taḥqīqāt-i Fārsī-yi Īrān ō Pākistān, 1414/1993); Muḥammad Riyāż, *Aḥwāl ō āṣār-i mīr sayyid 'Alī Hamadānī* (Lahore: Nadwat al-Muṣannafīn, 1972); Johann K. Teufel, *Eine Lebensbeschreibung des Scheichs 'Alī-i Hamadānī* (Leiden: E. J. Brill, 1962); Ernst, *Eternal Garden*; Richard Maxwell Eaton, *Sufis of Bijapur 1300–1700: Social Roles of Sufis in Medieval India* (Princeton: Princeton University Press, 1978).

73. See Qureishi, *The Administration of the Sultanate of Dehlī* (Karachi: Pakistan Historical Society, 1958), 190–191. This usage of *shaykh al-islām* is particular to South Asia. For the various meanings of the term in different societies, see Richard W. Bulliet "The Shaikh Al-Islām and the Evolution of Islamic Society," *Studia Islamica* 35 (1972): 53–67.

74. Ḥusaynī, *Jāmi' al-'ulūm*, 279 and 336. Every *tazkira* entry about Bukhārī mentions his affiliation with Naṣīr al-dīn Maḥmūd, giving it a position of prominence in his life relative to the *tazkira* author's association with the Chishtīya.

75. Ḥamīd Qalandar, *Khayr al-majālis*, Urdu trans. Mawlānā Aḥmad 'Alī (Delhi: Nāz Publishing House, n. d.), 164.

76. *Sirāj al-hidāya*, 188–189.

77. Ḥusaynī, *Jāmi' al-'ulūm*, 335–336, 192, 420.

78. Ḥusaynī, *Jāmi' al-'ulūm*, 230 and 584. Bukhārī claimed that Rukn al-dīn's body was moved by angels to his grandfather Bahā' al-dīn's tomb. It is unclear who built Rukn al-dīn's tomb, one of the finest examples of funerary architecture in South Asia. Some believe that Rukn al-dīn's tomb was originally built by Sultan Ghiyāṣ al-dīn Tughluq (r. 720/1320–725/1325). See Robert Hillenbrand, "Turco-Iranian Elements in the Medieval Architecture of Pakistan: The Case of the Tomb of Rukn-I 'Alam at Multan," *Muqarnas* 9 (1992): 148–174; and Welch and Crane, "The Tughluqs."

79. Welch and Crane, "The Tughluqs," 125.

Two: Pilgrimage and Travel

1. *Safar-nāma-yi Makhdūm-i jahāniyān* (MS. 1091, Persian and Arabic, Governmental Oriental Manuscripts Library, Madras).

2. For the *taẕkira* reports on Bukhārī, see Appendix D.

3. Bhaṭṭī, *Khizānat al-fawā'id al-Jalālīya*, 118a.

4. For a brief summary of Ibn Baṭṭūṭa's voyages, see the H. A. R. Gibb's foreword to *Travels of Ibn Battuta*, 1: ix-xvi.

5. Ibn Baṭṭūṭa, *Travels of Ibn Battuta*, 3:602; 2:413.

6. Richard Mortel, "The Ḥusaynid Amirate of Madīna during the Mamlūk Period," *Studia Islamica* 80 (1994): 97–123, 119.

7. Mortel, "The Ḥusaynid Amirate of Madīna during the Mamlūk Period" and "Zaydi Shi'ism and the Ḥasanid Sharifs of Mecca," *IJMES* 19, 4 (1987): 455–472.

8. Ḥusaynī, *Jāmi' al-'ulūm*, 284. Bukhārī implies that Mecca and Medina were under a single ruler. However, although there had been various attempts by one amirate to incorporate or interfere with the other, this does not seem to have been the case during the 740s/1340s. See Mortel, "The Ḥusaynid Amirate of Madīna during the Mamlūk Period" and "Zaydi Shi'ism and the Ḥasanid Sharifs of Mecca."

9. Ḥusaynī, *Jāmi' al-'ulūm*, 284. Laḥsā is more correctly spelled al-Aḥsā' or al-Ḥasā.' According to Mustawfī, "in former days Baḥrayn, together with Laḥsā, Qaṭīf, Khaṭṭ, Azar, Alārah, Farūq, Baynūnah, Sābūn, Dārīn and Ghābah were all counted as of the Arab kingdom. At the present day, however, the Island of Baḥrayn forms a part of Fārs, being of the kingdom of Īrān. The peninsula of Qaṭīf, and Laḥsā, with the other neighbouring places, however, at most times pay no allegiance to the Baḥrayn rulers" (Ḥamdallāh Mustawfī, *The Geographical Part of the* Nuzhat al-Qulūb *Composed by Ḥamd-allāh Mustawfī of Qazwīn in 740 (1340)*, trans. G. Le Strange [Leiden: Brill Imprimerie Orientale, 1919]), http://persian.packhum.org/persian/main, 124–136, accessed 7 July 2011). Mustawfī also describes Hormuz as a tributary state to the Ilkhānids. By the time Bukhārī traveled through the region, the Ilkhānid empire served by Mustawfī in its waning days had disintegrated completely.

10. Juan R. I. Cole, "Rival Empires of Trade and Imami Shiism in Eastern Arabia, 1300–1800," *IJMES* 19, 2 (1987): 177–180.

11. Ḥusaynī, *Jāmi' al-'ulūm*, 278.

12. Ḥusaynī, *Jāmi' al-'ulūm*, 543, 278, 253, and 280.

13. Ibn Hajar al-'Asqalānī, *al-Durar al-kāmina fi a'yān al-mī'at al-thāmina* (Hyderabad: Dā'irat al-Ma'ārif al-'Uthmānīya, 1974), 3:65–66; Tāj al-dīn al-Subkī, *Ṭabaqāt al-Shāfi'īya al-kubrā*, ed. Muṣṭafā 'Abd al-Qādir Aḥmad 'Aṭā (Beirut: Dār al-Kutub al-'Ilmīya, 1999/1420), 5:247–248.

14. E. Geoffroy, "Yāfi'ī," *Encyclopedia of Islam*, New Edition, vol. 11, (Leiden: Brill, 2002), 236a–b; al-Subkī, *Ṭabaqāt al-Shāfi'īya*, 5:246–247.

15. 'Abdallāh b. As'ab al-Yāfi'ī, *Mir'āt al-jinān* (Beirut: Dār al-Kutub al-'Ilmīya, 1997/1417), 4:231–246 and 249. On Iṣfahānī, see also al-Subkī, *Ṭabaqāt al-Shāfi'īya*, 5:274. Al-Subkī met Iṣfahānī and Maṭarī when he performed the hajj of 747. On Dhuhaybī, see also Abū Makhrama, *Tārīkh taghr 'Adan*, 198. On Ṭawāshī, see Muḥammad b. Aḥmad al-Fāsī, *al-'Iqd al-thamīn fī tārīkh al-balad al-āmīn* (Cairo: Maṭba'at al-Sunna al-Muḥammadīya, 1966), 5:108.

16. Stewart, *Islamic Legal Orthodoxy*, 103.

17. For the various religious institutions in Mecca at that time, see Mortel, "Madrasas in Mecca during the Medieval Period: A Descriptive Study Based on Literary Sources," *BSOAS* 60, 2 (1997): 236–252; and "*Ribāṭ*s in Mecca during the Medieval Period: A Descriptive Study Based on Literary

Sources," *BSOAS* 61, 1 (1998): 29–50. Mustawfī's description of the people of Mecca as mostly Ḥanafī is anomalous given the patronage of Shāfiʿism by the Mamlūks and the prevalence of Shīʿism in the local ruling house (Mustawfī, *The Geographical Part of the* Nuzhat al-Qulūb, 1–11).

18. Ḥusaynī, *Jāmiʿ al-ʿulūm*, 43 and 137.

19. C. E. Bosworth, "Legal and Political Sciences in the Eastern Iranian World and Central Asia in the Pre-Mongol Period," in *History of Civilizations of Central Asia: The Age of Achievement: Vol. 4: Part 1 - The Historical, Social and Economic Setting*, ed. M.S. Asimov and Clifford Edmund Bosworth (New Delhi: Motilal Banarsidass Publishers, 1999), 136.

20. Ḥusaynī, *Jāmiʿ al-ʿulūm*, 36.

21. Ḥusaynī, *Jāmiʿ al-ʿulūm*, 590.

22. Bhaṯṯī, *Khizānat al-fawāʾid al-Jalālīya*, 89a.

23. Bhaṯṯī, *Khizānat al-fawāʾid al-Jalālīya*, 258b.

24. Bhaṯṯī, *Khizānat al-fawāʾid al-Jalālīya*, 258b–259a.

25. Ḥusaynī, *Jāmiʿ al-ʿulūm*, 279 and 336.

26. Ḥusaynī, *Jāmiʿ al-ʿulūm*, 454.

27. Ibn Baṭṭūṭa, *Travels of Ibn Battuta*, 2:273–274. Gibb argues that Aḥmad Kūchak was Aḥmad al-Rifāʿī's great-great-grandson (Ibn Baṭṭūṭa, *Travels of Ibn Battuta*, 2:273–274 footnote 10).

28. Burhān al-dīn ʿAbdallāh Quṭb-i ʿālam, *Jāmiʿ al-ṭuruq*.

29. Ḥusaynī, *Jāmiʿ al-ʿulūm*, 420.

30. Bhaṯṯī, *Khizānat al-fawāʾid al-Jalālīya*, 16a.

31. See the various essays in Barbara D. Metcalf, ed., *Moral Conduct and Authority: The Place of Adab in South Asian Islam* (Berkeley: University of California Press, 1984).

32. Abū Makhrama makes no mention of this status and refers to Bukhārī as an imam (Abū Makhrama, *Tārīkh taghr ʿAdan*, 12, 58, 234). But some people were aware of Bukhārī being a sayyid since his hair was used by an old man in Mecca to make a *taʿwīẕ* (Ghaznawī, *Tuḥfat al-sarāʾir*, 13).

33. Ḥusaynī, *Jāmiʿ al-ʿulūm*, 35. See also Ḥusaynī, *Jāmiʿ al-ʿulūm*, 421–422, and Bhaṯṯī, *Khizānat al-fawāʾid al-Jalālīya*, 89a.

34. Mirzā Laʿl Bēg Badakhshī, *Ṣamarāt al-quds min shajarāt al-uns*, ed. Kamāl Hajj Sayyid Jawādī (Tehran: Pizhūhishgāh-i ʿUlūm-i Insānī wa Mutalaʿat-i Farhangī-yi Īrān, 1997), 695; *Sayr-nāma* (MS. Taṣawwuf 551, Andhra Pradesh Government Oriental Library, Hyderabad), 1–12; *Musāfir-nāma* (MS. Taṣawwuf 1826, Andhra Pradesh Government Oriental Library, Hyderabad), 1–10; Muḥammad Bukhārī, *Jawāhir al-awliyā*, 9, 222, 233, and 290.

35. The idea that someone with dark skin is unlikely to be a sayyid suggests that the South Asian Muslim community had a strong sense of the racial and color implications of claiming Arab descent.

36. Ḥusaynī, *Jāmiʿ al-ʿulūm*, 35.

37. Ḥusaynī, *Jāmiʿ al-ʿulūm*, 278–279.

38. Ḥusaynī, *Jāmiʿ al-ʿulūm*, 231 and 420.

39. Bhaṯṯī, *Khizānat al-fawāʾid al-Jalālīya*, 120a–b.

40. Ḥusaynī, *Jāmiʿ al-ʿulūm*, 559 and 335.

41. Ḥusaynī, *Jāmiʿ al-ʿulūm*, 559.

42. Ḥusaynī, *Jāmiʿ al-ʿulūm*, 22, 420; Burhān al-dīn ʿAbdallāh, *Jāmiʿ al-ṭuruq*; Niẓām Gharīb Yamanī, *Laṭāʾif-i Ashrafī fī bayān-i ṭawāʾif-i ṣūfī* (Delhi: Maṭbaʿ Nuṣrat al-Māṭābʿ-i Dihlī, [1880]).

43. *Tarjuma-yi khulāṣat al-mafākhir* (MS. I.O. Isl. 2271, British Library, London). See also Khuda Bakhsh Oriental Public Library, *Catalogue of the Arabic and Persian Manuscripts in the*

Khuda Bakhsh Oriental Public Library, vol. 8, Persian mss., *Biography, Romances, Tales and Anecdotes*, http://kblibrary.bih.nic.in/onlinecat.htm, 31–34, no. 670, accessed 7 July 2011; Wladimir Ivanow, *Descriptive Catalogue of the Persian Manuscripts in the Collection of the Asiatic Society of Bengal*, First Supplement, Bibliotheca Indica: 244 (Calcutta: Asiatic Society of Bengal, 1927), 67, no. 856; M. H. Qaisar Amrohvi and M. H. Razvi, *Catalogue of Manuscripts in the Maulana Azad Library: Ahsan Collection* (Aligarh: Maulana Azad Library, Aligarh Muslim University, 1983), 547, no. 920/37.

44. Quṭb al-dīn ʿAbdallāh b. Muḥammad b. Ayman al-Aṣfahīdī al-Dimashqī, *al-Risālat al-Makkīya fi khalwat al-ṣūfīya* or *fi ṭarīq al-sāda al-ṣūfīya* (MS. Del. Ar. 63/n. British Library, London; Persian translation, MS. T-121/8289, Punjab University, Lahore). See Carl Brockelmann, *Geschichte des Arabischen Literatur*, 2nd ed. (Leiden: Brill, 1943–1949), 2:227.

45. Ḥusaynī, *Jāmiʿ al-ʿulūm*, 464.

46. Ḥusaynī, *Jāmiʿ al-ʿulūm*, 463–464, and 486.

47. Quṭb al-dīn Dimashqī, *Risāla Makkīya*, Persian translation.

48. Ḥusaynī, *Jāmiʿ al-ʿulūm*, 578. The author's full name is Abū al-Qāsim al-Qāsim b. Firruh b. Khalaf al-Shāṭibī (d. 590/1194), not to be confused with the famous eighth-/fourteenth-century Andalusian Mālikī scholar, Abū Iṣḥāq al-Shāṭibī (Maria Eva Subtelny and Anas B. Khalidov, "The Curriculum of Islamic Higher Learning in Timurid Iran in the Light of the Sunni Revival under Shāh-Rukh," *Journal of the American Oriental Society* 115, 2 ([1995]: 228).

49. The *abdāl* (Ar. pl.: substitutes) are a fixed number of saints, usually given as forty, whose existence is necessary for the maintenance of the world. Their identities are hidden and when one dies another takes his or her place. Though human and (theoretically) mortal, their anonymity and wondrous abilities lend them an even greater supernatural air than most other saints have.

50. Bhaṯṯī, *Khizānat al-fawāʾid al-Jalālīya*, 243a–b.

51. Ḥusaynī, *Jāmiʿ al-ʿulūm*, 68.

52. Bhaṯṯī, *Khizānat al-fawāʾid al-Jalālīya*, 242b.

53. Ḥusaynī, *Jāmiʿ al-ʿulūm*, 27–28; *Sirāj al-hidāya*, 361.

54. Knysh, *Ibn ʿArabi*, 119.

55. Ḥusaynī, *Jāmiʿ al-ʿulūm*, 329.

56. Ḥusaynī, *Jāmiʿ al-ʿulūm*, 225–226, and 537. In relating this scene in 781/1380, Bukhārī adds that he has heard that prices in Mecca have gone down since his visit there. In the fourth/tenth century copyists were paid one dirham (silver coin) for each page copied (M. A. Beg, "Warrāḳ," *Encyclopaedia of Islam*, New Edition, vol. 11 [Leiden: Brill, 2002], 150a–151a).

57. Bhaṯṯī, *Khizānat al-fawāʾid al-Jalālīya*, 138; Ḥusaynī, *Jāmiʿ al-ʿulūm*, 423.

58. Ḥusaynī, *Jāmiʿ al-ʿulūm*, 278, 284, and 181–182; Bhaṯṯī, *Khizānat al-fawāʾid al-Jalālīya*, 220a, 228a; Ghaznawī, *Tuḥfat al-sarāʾir*, 18.

59. Mortel, "Madrasas in Mecca during the Medieval Period," 244–246, and 248–249.

60. Ḥusaynī, *Jāmiʿ al-ʿulūm*, 536; Bhaṯṯī, *Khizānat al-fawāʾid al-Jalālīya*, 261b.

61. Ḥusaynī, *Jāmiʿ al-ʿulūm*, 421, 578, 22, and 193; Burhān al-dīn ʿAbdallāh, *Jāmiʿ al-ṭuruq*, *khirqa* no. 7.21. In *Tuḥfat al-sarāʾir*, Bukhārī recounts that, before dying, Faqīh Baṣṣāl gave him a *khirqa* which was to be given to one of the Faqīh's sons, without specifying which one. Rukn al-dīn then appeared in a dream to say it should go to the youngest son (Ghaznawī, *Tuḥfat al-sarāʾir*, 27).

62. Abū Makhrama, *Tārīkh taghr ʿAdan*, 12, 58, and 234.

63. Ḥusaynī, *Jāmiʿ al-ʿulūm*, 22.

64. Bhaṯṯī, *Khizānat al-fawāʾid al-Jalālīya*, 261b; Burhān al-dīn ʿAbdallāh, *Jāmiʿ al-ṭuruq*, *khirqa* no. 7.22.

65. Abū Makhrama, *Tārīkh taghr 'Adan*, 21; Yāfi'ī, *Mir'āt al-jinān*, 4:94–98.

66. Ḥusaynī, *Jāmi' al-'ulūm*, 341.

67. Ḥusaynī, *Jāmi' al-'ulūm*, 530.

68. Ḥusaynī, *Jāmi' al-'ulūm*, 419.

69. Ḥusaynī, *Jāmi' al-'ulūm*, 35 and 419.

70. Ḥusaynī, *Jāmi' al-'ulūm*, 422.

71. Ibn Baṭṭūṭa followed the same path in the opposite direction in 732/1332 (Ibn Baṭṭūṭa, *Travels of Ibn Battuta*, 2: 409–411 and fig. 3).

72. Mustawfī, *The Geographical Part of the* Nuzhat al-Qulūb, 137–145. There are several towns by this name in modern Iran. Ibn Baṭṭūṭa also mentions a city named Shawānkāreh and Marco Polo lists Soncara as one of the "kingdoms" of Persia (Ibn Baṭṭūṭa, *Travels of Ibn Battuta*, 3:677–678; Marco Polo, *The Travels of Marco Polo*, ed. and trans. William Marsden and Manuel Komroff [New York: Modern Library, 2001], 35).

73. Ḥusaynī, *Jāmi' al-'ulūm*, 386, 422 and 530; Bhaṯṯī, *Khizānat al-fawā'id al-Jalālīya*, 44b, 254b and 259b. I have been unable to further identify this shaykh. Ibn Baṭṭūṭa met a Shaykh Sharaf al-dīn Mūsa b. Ṣadr al-dīn Sulaymān in Tustar in 727/1327 (Ibn Baṭṭūṭa, *Travels of Ibn Battuta*, 2:285).

74. Ibn Baṭṭūṭa, *Travels of Ibn Battuta*, 2:300–311.

75. Ḥusaynī, *Jāmi' al-'ulūm*, 323, and 457–458.

76. His (great-?) grandfather was Nāṣir al-dīn Samarqandī, author of *Nāfi,'* and the brother of Bukhārī's great-great-grandfather (Bhaṯṯī, *Khizānat al-fawā'id al-Jalālīya*, 293a). A Sayyid Ḥamīd al-dīn, perhaps the same individual, is also mentioned in *Risāla Makkīya Jalālīya*, attributed to Bukhārī (MS. Garret 12 W., Princeton University Library, Princeton, 1–3). Only a portion of this work survives and is mostly devoted to an explication of repentance. In the preface to the text, Bukhārī writes that he had traveled widely and met most of the *'ulamā'* and shaykhs of his time. He performed the pilgrimage to Mecca and there met a certain Sayyid Ḥamīd al-dīn, whom he calls a second Abū Ḥanīfa. Bukhārī goes on to explain that he was, as yet, no one's disciple because, although he was attached to the family of Bahā' al-dīn Zakarīyā through his father and grandfather, he had been unable to reach any shaykh of that line. But God finally gave him the means to reach the skirt of Shaykh Rukn al-dīn, grandson of Bahā' al-dīn. It is unclear whether this supports the *taẕkira* accounts that place Bukhārī's first pilgrimage before Rukn al-dīn's death in 735/1335 or whether the aforementioned Sayyid Ḥamīd al-dīn is the link to Rukn al-dīn.

77. Bhaṯṯī, *Khizānat al-fawā'id al-Jalālīya*, 260a, 261a, 264b, and 265b.

78. Ḥusaynī, *Jāmi' al-'ulūm*, 21, 422, and 530. According to Bukhārī's grandson, Burhān al-dīn 'Abdallāh, Qiwām al-dīn was the brother of Amīn al-dīn Kāzarūnī and had received Rukn al-dīn Abu al-Fatḥ's *khirqa* through him (Burhān al-dīn 'Abdallāh, *Jāmi' al-ṭuruq*, *khirqa* no. 7.8). However, there is no mention of this relationship in either *Khizānat al-fawā'id al-Jalālīya* or *Jāmi' al-'ulūm*. No doubt there is some confusion between Qiwām al-dīn, *khalīfa* of Rukn al-dīn, and Imām al-dīn, brother of Amīn al-dīn Balyānī Kāzarūnī.

79. 'Imād al-dīn Shaykh al-Ḥukamā'ī, Introduction to *Miftāḥ al-hidāya wa miṣbāḥ al-'ināya: Sīrat-nāma-yi shaykh Amīn al-dīn Muḥammad Balyānī* by Muḥammad b. 'Uṣmān (Tehran: Intishārāt-i Rawzana, 1376/1998), viii-ix.

80. J. Calmard, "Kāzarūn," *Encyclopaedia of Islam*, New Edition, vol. 4., (Leiden: Brill, 1978), 850b. For a discussion of the propagation of this idea, see al-Ḥukamā'ī, Introduction, ix–x.

81. Ḥusaynī, *Jāmi' al-'ulūm*, 416, 531; Bhaṯṯī, *Khizānat al-fawā'id al-Jalālīya*, 45a, 259a–b.

82. Ḥusaynī, *Jāmi' al-'ulūm*, 416, 531; Bhaṯṯī, *Khizānat al-fawā'id al-Jalālīya*, 45a, 259a–b.

83. al-Ḥukamā'ī, Introduction, x.

84. Mawlānā Nūr al-zamān Miṣbāḥī, *Taẕkira-i awliyā'-i Aḥmadābād* (Aḥmadābād: Nūr Academy, 1419/1998), 43 and 67–69. See also Muḥammad Naẕīr Aḥmad Na'īmī Murādābādī, *Ḥayāt-i ḥażrat Shāh-'ālam* (Aḥmadābād: Khānqāh-i Shāh-'ālam, 2009).

85. Burhān al-dīn 'Abdallāh, *Jāmi' al-ṭuruq*, *khirqa* no. 7.23.

86. Ḥusaynī, *Jāmi' al-'ulūm*, 22.

87. Ibn Baṭṭūṭa, *Travels of Ibn Battuta*, 2: 320–321.

88. Ḥusaynī, *Jāmi' al-'ulūm*, 164 and 319; Ghaznawī, *Tuḥfat al-sarā'ir*, 15.

89. For possible overland routes, see H. C. Verma, *Medieval Routes to India: Baghdad to Delhi: A Study of Trade and Military Routes* (Calcutta: Naya Prokash, 1978).

90. On Shams al-dīn Yaḥyā and Quṭb al-dīn Munawwar, see Sayyid Muḥammad b. Mubārak Kirmānī Mīr Khwurd, *Siyar al-awliyā,* Urdu trans. Ghulām Aḥmad Biryān and Ḥakīm Mahr Muḥammad Iqbāl Qādirī (Lahore: Mushtāq Book Corner, 1978), 327–340 and 354–366.

91. Ḥusaynī, *Jāmi' al-'ulūm*, 531.

92. Ḥusaynī, *Jāmi' al-'ulūm*, 425.

93. Burhān al-dīn 'Abdallāh, *Jāmi' al-ṭuruq*.

94. David N. Lorenzen, *Kabir Legends and Ananta-das's Kabir Parachai, With a Translation of the Kabir Parachai Prepared in Collaboration with Jagdish Kumar and Uma Thukral and with an Edition of the Niranjani Panthi Recension of This Work* (Albany: State University of New York Press, 1991), 69.

95. Peter Jackson, *The Delhi Sultanate*, 185 and 275–276; Baranī, *Tārīkh-i Fīrōz Shāhī*, 525.

96. Ḥusaynī, *Jāmi' al-'ulūm*, 279 and 336.

97. Nizami, English introduction to *Khayr al-majālis* by Ḥamīd Qalandar, 57 n. 2. Most of Nizami's sources on this point, however, are later than *Jāmi' al-'ulūm*.

98. Peter Jackson, *Delhi Sultanate*, 296–305.

99. Peter Jackson, *Delhi Sultanate*, 169.

100. Shams Sirāj 'Afīf, *Tārīkh-i Fīrōz Shāhī/The Tarikh-i-Firoz Shahi of Shams Siraj 'Afif*, ed. Wilāyat Ḥusayn, Bibliotheca Indica, vol. 119 (Calcutta: Asiatic Society of Bengal, 1891), 514–516.

101. Bhaṭṭī, *Khizānat al-fawā'id al-Jalālīya*, 255a; Ghaznawī, *Tuḥfat al-sarā'ir*, 31; Ḥusaynī, *Jāmi' al-'ulūm*, 36, and 280–281.

102. Bhaṭṭī, *Khizānat al-fawā'id al-Jalālīya*, 255a; Ghaznawī, *Tuḥfat al-sarā'ir*, 31; Ḥusaynī, *Jāmi' al-'ulūm*, 36, 280–281. The editor of *Jāmi' al-'ulūm* has interpreted this event as an indication that Bukhārī was in Medina at the time (Sarwar, *Muqaddama*, 10). However, from the parallel accounts in the other *malfūẓāt*, the reference to the *'ālam-i ṭayr*, and the need to be discreet in following the Shāfi'ī rule on funeral prayers, it is clear that Bukhārī's encounter with Maṭarī was a supernatural event that took place in Uch.

103. Ḥusaynī, *Jāmi' al-'ulūm*, 281.

104. Ḥusaynī, *Jāmi' al-'ulūm*, 36.

105. One indication of this sentiment with regard to the Chishtīya is *Hasht bihisht*, the extremely popular compilation of mostly retrospectively imagined *malfūẓāt*. It includes *malfūẓāt* of the first six Indian Chishtī saints up to Naṣīr al-dīn Maḥmūd Chirāgh-i Dihlī (*Hasht bihisht*, Urdu translation [Lahore: Shabīr Brothers, 2006]).

106. *Khizānat al-fawā'id al-Jalālīya* is a record of his teachings by a disciple who was with Bukhārī between 752/1351 and 767/1366. No mention is made in this text of any travels or significant activities on Bukhārī's part besides the instruction of his disciples. The only dates given are those contained in *waṣīyat-nāmas* (testaments or instructions) or *ijāzat-nāmas* (permits to teach or to pass on *khirqas*) to newly initiated or invested disciples. A certificate for Mawlānā Jamāl al-dīn Muḥammad b. Aḥmad b. Muḥammad b. Manṣūr al-Ma'barī (d. before 781/1379 and buried

in Delhi [Ḥusaynī, *Jāmiʿ al-ʿulūm*, 587]) is dated Wednesday 19 Rajab 767/1 April 1366. An *ijāzat-nāma*, dated Uch, Friday 24 Rajab 768/26 March 1367, was sent to Mawlānā Khwāja Qiwām al-dīn Muḥammad b. Ẓahīr al-dīn of Kara (near Benares), along with several letters of instruction. On 20 Jumādā I 769/12 January 1368, Shams al-dīn b. Naṣr-allāh b. Muḥammad al-Harawī of Kirmān, who had returned to Uch from a pilgrimage to Mecca and Medina, received a *shajara* (pedigree) for his *khirqa*. Finally, a certificate for Qāżī Shihāb al-dīn ʿAbd al-Rashīd b. Zayn al-dīn Ibrāhīm al-Farajī is dated Uch, 19 Shawwāl 770/27 May 1369. As all of these texts were written in Uch, it seems that Bukhārī cannot have left home for extended periods during these years (Bhaṯṯī, *Khizānat al-fawāʾid al-Jalālīya*, MS. 15427 (Kitābkhāna-yi Dātā Ganj Bakhsh, Islamabad), 264a–268a; MS. 2557 (Kitābkhāna-yi Dātā Ganj Bakhsh, Islamabad), 246a–255a; MS. I.O. Isl. 577 (British Library, London), 209b–218a; *Risāla fi lubs khirqat al-mashāʾikh al-ṣūfīya*, MS. 312 (d) (Government Oriental Manuscripts Library, Madras).

Three: Book-Learning and Islamic Law

1. For an overarching examination of *ʿilm* in Islamic society, see Franz Rosenthal, *Knowledge Triumphant: The Concept of Knowledge in Medieval Islam* (Boston: Brill, 2006).

2. Ḥusaynī, *Jāmiʿ al-ʿulūm*, 538. For various opinions on the relationship between *ʿilm* and *ʿamal*, most corresponding to Bukhārī's views, see Rosenthal, *Knowledge Triumphant*, 240–251.

3. Ḥusaynī, *Jāmiʿ al-ʿulūm*, 43. In another version of the same statement, Bukhārī replaces *awrād* with the practice of seclusion (*khalwat*) (Ḥusaynī, *Jāmiʿ al-ʿulūm*, 137).

4. For the process by which legal learning came to dominate the possible meanings of *ʿilm*, see C. Turner, "The Ubiquitous *Faqīh*: A Reconsideration of the Terms *Īmān*, *Islām* and *ʿIlm* and Their Role in the Rise to the Predominance of the Jurist in the Islamic World of Learning," *CMEIS Occasional Paper No. 54, February 1996* (Durham: University of Durham Centre for Middle Eastern and Islamic Studies, 1996).

5. Bhaṯṯī, *Khizānat al-fawāʾid al-Jalālīya*, 10b.

6. Bhaṯṯī, *Khizānat al-fawāʾid al-Jalālīya*, 19a.

7. Ḥusaynī, *Jāmiʿ al-ʿulūm*, 4–5.

8. Another of his *malfūẓāt*, *Khizāna-yi jawāhir-i Jalālīya,* is almost wholly devoted to such material (Fażlallāh b. Żiyāʾ al-ʿAbbāsī, *Khizāna-yi jawāhir-i Jalālīya* (MS. 5193, MS. 2463, and MS. 1749, Kitābkhāna-yi Dātā Ganj-bakhsh, Islamabad).

9. My identification of these works, totaling approximately 200, and my classification of them into broad topical categories are necessarily tentative and incomplete since Bukhārī and the compilers of his *malfūẓāt* used abbreviated titles for books and their authors.

10. Zafarul Islam, "Origin and Development."

11. William Smyth, "The Making of a Textbook," *Studia Islamica* 78 (1993): 99.

12. Paul L. Heck, "The Epistemological Problem of Writing in Islamic Civilization: al-Ḫaṭīb al-Baġdādī's (d. 463/1071) *Taqyīd al-ʿilm*," *Studia Islamica* 94 (2002): 85–114.

13. K. A. Nizami, "Development of the Muslim Educational System in Medieval India," *Islamic Culture* 70, 4 (October 1996): 35.

14. K. A. Nizami, *Some Aspects of Religion and Politics in India during the Thirteenth Century* (Bombay: Asia Publishing House, 1961), 151 footnote 1.

15. See Shahab Ahmed and Nenad Filipovic, "The Sultan's Syllabus: A Curriculum for the Ottoman Imperial *Madreses* Prescribed in a *Fermān* of Qānūnī I Süleymān, Dated 973 (1565)," *Studia Islamica* 98/99 (2004): 183–218; and Maria Eva Subtelny and Anas B. Khalidov, "The Curriculum of Islamic Higher Learning in Timurid Iran in the Light of the Sunni Revival under Shāh-Rukh," *Journal of the American Oriental Society* 115, 2 (1995): 210–236.

16. Ghaznawī, *Tuḥfat al-sarā'ir*, 14–15.

17. For example, Naṣīr al-dīn Maḥmūd quoted *Mashāriq al-anwār*, *al-Maṣābīḥ*, *al-Hidāya*, Qudūrī, Pazdawī, and *'Awārif al-ma'ārif* in his teachings (Nizami, English introduction to *Khayr al-majālis*, 9–10.)

18. Nizami, *Some Aspects of Religion*, 151 footnote 1.

19. Bhaṭṭī, *Khizānat al-fawā'id al-Jalālīya* (MS. I.O. Isl. 577, British Library, London), 218a–218b. For the sake of brevity I have removed many honorifics, prayers, and blessings from this extract.

20. Rukn al-dīn b. 'Imād al-dīn Kāshānī, *Shamā'il al-atqiyā*,' ed. Mawlawī Ḥakīm Ghulām Murtażā (Hyderabad: Ashraf Press, 1928).

21. Ernst, *Eternal Garden*, 75.

22. Muḥammad Mujīr b. Wajīh al-dīn, *Miftāḥ al-jinān* (MS. I.O. Isl. 927, British Library, London).

23. Other *malfūẓāt* with similar structures include *Durar-i niẓāmī*, devoted to the teachings of Niẓām al-dīn Awliyā,' and *Aḥsan al-aqwāl*, about Burhān al-dīn Gharīb (K. A. Nizami, "*Durar-i-Nizami*—A Unique but Less-known *Malfuz* of Shaikh Nizam-u'd-din Auliya," in *Historical Studies—Indian and Islamic*, vol. 1, *On Sources and Source Material* (New Delhi: Idarah-i Adabiyat-i Dilli, 1995), 48; Nizami, "*Ahsan-al-Aqwal*, a *Malfuz* of Shaikh Burhan-u'd-din Gharib," *Journal of the Pakistan Historical Society* (January 1955), reprinted in *Historical Studies*, 72; Ernst, *Eternal Garden*, 73–74.)

24. *Sirāj al-hidāya*, 18.

25. *Sirāj al-hidāya*, 19.

26. Ernst, *Eternal Garden*, 251–263.

27. Muḥammad Mujīr, *Miftāḥ al-jinān*, 2a-2b.

28. William A. Graham, "Traditionalism in Islam: An Essay in Interpretation," *Journal of Interdisciplinary History* 23, no. 3 (Winter 1993): 500.

29. Jonathan Culler, "Presupposition and Intertextuality," *MLN: Modern Languages Notes* 91, 6 (December 1976): 1382.

30. Ernst, "The Interpretation of the Classical Sufi Tradition in India: The *Shamā'il al-atqiyā'* of Rukn al-Dīn Kāshānī," *Sufi* 22 (Summer 1994): 6.

31. Ḥusayn, editor's introduction to *Sirāj al-hidāya*.

32. Muhammad Khalid Masud, Brinkley Messick, and David S. Powers, "Muftis, Fatwas, and Islamic Legal Interpretation," in *Islamic Legal Interpretation: Muftis and Their Fatwas*, ed. Masud, Messick, and Powers (Cambridge: Harvard University Press, 1996), 11. For an overview of South Asian *fiqh* texts, see Muḥammad Isḥāq Bhaṭṭī, *Barr-i ṣaghīr Pāk-ō-Hind meṉ 'ilm-i fiqh* (Lahore: Idāra-yi Ṣaqāfat-i Islāmīya, 1973).

33. Zafarul Islam, "Origin and Development" and "Works of Legal Nature."

34. Alan M. Guenther, "Hanafi *Fiqh* in Mughal India: The *Fatāwā-i 'Ālamgīrī*," in *India's Islamic Traditions, 711–1750*, ed. Richard M. Eaton (New Delhi: Oxford University Press, 2003), 215.

35. Ṣadr al-dīn Ya'qūb Muẓẓafar Karāmī, *Fiqh-i Fīrōz Shāhī* (MS. I.O. Isl. 2987, British Library, London). For a discussion of the legal contents of this text, see Zafarul Islam, "Origin and Development," 233–239.

36. The ongoing tradition of citation and commentary on a fairly stable body of legal texts is made apparent by the list of works used by the famous seventeenth-century legal text *Fatāwā-i 'Ālamgīrī* (Mujīb Allāh Nadwī, *Fatāwā-i 'Ālamgīrī kē mu'allifīn* [Lahore: Markaz-i Taḥqīq-i Dayāl Singh Trust Library, 1407/1987], 14–18).

37. Another very interesting example of the collapse of the distinction between *fatāwā* compilation, Sufi writing, and other Islamic genres is *Fawā'id-i Fīrōz Shāhī*, composed by Sharaf al-dīn

b. Muḥammad al-ʿAṭāʾī (MS. Or. 11,322, British Library, London; Zafarul Islam, "Works of Legal Nature," 332–333.). Though often discussed in the same terms as *Fiqh-i Fīrōz Shāhī* (and sometimes confused with it), *Fawāʾid-i Fīrōz Shāhī* is a great deal more than the "legal compendium" it is described as. Beyond providing legal rulings on all the standard topics of *fatāwā* compilation, such as juridical processes, commercial transactions, criminal liabilities, ritual requirements, etc., it addresses a much wider variety of topics. These include a description of appropriate behaviors that ranges from strictly ethical concerns to piety, manners, and customs. Thus, opinions on the legality of different foods are combined with information on the blessings accrued from the angels because of the presence of certain comestibles (e.g., olives, honey, and coriander seed) in one's house. This is followed by a discussion of hospitality, feasting, manners of hosts and guests, and the virtues of particular dishes. Different kinds of games and pastimes, clothing, and medical information are all described and chapters are devoted to the stations of the Sufi path and the relationship between Sufi masters and their disciples. In accordance with its wide range of topics, *Fawāʾid-i Fīrōz Shāhī* draws upon legal texts, Sufi handbooks, and other works such as the ethical treatise *Akhlāq-i Nāṣirī*.

38. Bhaṯṯī, *Khizānat al-fawāʾid al-Jalālīya* (MS. I.O. Isl. 577, British Library, London), 1b.

39. Abū Makhrama, *Tārīkh taghr ʿAdan*, 12, 58, 234.

40. ʿAfīf, *Tārīkh-i Fīrōz Shāhī*, 514–516.

41. Nizami, *The Life and Times of Shaikh Nasir-u'd-din*, 8.

42. Welch, "A Medieval Center of Learning: The Hauz Khas Madrasa in Delhi," *Muqarnas* 13 (1996): 165–190.

43. Bhaṯṯī, *Khizānat al-fawāʾid al-Jalālīya*, 16b.

44. Ḥusaynī, *Jāmiʿ al-ʿulūm*, 194 and 493. It is not necessary to have all the ʿulama as disciples; some well-respected ones will do.

45. Bhaṯṯī, *Khizānat al-fawāʾid al-Jalālīya*, 16a.

46. Sharaf al-dīn Manērī, *Maktūbāt-i dō ṣadī*, Urdu trans. Ḥakīm Sayyid Shāh Qasīm al-dīn Aḥmad Sharafī Firdawsī and Sayyid Shah Muḥammad Sayf al-dīn Firdawsī (Lahore: Seerat Foundation, 2003), 38 and 153–155.

47. Manērī, *Maktūbāt-i dō ṣadī*, 588.

48. Manērī, *Maktūbāt-i dō ṣadī*, 32 and 555.

49. Manērī, *Maktūbāt-i dō ṣadī*, 38.

50. Manērī, *Maktūbāt-i dō ṣadī*, 518.

51. Manērī, *Maktūbāt-i dō ṣadī*, 555 and 586.

52. Manērī, *Maktūbāt-i dō ṣadī*, 153–154.

53. Manērī, *Maktūbāt-i dō ṣadī*, 65, 117 and 588.

54. Manērī, *Maktūbāt-i dō ṣadī*, 32–35.

55. Ḥusaynī, *Jāmiʿ al-ʿulūm*, 164 and 319; Ghaznawī, *Tuḥfat al-sarāʾir*, 15. Alor was another ancient town not far from Bhakkar. See "Aror" in *Imperial Gazetteer of India*, New Edition (Oxford: Clarendon Press, 1908), 6:4.

56. Ḥusaynī, *Jāmiʿ al-ʿulūm*, 357.

57. Ghaznawī, *Tuḥfat al-sarāʾir*, 16.

58. See Carl Ernst, *Words of Ecstasy in Sufism* (Albany: State University of New York Press, 1984).

59. Ḥusaynī, *Jāmiʿ al-ʿulūm*, 65.

60. In South Asia such groups are known as *qalandars*, *malangs*, *ḥaydarīs*, and *jalālīs*. See Simon Digby, "Qalandars and Related Groups: Elements of Social Deviance in the Religious Life of the Delhi Sultanate of the Thirteenth and Fourteenth Centuries," in *Islam in Asia*, vol. 1, *South Asia*, ed. Yohannan Friedmann (Boulder: Westview Press, 1984); and Ahmet T. Karamustafa, *God's Unruly Friends: Dervish Groups in the Islamic Later Middle Period, 1200–1550* (Salt Lake City: The University of Utah Press, 1994).

61. Ḥusaynī, *Jāmi' al-'ulūm*, 454; Bhaṯṯī, *Khizānat al-fawā'id al-Jalālīya*, 262b–263a.

62. Paul Jackson, *The Way of a Sufi*, 137–140, and Paul Jackson, introduction to *Sharafuddin Maneri: The Hundred Letters* (New York: Paulist Press, 1980), 3; Sayyid Muṭī' al-imām, *Shaykh Sharaf al-dīn*, 147; Rizvi, *A History of Sufism in India*, 1:231.

63. *Muqarrar-nāma* or *Naṣā'iḥ-i makhdūm-i jahāniyān* (MS. 1089, Arabic and Persian, Government Oriental Manuscripts Library, Madras). This text is addressed to Tāj al-dīn Aḥmad Mu'īn Siyāh-pōsh 'Alawī, a resident of Sultānpūr, near Delhi. He had requested some words from "Makhdūm-i jahāniyān Jahāngīr" and received these pages on the first of Rajab 776/Wednesday 6 December 1374 through the good offices of Mawlānā 'Izz al-dīn. The work is divided into short sections, each beginning *muqarrar farzandī bād* (My son, it is certain).

64. *Muqarrar-nāma*, 7 and 42.

65. Bhaṯṯī, *Khizānat al-fawā'id al-Jalālīya*, 12b–13a.

66. Bhaṯṯī, *Khizānat al-fawā'id al-Jalālīya*, 16a.

67. *Muqarrar-nāma*, 43.

68. *Muqarrar-nāma*, 14.

Four: Ritual and Practice

1. Ḥusaynī, *Jāmi' al-'ulūm*, 8.

2. Bhaṯṯī, *Khizānat al-fawā'id al-Jalālīya*, 56a. Following Bukhārī's example, I use the term *darwēsh* rather than "mystic" or "Sufi" to refer to those participating in the Sufi way of life. The other terms commonly used by Bukhārī were *faqīr* (poor) and *sālik* (wayfarer).

3. Ḥusaynī, *Jāmi' al-'ulūm*, 225.

4. Ḥusaynī, *Jāmi' al-'ulūm*, 199 and 213.

5. Ḥusaynī, *Jāmi' al-'ulūm*, 213.

6. Bhaṯṯī, *Khizānat al-fawā'id al-Jalālīya*, 45a–47a.

7. Bhaṯṯī, *Khizānat al-fawā'id al-Jalālīya*, 45a–47a. In *Laṭā'if-i Ashrafī*, Ashraf Jahāngīr Simnānī describes Bukhārī inculcating the *ẕikr* by touching his head to the initiate's head and saying the creed in a loud voice and a single breath, while prolonging it to such an extent that his companions lost their breath (Yamanī, *Laṭā'if-i Ashrafī*, 294). This passage is identical, however, to an account of Ṣadr al-dīn 'Ārif's method of implanting the *ẕikr* in *Khizānat al-fawā'id al-Jalālīya* (Bhaṯṯī, 45b). Simnānī also credited Bukhārī with teaching him the *mashrab-i shaṭṭār*, apparently an explanation of *ẕikr* based on letter symbolism (Yamanī, *Laṭā'if-i Ashrafī*, 298). It is unclear how this might relate to the Shaṭṭārī order which was not introduced into South Asia until the ninth/fifteenth century (Rizvi, *A History of Sufism in India*, 2:150–173). Bukhārī's *malfūẓāt* make no mention of the Shaṭṭārī order nor of its methods of *ẕikr*.

8. Ḥusaynī, *Jāmi' al-'ulūm*, 212.

9. Ḥusaynī, *Jāmi' al-'ulūm*, 199.

10. Ḥusaynī, *Jāmi' al-'ulūm*, 181, 199, and 225.

11. Ḥusaynī, *Jāmi' al-'ulūm*, 203.

12. Ḥusaynī, *Jāmi' al-'ulūm*, 199.

13. Ḥusaynī, *Jāmi' al-'ulūm*, 179.

14. Ghaznawī, *Tuḥfat al-sarā'ir*, 7–8.

15. Ḥusaynī, *Jāmi' al-'ulūm*, 178.

16. Ḥusaynī, *Jāmi' al-'ulūm*, 159.

17. Ghaznawī, *Tuḥfat al-sarā'ir*, 7–8; *Sirāj al-hidāya*, 168.

18. Ḥusaynī, *Jāmi' al-'ulūm*, 178.

19. Ernst and Lawrence, *Sufi Martyrs of Love*, 34–46.

20. Leonard Lewisohn, "The Sacred Music of Islam: Samāʿ in the Persian Sufi Tradition," *British Journal of Ethnomusicology* 6 (1997): 1–33; Arthur Gribetz, "The *Samāʿ* Controversy: Sufi vs. Legalist," *Studia Islamica* 74 (1991): 43–62.

21. Lewisohn, "The Sacred Music of Islam," 8.

22. Iqtidar Husain Khan, "The *Pīr* and *Murīd*: A Case Study of the *Ṣūfīs* of Suhrawardī *Silsilah* in India during the Thirteenth and Fourteenth Centuries," *Hamdard Islamicus* 21 (1998): 26.

23. Ḥusaynī, *Jāmiʿ al-ʿulūm*, 220.

24. Abū Ḥāmid al-Ghazālī, *Al-Ghazālī's Path to Sufism and His Deliverance from Error: An Annotated Translation of Al Munqidh min al-Dalāl*, trans. R. J. McCarthy (Louisville: Fons Vitae, 2000), 52 and 57.

25. Ḥusaynī, *Jāmiʿ al-ʿulūm*, 361.

26. Yamanī, *Laṭā'if-i Ashrafī*, 392.

27. Furthermore, Rizvi points out that *Laṭā'if-i Ashrafī* is not necessarily always the most reliable of sources (Rizvi, *A History of Sufism in India*, 1: 266–267).

28. Ḥusaynī, *Jāmiʿ al-ʿulūm*, 228.

29. Digby, "Qalandars and Related Groups"; Karamustafa, *God's Unruly Friends*.

30. Ḥusaynī, *Jāmiʿ al-ʿulūm*, 153 and 361.

31. Ḥusaynī, *Jāmiʿ al-ʿulūm*, 180.

32. Ḥusaynī, *Jāmiʿ al-ʿulūm*, 383.

33. Ḥusaynī, *Jāmiʿ al-ʿulūm*, 35 and 421–422; Bhaṯṯī, *Khizānat al-fawā'id al-Jalālīya*, 89a.

34. Ḥusaynī, *Jāmiʿ al-ʿulūm*, 335–336, 192, 420, 35, 278–279, 36, and 280–281; Bhaṯṯī, *Khizānat al-fawā'id al-Jalālīya*, 255a; Ghaznawī, *Tuḥfat al-sarā'ir*, 31.

35. Ḥusaynī, *Jāmiʿ al-ʿulūm*, 55.

36. Ḥusaynī, *Jāmiʿ al-ʿulūm*, 55.

37. Ghaznawī, *Tuḥfat al-sarā'ir*, 45–46.

38. Ghaznawī, *Tuḥfat al-sarā'ir*, 25–26.

39. Ghaznawī, *Tuḥfat al-sarā'ir*, 11 and 32.

40. Michael Sells, *Early Islamic Mysticism: Sufi, Qur'an, Miʿraj, Poetic and Theological Writings* (New York: Paulist Press, 1996), 151.

41. Manērī, *Maktūbāt-i dō ṣadī*, 305–306.

42. Ghaznawī, *Tuḥfat al-sarā'ir*, 27.

43. Ḥusaynī, *Jāmiʿ al-ʿulūm*, 280.

44. Bhaṯṯī, *Khizānat al-fawā'id al-Jalālīya*, 236b–237b.

45. Ghaznawī, *Tuḥfat al-sarā'ir*, 51; Ḥusaynī, *Jāmiʿ al-ʿulūm*, 580.

46. Ḥusaynī, *Jāmiʿ al-ʿulūm*, 8 and 138–140.

47. Bhaṯṯī, *Khizānat al-fawā'id al-Jalālīya*, 285a–288b, 311b, 335b and 341a.

48. Bhaṯṯī, *Khizānat al-fawā'id al-Jalālīya*, 314b, 334b, 335b, 339a, 340b and 343b.

49. Richard Bulliet suggests that the Sufis achieved their monopoly on amulet making in the thirteenth and fourteenth centuries, a change from an earlier period when amulets were produced by other segments of society. Earlier amulets were sometimes block printed but this was incompatible with the transference of blessing achieved by the handwriting of a saint (Richard W. Bulliet, "Medieval Arabic *Tarsh*: A Forgotten Chapter in the History of Printing," *Journal of the American Oriental Society* 107, 3 [1987]: 438–439).

50. Bhaṯṯī, *Khizānat al-fawā'id al-Jalālīya*, 335a.

51. For the construction and history of these arrangements of numbers, which were credited with magical and divinatory powers from the seventh/thirteenth century onward, see J. Sesiano, "Wafḳ," *Encyclopedia of Islam*, New Edition (Leiden: Brill, 2002), 11:28a–31a; and Schuyler Cam-

mann, "Islamic and Indian Magic Squares. Part 1," *History of Religions* 8, 3 (1969): 181–209, and "Islamic and Indian Magic Squares. Part 2," *History of Religions* 8, 4 (1969): 271–299.

52. The use of letters, symbols, and magic squares in protective amulets or talismans is by no means unique to this context. Similar objects were used by various communities of the Near East as well as in Byzantine culture. For a sweeping, and dated, overview of the topic, see Sir E. A. Wallis Budge, *Amulets and Talismans* (New Hyde Park: University Books, 1961).

53. Ghaznawī, *Tuḥfat al-sarā'ir*, 13.

54. Bhaṯṯī, *Khizānat al-fawā'id al-Jalālīya*, 338b, 292a, and 293a.

55. Bhaṯṯī, *Khizānat al-fawā'id al-Jalālīya*, 260a–b.

56. Ghaznawī, *Tuḥfat al-sarā'ir*, 10.

57. For Bahā' al-dīn's instructions for several prayers see Huda, *Striving for Divine Union*, 157–164 and 173–178.

58. James Robson, "The Magical Use of the Koran," *Transactions of the Glasgow University Oriental Society* 6 (1929–1933): 51–61.

59. Nizami, "Some Aspects of Khānqāh Life," 63.

60. Muḥammad Bukhārī, *Jawāhir al-awliyā'.*

61. Constance E. Padwick, *Muslim Devotions: A Study of Prayer-Manuals in Common Use* (London: S.P.C.K, 1961).

62. Padwick, *Muslim Devotions*, 23, 25, 96, 106, 110, and 113.

63. Padwick, *Muslim Devotions*, 76, 96, and 97.

64. Padwick, *Muslim Devotions*, 25, 110, and 113.

65. A. J. Arberry, *Sufism: An Account of the Mystics of Islam* (London: Allen and Unwin, 1950), 120–121.

66. Bulliet, "Medieval Arabic *Tarsh*," 438.

67. For examples, see Gerhard Böwering, "Règles et rituels soufis," in *Les Voies D'Allah,* ed. Alexandre Popovic and Gilles Veinstein (Paris: Fayard 1996), 152–156; Ernst, *The Shambala Guide to Sufism*, 143.

68. The *tazkira* texts list many disciples (*murīds*) of Bukhārī and indicate that his brother, Sayyid Ṣadr al-dīn Rāju-qattāl, was his *khalīfa*, or primary successor. Bukhārī himself hardly ever referred to anyone as his *murīd* or *khalīfa*. Rather, he preferred familial terms, such as brother/sister or son/daughter, because he did not view himself as having the kind of authority necessary to take on a *murīd*. "I accept the old in brotherhood, and the young as sons. I am not a shaykh, I am a representative (*wakīl*)" (Ḥusaynī, *Jāmi' al-'ulūm*, 568–569).

69. As a rule, Bukhārī disapproved of shaving the head, especially the eyebrows, as well as other modes of extreme appearance modification, such as wearing leather or iron chains, favored by *qalandar*s and *ḥaydarī*s.

70. Bhaṯṯī, *Khizānat al-fawā'id al-Jalālīya*, 262b–263a.

71. "Bay'a," *Encyclopaedia of Islam*, New Edition, vol. 1 (Leiden: Brill, 1960), 1113.

72. G. G. Arnakis, "Futuwwa Traditions in the Ottoman Empire: Akhis, Bektashi Dervishes and Craftsmen," *Journal of Near Eastern Studies* 12, 4 (October 1953): 240. Gibb suggests that the haircut is a reference to the Quranic (96:16) description of the forelock as "lying, sinful" (*Travels of Ibn Battuta*, 2:286, footnote 56).

73. Ḥamīd Qalandar, *Khayr al-majālis*, 134.

74. J. L. Austin, *How to Do Things with Words* (Cambridge : Harvard University Press, 1962).

75. Frits Staal, "From Meanings to Trees," *Journal of Ritual Studies* 7, 2 (Fall 1993): 14–15. See also Staal, "The Meaninglessness of Ritual," *Numen* 26, 1 (June 1979): 2–22.

76. Ḥusaynī, *Jāmi' al-'ulūm*, 426.

77. See my essay on "Ritual," in *Key Themes for the Study of Islam*, ed. Jamal J. Elias (Oxford: Oneworld Publications, 2010), 304–320.

78. Manērī, *The Hundred Letters*, 33.

79. Yamanī, *Laṭā'if-i Ashrafī*, 324. This is also the view of Burhān al-dīn Gharīb (Kāshānī, *Shamā'il al-atqiyā*,' MS. I.O. Isl. 1322, British Library, London, 27b).

80. 'Umar b. Muḥammad Shihāb al-dīn Suhrawardī, *'Awārif al-ma'ārif*, Urdu trans. Sayyid Rashid Aḥmad Arshad (Lahore: Asad Publications, 1973), 135.

81. Ḥusaynī, *Jāmi' al-'ulūm*, 426–427.

82. Yamanī, *Laṭā'if-i Ashrafī*, 324.

83. Najm al-dīn Kubrā, *La Pratique du Soufisme: Quatorze petits traités*, French trans. Paul Ballanfat (Nimes: Éditions de l'éclat, 2002), 238–9. Shihāb al-dīn Suhrawardī also cited the story of Umm Khālid as the Prophetic basis for investiture (Ohlander, *Sufism in an Age of Transition*, 210). Manērī goes further and traces the practice of investiture back to Adam, who dressed his son Seth in a garment of leaves, and to Shu'ayb, who gave Moses a blanket (Manērī, *The Hundred Letters*, 90–91).

84. Kubrā, *La Pratique du Soufisme*, 237–244.

85. Kubrā, *La Pratique du Soufisme*, 239.

86. Ḥusaynī, *Jāmi' al-'ulūm*, 173.

87. Bhaṯṯī, *Khizānat al-fawā'id al-Jalālīya*, 260a.

88. Ghaznawī, *Tuḥfat al-sarā'ir*, 25.

89. Ḥusaynī, *Jāmi' al-'ulūm*, 350.

90. Bhaṯṯī, *Khizānat al-fawā'id al-Jalālīya*, 230b; *Sirāj al-hidāya*, 122–123. For similar lists see Gerhard Böwering, "The *Adab* Literature of Classical Sufism: Ansari's Code of Conduct," in *Moral Conduct and Authority*, ed. B. D. Metcalf (Berkeley: University of California Press, 1984), 62–87; and Elias, "The Sufi Robe (*Khirqa*) as a Vehicle of Spiritual Authority," 275–290.

91. Bhaṯṯī, *Khizānat al-fawā'id al-Jalālīya*, 231a.

92. Ibn Baṭṭūṭa, *Travels of Ibn Battuta*, 2:297.

93. Bhaṯṯī, *Khizānat al-fawā'id al-Jalālīya*, 230a.

94. Ḥusaynī, *Jāmi' al-'ulūm*, 560.

95. Bhaṯṯī, *Khizānat al-fawā'id al-Jalālīya*, 229b. It is interesting to note that in Bukhārī's conversation with Naṣīr al-dīn Maḥmūd Awadhī, discussed in Chapter 1, the *kulāh* was a sign of *not* being a *darwēsh* and is contrasted with *libās-i darwēshān* (the clothes of the *darwēsh*es).

96. Ḥusaynī, *Jāmi' al-'ulūm*, 18.

97. Ḥusaynī, *Jāmi' al-'ulūm*, 40, 173, and 350.

98. Ḥusaynī, *Jāmi' al-'ulūm*, 22.

99. Bhaṯṯī, *Khizānat al-fawā'id al-Jalālīya*, 257a–b.

100. Ḥusaynī, *Jāmi' al-'ulūm*, 21–22, 425, 583.

101. Ernst states that the *khirqa-yi tabarruk* is "available to those who are not at the point of becoming disciples but who are drawn to Sufism," i.e., for those at a lower stage on the spiritual path (Ernst, *The Shambala Guide to Sufism*, 144). However, we know that Bukhārī received many cloaks of blessing after being his father's disciple and at a point in his life when he was well along in his career as a Sufi. He also bestowed such *khirqa*s on people who had already been initiated by someone else. Thus the *khirqa-yi tabarruk* is for those who are not yet *murīd*s and for those who are already someone else's *murīd*s.

102. Bhaṯṯī, *Khizānat al-fawā'id al-Jalālīya*, 256b. That shaykhs were sometimes forced to bestow *khirqa*s suggests the value placed on the possession of a *khirqa* and the vulnerability of Sufi shaykhs to external pressure, perhaps social or economic, or even the threat of physical violence.

103. Ḥusaynī, *Jāmi' al-'ulūm*, 520.

Five: Money, Non-Muslims, Women, and Saints

1. Nizami, *Some Aspects of Religion*, 244–257.
2. Ḥusaynī, *Jāmi' al-'ulūm*, 327.
3. Bhaṯṯī, *Khizānat al-fawā'id al-Jalālīya*, 239a.
4. Ḥusaynī, *Jāmi' al-'ulūm*, 462.
5. Bhaṯṯī, *Khizānat al-fawā'id al-Jalālīya*, 240a.
6. Ḥusaynī, *Jāmi' al-'ulūm*, 426.
7. *Sirāj al-hidāya*, 111–112. Also quoted and translated in Nizami, *Some Aspects of Religion*, 250–251.
8. *Sirāj al-hidāya*, 262.
9. Ḥusaynī, *Jāmi' al-'ulūm*, 566, and 251–252.
10. Ḥusaynī, *Jāmi' al-'ulūm*, 370, 566, and 258; Ghaznawī, *Tuḥfat al-sarā'ir*, 17.
11. Ḥusaynī, *Jāmi' al-'ulūm*, 201, 204.
12. Bhaṯṯī, *Khizānat al-fawā'id al-Jalālīya*, 239a–b.
13. Bhaṯṯī, *Khizānat al-fawā'id al-Jalālīya*, 238a.
14. Bhaṯṯī, *Khizānat al-fawā'id al-Jalālīya*, 242a. For descriptions of the financial bases and personnel of Egyptian Sufi institutions of the same time period, see Leonor Fernandes, *The Evolution of a Sufi Institution in Mamluk Egypt: The Khanqah*, Islamkundliche Untersuchungen Band 134 (Berlin: Klaus Schwarz Verlag, 1988). On *khānqāhs* in Iran, see Muḥsin Kīyānī, *Tārīkh-i khānqāh dar Īrān* (Tehrān: Kitābkhāna-yi Ṭaḥūrī, 1369/1990).
15. Bhaṯṯī, *Khizānat al-fawā'id al-Jalālīya*, 240a–b.
16. Ḥusaynī, *Jāmi' al-'ulūm*, 566.
17. Riazul Islam, "Ideas on *kasb* in South Asian Sufism (mainly Fourteenth Century)," *The Indian Historical Review* 17, 1–2 (1997) 90–98.
18. *Sirāj al-hidāya*, 51.
19. Riazul Islam, "Ideas on *kasb*," 106–107.
20. Ḥusaynī, *Jāmi' al-'ulūm*, 303.
21. *Sirāj al-hidāya*, 107.
22. Ḥusaynī, *Jāmi' al-'ulūm*, 54.
23. Ghaznawī, *Tuḥfat al-sarā'ir*, 6.
24. Ḥusaynī, *Jāmi' al-'ulūm*, 585 and 360.
25. Ghaznawī, *Tuḥfat al-sarā'ir*, 49.
26. Ḥusaynī, *Jāmi' al-'ulūm*, 191–192.
27. Ḥusaynī, *Jāmi' al-'ulūm*, 15.
28. *Waẓīfa* can also mean a "devotional text or litany," part of the daily Sufi routine, but this does not appear to be its meaning in this case (T. De Jong, "Waẓīfa," *Encyclopedia of Islam*, New Edition, vol. 11 [Leiden: Brill, 2002], 184a–185b).
29. Ḥusaynī, *Jāmi' al-'ulūm*, 174 and 194.
30. Ḥusaynī, *Jāmi' al-'ulūm*, 15, 134, 137, 194, 314, 458, 579 and 585–586.
31. Ḥusaynī, *Jāmi' al-'ulūm*, 584.
32. It is only in later texts such as *Qaṣr-i 'ārifān*, completed in 1291/1874, that he is referred to as Uchchī (Aḥmad 'Alī Chishtī, *Qaṣr-i 'ārifān*, Urdu trans. Iqbāl Aḥmad Fārūqī [Lahore: Maktaba-yi Maẓhar-i Fayż Rižā, 1407/1977], 154).
33. First-generation immigrants were known by their place of origin, e.g., Mu'īn al-dīn *Sijzī*, Bakhtiyār Kākī *Ūshī*, Ashraf Jahāngīr *Simnānī*, but later generations were often given the names of their Indian homes: Rukn al-dīn *Multānī*, Naṣīr al-dīn Maḥmūd *Awadhī*, Yaḥyā *Manērī*. But

rather than Uch renaming the Bukhārī family, it was the city that took on their name so that even today a portion of the town is known as Uch Bukhāriyān̲.

34. Ḥusaynī, *Jāmi' al-'ulūm*, 584. For comments on this legend and its role in the Islamic sacralization of India, see Ernst, *Eternal Garden*, 28–29.

35. Abu Makhrama, *Tārīkh taghr 'Adan*, 58.

36. Ghaznawī, *Tuḥfat al-sarā'ir*, 18.

37. Richard M. Eaton, *The Rise of Islam and the Bengal Frontier* (Berkeley: University of California Press, 1993), 113–134.

38. H. A. Rose, *A Glossary of the Tribes and Castes of the Punjab and North-West Frontier Province*, 3 vols. (1883; reprint, Patiala: Languages Department Punjab, 1970).

39. Rose, *Glossary of the Tribes*, 1:533, 3:173, and 2:496.

40. Rose, *Glossary of the Tribes*, 2:498, 3:130, 3:173, 2:153, 2:103, 2:158, and 2:283.

41. One approach to this type of information is modeled by Eaton's examination of the claims of various Jatt clans to have been converted by Farīd al-dīn Mas'ūd. Following Richard Bulliet's approach to conversion in Iran, Eaton used changes in the prevalence of Muslim names in genealogies to date the actual period of Islamization of particular tribes. Finding this to be centuries after the death of Farīd al-dīn, Eaton "hypothesize[s] that the agent of the clans' conversion, instead of Bābā Farīd himself, was the shrine of Bābā Farīd as a highly complex religious and social institution" (Richard M. Eaton, "The Political and Religious Authority of the Shrine of Bābā Farīd," in *Moral Conduct and Authority*, ed. Barbara Metcalf [Berkeley: University of California Press, 1984], 346).

42. Ḥusaynī, *Jāmi' al-'ulūm*, 563, 546.

43. Ghaznawī, *Tuḥfat al-sarā'ir*, 18.

44. Ḥusaynī, *Jāmi' al-'ulūm*, 560.

45. Ḥusaynī, *Jāmi' al-'ulūm*, 108; Ghaznawī, *Tuḥfat al-sarā'ir*, 44.

46. Richard M. Eaton, "Sufi Folk Literature and the Expansion of Indian Islam," *History of Religions* 14 (1974): 117–127.

47. See Amrit Rai, *A House Divided: The Origin and Development of Hindi / Hindavi* (Delhi: Oxford University Press, 1984), especially 130–171.

48. *Sirāj al-hidāya*, 205–206.

49. *Sirāj al-hidāya*, ed. Ḥusayn, 381; MS. 430 (333), Arabic and Persian, Government Oriental Manuscripts Library, Madras, 219b; MS. I.O. Isl. 1038, British Library, London, 130a.

50. For the history of Hindawī, see Rai, *A House Divided.* On Siraiki, see Christopher Shackle, "Siraiki: A Language Movement in Pakistan," *Modern Asian Studies* 11, 3 (1977): 379–403; and George Grierson, "Indo-Aryan Vernaculars" *Bulletin of the School of Oriental Studies*, 1, 2 (1918): 47–81, where "Lahndā" is the term used for the language and dialects of the Uch and Multan regions.

51. Ḥusaynī, *Jāmi' al-'ulūm*, 426–427.

52. Ḥusaynī, *Jāmi' al-'ulūm*, 558. Fīrōz Shāh is known as one of the more bigoted or pious—depending on one's viewpoint—Sultans of Delhi.

53. Jamālī, *Siyar al-'ārifīn*, 231–232. Rājū-qattāl was also one of the nicknames of the Chishtī saint Gīsūdarāz Sayyid Muḥammad Ḥusaynī (1321–1422), a *khalīfa* of Naṣīr al-dīn Maḥmūd Chirāgh-i Dihlī.

54. Jamālī, *Siyar al-'ārifīn*, 235.

55. Jamālī, *Siyar al-'ārifīn*, 234.

56. 'Abd al-Ḥaqq Muḥaddiṣ Dihlawī, *Akhbār al-akhyār* (Gambat Żila' Khayrpūr: Fārūq Academy, 1977), 143.

57. This anecdote has been retold and transmitted by a number of modern scholars. One example of its appearance in Western scholarship is in Alessandro Bausani, "Can Monotheism Be Taught?

(Further Considerations on the Typology of Monotheism)," *Numen* 10, 3 (December 1963): 192–193. Bausani's source was S. M. Ikrām, *Āb-i kawsar: Islāmī Hind ō Pākistān kī mazhabī awr 'ilmī tārīkh 'ahd-i Mughlīya sē pehlē* (Karachi, 1952), 320–321.

58. For a description of their shrines in Ahmadabad, see Z. A. Desai, "The Major Dargahs of Ahmadabad," in *Muslim Shrines in India: Their Character, History and Significance*, ed. Christian W. Troll (Delhi: Oxford University Press, 1989), 83–89.

59. Lak'hnawī, *Nuzhat al-khawāṭir*, 2:35. *Sawāl ō jawāb* confirms that Bukhārī married his cousin (Riżawī, *Sawāl ō jawāb*, 233a).

60. Ḥusaynī, *Jāmi' al-'ulūm*, 203.

61. Ḥusaynī, *Jāmi' al-'ulūm*, 470.

62. Ḥusaynī, *Jāmi' al-'ulūm*, 106–107. In both of these events, to be weak (*ża'īf*) seems to be equated with impotence. The ages of the elderly are often exaggerated beyond probability and usually expressed in round numbers, such as 120, 130, and 140.

63. Ḥusaynī, *Jāmi' al-'ulūm*, 218.

64. Ḥusaynī, *Jāmi' al-'ulūm*, 104, 361, 35, and 357.

65. Ḥusaynī, *Jāmi' al-'ulūm*, 563 and 546.

66. Ḥusaynī, *Jāmi' al-'ulūm*, 35, 260–261, and 358.

67. Ghaznawī, *Tuḥfat al-sarā'ir*, 27. These two women cannot be identical since the one from Sīwistān died some years before 777/1376 and the one from Uch was still alive in 781/1379.

68. Ghaznawī, *Tuḥfat al-sarā'ir*, 33; Ḥusaynī, *Jāmi' al-'ulūm*, 558; 'Afīf, *Tārīkh-i Fīrōz Shāhī*, 241.

69. For example, al-Ḥākim al-Tirmidhī, *The Concept of Sainthood in Early Islamic Mysticism: Two Works by Al-Ḥākim Al-Tirmidhī*, trans. Bernd Radtke and John O'Kane (Richmond: Curzon Press, 1996).

70. Bhaṯṯī, *Khizānat al-fawā'id al-Jalālīya*, 219b.

71. Many of these *karāmāt* can already be found in Tirmidhī's early summary of the external signs of the *awliyā'*: "The second sign is that they possess the power of that which is due; no one can oppose them without being overwhelmed by the power of that which is due to God. The third sign is that they are endowed with clairvoyance, and the fourth sign is that they receive divine inspiration. The fifth sign is that whoever contends with them is cast down and comes to an evil end. And the sixth sign is that all tongues agree in praising them, except for those who are afflicted with jealousy of them. And the seventh sign is that their prayers are answered and they are manifestly capable of miracles such as traveling distances over the earth and walking on water. And they converse with Khaḍir (Khiḍr)" (al-Tirmidhī, *The Concept of Sainthood*, 124–125). For descriptions of the many varieties of *karāmāt*, see Richard Gramlich, *Die Wunder der Freunde Gottes* (Stuttgart: Steiner Verlag Wiesbaden, 1987).

72. Bhaṯṯī, *Khizānat al-fawā'id al-Jalālīya*, 47a. This is why Naṣīr al-dīn Maḥmūd instructed Bukhārī to keep his (Naṣīr al-dīn's) miraculous weekly visits to Mecca a secret.

73. Ḥusaynī, *Jāmi' al-'ulūm*, 231–232.

74. Ḥusaynī, *Jāmi' al-'ulūm*, 568. In this case Bukhārī is also placing himself among the shaykhs and *awliyā'*.

75. See Desiderio Pinto, *Piri-Muridi Relationship: A Study of the Nizamuddin Dargah* (New Delhi: Manohar Publishers, 1995); and Arthur Buehler, *Sufi Heirs to the Prophet: The Indian Naqshbandiyya and the Rise of the Mediating Sufi Shaykh* (Columbia: University of South Carolina Press, 1998).

76. Ḥusaynī, *Jāmi' al-'ulūm*, 426.

77. Ḥusaynī, *Jāmi' al-'ulūm*, 181–182. *Abdāl* (pl. of *badal*, substitute) are usually identified as forty or seventy individuals in the hierarchy of saints. Bukhārī gives several lists of the ranks of

saints. One is quoted from Yāfi'ī's *Rawżat al-riyāḥīn*: three hundred *awliyā,* seventy *nujabā,* forty *awtād al-arż*, ten *nuqabā,* seven *'urafā,* three *mukhtārūn*, and one *ghawṣ*. Another list, which can be used as a prayer, is *nuqabā, nujabā, ruqabā, nukabā,' akhyār, abdāl, awtād, ghawṣ* and *quṭb* (Bhaṭṭī, *Khizānat al-fawā'id al-Jalālīya*, 221a–b and 317b).

78. Bhaṭṭī, *Khizānat al-fawā'id al-Jalālīya*, 220a and 228a; Ḥusaynī, *Jāmi' al-'ulūm*, 181–182; Ghaznawī, *Tuḥfat al-sarā'ir*, 18.

79. Ḥusaynī, *Jāmi' al-'ulūm*, 261.

80. Bhaṭṭī, *Khizānat al-fawā'id al-Jalālīya*, 243b.

81. The only exception is Muḥammad Mutaqī Bayābānī, grandson of Shaykh Amīn al-dīn Kāzarūnī. By his descent he is part of the shaykh group, but by virtue of being a hermit in the wilderness he falls into the socially marginal group (Ḥusaynī, *Jāmi' al-'ulūm*, 37).

82. A dramatically literal interpretation of the parallel between saints and menstruating women is found in an anecdote about Aḥmad Ma'shūq, a disciple of Shaykh Ṣadr al-dīn 'Ārif. Aḥmad Ma'shūq was so intoxicated by love that he no longer performed the ritual prayers. The local 'ulama berated him, argued with him, and eventually had him beaten for his recalcitrance. But when his blood began to flow he was vindicated in his claim of exemption from prayer, just like a menstruating woman. (Jamālī, *Siyar al-'ārifīn*, 183.)

83. Ḥusaynī, *Jāmi' al-'ulūm*, 327.

84. Ḥusaynī, *Jāmi' al-'ulūm*, 558.

85. Bhaṭṭī, *Khizānat al-fawā'id al-Jalālīya*, 221b, 292a and 293a.

86. Yamanī, *Laṭā'if-i Ashrafī*, 331.

87. Mīr Khwurd, *Siyar al-awliyā,* 289.

88. Vincent J. Cornell, *Realm of the Saint: Power and Authority in Moroccan Sufism* (Austin: University of Texas Press, 1998), 272–273.

89. Cornell, *Realm of the Saint*, 273.

90. Ḥusaynī, *Jāmi' al-'ulūm*, 182 and 559.

91. Cornell, *Realm of the Saint*, 94.

92. Ḥusaynī, *Jāmi' al-'ulūm*, 578.

93. Ḥusaynī, *Jāmi' al-'ulūm*, 542.

94. Ḥusaynī, *Jāmi' al-'ulūm*, 426. It is unclear why this evidence of the Prophet's favor was a matter for secrecy when the Prophet's statement to him in Medina is discussed openly and repeated several times in the different sources.

95. *Sirāj al-hidāya*, 362.

96. Ḥusaynī, *Jāmi' al-'ulūm*, 160.

97. Ḥusaynī, *Jāmi' al-'ulūm*, 194.

Six: A Public Figure

1. Peter Hardy, *Historians of Medieval India: Studies in Indo-Muslim Historical Writing* (London: Luzac and Company Ltd, 1960), 20.

2. Mohammad Habib, "Life and Thought of Ziauddin Barani," *Medieval India Quarterly* 3, 3–4 (1958): 241.

3. Habib, "Ziauddin Barani," 201 footnote 1.

4. S. Nurul Hasan, "Sahifa-i-Na't-i-Muhammadi of Zia-ud-din Barani," *Medieval India Quarterly*, 1, 3–4 (1954): 100–106.

5. Bhaṭṭī, *Khizānat al-fawā'id al-Jalālīya*, 196b–198b.

6. Peter Hardy, "Didactic Historical Writing in Indian Islam: Ziyā al-Dīn Baranī's Treatment of the Reign of Sultan Muḥammad Tughluq (1324–1351)," in *Islam in Asia*, vol. 1, *South Asia*, ed.

Yohannan Friedmann (Jerusalem: the Magnes Press, The University of Jerusalem, 1984), 59 footnote 76.

7. According to 'Afīf, Ibn Māhrū received the *iqṭā's* (land revenues, fiefs) of Multan, Bhakkar, and Sīwistān and was placed in charge of those regions by Fīrūz ('Afīf, *Tārīkh-i Fīrōz Shāhī*, 414). Peter Jackson argues that Ibn Māhrū was appointed to Multan in 751/1352 during Muḥammad b. Tughluq's fatal campaign in Sind and served there until his death sometime before 772/1370 (Jackson, *Delhi Sultanate*, 154–155, 270 footnote 91, and 329).

8. 'Ayn al-mulk ibn Māhrū, *Inshā'-i Māhrū (Letters of 'Ain ud-Dīn 'Ain ul-Mulk Abdullah bin Mahru)*, ed. 'Abdur Rashid and Muḥammad Bashir Husain (Lahore: Research Society of Pakistan, University of the Panjab, 1970), 51–55.

9. Riazul Islam, "The Rise of the Sammas in Sind (Based on Contemporary Sources)," *Islamic Culture* 22 (1948): 359–382.

10. Ibn Māhrū, *Inshā*, 186–187; Riazul Islam, "Rise of the Sammas," 370.

11. The *shaykh al-islām* was the state-appointed head of the Sufi orders, either throughout the empire or of a particular region. Ṣadr al-dīn's appointment was on the imperial, rather than local, level (Nizami, "Early Indo-Muslim Mystics," *Islamic Culture* 22 [1948]: 390).

12. Riazul Islam, "Rise of the Sammas," 371.

13. Riazul Islam, "Rise of the Sammas," 371–372.

14. 'Afīf, *Tārīkh-i Fīrōz Shāhī*, 240.

15. 'Afīf, *Tārīkh-i Fīrōz Shāhī*, 241.

16. 'Afīf, *Tārīkh-i Fīrōz Shāhī*, 241.

17. Riazul Islam, "Rise of the Sammas," 377; Islam's translation and parenthetical additions.

18. Riazul Islam, "Rise of the Sammas," 377.

19. *Sirāj al-hidāya*, ed. Ḥusayn, 320; *Sirāj al-hidāya* (MS. 430 [333]), 203a–b. Both versions have Bahman instead of Bānhbīna. Riazul Islam, "Rise of the Sammas," 378–379.

20. Riazul Islam, "Rise of the Sammas," 380 footnote 4.

21. Peter Jackson, *Delhi Sultanate*, 304, 311 footnote 105.

22. Ḥusaynī, *Jāmi' al-'ulūm*, 437.

23. Ḥusaynī, *Jāmi' al-'ulūm*, 370, 437, 230, 575.

24. 'Abd al-Raḥmān Chishtī, *Mir'āt al-asrār*, 1:535–536.

25. *Sayr-nāma*, 1–12; *Musāfir-nāma*.

26. Muḥammad Bukhārī, *Jawāhir al-awliyā*,' 61 and 222.

27. Peter Jackson, *Delhi Sultanate*, 296.

28. Welch, "Shrine," 166–178; Annemarie Schimmel, *Islam in the Indian Subcontinent*, 49.

29. *Sirāj al-hidāya*, 147, 162, and 206. Firishta writes that Bukhārī visited Egypt, Syria, Jerusalem, Khurāsān, Balkh, and Bukhara (*Gulshan-i Ibrāhīmī* or *Tārīkh-i Firishta* [Lucknow: Nawal Kishawr, 1281/1864–65], 2:415).

30. *Sirāj al-hidāya*, 206.

31. 'Afīf, *Tārīkh-i Fīrōz Shāhī*, 514–516.

32. *Sirāj al-hidāya*, 334.

33. Ḥusaynī, *Jāmi' al-'ulūm*, 15.

34. Ghaznawī, *Tuḥfat al-sarā'ir*, 16.

35. Jamālī, *Siyar al-'ārifīn*, 227.

36. Ḥusaynī, *Jāmi' al-'ulūm*, 230.

37. Peter Jackson, *Delhi Sultanate*, 188, 304; *Sirāj al-hidāya*, 106, 146, 159, 190, 206, 360, and 523.

38. *Sirāj al-hidāya*, 213.

39. Ghaznawī, *Tuḥfat al-sarā'ir*, 16.

40. Ḥusaynī, *Jāmiʿ al-ʿulūm*, 11.

41. Ghaznawī, *Tuḥfat al-sarā'ir*, 16.

42. Ghaznawī, *Tuḥfat al-sarā'ir*, 3.

43. Yamanī, *Laṭā'if-i Ashrafī*, 390–392.

44. ʿAbd al-Raḥmān Chishtī, *Mir'āt al-asrār*, 1:413–414; Rizvi, *A History of Sufism in India*, 1:266–270; Lawrence, *Notes From a Distant Flute*, 52–55.

45. Dihlawī, *Akhbār al-akhyār*, 143.

46. Muṭīʿ al-Imām, *Sharaf al-dīn Manērī*, 147–148.

47. Paul Jackson, *The Way of a Sufi*, 137–140, and *The Hundred Letters*, 3.

48. Muḥammad Ṣādiq Dihlawī Kashmīrī Hamadānī, *Kalimāt al-ṣādiqīn: Taẕkira-i ṣūfiyān madfūn dar Dihlī tā sāl-i 1023 hijrī qamarī/The Kalimāt al-Ṣādiqīn: A Hagiography of Ṣufis Buried at Delhi until 1614 A. D.*, ed. Muḥammad Salīm Akhtar (Islamabad: Markaz-i taḥqīqāt-i fārsī-yi Īrān ō Pākistān, 1988), 95–96.

49. Badakhshī, *Ṣamarāt al-quds*, 869.

50. Miṣbāḥī, *Taẕkira-i awliyā'-i Aḥmadābād*, 67–69.

51. Miṣbāḥī, *Taẕkira-i awliyā'-i Aḥmadābād*, 43.

52. Dihlawī, *Akhbār al-akhyār*, 159.

53. Though Ḥusaynī consistently uses the expression *qadam būs* (kiss the feet) every time someone meets Bukhārī, this should probably not to be taken literally. The Suhrawardī order did not approve of the Chishtī practice of prostration before the shaykh. F. Steingass' *Persian-English Dictionary* suggests these alternate meanings of *qadam būsī*: "touching the feet of the person respectfully approached with the right hand, and then kissing the latter; respectful salutation; obeisance."

54. Abha Rani, *The Tughluq Architecture of Delhi* (Varanasi: Bharati Prakashan 1991), 81.

55. Anthony Welch, "The Shrine of the Holy Footprint," *Muqarnas* 13 (1996): 177 footnote 10. For an overview of Delhi at this time see M. Athar Ali, "Capital of the Sultans: Delhi during the Thirteenth and Fourteenth Centuries" in *Delhi Through the Ages*, ed. R. E. Frykenberg (Delhi: Oxford University Press, 1993), 21–31.

56. ʿAfīf, *Tārīkh-i Fīrōz Shāhī*, 514. Ḥusaynī states that Bukhārī stayed at the tomb of Fīrōz Khān. Sajjād Ḥusayn, editor of the Delhi edition of *Jāmiʿ al-ʿulūm*, identifies this as the tomb of Fatḥ Khān (Ḥusaynī, *Jāmiʿ al-ʿulūm*, ed. Sajjād Ḥusayn [New Delhi: Indian Council of Historical Research, 1987]), 25 footnote 2). Besides the confusion of tombs there is also some confusion about these two princes. Fatḥ Khān is sometimes identified as Fīrōz Shāh's son and sometimes as his grandson, the son of the Sultan's eldest son Fīrōz Khān (Rani, *Tughluq Architecture*, 42; Welch, "Shrine," 170–171; Peter Jackson, *Delhi Sultanate*, 332 and 335). The year of his death is variously listed as 776/1374, 777/1376, and 778/1376 (Jackson, *Delhi Sultanate*, 169 footnote 116).

57. Welch, "Shrine," 170; Rani, *Tughluq Architecture*, 42–3; Nizami, *Royalty in Medieval India* (New Delhi: Munshiram Manoharlal Publishers, 1997), 131.

58. Welch, "Shrine," 177 footnote 4; Rani, *Tughluq Architecture*, 42; Perween Hassan, "The Footprint of the Prophet," *Muqarnas* 10 (1993): 335–343.

59. Ḥusaynī, *Jāmiʿ al-ʿulūm*, 581 and 586.

60. Ḥusaynī, *Jāmiʿ al-ʿulūm*, 14, 15, and 20.

61. Ḥusaynī, *Jāmiʿ al-ʿulūm*, 534–535, 546, and 574; Riżawī, *Sawāl ō jawāb*, 233a.

62. Ḥusaynī, *Jāmiʿ al-ʿulūm*, 545–546, 206, 313, 569, and 585.

63. Nizami, "Early Indo-Muslim Mystics," 390.

64. Ḥusaynī, *Jāmiʿ al-ʿulūm*, 581. For a detailed description of the Ḥauẓ-i Khāṣṣ, see Welch, "A Medieval Center of Learning in India."

65. Ḥusaynī, *Jāmiʿ al-ʿulūm*, 149–150.
66. Ḥusaynī, *Jāmiʿ al-ʿulūm*, 253.
67. Ḥusaynī, *Jāmiʿ al-ʿulūm*, 581–586.
68. Ḥusaynī, *Jāmiʿ al-ʿulūm*, 210 and 252.
69. Ḥusaynī, *Jāmiʿ al-ʿulūm*, 524–527.
70. Ḥusaynī, *Jāmiʿ al-ʿulūm*, 551–556.
71. Ḥusaynī, *Jāmiʿ al-ʿulūm*, 553 and 589.
72. Peter Jackson, *Delhi Sultanate*, 168.
73. Ḥusaynī, *Jāmiʿ al-ʿulūm*, 19.
74. Ḥusaynī, *Jāmiʿ al-ʿulūm*, 314 and 258.
75. Peter Jackson, *Delhi Sultanate*, 168.
76. Ḥusaynī, *Jāmiʿ al-ʿulūm*, 285–286.
77. Ḥusaynī, *Jāmiʿ al-ʿulūm*, 313.
78. ʿAfīf, *Tārīkh-i Fīrōz Shāhī*, 514–515.
79. Ḥusaynī, *Jāmiʿ al-ʿulūm*, 527.
80. Ḥusaynī, *Jāmiʿ al-ʿulūm*, 560–561. Burton took a skeptical view of such courtesies in more recent times: "So tenacious of respect are most of the chief Pirs, that they would never rise to any of the Ameers, or condescend to treat them with civility; the prince, on his side, was glad to make an easy show of religious humility, and stoop to conquer when forcible victory would have been valueless" (Burton, *Sindh*, 206–207).
81. Ḥusaynī, *Jāmiʿ al-ʿulūm*, 545–551.
82. Ḥusaynī, *Jāmiʿ al-ʿulūm*, 553–588.
83. Ḥusaynī, *Jāmiʿ al-ʿulūm*, 581–590.
84. Peter Jackson, *Delhi Sultanate*, 305–313.

Seven: Legacy

1. These comments apply mostly to Sufi saints who, like Bukhārī, functioned as shaykhs and teachers. There are also numerous saints who are known only as the occupant of a venerated and miracle-working shrine.
2. For a recent description of their shrines in Ahmadabad, see Desai, "The Major Dargahs of Ahmadabad," 83–89.
3. Peter Jackson, *Delhi Sultanate*, 188, 308, 318.
4. Miṣbāḥī, *Taẕkira-i awliyāʾ-i Aḥmadābād*, 169. Muẓaffar Shāh is not identical to either of the Ẓafar Khāns who were governors of Gujarat under Fīrōz and one of whose conversation with Bukhārī is mentioned above.
5. Muḥammad Ghawṣī Shaṭṭārī, *Gulzār-i abrār*, Urdu translation by Fażl Aḥmad Jēwarī under the title *Aẕkār al-abrār* (Agra: Maṭbaʿ-yi mufīd-i ʿāmm, 1326 AH), 147.
6. Miṣbāḥī, *Taẕkira-i awliyāʾ-i Aḥmadābād*, 178. For more on the descendents and disciples of this family, see Badakhshī, *Ṡamarāt al-quds*, 839–847.
7. Schimmel, *Islam in the Indian Subcontinent*, 66–67.
8. See Ghulām Sarwar's introduction to Muḥammad Bukhārī, *Jawāhir al-awliyā*, 20, for a discussion of this sometimes violent conflict.
9. Burhān al-dīn ʿAbdallāh, *Jāmiʿ al-ṭuruq*. Sayyid Sharaf al-dīn al-Mashhadī and Sayyid Sikandar b. Masʿūd settled in Gujarat (Desai, "The Major Dargahs of Ahmadabad," 77).
10. Yamanī, *Laṭāʾif-i Ashrafī*, 392.
11. Dihlawī, *Akhbār al-akhyār*, 155–156; Chishtī, *Mirʾāt al-asrār*, 543–546.
12. Chishtī, *Mirʾāt al-asrār*, 538.

13. Badakhshī, *Ṣamarāt al-quds*, 786–787.

14. Rizvi, *History of Sufism in India*, 1:316–317

15. Khan, *Uchchh, History and Architecture*, 55.

16. U. S. Department of State, Embassy of the United States, "U.S. Grants $50,000 For Uch Sharif Shrine Conservation," press release 10/19/2007, Islamabad, Pakistan (http://islamabad.us embassy.gov/pakistan/press_releases_2007.html, accessed 12 May 2008); U.S. Department of State, Bureau of Educational and Cultural Affairs, "Ambassador's Fund For Cultural Preservation Project Listing: Conservation of Shrine Hazrat Jalal-ud-Din Bukhari in Uch Sharif" (http.//www.exchanges .state.gov/culprop/afcp/project_listings/, accessed 7 July 2011); "Grant for Uch Shrine," *Dawn*, Saturday October 20, 2007 / Shawwal 7, 1428.

17. U. S. Department of State, Embassy of the United States, "U.S. Ambassador Visits Uch Sharif To Mark Completion Of Shrine Conservation," press release, 5/22/2009, Islamabad, Pakistan (http://islamabad.usembassy.gov/pr-09052201.html, accessed 16 January 2011); U.S. Department of State, Bureau of International Information Programs, "Preserving the Hazrat Jalaluddin Bukhari Shrine in Pakistan: Embassy program helped preserve unique religious and architectural treasure," 8 April 2010 (http://www.america.gov/st/peopleplace-english/2010/April/20100401093 220kJleinaDO.5313486.html, accessed 7 July 2011).

18. On Dātā Ganj Bakhsh's *'urs*, see Qamar-ul Huda, "Celebrating Death and Engaging in Texts at Dātā Ganj Bakhsh's *'Urs*," *The Muslim World* 90 (2000): 377–394.

19. Nawaz Sharif was Chief Minister of Punjab from 1985 to 1988 and Prime Minister of Pakistan from 1990 to 1993 and from 1997 to 1999. His brother Shahbaz Sharif served as Chief Minister of Punjab, 1997–1999, and from 2008 onward. For a discussion of the Pakistani state's changing attitude towards, and involvement in, the management of shrines and *'urs* celebrations, see Katherine Pratt Ewing, *Arguing Sainthood: Modernity, Psychoanalysis, and Islam* (Durham: Duke University Press, 1997), especially 65–90. See also Christian W Troll, ed., *Muslim Shrines in India: Their Character, History and Significance* (Delhi: Oxford University Press, 1989).

20. For recommendations that the U. S. pursue a strategy of supporting Sufis and Sufism as "the world's best weapons against al-Qaeda and other Islamists" by preserving and restoring shrines, see "The enemy of my enemy. . . ," *U. S. News & World Report*, 25 April 2005; and Zeyno Baran, ed., *Understanding Sufism and Its Potential Role in US Policy* (Nixon Center Conference Report, March 2004), 25.

21. Schimmel, *Islam in the Indian Subcontinent*, 127.

22. For a summary of different theories on the identity and path of this river and the date of its disappearance, see Shihāb, *Khiṭṭa-yi pāk*, 37–41 footnote 3.

23. Bruce B. Lawrence, "The Chishtīya of Sultanate India: A Case Study in Biographical Complexities in South Asian Islam," in *Charisma and Sacred Biography*, ed. Michael A. Williams, *JAAR Thematic Studies* 48, nos. 3–4 (1982), 52.

24. Lawrence, "The Chishtīya of Sultanate India," 64.

25. Ḥusaynī, *Jāmiʿ al-ʿulūm*, 436.

26. Ḥusaynī, *Jāmiʿ al-ʿulūm*, 385–386.

Conclusion

1. Two examples of this dichotomous approach can be found in the pages of the *New York Times*: Thomas L. Friedman, "The Power of Green," *New York Times Magazine*, 15 April 2007; Waleed Ziad, "In Pakistan, Islam Needs Democracy," Op-Ed Contributor, *New York Times*, 16 February 2008.

2. See "The enemy of my enemy. . . ," and Baran, ed., *Understanding Sufism*, 25.

3. A recent example of the literary use of these two brothers to represent two oppositional worldviews is the novel *Moth Smoke* by the Pakistani writer Mohsin Hamid (New York: Farrar, Straus and Giroux, 2000).

4. For example, in March 2009, the Pakistani Taliban detonated explosives at the tomb of Raḥmān Bābā, a seventeenth-century Sufi poet, destroying much of his shrine complex. Their stated justification was the refusal of the shrine administration to restrict women's access to the site. (Ali Hazrat Bacha, "Pashtun poet Rehman Baba's mausoleum bombed," *Dawn*, 5 March 2009; "Sufi Shrine 'blown up by Taleban,'" BBC News, March 5, 2009, http://news.bbc.co.uk/2/hi/7925867.stm, accessed 7 July 2011.)

5. A recent example of the weakness of such a dichotomous approach to understanding Islam in South Asia is the assassination of Salmaan Taseer, governor of Punjab, on 4 January 2011 for his call to reform Pakistan's draconian blasphemy law. Taseer's assassin is a member of the Barelvi movement which is closely identified with Sufism and frequently characterized as "moderate" and non-violent. Much of the leadership and the rank-and-file of the movement came out in support of the assassination, to the surprise of outside observers. ("The crumbling centre: Pakistan's religious mainstream makes common cause with militants," *The Economist*, 13 January 2011; "Salmaan Taseer, Aasia Bibi and Pakistan's struggle with extremism," *The Guardian*, 8 January 2011.)

Appendix B: The Malfūẓāt of Jalāl al-dīn Bukhārī

1. Bhaṯṯī, *Khizānat al-fawā'id al-Jalālīya* (MS. 15427, Kitābkhāna-yi Dātā Ganj-bakhsh, Islamabad), 2a–b, 268a; (MS. 2557, Kitābkhāna-yi Dātā Ganj-bakhsh, Islamabad), 2a, 254b; (MS. 577, India Office. British Library, London), 2a, 218b.

2. Bhaṯṯī, *Khizānat al-fawā'id al-Jalālīya*, 1a. *Rāḥat al-qulūb* is believed to be retrospectively imagined (Mohammad Habib, "Chishti Mystic Records of the Sultanate Period," *Medieval India Quarterly* 1, 2 [1950]: 1–42).

3. Sarwar's edition is based on the following manuscripts: MS., Kitābkhāna-yi Sind'hī Adabī Board, Hyderabad, Pakistan, copied by the son of Shaykh 'Abbās Qurayshī, 526 pages; MS., Kitābkhāna-yi nawshāhiya, Sāhan-pul, Gujarat, 292 folios; MS. 1313, Kitābkhāna-yi Dātā Ganj-bakhsh, Islamabad, copied by Ibrāhīm, completed 29 Jumādā I 1102/28 February 1691, 862 pages (Sarwar, *Muqaddama-yi khulāṣat al-alfāẓ-i jāmi' al-'ulūm*, 1–3).

4. Ḥusayn's edition is based on two manuscripts, one from the Ẕakhīra-yi Nawādir-i Kutub in Delhi and the other from the Ẕakhīra-yi Kutub-i Nādira in Rampur, as well as the 1891 Urdu translation (Ḥusayn, introduction to *Jāmi' al-'ulūm*, 47).

5. Ḥusaynī, *Jāmi' al-'ulūm*, 1–2 and 8.

6. Wladimir Ivanow, *Concise Descriptive Catalogue of the Persian Manuscripts in the Collection of the Asiatic Society of Bengal*, Bibliotheca Indica: 240 (Calcutta: Asiatic Society, 1985), 574, no. 1209.

7. Nizami, English introduction to *Khayr al-majālis* by Ḥamīd Qalandar, 3.

8. Qādirī, *Makhdūm-i jahāniyān Jahāngasht*, 238.

9. Ḥusayn's edition is based on five manuscripts: incomplete manuscript at Jawahar Museum, Maulana Azad Library, Aligarh; MS. 1060, Raza Library, Rampur, copied by Mawlānā Farżallāh b. Mawlānā 'Abdallāh b. Mawlānā Karamallāh Qurayshī Narnūlī, 27 Safar 1026/6 March 1617; MS. 1059, Raza Library, Rampur, copied by Shahrallāh b. Aḥmad al-Qurayshī al-Badā'unī; MS., personal collection of Professor Khalīq Aḥmād Niẓāmī, Aligarh University, copied by Ibrāhīm; MS., Muftī Ilāhī Bakhsh Academy, Kandhla, District Muzaffarnagar (Ḥusayn, introduction to *Sirāj al-hidāya*, xiv and 14–15).

10. Riazul Islam, "Collections of the Malfuzat of Makhdum-i-Jahanian (1307–1388) of Uchh," *Proceedings of the All Pakistan History Conference, First Session* (Karachi: Pakistan Historical Society, 1951): 214; Riazul Islam, "Rise of the Sammas," *Islamic Culture* 22 (1948): 378; Maḥmūd Ḥasan Siddiqui, *The Memoirs of Sufis Written in India* (Baroda: Maharaja Sayajirao University of Baroda, 1979), 28.

11. Ivanow, *Concise Descriptive Catalogue*, 576, no. 1210.

12. Riazul Islam, "Collections of the Malfuzat," 215–216; "Rise of the Sammas," 359–382.

13. Riżawī, *Sawāl o jawāb*, 233a.

14. Ḥusaynī, *Jāmi' al-'ulūm*, 534–535, 546, and 574.

Appendix C: Works Attributed to Jalāl al-dīn Bukhārī

1. Bruce B. Lawrence, *Notes from a Distant Flute: The Extant Literature of Pre-Mughal Indian Sufism* (Tehran: Imperial Academy of Philosophy, 1978), 69.

2. Ḥusaynī, *Jāmi' al-'ulūm*, 7 and 8.

3. It is unclear who this Sayyid Ḥamīd al-dīn was; he cannot be the same as Sayyid Ḥamīd al-dīn Maḥmūd al-Samarqandī whom Bukhārī met in Shiraz (See Chapter 2).

4. *Safar-nāma* (MS. 1091, Persian and Arabic, Government Oriental Manuscripts Library, Madras), 1.

5. *Safar-nāma*, 47.

Appendix D: *Tazkira* Entries on Jalāl al-dīn Bukhārī

1. See Siddiqui, *The Memoirs of Sufis Written in India*, 21–28.

2. My choice of texts to examine is largely based on availability. I have tried to focus on some of the earliest, best known, and most often cited works.

3. Hermansen and Lawrence, "Indo-Persian Tazkiras," 176–198.

4. Ḥāmid b. Fażlallāh Jamālī, *Siyar al-'ārifīn*, Urdu trans. Muḥammad Ayyūb Qādirī (Lahore: Markazī Urdu Board, 1976).

5. Jamālī, *Siyar al-'ārifīn*, 224–226 and 237–238.

6. Jamālī, *Siyar al-'ārifīn*, 228–229.

7. Jamālī, *Siyar al-'ārifīn*, 228.

8. Jamālī, *Siyar al-'ārifīn*, 227.

9. Jamālī, *Siyar al-'ārifīn*, 235. The Sumras were the ruling tribe of Thatta and lower Sind before the Sammas displaced them around 752/1351–1352. But, as far as I know, there was no ruler in Uch by that name. See Riazul Islam, "Rise of the Sammas"; Arshad Islam, "Sūmrah and Sammah Rule in Sind (c. 1051–1520 C. E.)," *Journal of the Pakistan Historical Society* 46, 2 (1998): 69–78.

10. Jamālī, *Siyar al-'ārifīn*, 234.

11. Jamālī, *Siyar al-'ārifīn*, 236–237.

12. Muḥammad Ghawṣī Shaṭṭārī, *Azkār al-abrār*, Urdu translation of *Gulzār-i abrār* by Fażl Aḥmad Jēwarī (Agra: Maṭba'-i Mufīd-i 'Āmm, 1326/1908).

13. Shaṭṭarī, *Azkār al-abrār*, 112–114.

14. Badakhshī quotes a Sayyid Shams al-dīn Mashhadī (see below). These two individuals are probably the same.

15. 'Abd al-Ḥaqq Muḥaddis̱ Dihlawī, *Akhbār al-akhyār* (Gambaṯ Ẓila' Khayrpūr: Fārūq Academy, 1977).

16. This work was completed in 842/1438 and therefore precedes any of the *tazkiras* examined here (Muḥammad Bihāmad Khānī, *Tarikh-i-Muhammadi: Portion Dealing with the Account of*

Sultan Firoz Shah, His Successors, and the Minor Kingdoms, from AH 752/AD 1351 to AH 842/AD 1438, trans. Muhammad Zaki [Aligarh: Aligarh Muslim University Press, 1972], ix). Muḥammad Bihāmad Khān was a disciple of Shaykh Yusuf Budh Īrajī (d. 834/1430–1431), who had received *khilāfat* and *ijāzat* from Bukhārī and from Bukhārī's brother Rājū-qattāl (Dihlawī, *Akhbār al-akhyār*, 155).

17. Dihlawī, *Akhbār al-akhyār*, 142.
18. Dihlawī, *Akhbār al-akhyār*, 143.
19. Dihlawī, *Akhbār al-akhyār*, 142.
20. Mirzā La'l Bēg Badakhshī, *S̱amarāt al-quds min shajarāt al-uns*, ed. Kamāl Ḥajj Sayyid Jawādī (Tehrān: Pizhūhishgāh-i 'Ulūm-i Insānī wa Mutala'at-i Farhangī-yi Īrān, 1997).
21. Badakhshī, *S̱amarāt al-quds*, 698–701 and 703.
22. Badakhshī, *S̱amarāt al-quds*, 689–690. It is unclear whether *I'timād al-murīdīn* is still extant; I have seen no mention of it in catalogues.
23. Badakhshī, *S̱amarāt al-quds*, 690–691.
24. Badakhshī, *S̱amarāt al-quds*, 703–705.
25. Badakhshī, *S̱amarāt al-quds*, 703.
26. Badakhshī, *S̱amarāt al-quds*, 690 and 692.
27. Badakhshī, *S̱amarāt al-quds*, 695.
28. Badakhshī, *S̱amarāt al-quds*, 696–697.
29. Abū al-Qāsim Firishta, *Gulshan-i Ibrāhīmī* or *Tārīkh-i Firishta* (Lucknow: Nawal Kishawr, 1281/1864–1865).
30. Firishta, *Gulshan-i Ibrāhīmī*, 2:415–417.
31. 'Abd al-Raḥmān Chishtī, *Mir'āt al-asrār*, Urdu trans. Waḥīd Bakhsh Siyāl (Lahore: Sufi Foundation, 1402/1982).
32. Chishtī, *Mir'āt al-asrār*, 1: 410–414.
33. Chishtī, *Mir'āt al-asrār*, 1: 411–412.
34. Mian Muhammad Saeed, *The Sharqi Sultanate of Jaunpur: A Poltical and Cultural History* (Pakistan: University of Karachi, 1972), 50–52. Ikram, *Muslim Rule in India and Pakistan*, 112.
35. Chishtī, *Mir'āt al-asrār*, 1: 415.
36. Saeed, *The Sharqi Sultanate*, 30–33.
37. Khwāja Gul Muḥammad Aḥmadpūrī, *Ẕikr al-aṣfiyā': Takmila-yi siyar al-awliyā,'* Urdu trans., Mas'ūd Ḥasan Shihāb (Bahāwalpūr: Maktaba-yi Ilhām, 1978).
38. Aḥmadpūrī, *Ẕikr al-aṣfiyā,'* 36, 50.
39. Aḥmadpūrī, *Ẕikr al-aṣfiyā,'* 68.
40. Aḥmadpūrī, *Ẕikr al-aṣfiyā,'* 33.
41. Aḥmadpūrī, *Ẕikr al-aṣfiyā,'* 47.
42. Aḥmadpūrī, *Ẕikr al-aṣfiyā,'* 51–56.

BIBLIOGRAPHY

1. Early Works: Pre-1900

'Abbāsī, Fażlallāh b. Żiyā'. *Khizāna-yi jawāhir-i Jalālīya*. MS. 5193, MS. 2463, and MS. 1749. Kitābkhāna-yi Dātā Ganj-bakhsh, Islamabad.

Abū Makhrama. *Arabische Texte zur Kenntnis der Stadt Aden im Mittelalter (Tārīkh taghr 'Adan)*. Edited by Oscar Lofgren. Arbeten Utgivna med Understod av Vilhelm Ekmans Universitetsfond, no. 42:2. Uppsala: Almqvist & Wiksells Boktryckeri, 1936.

'Afīf, Shams-i Sirāj. *Tārikh-i Fīrōz Shāhī/The Tarikh-i-Firoz Shahi of Shams Siraj 'Afif*. Edited by Wilāyat Ḥusayn (Maulvi Vilayat Husain). Bibliotheca Indica: 119. Calcutta: Asiatic Society of Bengal, 1891.

———. *Medieval India in Transition: Tarīkh-i Fīrōz Shāhī: A First-Hand Account*. Translated by R. C. Jauhri. New Delhi: Sundeep Prakashan, 2001.

Aḥmadpūrī, Khwāja Gul Muḥammad. *Ẕikr al-aṣfiyā': Takmila-i siyar al-awliyā'*. Urdu translation by Mas'ūd Ḥasan Shihāb. Bahāwalpūr: Maktaba-yi Ilhām, 1978.

al-'Asqalānī, Aḥmad Ibn Hajjar. *al-Durar al-kāmina fi a'yān al-mī'at al-thāmina*. Hyderabad: Dā'irat al-Ma'ārif al-'Uthmānīya, 1974.

al-'Aṭā'ī, Sharaf al-dīn b. Muḥammad. *Fawā'id-i Fīrōz Shāh*. MS. Or. 11, 322. British Library, London. Incomplete at beginning.

Badakhshī, Mirza La'l Bēg. *Ṣamarāt al-quds min shajarāt al-uns*. Edited by Kamāl Ḥajj Sayyid Jawādī. Tehrān: Pizhūhishgāh-i 'Ulūm-i Insānī wa Mutala'at-i Farhangī-yi Īrān, 1997.

al-Badā'unī, 'Abd al-Qādir b. Malūk Shāh. *Muntakhab al-tawārīkh*. 2 vols. Edited by Aḥmad 'Alī. Calcutta: Asiatic Society of Bengal, 1868.

———. *Muntakhab al-Tawārīkh*. Translated by George S. A. Ranking. 2 vols. Bibliotheca Indica: 97. Calcutta: Asiatic Society of Bengal, 1898.

Bahā' al-dīn Zakarīyā Multānī. *al-Awrād*. Edited by Muḥammad Mīyān Ṣiddīq. Islamabad: Markaz-i Taḥqīqāt-i Fārsī-yi Īrān ō Pākistān, 1978/1398.

Baranī, Żiyā' al-dīn. *Tārīkh-i Firōz Shāhī/Tarikh-i Feroz-Shahi of Ziaa al-Din Barni, Commonly Called Ziaa-i Barni*. Edited by Sayyid Aḥmad Khān. Bibliotheca Indica, New Series: 33. Calcutta: Asiatic Society of Bengal, 1862.

———. *Fatāwā-i jahāndārī*. Translated by Mohammad Habib and Afsar Umar Salim Khan. *Medieval India Quarterly*. 3, 3–4 (1958): 151–196.

Bhaṯṯī, Aḥmad Bahā' b. Ya'qūb. *Khizānat al-fawā'id al-Jalālīya*. MS 15427. Kitābkhāna-yi Dātā Ganj-bakhsh, Islamabad.

Bukhārī, Jalāl al-dīn. *Risāla Makkīya Jalālīya*. MS. Garret 12 W. Princeton University Library, Princeton.

———, [attributed]. *Muqarrar-nāma* or *Naṣā'iḥ-yi Makhdūm-i jahāniyān*. MS. 1089, Arabic and Persian. Government Oriental Manuscripts Library, Madras.

———, [attributed]. *Musāfir-nāma*. MS. 1826. Taṣawwuf. Andhra Pradesh Oriental Manuscripts Library, Hyderabad.

——, [attributed]. *Safar-nāma-yi Makhdūm-i jahāniyān*. MS. 1091. Arabic and Persian. Government Oriental Manuscripts Library, Madras.

——, [attributed]. *Sayr-nāma*. MS. 551. Taṣawwuf. Folios 1–12. Andhra Pradesh Oriental Manuscripts Library, Hyderabad.

Bukhārī, Muḥammad Bāqir b. ʻUs̱mān. *Jawāhir al-awliyā'*. Edited by Ghulām Sarwar. Islamabad: Markaz-i Taḥqīqāt-i Fārsī-yi Īrān ō Pākistān, 1396/1976.

Bukhārī, Shāh Isma'īl. *Nasab-nāma*. MS. 123. Taṣawwuf. Andhra Pradesh Government Oriental Library, Hyderabad, India. 11 folios.

Burhān al-dīn 'Abdallāh Quṭb-i 'ālam. *Jāmi' al-ṭuruq*. MS. 1549. Taṣawwuf. Andhra Pradesh Government Oriental Manuscripts Library, Hyderabad, India.

Burton, Richard Francis. *Sindh, and the Races That Inhabit the Valley of the Indus*. London: W. H. Allen, 1851.

Chishtī, 'Abd al-Raḥmān b. 'Abd al-rasūl. *Mir'āt al-asrār*. Urdu translation by Waḥīd Bakhsh Siyāl. 2 vols. Lahore: Sufi Foundation, 1402/1982.

Chishtī, Aḥmad 'Alī. *Qaṣr-i 'ārifān*. Urdu translation by Iqbāl Aḥmad Fārūqī. Lahore: Maktaba-yi Maẓhar-i Fayż Riżā, 1407/1977.

Dihlawī, 'Abd al-Ḥaqq Muḥaddis̱. *Akhbār al-akhyār*. Gambaṯ Żila' Khayrpūr: Fārūq Academy, 1977.

——. *Akhbār al-akhyār*. Urdu translation by Iqbāl al-dīn Aḥmad. Karachi: Dār al-Ishā'at, 1963.

Dihlawī, Amīr Ḥasan 'Alā' Sijzī (d. 737). *Fawā'id al-fu'ād: Malfūẓāt-i khwāja Niẓām al-dīn Awliyā' Badāyūnī (mutawaffā 725 hijrī)*. Edited by Muḥammad Laṭīf Malik. Tehran: Intishārāt-i Rawzaneh, 1998.

——. *Fawā'id al-Fu'ād: Spiritual and Literary Discourses of Shaikh Niẓāmuddīn Awliyā*. Islamic Heritage in Cross-Cultural Perspectives, no. 2. Translated by Ziya-ul-Hasan Faruqi. New Delhi: D. K. Printworld (P) Ltd., 1996.

——. *Morals for the Heart*. Translated by Bruce B. Lawrence. New York: Paulist Press, 1992.

Dimashqī, Quṭb al-dīn 'Abdallāh al-Aṣfahīdī. *al-Risālat al-Makkīya fi khalwat al-ṣūfiya* or *fi ṭarīq al-sādat al-ṣūfiya*. MS. Del. Ar. 63/n. British Library, London.

——. *Risāla Makkīya*. Persian translation. MS T-121/8289. Punjab University Library, Lahore. 132 folios.

Elliot, H. M., and John Dowson. *The History of India as told by its own Historians, The Muhammadan Period*. Vols. 1 and 2. 1869. Reprint. New York: AMS Press, 1966.

al-Fāsī, Muḥmmad b. Aḥmad. *al-'Iqd al-thamīn fi tārīkh al-balad al-āmīn*. Cairo: Maṭba'at al-Sunna al-Muḥammadīya, 1966.

Firishta, Abū al-Qāsim. *Gulshan-i Ibrāhīmī: Tārīkh-i Firishta*. Lucknow: Nawal Kishawr, 1281/1864–65.

——. *History of the Rise of the Mahomedan Power in India, Till the Year A.D. 1612*. Translated by John Briggs. London: Longman, Rees, Orme, Brown, and Green, 1829.

——. *Mashāhīr-i mashā'ikh-i Hind*. Urdu translation of Chapter 12 of *Tārīkh-i Firishta* by Muḥammad Shafī' al-dīn Khān. Murādabad, 1334 AH.

Firōz Shāh Tughluq. *Futūḥāt-i Fīrōz Shāhī*. Edited by Shaikh Abdur Rashid. Aligarh: Aligarh Muslim University, 1954.

——. "The Victories of Sulṭān Firūz Shāh of Tughluq Dynasty (English Translation of Futūḥāt-i-Firūz Shāhī)." Translated by N. B. Roy. *Islamic Culture* 15 (1941): 449–469.

Ghawṣī Shaṭṭārī, Muḥammad. *Gulzār-i abrār*. Urdu translation by Fażl Aḥmad Jēwarī. Agra: Maṭba'-i Mufīd-i 'Āmm, 1326/1908.

al-Ghazālī, Abū Ḥāmid. *Al-Ghazālī's Path to Sufism and His Deliverance from Error: An Annotated Translation of Al Munqidh min al-Dalāl.* Translated by R. J. McCarthy. Louisville: Fons Vitae, 2000.

Ghaznawī, Muḥammad. *Tuḥfat al-sarā'ir.* MS. 1090. Arabic and Persian. Government Oriental Manuscripts Library, Madras.

Gīlānī, 'Abd al-Qādir. *Utterances of Shaikh 'Abd al-Qādir al-Jīlānī (Malfūẓāt).* Translated by Muhtar Holland. Houston: Al-Baz Publishing, 1992.

Hamadānī, Muḥammad Ṣādiq Dihlawī Kashmīrī. *Kalimāt al-ṣādiqīn: Taẕkira-i ṣūfiyān madfūn dar Dihlī ta sāl-i 1023 hijrī qamrī/The Kalimāt al-Ṣādiqīn: A Hagiography of Ṣufis Buried at Delhi until 1614 A.D.* Edited by Muḥammad Salīm Akhtar. Islamabad: Markaz-i Taḥqīqāt-i Fārsī-yi Īrān ō Pākistān, 1988.

Ḥamīd Qalandar. *Khayr al-majālis: Malfūẓāt-i ḥażrat shaykh Naṣīr al-dīn Maḥmūd Chirāgh-i Dihlī.* Edited by Khalīq Aḥmad Nizāmī. Aligarh: The Aligarh Muslim University, 1959.

———. *Khayr al-majālis.* Urdu translation by Mawlana Aḥmad 'Alī. Delhi: Nāz Publishing House, n.d.

Hasht bihisht. Urdu translation. Lahore: Shabīr Brothers, 2006.

Ḥusaynī, Sayyid 'Alā' al-dīn 'Alī b. Sa'd al-Qurayshī. *Khulāṣat al-alfāẓ-i jāmi' al-'ulūm.* Edited by Ghulām Sarwar. Islamabad: Markaz-i Taḥqīqāt-i Fārsī-yi Īrān ō Pākistān, 1412/1992.

———. *Jāmi' al-'ulūm.* Edited by Sajjād Ḥusayn. New Delhi: Indian Council of Historical Research, 1987.

Ibn Baṭṭūṭa, Muḥammad ibn 'Abdallāh. *The Travels of of Ibn Battuta, A.D. 1325–1354.* Translated by H. A. R. Gibb. 5 vols. Cambridge: Published for the Hakluyt Society at the University Press, 1958–2000.

Ibn Māhrū, 'Ayn al-mulk. *Inshā'-i Māhrū/Letters of 'Ain ud-Dīn 'Ain ul-Mulk Abdullah bin Mahru).* Edited by 'Abdur Rashid and Muḥammad Bashir Husain. Lahore: Research Society of Pakistan, University of the Panjab.

———. *Insha'-i Māhrū.* MS. 208. Taṣawwuf. Andhra Pradesh Government Oriental Library. Hyderabad, India.

'Iṣāmī. *Futūḥ al-salāṭīn.* Edited by A. S. Usha. Madras: University of Madras, 1948.

———. *Futūḥ as-Salāṭīn or Shāh Nāmah-i Hind of 'Iṣāmī.* Translated by Mahdi Husain. 3 vols. New York: Asia Publishing House, 1977.

[Isfandiyār, Kaykhusraw]. *Dabistān-i maẕāhib.* 2 vols. Edited by Raḥīm Riżāzāda Malik. 2 vols. Tehran: Kitābkhāna-yi Ṭāhūrī, 1983.

Jamālī, Ḥāmid b. Fażlallāh. *Siyar al-'ārifīn.* Urdu translation by Muḥammad Ayūb Qādrī. Lahore: Markazī Urdu Board, 1976.

al-Kalābādhī, Abū Bakr Muḥammad ibn Isḥāq. *The Doctrine of the Ṣūfīs.* Translated by A. J. Arberry. Cambridge: The University Press, 1935.

Karāmī, Ṣadr al-dīn Ya'qūb Muẓaffar. *Fiqh-i Fīrōz Shāhī.* MS. I.O. Isl. 2987. British Library, London.

Kāshānī, Rukn al-dīn b. 'Imād al-dīn. *Shamā'il al-atqiyā'.* MS. I.O. Isl. 1322. British Library, London.

———. *Shamā'il al-atqiyā'.* Edited by Mawlawī Ḥakīm Ghulām Murtażā. Hyderabad: Ashraf Press, 1928.

Kubrā, Najm al-dīn. *La Pratique du Soufisme: quatorze petits traités.* French translation by Paul Ballanfat. Nimes: Éditions de l'éclat, 2002.

Lāhōrī, Ghulām Sarwar. *Ḥadīqat al-awliyā'.* Lahore: Islamic Book Foundation, 1396/1976.

———. *Khazīnat al-asfiyā'*. Urdu Translation. Lahore: Maktaba-yi Nabawīya, 1990.

al-Lak'hnawī, 'Abd al-Ḥayy b. Fakhr al-dīn al-Ḥasanī. *Nuzhat al-khawāṭir wa bahjat al masāmi' wa al-nawāzir*. 10 vols. Hyderabad: Maṭba'at Dā'irat al-Ma'ārif al-'Usmānīya, 1366/1947.

Maḥmūd b. 'Usmān. *Miftāḥ al-hidāya wa miṣbāḥ al-'ināya: Sīrat-nāma-yi shaykh Amīn al-dīn Muḥammad Balyānī*. Edited by 'Imād al-dīn Shaykh al-Ḥukamā'ī. Intishārāt-i Rawzanah, 1376/1997.

Majma' al-awliyā' wa maḥfil al-aṣfiyā'. MS. I.O. 1647, British Library, London.

Manba' al-sādāt. MS. Or. 2,014. British Library, London.

Manērī, Sharaf al-dīn Aḥmad ibn Yaḥyā. *Sharafuddin Maneri: The Hundred Letters*. Translated and edited by Paul Jackson. New York: Paulist Press, 1980.

———. *Maktūbāt-i dō ṣadī*. Urdu translation by Sayyid Shāh Qasīm al-dīn Aḥmad Sharafī Firdawsī. Lahore: Seerat Foundation, 2003.

Minhāj-i Sirāj, Minhāj al-dīn Abū 'Umar-i 'Usmān. *Ṭabaqāt-i Nāṣirī yā Tārīkh-i Īrān ō Islām*. Edited by 'Abd al-Ḥayy Ḥabībī. Tehran: Dunyā-yi Kitāb, 1363.

———. *Ṭabaqāt-i Nāṣirī*. Edited by W. Nassau Lees. Bibliotheca Indica. Calcutta: Asiatic Society of Bengal, 1864.

———. *Ṭabaqāt-i Nāṣirī. A General History of the Muhammadan Dynasties of Asia*. Translated by H. G. Raverty. 2 vols. Bibliotheca Indica. London: Asiatic Society of Bengal, 1881.

Mīr Khwaurd, Sayyid Muḥammad b. Mubārak 'Alawī Kirmānī. *Siyar al-awliyā'*. Lahore: Markaz-i Taḥqīqāt-i Fārsī-yi Īrān ō Pākistān.

———. *Siyar al-awliyā'*. Urdu translation by Ghulām Aḥmad Biryān and Ḥakīm Mahr Muḥammad Iqbāl Qādrī. Lahore: Mushtāq Book Corner, 1978.

———. *Siyar al-awliyā'*. Urdu translation by I'jāz al-Ḥaqq Quddūsī. Lahore: Markazī Urdū Board, n. d.

Miṣbāḥī, Mawlānā Nūr al-zamān. *Tazkira-i awliyā'-i Aḥmadābād*. Aḥmadābād: Nūr Academy, 1419/1998.

Muḥammad Bihāmad Khānī. *Tārīkh-i Muḥammadī: Portion Dealing with the Account of Sultan Firoz Shah, his Successors, and the Minor Kingdoms, from AH 752/AD 1351 to AH 842/1438*. Translated by Muhammad Zakī. Aligarh: Aligarh Muslim University Press, 1972.

Muḥammad Mujīr b. Wajīh al-dīn. *Miftāḥ al-jinān*. MS. I.O. Isl. 927. British Library, London.

Mustawfī, Ḥamdallāh. *The Geographical Part of the* Nuzhat al-Qulūb *Composed by Ḥamd-allāh Mustawfī of Qazwīn in 740 (1340)*. Translated by G. Le Strange. Leiden: Brill Imprimerie Orientale, 1919. In Persian Literature in Translation, Packard Humanities Institute, http://persian.packhum.org/persian/main. Accessed July 6, 2011.

Polo, Marco. *The Travels of Marco Polo*. Edited and revised from William Marsden's translation, by Manuel Komroff, introduction by Jason Goodwin. New York: Modern Library, 2001.

Riżawī, Muḥammad b. Jalāl Shāhī. *Sawāl ō jawāb*. MS. H-125. Punjab University Library, Lahore.

Rūmī, Jalāl al-dīn. *Signs of the Unseen: The Discourses of Jalaluddin Rumi*. Translated by W. M. Thackston. Putney, Vt.: Threshold Books, 1994.

Ṣalāḥ al-dīn, Shāh. *Mazhar-i Jalālī*. MS. 2–F/8295. Punjab University Library, Lahore. 36 folios.

al-Sha'rānī, 'Abd al-Wahhāb. *al-Ṭabaqāt al-kubrā*. Beirut: Dār al-Jīl, 1988.

Sirāj al-hidāya: Malfūẓāt-i Ḥusayn al-ma'rūf bi Jalāl al-dīn Makhdūm-i jahāniyān Jahāngasht. Edited by Qāżī Sajjād Ḥusayn. New Delhi: Indian Council of Historical Research, 1983.

Sīrat-i Fīrōz Shāhī. Translated by Muḥammad Ḥamīd Qurayshī. Appended to *A Memoir on Kotla Firoz Shah, Delhi* by James Alfred Page. Delhi: Manager of Publications, 1937.

Sirhindī, Yaḥyā. *The Tārīkh-i Mubārak-shāhī*. Translated by K. K. Basu. Gaekwad's Oriental Series: 63. Baroda: Oriental Institute, 1932.

al-Subkī, Tāj al-dīn. *Ṭabaqāt al-Shāfi'īya al-kubrā*. Edited by 'Abd al-Fattāḥ Muḥammad al-Ḥilw and Maḥmūd Muḥammad al-Ṭanāḥī. Reprint. Jīzah [Cairo]: Hajar lil-Ṭibā'a wa al-Nashr, 1992.

———. *Ṭabaqāt al-Shāfi'īya al-kubrā*. Edited by Muṣṭafā 'Abd al-Qādir Aḥmad 'Aṭā. Beirut: Dār al-Kutub al-'Ilmīya, 1999/1420.

Suhrawardī, 'Umar b. Muḥammad Shihāb al-dīn. *'Awārif al-ma'ārif*. Urdu translation by Sayyid Rashid Aḥmad Arshad. Lahore: Asad Publications, 1973.

Tarjuma-yi khulāṣat al-mafākhir. MS. I.O. Isl. 2271. British Library, London.

al-Tirmidhī, al-Ḥākim. *The Concept of Sainthood in Early Islamic Mysticism: Two Works by Al-Ḥākim Al-Tirmidhī*. Translated by Bernd Radtke and John O'Kane. Richmond: Curzon Press, 1996.

Wāriṣ Shāh. *Hīr Wāriṣ Shāh: Matn wa Urdu tarjuma*. Edition and accompanying Urdu translation by Ḥamīdallāh Shāh Hāshmī. Lahore: Dāniyāl, 2000.

———. *Hīr Vāriṣ Śāh: poème panjabi du XVIIIe siecle*. Introduction, transliteration, French translation, and commentary by Denis Matringe. Pondichéry: Institut Français, 1988.

al-Yāfi'ī, 'Abdallāh b. As'ab. *Mir'āt al-jinān*. Beirut: Dār al-Kutub al-'Ilmīya, 1997/1417.

Yamanī, Niẓām Gharīb. *Laṭā'if-i Ashrafī fī bayān-i ṭawā'if-i ṣūfī*. Delhi: Maṭba' Nuṣrat al-Māṭāb'-i Dihlī, [1880].

2. Modern Secondary Scholarship

Ahmad, Aziz. *An Intellectual History of Islam in India*. Edinburgh: Edinburgh University Press, 1969.

———. "The Sufi and Sultan in Pre-Mughal Muslim India." *Der Islam* 38 (1962): 142–141.

Ahmad, Nazir. "The Oldest Persian Translation of the 'Awarifu'l-Ma'ārif." *Indo-Iranica* (Calcutta) 25, 3–4 (1972): 19–50.

Ahmad, Qeyamuddin. "Barani's References to the Hindus in the *Tārīkh-i Fīruz Shāhi*—Territorial and Other Dimensions." *Islamic Culture* 56 (1982): 295–302.

Ahmed, Shahab and Nenad Filipovic. "The Sultan's Syllabus: A Curriculum for the Ottoman Imperial *Madreses* Prescribed in a *Fermān* of Qānūnī I Süleymān, Dated 973 (1565)," *Studia Islamica* 98/99 (2004): 183–218.

Alam, Muzaffar. "*Shari'a* and Governance in the Indo-Islamic Context." In *Beyond Turk and Hindu: Rethinking Religious Identities in Islamicate South Asia*. Edited by David Gilmartin and Bruce Lawrence. Gainsville: University Press of Florida, 2000.

Algar, Hamid. "Kāzarūnī," *Encyclopaedia of Islam*. New Edition. Vol. 4. Leiden: Brill, 1978. 851a–852a.

Ali, M. Athar. "Capital of the Sultans: Delhi during the Thirteenth and Fourteenth Centuries." In *Delhi through the Ages: Selected Essays in Urban History, Culture and Society*. Edited by R. E. Frykenberg. Delhi: Oxford University Press, 1993.

Ali, Mir Hasan. "Haḍrat Sayyid Jalal Mir Surkh Bukhari of Uch Sharif." *Journal of the Pakistan Historical Society* 29, 1 (1981): 40–49.

Ansari, A. S. Bazmee. "Djalāl al-Dīn Ḥusayn al-Bukhārī". *Encyclopaedia of Islam*. New Edition. Vol. 2. Leiden: Brill, 1965. 392a–393b.

Arberry, A. J. *Sufism: An Account of the Mystics of Islam*. London: Allen and Unwin, 1950.

Arnakis, G. G. "Futuwwa Traditions in the Ottoman Empire: Akhis, Bektashi Dervishes and Craftsmen." *Journal of Near Eastern Studies* 12, 4 (1953): 232–247.

Askari, S. H. *Maktub and Malfuz Literature as a Source of Socio-Political History*. Patna: Khuda Bakhsh Oriental Public Library, 1981.

Aslam, Muḥammad. *Malfūẓātī adab kī tārīkhī ahmīyat*. Lahore: Idāra-yi Taḥqīqāt-i Pākistān, Punjab University, 1995.

Austin, J. L. *How to Do Things with Words*. Cambridge: Harvard University Press, 1962.

Āʿẓamī, Shuʿayb. *Fārsī adab ba-ʿahd-i salāṭīn-i Tughluq*. Delhi: Nuʿmānī Press, 1985.

Banerjee, Jamini Mohan. *History of Firuz Shah Tughluq*. Delhi: Munshiram Manoharlal, 1967.

Baloch, N. A. "Tadhkirah-i-Mashaikh-i-Siwistan: An Unpublished Work and a New Source of Information on the Burial Place of Sultan Muhammad b. Tughluq at Sehwan, in Sind." *Sind University Research Journal. Arts Series. Humanities and Social Sciences* 9 (1970): 30–36.

Banga, Indu. "Gender Relations in Medieval India." In *The State and Society in Medieval India*. Edited by J. S. Grewal. *History of Science, Philosophy and Culture in Indian Civilization*. Vol. VII, Part I. New Delhi: Oxford University Press, 2005. 443–474.

Baran, Zeyno, ed. *Understanding Sufism and its Potential Role in US Policy*. Nixon Center Conference Report. Washington: The Nixon Center, March 2004.

Bashir, Shahzad. *Messianic Hopes and Mystical Visions: The Nūrbakhshīya between Medieval and Modern Islam*. Columbia: University of South Carolina Press, 2003.

———. "Enshrining Divinity: The Death and Memorialization of Fazlallāh Astarābādī in Ḥurūfī Thought." *Muslim World* 90, 3 (2000): 289–308.

Bausani, Alessandro. *L'Islam in India: Tipologia di un contatto religioso*. Roma: Accademia Nazionale dei Lincei, 1973.

———. "Can Monotheism Be Taught? (Further Considerations on the Typology of Monotheism)." *Numen* 10, 3 (December 1963): 167–201.

"Bayʿa". *Encyclopaedia of Islam*. New Edition. Vol. 1. Leiden: Brill, 1960. 1113.

Beg, M. A. "Warrāḳ." *Encyclopaedia of Islam*. New Edition. Vol. 11., 2002. 150a–151a.

Behl, Aditya. "The Politics of 'Other People's Myths.'" In *Notes from a Mandala: Essays in the History of Indian Religions in Honour of Wendy Doniger*. Edited by Laurie L. Patton and David L. Haberman. Newark: University of Delaware Press, 2010.

Bhaṭṭī, Muḥammad Isḥāq. *Barr-i ṣaghīr Pāk-ō-Hind meṉ ʿilm-i fiqh*. Lahore: Idāra-yi Ṣaqāfat-i Islāmīya, 1973.

Bosworth, C. E. "Legal and Political Sciences in the Eastern Iranian World and Central Asia in the Pre-Mongol Period." In *History of Civilizations of Central Asia: The Age of Achievement: Vol 4: Part 1—The Historical, Social and Economic Setting*. Edited by M. S. Asimov and Clifford Edmund Bosworth. New Delhi: Motilal Banarsidass Publishers, 1999. 133–141.

Böwering, Gerhard. "From the Word of God to the Vision of God: Muḥammad's Heavenly Journey in Classical Ṣūfī Qur'ān Commentary." In *Le voyage initiatique en terre d'Islam: ascensions célestes et itinéraires spirituels*. Edited by Mohammad Ali Amir-Moezzi. Louvain: Peeters, 1996. 205–221.

———. "Règles et rituels soufis." In *Les Voies D'Allah*. Edited by Alexandre Popovic and Gilles Veinstein. Paris: Fayard 1996.

———. "The *Adab* Literature of Classical Sufism: Ansari's Code of Conduct." In *Moral Conduct and Authority: The Place of Adab in South Asian Islam*. Edited by Barbara D. Metcalf. Berkeley: University of California Press, 1984.

Broadbridge, Anne F. *Kingship and Ideology in the Islamic and Mongol Worlds*. Cambridge: Cambridge University Press, 2008.

Budge, Sir E. A. Wallis. *Amulets and Talismans*. New Hyde Park: University Books, 1961.

Buehler, Arthur. *Sufi Heirs to the Prophet: The Indian Naqshbandiyya and the Rise of the Mediating Sufi Shaykh*. Columbia: University of South Carolina Press, 1998.

Bulliet, Richard W. "Medieval Arabic *Tarsh*: A Forgotten Chapter in the History of Printing." *Journal of the American Oriental Society* 107, 3 (1987): 427–438.

———. "The Shaikh Al-Islām and the Evolution of Islamic Society." *Studia Islamica* 35 (1972): 53–67.

Calmard, J. "Kāzarūn." *Encyclopaedia of Islam*. New Edition. Vol. 4. Leiden: Brill, 1978. 850b–851a.

Callewaert, Winand M. and Rupert Snell, eds. *According to Tradition: Hagiographical Writing in India*. Wiesbaden: Harrasowitz Verlag, 1994.

Cammann, Schuyler. "Islamic and Indian Magic Squares." *History of Religions* 8, 3 (1969): 181–209 and 8, 4 (1969): 271–299.

Cole, Juan R. I. "Rival Empires of Trade and Imami Shiism in Eastern Arabia, 1300–1800." *International Journal of Middle East Studies* 19, 2 (May, 1987): 177–203

Cornell, Vincent J. *Realm of the Saint: Power and Authority in Moroccan Sufism*. Austin: University of Texas Press, 1998.

Crook, Nigel. ed. *The Transmission of Knowledge in South Asia: Essays on Education, Religion, History and Politics*. Delhi: Oxford University Press, 1996.

Culler, Jonathan. "Presupposition and Intertextuality." *MLN: Modern Languages Notes* 91, 6 *Comparative Literature* (December 1976): 1380–1396.

Currie, P. M. *The Shrine and Cult of Mu'īn al-Dīn Chishtī of Ajmer*. Oxford University. South Asian Studies Series. Delhi: Oxford University Press, 1989.

Daftary, Farhad. *A Short History of the Ismailis: Traditions of a Muslim Community*. Edinburgh University Press, 1998.

Dallapiccola, Anna Libera, and Stephanie Zingel-Avé Lallemant, eds. *Islam and Indian Regions*. Vol. 1. Stuttgart: Franz Steiner Verlag, 1993.

Danner, Victor. "The Shādhiliyya and North African Sufism." In *Islamic Spirituality II: Manifestations*. Edited by Seyyed Hossein Nasr. New York: Crossroad, 1991.

De Jong, T. "Waẓīfa, 2." *Encyclopaedia of Islam*. New Edition. Vol. 11. Leiden: Brill, 2002. 184a–185b.

Denny, F. M. "Wird." *Encyclopaedia of Islam*. New Edition. Vol. 11. Leiden: Brill, 2002. 209b–210a.

Desai, Z. A. "India and the Near East during 13th and 15th centuries." In *A Quest for Truth: A Collection of Research Articles of Dr Z. A. Desai*. Ahmadabad: Hazrat Pir Mohammed Shah Dargah Sharif Trust, 2004. 108–120.

———. *Malfuz Literature as a Source of Political, Social and Cultural History of Gujrat and Rajasthan*. Patna: Khuda Bakhsh Oriental Public Library, 1991.

________. "The Major Dargahs of Ahmadabad." In *Muslim Shrines in India: Their Character, History and Significance*. Edited by Christian W. Troll. Delhi: Oxford University Press, 1989.

Devahuti. *Bias in Indian Historiography*. Delhi: Indian History and Culture Society, 1980.

DeWeese, Devin. "Sacred Places and 'Public' Narratives: The Shrine of Aḥmad Yasavī in Hagiographical Traditions of the Yasavī Ṣūfī Order, 16th–17th Centuries." *The Muslim World* 90, 3 (2000): 353–374.

Dhillon, Sukhninder Kaur. *Religious History of Early Medieval Punjab*. New Delhi: National Book Organization, 1991.

Digby, Simon. "The Sufi *Shaykh* and the Sultan: A Conflict of Claims to Authority in Medieval India." *Iran* 28 (1990): 71–81.

———. "The Sufi Shaikh as a Source of Authority in Mediaeval India." In *Islam and Society in South Asia/Islam et Société en Asie du Sud*. Edited by Marc Gaborieau. Paris: Éditions de l'École des Hautes Études en Sciences Sociales, 1986.

——. "Qalandars and Related Groups: Elements of Social Deviance in the Religious Life of the Delhi Sultanate of the Thirteenth and Fourteenth Centuries." In *Islam in Asia*, Vol. 1, *South Asia*. Edited by Yohanan Friedmann. Boulder: Westview Press, 1984.

Eaton, Richard M. *Essays on Islam and Indian History*. New Delhi: Oxford University Press, 2000.

——. "Temple Desecration and Indo-Muslim States." In *Beyond Turk and Hindu: Rethinking Religious Identities in Islamicate South Asia*. Edited by David Gilmartin and Bruce Lawrence. Gainsville: University Press of Florida, 2000.

——. Review of *Eternal Garden: Mysticism, History, and Politics at a South Asian Sufi Center*, by Carl W. Ernst. *The Journal of Asian Studies* 53, 1 (1994): 249–251.

——. *The Rise of Islam and the Bengal Frontier*. University of California Press, 1993.

——. "The Political and Religious Authority of the Shrine of Baba Farid in Pakpattan, Punjab." In *Moral Conduct and Authority: the Place of Adab in South Asian Islam*. Edited by Barbara D. Metcalf. Berkeley: University of California Press, 1984.

——. *Sufis of Bijapur 1300–1700: Social Roles of Sufis in Medieval India*. Princeton: Princeton University Press, 1978.

——. "Sufi Folk Literature and the Expansion of Indian Islam." *History of Religions* 14 (1974): 117–127.

Elias, Jamal J. "The Sufi Robe (*Khirqa*) as a Vehicle of Spiritual Authority." In *Robes of Honor: The Medieval World of Investiture*. Edited by Stewart Gordon. New York: Palgrave, 2001.

——. "A Second 'Alī: The Making of Sayyid 'Alī Hamadānī in Popular Imagination." *The Muslim World* 90, 3 (2000): 395–415.

——. *Throne Carrier of God: The Life and Thought of 'Alā' ad-dawla as-Simnānī*. Albany: State University of New York Press, 1995.

Ernst, Carl W. *The Shambala Guide to Sufism*. Boston: Shambala, 1997.

——. "The Interpretation of the Classical Sufi Tradition in India: The *Shamā'il al-atqiyā'* of Rukn al-Dīn Kāshānī." *Sufi* 22 (Summer 1994): 5–10.

——. *Eternal Garden: Mysticism, History and Politics at a South Asian Sufi Center*. Albany: State University of New York Press, 1992.

——. *Words of Ecstasy in Sufism*. Albany: State University of New York Press, 1984.

Ernst, Carl W. and Bruce B. Lawrence. *Sufi Martyrs of Love: The Chishti Order in South Asia and Beyond*. New York: Palgrave Macmillan, 2002.

Ewing, Katherine Pratt. *Arguing Sainthood: Modernity, Psychoanalysis and Islam*. Durham: Duke University Press, 1997.

Fernandes, Leonor. *The Evolution of a Sufi Institution in Mamluk Egypt: The Khanqah*. Islamkundliche Untersuchungen Band 134. Berlin: Klaus Schwarz Verlag, 1988.

——. "Mamluk Politics and Education: The Evidence from Two Fourteenth Century Waqfiyya." *Annales Islamologiques* 23 (1987): 87–98.

——. "Some Aspects of the *Zāwiya* in Egypt at the Eve of the Ottoman Conquest." *Annales Islamologiques* 19 (1983): 9–17.

——. "Three Ṣūfī Foundations in a 15th Century Waqfiyya." *Annales Islamologiques* 17 (1981): 141–156.

Friedmann, Yohanan, ed. *Islam in Asia*. Vol. 1. *South Asia*. Boulder: Westview Press, 1984.

Frykenberg, R. E., ed. *Delhi through the Ages: Selected Essays in Urban History, Culture and Society*. New Delhi: Oxford University Press, 1993.

Geijbels, Matthew. "Aspects of the Veneration of Saints in Islam, with Special Reference to Pakistan." *The Muslim World* 68 (1978): 176–186.

Geoffroy, E. "Yāfi'ī." *Encyclopaedia of Islam*. New Edition. Vol. 11. Leiden: Brill, 2002. 236a–236b.

Gilmartin, David and Bruce Lawrence, eds. *Beyond Turk and Hindu: Rethinking Religious Identities in Islamicate South Asia.* Gainsville: University Press of Florida, 2000.

Gaborieau, Marc, ed. *Islam and Society in South Asia/Islam et Société en Asie du Sud.* Paris: Éditions de l'École des Hautes Études en Sciences Sociales, 1986.

Gordon, Stewart, ed. *Robes of Honour:* Khil'at *in Pre-Colonial and Colonial India.* New Delhi: Oxford University Press, 2003.

———, ed. *Robes of Honor: The Medieval World of Investiture.* New York: Palgrave, 2001.

Graham, William A. "Traditionalism in Islam: An Essay in Interpretation." *Journal of Interdisciplinary History* 23, 3 (1993): 495–522.

Gramlich, Richard. *Die Wunder der Freunde Gottes: Theologien und Erscheinungsformen des Islamischen Heiligenwunders.* Stuttgart: Steiner Verlag Wiesbaden, 1987.

———. *Die Schiitischen Derwischorden Persiens.* Vol. 1. *Die Affiliationen.* Abhandlungen fur die Kunde des Morgenlandes: 34, 1. Wiesbaden, 1965.

Grewal, J. S. *The State and Society in Medieval India.* Vol. VII, Part I. *History of Indian Science, Philosophy and Culture in Indian Civilization.* New Delhi: Oxford University Press, 2005.

Gribetz, Arthur. "The *Samā'* Controversy: Sufi vs. Legalist." *Studia Islamica* 74 (1991): 43–62.

Grierson, George. "Indo-Aryan Vernaculars." *Bulletin of the School of Oriental Studies* 1, 2 (1918).

Guenther, Alan M. "Hanafi *Fiqh* in Mughal India: The *Fatāwā-i 'ālamgīrī.*" In *India's Islamic Traditions, 711–1750.* Edited by Richard M. Eaton. New Delhi: Oxford University Press, 2003.

Habib, Mohammad. "Life and Thought of Ziauddin Barani." *Medieval India Quarterly* 3, 3–4 (1958).

———. "Chishti Mystic Records of the Sultanate Period." *Medieval India Quarterly* 1, 2 (1950): 1–42.

Habib, Mohammad and Afsar Umar Salim Khan. *The Political Theory of the Delhi Sultanate (Including a Translation of Ziauddin Barani's Fatawa-i Jahandari, Circa, 1358–9 A.D.). Medieval India Quarterly* 3, 3–4 (1958): 117–252.

Habib, Mohammad and Khaliq Ahmad Nizami, eds. *A Comprehensive History of India.* Vol. 5. *The Delhi Sultanat (A.D. 1206–1526).* New Delhi: People's Publishing House, 1970.

Haig, T. W. and C. E. Bosworth. "Sind: History in the Pre-Modern Period." *Encyclopaedia of Islam.* New Edition. Vol. 9. Leiden: Brill, 1997. 632b–635b.

Hambly, Gavin. "From Baghdad to Bukhara, from Ghazna to Delhi: The *Khil'a* Ceremony in the Transmission of Kingly Pomp and Circumstance." In *Robes of Honor: The Medieval World of Investiture.* Edited by Stewart Gordon. New York: Palgrave, 2001.

Hamid, Farooq. "The Hagiographic Process: The Case of Medieval Chishti Sufi Farīd al-Dīn Mas'ūd Ganj-i Shakar (d. 664/1265)." *The Muslim World* 90, 3 (2000): 421–437.

Ḥāmid, Khān. *Ḥażrat Sakhī Sarwar.* Lahore: Maḥkama-i Awqāf, 1978.

Haq, S. Moinul. "The Suhrawardīs." *Journal of the Pakistan Historical Society* 22 (1974): 71–103.

Hardy, Peter. "Didactic Historical Writing in Indian Islam: Ziyā al-Dīn Baranī's Treatment of the Reign of Sultan Muḥammad Tughluq (1324–51)." In *Islam in Asia.* Volume 1. *South Asia.* Edited by Yohanan Friedmann, Jerusalem: Magnes Press, 1984.

———. "Dihlī Sultanate." *Encyclopaedia of Islam.* New Edition. Vol. 2. Leiden: Brill, 1965. 266b–274a.

———. *Historians of Medieval India: Studies in Indo-Muslim Historical Writing.* London: Luzac and Company Ltd., 1960.

Hasan, Mohibbul, ed. *Historians of Medieval India.* New Delhi: Jamia Millia Islamia, 1968.

Hasan, S. Nurul. "Sahifa-i-na't-i-Muhammadi of Zia-ud-din-Barani." *Medieval India Quarterly* 1, 3–4 (1954): 100–106.

Hassan, Perween. "The Footprint of the Prophet." In *Essays in Honor of Oleg Grabar. Muqarnas* 10 (1993): 335–343.
Heck, Paul L. "The Epistemological Problem of Writing in Islamic Civilization: al-Ḫaṭīb al-Baġdādī's (d. 463/1071) *Taqyīd al-'ilm*." *Studia Islamica* 94 (2002): 85–114.
Hermansen, Marcia K. "Religious Literature and the Inscription of Identity: The Sufi Tazkira Tradition in Muslim South Asia." *The Muslim World* 87, 3–4 (1997): 315–329.
———. "Visions as 'Good to Think': A Cognitive Approach to Visionary Experience in Islamic Sufi Thought." *Religion* 27 (1997): 25–43.
Hermansen, Marcia K. and Bruce B. Lawrence. "Indo-Persian Tazkiras as Memorative Communications." In *Beyond Turk and Hindu: Rethinking Religious Identities in Islamicate South Asia*. Edited by David Gilmartin and Bruce Lawrence. Gainsville: University Press of Florida, 2000.
Hillenbrand, Robert. "Turco-Iranian Elements in the Medieval Architecture of Pakistan: The Case of the Tomb of Rukn-I 'Alam at Multan." *Muqarnas* 9 (1992): 148–174.
Hoḍīvālā, Shāhpūrshāh Hormasjī. *Studies in Indo-Muslim History*. Vol. 2. *A Critical Commentary on Eliot and Dowson's History of India*. Bombay: Popular Book Depot, 1957.
Hodgson, Marshall G. S. *The Venture of Islam: Conscience and History in a World Civilization*. 3 Volumes. Chicago: The University of Chicago Press, 1974.
Hoffman, Valerie. "Eating and Fasting for God in the Sufi Tradition." *Journal of the American Academy of Religion* 63, 3 (1995): 465–484.
Huda, Qamar-ul. *Striving for Divine Union: Spiritual Exercises for Suhrawardī Ṣūfīs*. London: RoutledgeCurzon, 2003.
———. "Celebrating Death and Engaging in Texts at Dātā Ganj Bakhsh's *'Urs*." *The Muslim World* 90, 3 (2000): 377–394.
Ikram, S. M. *Āb-i kawsar: Islāmī Hind ō Pākistān kī mazhabī awr 'ilmī tārīkh 'ahd-i Mughlīya sē pehlē*. 5th edition. Lahore: Idāra-yi Ṣaqāfat-i Islāmīya, 1964.
———. *Muslim Rule in India and Pakistan (711–1858 A.C.)*. Lahore: Star Book Depot, 1961.
Imamuddin, S. M. "Education under the Mughals in India (1526–1707 A.D.)." *Islamic Quarterly* 26 (1982): 185–193.
Islam, Arshad. "Sūmrah and Sammah rule in Sind (c. 1051–1520 C. E.)." *Journal of the Pakistan Historical Society* 46, 2 (1998): 69–78.
———. "Development of Islamic Education and Learning in Sindh (712–1526)." *Journal of the Pakistan Historical Society* 44, 1 (1996): 101–108.
Islam, Riazul. *Sufism in South Asia: Impact on Fourteenth Century Muslim Society*. Oxford: Oxford University Press, 2002.
———. "A Note on the Position of Non-Muslim Subjects in the Sultanate of Delhi under the Khaljis and the Tughluqs." *Journal of the Pakistan Historical Society* 45, 3 (1997): 215–229.
———. "A Note on Zanbil: The Practice of Begging among Sufis in South Asia (Mainly 14th Century)." *Journal of the Pakistan Historical Society* 44, 1 (1996): 5–11.
———. "South Asian Sufis and Their Social Linkage (Mainly 14th Century)." In *Cultural Interaction in South Asia: A Historical Perspective*. Edited by S. A. I. Tirmizi. New Delhi: Hamdard Institute of Historical Research (1993).
———. "Ideas on *Kasb* in South Asian Sufism (Mainly Fourteenth Century)." *The Indian Historical Review* 17, 1–2 (1990–1991, 1993): 90–121.
———. "Collections of the Malfuzat of Makhdum-i-Jahanian (1307–1388) of Uchh." In *The Proceedings of the All-Pakistan History Conference, 1951*. Karachi: Pakistan Historical Society.
———. "A Review of the Reign of Fīrōz Shāh (1351–88 A.C.)." *Islamic Culture* 23 (1949): 281–297.

———. "The Rise of the Sammas in Sind (Based on Contemporary Sources)." *Islamic Culture* 22 (1948): 359–382.

Islam, Zafarul. "Origin and Development of *Fatāwā* Compilation in Medieval India." *Studies in History* 12, 2 (1996): 223–241.

———. "Works of Legal Nature in the Reign of Firuz Shah Tughluq." In *Bias in Indian Historiography*. Edited by Devahuti. Delhi: Indian History and Culture Society, 1980.

Jackson, Paul. *The Way of a Sufi: Sharafuddin Maneri*. Delhi: Idarah-i Adabiyat-i Delli, 1987.

———. "Shaikh Shrafuddin [*sic*] Maneri as Spiritual Master." In *Spiritual Masters: Christianity and Other Religions*. Studia missionalia. Vol. 36. Rome: Gregorian University Press, 1987.

Jackson, Peter. *The Delhi Sultanate: A Political and Military History*. Cambridge: Cambridge University Press, 1999.

Jauhri, R. C. "Learning and Literature during the Reign of Firoz Shah Tughluq (1351–88)." *Islamic Culture* 41 (1967): 241–246.

Kalīm, Muḥammad Dīn. *Suhrawardī awliyā'-i Lāhōr*. Lahore: Maktaba-yi Tārīkh, 1969.

———. *Lāhōr kē awliyā'-i Chisht*. Lahore: Maktaba-yi Tārīkh, 1968.

Karamustafa, Ahmet T. *God's Unruly Friends: Dervish Groups in the Islamic Later Middle Period, 1200–1550*. Salt Lake City: University of Utah Press, 1994.

Khan, Ahmad Nabi. *Multan: History and Architecture*. Islamabad: Institute of Islamic History, Culture and Civilization, Islamic University, 1983.

———. *Uchchh, History and Architecture*. Islamabad: National Institute of Historical and Cultural Research, 1980.

Khan, Iqtidar Husain. "The *Pīr* and *Murīd*: A Case Study of the *Ṣūfīs* of Suhrawardī *Silsilah* in India during the Thirteenth and Fourteenth Centuries." *Hamdard Islamicus* 21, 3 (1998): 23–36.

Khan, M. N. A. "Muslim Educational System in the Deccan during the Mediaeval Period and the Synthesis of its Culture." *Salar Jung Bi-Annual Research Journal* 17–18 (1982–83): 75–80.

Khan, Masud Ahmad. "Khanqahs: Centres of Learning." In *Sufis, Sultans and Feudal Orders: Professor Nurul Hasan Commemoration Volume*. Edited by Mansura Haidar. New Delhi: Manohar, 2004. 71–106.

Kiyānī, Muḥsin. *Tārīkh-i khānqāh dar Īrān*. Tehrān: Kitābkhāna-yi Ṭahūrī, 1369/1990.

Khudā Bakhsh Janūbī Ayshyā'ī 'Ilāqā'ī Sēmīnār. *Taṣawwuf barr-i ṣaghīr mēṉ: Taṣawwuf kē nādir makhṭūṭāt par janūbī ayshyā'ī 'ilāqā'ī sēmīnār mun'aqada 1985 kē mulāqāt*. Patna: Khudā Bakhsh Oriental Public Library, 1992.

Knysh, Alexander D. *Ibn 'Arabi in the Later Islamic Tradition*. Albany: State University of New York Press, 1999.

Krenkow, F. "al-Yāfi'ī." *Encyclopaedia of Islam*. 1st edition. Vol. 3. Leiden: Brill, 1913–1938. 1145a.

Lal, K. S. *Growth of Muslim Population in Medieval India (A. D. 1000–1800)*. Delhi: Research Publications, 1973.

Lari, Suhail Zaheer. *A History of Sindh*. Karachi: Oxford University Press, 1994.

Lawrence, Bruce B. "Early Indo-Muslim Saints and Conversion." In *Islam in Asia*. Vol. 1. *South Asia*. Edited by Yohanan Friedmann. Boulder: Westview Press, 1984.

———. "The Chishtīya of Sultanate India: A Case Study in Biographical Complexities in South Asian Islam." In *Charisma and Sacred Biography*. Edited by Michael A. Williams. *JAAR Thematic Studies* 48, 3–4 (1982): 47–67. Reprinted as "The Earliest Chishtiyya and Shaikh Niẓām ud-Dīn Awliyā." In *Delhi Through the Ages: Selected Essays in Urban History, Culture and Society*. Edited by R. E. Frykenberg. Delhi: Oxford University Press, 1993.

———, ed. *The Rose and the Rock: Mystical and Rational Elements in the Intellectual History of South Asian Islam*. Durham: Duke University Program in Comparative Area Studies, 1979.

———. *Notes from a Distant Flute: The Extant Literature of Pre-Mughal Indian Sufism*. Tehran: Imperial Academy of Philosophy, 1978.

Leiser, Gary. "Notes on the Madrasa in Medieval Islamic Society." *The Muslim World* 76 (1986): 16–23.

Lewisohn, Leonard. "The Sacred Music of Islam: Samā' in the Persian Sufi Tradition." *British Journal of Ethnomusicology* 6 (1997): 1–33.

Lorenzen, David N. *Kabir Legends and Ananta-das's Kabir Parachai, with a Translation of the Kabir Parachai Prepared in Collaboration with Jagdish Kumar and Uma Thukral and with an Edition of the Niranjani Panthi Recension of This Work*. Albany: State University of New York Press, 1991.

Luniya, B. N. *Some Historians on Medieval India*. Agra: Lakshmi Narain Agarwal, 1969.

Maclean, Derryl N. *Religion and Society in Arab Sind*. Leiden: Brill, 1989.

Madan, T. N. ed. *Muslim Communities of South Asia: Culture, Society and Power*. Delhi: Institute of Economic Growth, 2001.

Mahajan, Vidya Dhar. *The Sultanate of Delhi*. S. Chand & co., 1963.

Makdisi, George. *Religion, Law and Learning in Classical Islam*. Hampshire: Varorium, 1991.

———. "The Diary in Islamic Historiography: Some Notes." *History and Theory* 25 (1986): 173–185.

Masud, Muhammad Khalid, Brinkley Messick, and David S. Powers. "Muftis, Fatwas, and Islamic Legal Interpretation." In *Islamic Legal Interpretation: Muftis and Their Fatwas*. Edited by Masud, Messick, and Powers. Cambridge: Harvard University Press, 1996.

Matringe, Denis. "The Future Has Come Near, the Past Is Far Behind": A Study of Saix Farīd's Verses and Their Sikh Commentaries in the Adi Granth." In *Islam and Indian Regions*. Vol. 1. Edited by Anna Libera Dallapiccola and Stephanie Zingel-Avé Lallemant. Stuttgart: Franz Steiner Verlag, 1993.

Metcalf, Barbara D., ed. *Moral Conduct and Authority: The Place of Adab in South Asian Islam*. Berkeley: University of California Press, 1984.

Mojaddedi, J. A. *The Biographical Tradition in Sufism: The Ṭabaqāt Genre from al-Sulamī to Jāmī*. Richmond, Surrey: Curzon Press, 2001.

Mortel, Richard. "*Ribāṭs* in Mecca during the Medieval Period: A Descriptive Study Based on Literary Sources." *Bulletin of the School of Oriental and African Studies* 61, 1 (1998): 29–50.

———. "Madrasas in Mecca during the Medieval Period: A Descriptive Study Based on Literary Sources." *Bulletin of the School of Oriental and African Studies* 60, 2 (1997): 236–252.

———. "The Ḥusaynid Amirate of Madīna during the Mamlūk Period." *Studia Islamica* 80 (1994): 97–123.

———. "Zaydi Shi'ism and the Ḥasanid Sharifs of Mecca." *International Journal of Middle East Studies* 19, 4 (1987): 455–472.

Mottahedeh, Roy P. *Loyalty and Leadership in an Early Islamic Society*. Princeton: Princeton University Press, 1980.

Motzki, Harald. "Child Marriage in Seventeenth-Century Palestine." In *Islamic Legal Interpretation: Muftis and Their Fatwas*. Edited by Masud, Messick, and Powers. Cambridge: Harvard University Press, 1996.

Mughal, Mohammad Rafique. *Ancient Cholistan: Archaeology and Architecture*. Lahore: Ferozsons, 1997.

Mujeeb, M. *The Indian Muslims*. London: George Allen and Unwin Ltd., 1967.

Murādābādī, Muḥammad Naẕīr Aḥmad Na'īmī. *Ḥayāt-i ḥażrat Shāh-i 'alam.* Aḥmadābād: Khānqāh-i Shāh-i 'ālam, 2009.

Muṭī' al-Imām, Sayyid. *Shaykh Sharaf al-dīn ibn Yaḥyā Manērī wa sahm-i ū dar mutaṣṣawafāna-yi fārsī.* Islamabad: Markiz-i Taḥqīqāt-i Fārsī-yi Īrān ō Pākistān, 1414/1993.

Nadwī, Mujīb Allāh. *Fatāwā-i 'Ālamgīrī kē mu'allifīn.* Lahore: Markaz-i Taḥqīq-i Dayāl Singh Trust Library, 1407/1987.

Nasr, Seyyed Hossein. "The Traditional Texts used in Persian Madrasahs." In *Encyclopaedic Survey of Islamic Culture.* Vol 13. *Educational Developments in the Muslim World.* Edited by Mohamed Taher. New Delhi: Anmol Publications, 1997.

———. "Oral Transmission and the Book in Islamic Education: The Spoken and the Written Word." *Journal of Islamic Studies* 3, 1 (1992): 1–14.

Nigam, S. B. P. "Organisation of Turkish Nobility in India (1206–1398)." *Islamic Culture* 29 (1965): 271–283.

Nijjar, Bakhshish Singh. "Mamluk Administration." In *History of the Punjab (AD 1000–1526).* Vol. 3. Edited by Fauja Singh. Patiala: Punjabi University, 1972.

Nizami, Khaliq Ahmad. *Royalty in Medieval India.* New Delhi: Munshiram Manoharlal, 1997.

———. "Development of the Muslim Educational System in Medieval India." *Islamic Culture* 70, 4 (1996): 27–52.

———. "*Durar-i-Nizami*—A Unique but Less-known *Malfuz* of Shaikh Nizam-u'd-din Auliya." In *Historical Studies—Indian and Islamic.* Vol. 1. *On Sources and Source Material.* New Delhi: Idarah-i Adabiyat-i Dilli, 1995.

———. "*Sarur-u's-Sudur*, a *Malfuz* of Shaikh Hamid-u'd-din of Nagaur." In *Historical Studies — Indian and Islamic.* Vol. 1. *On Sources and Source Material.* New Delhi: Idarah-i Adabiyat-i Dilli, 1995.

———. "Ṣūfīya-yi Hind kā ēk nādir taẕkira "Mārij al-wilāya"." In *Taṣawwuf barr-i ṣaghīr mēṉ: Taṣawwuf kē nādir makhṭūṭāt par janūbī ayshyā'ī 'ilāqā'ī sēmīnār mun'aqada 1985 kē mulāqāt.* Khudā Bakhsh Janūbī Ayshyā'ī 'Ilāqā'ī Sēmīnār. Patna: Khudā Bakhsh Oriental Public Library, 1992. 30–37.

———. *The Life and Times of Shaikh Nasir-u'd-din Chiragh-i-Dehli.* Delhi: Idarah-i Adabyat-i Delli, 1991.

———. "The Impact of Ibn Taimiyya on South Asia." *Journal of Islamic Studies* 1 (1990): 120–149.

———. "Ahsan-al-Aqwal, a malfuz of Shaikh Burhan-u'd-din Gharib." *Journal of the Pakistan Historical Society* (January 1955). Reprinted in *Historical Studies—Indian and Islamic.* Vol. 1. *On Sources and Source Material.* New Delhi: Idarah-i Adabiyat-i Dilli, 1995.

———. *State and Culture in Medieval India.* New Delhi: Adam Publishers, 1985.

———. *Some Aspects of Religion and Politics in India during the Thirteenth Century.* Bombay: Asia Publishing House, 1961.

———. *Salāṭīn-i Dihlī kē maẕhabī ruḥjānāt.* Delhi: Idāra-yi Adabīyāt-i Dillī, 1958.

———. "Some Aspects of Khānqāh Life in Medieval India." *Studia Islamica* 8 (1957): 51–69.

———. *The Life and Times of Shaikh Farid-u'd-Din Ganj-i-Shakar.* Delhi: Idarah-i Adabiyat-i Delli, 1955.

———. "Shattari Saints and Their Attitude Towards the State." *Medieval India Quarterly* 1, 2 (1950): 56–70.

———. "Early Indo-Muslim Mystics and Their Attitude towards the State." Parts 1–5. *Islamic Culture* 22 (1948): 387–398; 23 (1949): 13–21, 162–170, 312–321; 24 (1950): 60–71.

Oddie, G. A., ed. *Religion in South Asia: Religious Conversion and Revival Movements in South Asia in Medieval and Modern Times.* 2nd edition. New Delhi: Manohar, 1991.

Ohlander, Erik S. *Sufism in an Age of Transition: 'Umar al-Suhrawardī and the Rise of the Islamic Mystical Brotherhoods*. Leiden: Brill, 2008.

Padwick, Constance E. *Muslim Devotions: A Study of Prayer-Manuals in Common Use*. London: S.P.C.K, 1961.

Pedersen, J. "Some Aspects of the History of the Madrasa." In *Encyclopaedic Survey of Islamic Culture*. Vol 3. *Educational Developments in the Muslim World*. Edited by Mohamed Taher. New Delhi: Anmol Publications, 1997.

Pinto, Desiderio. *Piri-Muridi Relationship: A Study of the Nizamuddin Dargah*. New Delhi: Manohar Publishers, 1995.

Popovic, Alexandre and Gilles Veinstein, eds. *Les Voies D'Allah*. Paris: Fayard, 1996.

Qādirī, Muḥammad Ayyūb. *Makhdūm-i jahāniyān Jahāngasht: Mufaṣṣal-i ḥālāt ō sawāniḥ-yi Jalāl al-dīn Makhdūm-i jahāniyān Jahāngasht Bukhārī Uchī*. Karachi: Idāra-yi Taḥqīq ō Taṣnīf, 1963.

Qureshi, Ishtiaq Husain. *The Muslim Community of the Indo-Pakistan Subcontinent (610–1947)*. The Hague: Mouton and Co., 1962.

———. *The Administration of the Sultanate of Dehlī*. 4th Edition (Revised). Karachi: Pakistan Historical Society, 1958.

Radtke, B. et al. "Walī". *Encyclopaedia of Islam*. New Edition. Vol. 11. Leiden: Brill, 2002. 109b-125a.

Rai, Amrit. *A House Divided: The Origin and Development of Hindi/Hindavi*. Delhi: Oxford University Press, 1984.

Rani, Abha. *The Tughluq Architecture of Delhi*. Varanasi: Bharati Prakashan, 1991.

Rashid, Shaykh Abdur. "Inshā'-i-māhrū or Tarassul-i-'Ain-ul-Mulk." *Islamic Culture* 16 (1942): 279–290.

Reynolds, Dwight F. ed. *Interpreting the Self: Autobiography in the Arabic Literary Tradition*. Berkeley: University of California Press, 2001.

Richards, J. F. "The Islamic Frontier in the East: Expansion into South Asia." *South Asia* 4 (1974): 91–109.

Rizvi, Saiyid Athar Abbas. "Islamic Proselytisation: Seventh to Sixteenth Centuries." In *Religion in South Asia: Religious Conversion and Revival Movements in South Asia in Medieval and Modern Times*. Edited by G. A. Oddie. 2nd Edition. New Delhi: Manohar, 1991.

———. *A History of Sufism in India*. 2 vols. New Delhi: Munshiram Manoharlal, 1978.

———. *A Socio-Intellectual History of the Isnā 'Asharī Shī'īs in India, 16th–19th century AD*. 2 vols. Canberra: Ma'rifat Publishing House, 1968.

Riyāż, Muḥammad. *Aḥwāl ō āṣār-i mīr sayyid 'Alī Hamadānī*. Lahore: Nadwat al-Muṣannafīn, 1972.

Robinson, Francis. *Islam and Muslim History in South Asia*. New Delhi: Oxford University Press, 2000.

———. "Islam and the Impact of Print in South Asia." In *The Transmission of Knowledge in South Asia: Essays on Education, Religion, History and Politics*. Edited by Nigel Crook. Delhi: Oxford University Press, 1996.

Robson, James. "The Magical Use of the Koran." *Transactions of the Glasgow University Oriental Society* 6 (1929–1933): 51–61.

Rosenthal, Franz. *Knowledge Triumphant: The Concept of Knowledge in Medieval Islam*. Boston: Brill, 2006.

Saeed, Mian Muhammad. *The Sharqi Sultanate of Jaunpur: A Poltical and Cultural History*. Pakistan: University of Karachi, 1972.

Ṣafā, Ẕabīh Allāh. *Tārīkh-i adabīyāt dar Īrān*. 5 vols. Tehran: Ibn-i Sīnā/Intishārāt-i Dānishgāh-i Tihrān, 1953–83.

Sakhāwat, Mirzā. *Tazkira-yi ḥażrat sayyid Jalāl al-dīn Makhdūm-i jahāniyān Jahāngasht*. Hyderabad: Institute of Individualist Cultural Studies, 1962.
Salim, Muhammad. *Shaykh Baha al-Din Zakariyya of Multan*. Karachi: Pakistan Historical Society, Memoir No. 12, 1969.
Sarwar, Ghulām. *Muqaddama-yi khulāṣat al-alfāẓ jāmi' al-'ulūm*. Islamabad: Markaz-i Taḥqīqāt-i Fārsī-yi Īrān ō Pākistān, 1412/1992.
Schimmel, Annemarie. *Islam in the Indian Subcontinent*. Leiden-Koln: Brill, 1980.
Sells, Michael. *Early Islamic Mysticism: Sufi, Qur'an, Mir'aj, Poetic and Theological Writings*. New York: Paulist Press, 1996.
Sesiano, J. "Wafḳ." *Encyclopaedia of Islam*. New Edition. Vol. 11. Leiden: Brill, 2002. 28a-31a.
Shackle, Christopher. "Early Vernacular Poetry in the Indus Valley: Its Contexts and Its Character." In *Islam and Indian Regions*. Vol. 1. Edited by Anna Libera Dallapiccola and Stephanie Zingel-Avé Lallemant. Stuttgart: Franz Steiner Verlag, 1993.
———. "Siraiki: A Language Movement in Pakistan." *Modern Asian Studies* 11, 3 (1977): 379–403.
Shackle, Christopher and Zawahir Moir. *Ismaili Hymns from South Asia: An Introduction to the Ginans*. London: School of Oriental and African Studies, University of London, 1992.
Sharda, S. R. *Sufi Thought: Its Development in Panjab and Its Impact on Panjabi Literature from Baba Farid to 1850 AD*. New Delhi: Munshiram Manoharlal Publishers, 1974.
Sharif, Miraj Muhammad. "The Sultan and the 'Ulama' in the Turkish Sultanate of Delhi (1206–1413)." *Iqbal* 13, 3 (1965): 31–60.
Shihāb, Mas'ūd Ḥasan. *Khiṭṭa-yi pāk: Ūch*. 3rd Edition. Bahawalpur: Urdu Academy, 1993.
Siddiqui, Iqtidar Husain. "The 13th and 14th-Century Farmāns Concerning the Conduct of Governors under the Sultans of Delhi." *Islamic Culture* 65, 2–3 (April-July 1991): 119–146.
———. "The Early Chishti Dargahs." In *Muslim Shrines in India: Their Character, History and Significance*. Edited by Christian W. Troll. Delhi: Oxford University Press, 1989.
Siddiqui, Mahmud Husain. *The Memoirs of Sufis Written in India*. Baroda: Maharaja Sayajirao University of Baroda, 1979.
Smyth, William. "The Making of a Textbook." *Studia Islamica* 78 (1993): 99–115.
Sourdel, Dominique. "Robes of Honor in 'Abbasid Baghdad during the Eighth to Eleventh Centuries." In *Robes of Honor: The Medieval World of Investiture*. Edited by Stewart Gordon. New York: Palgrave, 2001.
Staal, Frits. "From Meanings to Trees." *Journal of Ritual Studies* 7, 2 (1993): 11–29.
———. "The Meaninglessness of Ritual." *Numen* 26, 1 (1979): 2–22.
Steinfels, Amina M. "Ritual." In *Key Themes for the Study of Islam*. Edited by Jamal J. Elias. Oxford: Oneworld Publications, 2010.
———. "His Master's Voice: The Genre of *Malfūẓāt* in South Asian Sufism." *History of Religions* 44, 1 (2004): 56–69.
Stewart, Devin J. *Islamic Legal Orthodoxy: Twelver Shiite Responses to the Sunni Legal System*. Salt Lake City: The University of Utah Press, 1998.
Subtelny, Maria Eva and Anas B. Khalidov. "The Curriculum of Islamic Higher Learning in Timurid Iran in the Light of the Sunni Revival under Shāh-Rukh." *Journal of the American Oriental Society* 115, 2 (1995): 211–236.
Teufel, Johann K. *Eine Lebensbeschreibung des Scheichs 'Alī-i Hamadānī*. Leiden: Brill, 1962.
Troll, Christian W., ed. *Muslim Shrines in India: Their Character, History and Significance*. Delhi: Oxford University Press, 1989.
Turner, C. "The Ubiquitous *Faqīh*: A Reconsideration of the Terms *Īmān*, *Islām* and *'Ilm* and Their Role in the Rise to the Predominance of the Jurist in the Islamic World of Learning." *CMEIS*

Occasional Paper No. 54, February 1996. Durham: University of Durham Centre for Middle Eastern and Islamic Studies, 1996.

Verma, H. C. *Medieval Routes to India: Baghdad to Delhi: A Study of Trade and Military Routes*. Calcutta: Naya Prokash, 1978.

Walī, 'Abdu'l. "Life and Letters of Malik 'Aynu'l-Mulk Māhrū." *Journal of the Asiatic Society of Bengal* N, 19 (1923): 253–290.

Welch, Anthony. "The Shrine of the Holy Footprint in Delhi." *Muqarnas* 14 (1997): 166–178.

———. "A Medieval Center of Learning: The Hauz Khas Madrasa in Delhi." *Muqarnas* 13 (1996): 165–190.

Welch, Anthony and Howard Crane. "The Tughluqs: Master Builders of the Delhi Sultanate." *Muqarnas* 1 (1983): 123–166.

Werbner, Pnina. "The Ranking of Brotherhoods: The Dialectics of Muslim Caste among Overseas Pakistanis." In *Muslim Communities of South Asia: Culture, Society and Power*. Edited by T. N. Madan. 3rd enlarged edition. *Contributions to Indian Sociology, Occasional Studies No. 6*. Delhi: Institute of Economic Growth, 2001.

Wikeley, J. M. *Punjabi Musalmans*. Revised by R. R. Zafar. Lahore: Pakistan National Publishers, 1968.

Williams, Michael A., ed. *Charisma and Sacred Biography*. JAAR Thematic Studies 48, 3–4 (1982).

Wink, André. *Al-Hind: The Making of the Indo-Islamic World*. 3 vols. Leiden: Brill, 1991–2004.

Yusuf, K. M. "The Judiciary in India under the Sultans of Delhi and the Mughal Emperors." *Indo-Iranica* (Calcutta) 18, 4 (1965): 1–12.

Zaydī, Shamīm Maḥmūd. *Aḥwāl ō āṣār-i shaykh Bahā' al-dīn Zakarīyā' Multānī wa Khulāṣat al-'ārifīn*. Rawalpindi: Markaz-i Taḥqīqāt-i Fārsī-yi Īrān ō Pākistān, 1984.

3. Atlases, Bibliographies, Catalogues, and Other Reference Works

Amrohvi, M. H. Qaiṣar and M. H. Razvi. *Catalogue of Manuscripts in the Maulana Azad Library, Aligarh Muslim University, Aligarh: Ahsan Collection*. Aligarh: Maulana Azad Library, Aligarh Muslim University, 1983.

Artur, Antonio-Paulo Ubieto. *Tablas Teoricas de Equivalencia Diaria entre los Calendarios Islámicos y Christiano: Theoretical Tables of Daily Equivalence between the Islamic and Christian Calendars*. 2 vols. Obras Auxiliares, 6. Zaragoza: Anubar Ediciones, 1984.

Baness, J. Frederick. *Index Geographicus Indicus*. Calcutta: W. Newman and Co., 1881.

Brockelmann, Carl. *Geschichte des arabischen Literatur*. 2nd edition. With *Supplementenband*. Leiden: Brill, 1943–49.

Dutt, Ashok K. and M. Margeret Geib. *Fully Annotated Atlas of South Asia*. Boulder: Westview Press, 1987.

Habib, Irfan. *An Atlas of the Mughal Empire*. New Delhi: Oxford University Press, 1982.

Hadi, Nabi. *Dictionary of Indo-Persian Literature*. New Delhi: Indira Gandhi National Centre for the Arts, 1995.

Ibbetson, Denzil. *Panjab Castes*. Lahore: Government Printing, 1916.

The Imperial Gazetteer of India. New Edition. Oxford: Clarendon Press, 1908.

The Imperial Gazetteer of India. New Edition. Vol. 26. *Atlas*. Oxford: Clarendon Press, 1909.

Ivanow, Wladimir. *Descriptive Catalogue of the Persian Manuscripts in the Collections of the Asiatic Society of Bengal*. First Supplement. Bibliotheca Indica: 244. Calcutta: Asiatic Society of Bengal, 1927.

———. *Concise Descriptive Catalogue of the Persian Manuscripts in the Collection of the Asiatic Society of Bengal*. Bibliotheca Indica: 240. Calcutta: Asiatic Society, 1924.

Khuda Bakhsh Oriental Public Library. *Catalogue of the Arabic and Persian Manuscripts in the Khuda Bakhsh Oriental Public Library*. http://kblibrary.bih.nic.in/onlinecat.htm. Accessed July 6, 2011.

Moghadam, Mohamad E. and Yahya Armajani. *Descriptive Catalog of the Garrett Collection of Persian, Turkish, and Indic Manuscripts in the Princeton University Library*. Princeton: Princeton University Press, 1939.

Massy, Charles Francis. *Chiefs and Families of Note in the Panjab*. Allahabad: Pioneer Press, 1890.

Rose, H. A. *A Glossary of the Tribes and Castes of the Punjab and North-West Frontier Province*. First published 1883. Reprint. Patiala: Languages Department Punjab, 1970.

Schwartzberg, Joseph E. *A Historical Atlas of South Asia*. Chicago: University of Chicago Press, 1978.

Sezgin, Fuat. *Geschichte des arabischen Schrifttums*. Leiden: Brill, 1967.

Storey, C. A. *Persian Literature. A Bio-Bibliographical Survey*. 2 vols. London: Luzac and Co. Ltd., 1927–71.

INDEX

'Abbāsī, FaŻlallāh b. żiyā', 145; *Khizāna-yi jawāhir-i Jalālīya*, 9, 86, 145, 167–68, 179, 181, 202n8
'Abbāsid Caliphate, 1, 41, 131
abdāl, 49, 86, 108, 117–18, 174, 199n49, 211n77. *See also* saints
Abū al-Ghayth b. Jamīl, 51, 162
Abū Ḥanīfa, 41, 133, 169, 188, 190
Abū Makhrama, 51, 76, 108, 181
Aden, 25, 28, 37, 39, 42, 51, 66, 108
Afghanistan, 147, 194n26
'Afīf, Sirāj, 59, 76, 128–30, 132–33, 141–42
Aḥmad Bihārī, 79
Aḥmad Kanbu, 98
Aḥmad K'haṯṯū Sarkhēzī, 54, 136–37
Aḥmad b. Tātār, 144–45
Aḥmadpūrī, Khwāja Gul Muḥammad, 178–79
Ahmed, Aziz, 32
Ahmedpur East, 148
'Ā'isha b. Abī Bakr, 139
Ajmer, 21
Ajūdhān, 21, 22, 116, 146
Akhbār al-akhyār (Dihlawī), 135, 175–79
Akhī Rāj-girī, 146
Akhsīkatī, Ḥusām al-dīn Muḥammad, 67, 186
'Alā' al-dīn, Ṣadr-i jahān, 139–40, 142
'Alā' al-Ḥaqq Bangālī, 135, 178
alchemy, 107
Alexander the Great, 170
'Alī b. Abī Ṭālib, 16, 55, 99, 126, 132, 146
'Alī al-Hādī, 15
'ālim/'ālima. *See* 'ulama
Alor, 78, 204n55
amulets. See *ta'wīẓ*
Ansari, Bazmee, 10
anti-nomian behavior, 6, 45, 79, 114. See also *qalandar*
'Aqīdat al-Nasafī (Nasafī), 67–68, 187
Arabia, 4, 16, 35–37, 39–57, 90, 115, 131–32, 138, 178
Arabic language: study of, 42, 51, 63, 68, 71, 76, 80, 152, 189; texts in, 4, 23, 39, 48, 50, 67, 70–71, 74–76, 111, 155, 165; as trans-regional language of scholarship, 39, 56–57; use in ritual and prayer, 39, 89–90, 94–97, 112–13
Arba'īn-i ṣūfīya (Bukhārī), 67
Arberry, A. J., 92
asceticism, 27, 42, 53, 79, 151
'Aṭā'allāh, Mawlānā, 145
Austin, J. L., 96
'Awārif al-ma'ārif (Suhrawardī), 6, 32, 51, 53, 67–68, 73, 84, 100, 115–16, 181
awrād, 63–66, 68–69, 82–83, 88–89, 91, 95, 150, 167–68, 169, 181–82. *See also* prayer
Awrād-i shaykh kabīr (Bahā' al-dīn Zakarīyā), 68, 91, 181
Awrangzēb, 154
Awzjandī, Imām Fakhr al-dīn Ḥusayn, 104, 185
'Ayn al-'ilm, 65, 182

Bābā Farīd. *See* Farīd al-dīn Mas'ūd
Badakhshī, Mirzā La'l Bēg, 176–77
Badr al-dīn Yamanī, 175, 177–78
Badr-i 'ālam, Pīr, 146
Baghawī, Abū Muḥammad al-, 23; *Maṣābīḥ al-sunna*, 23, 53, 67, 68, 169, 184
Baghdad, 20, 132
Baghdādī, al-Khaṭīb al-, 67, 187
Bahā' al-dīn 'Allāma, 23, 26
Bahā' al-dīn Zakarīyā Multānī, 19–21, 26, 28–29, 32–33, 47, 69, 84–85, 89–91, 95, 103–4, 107, 118, 120, 127–28, 139, 147, 169, 175–77; *Awrād-i shaykh kabīr*, 68, 91, 181
Bahādur b. Muẓaffar, Sultan, 145
Bahawalpur, 148
Bahrain, 41, 52
Balyānī, Amīn al-dīn Kāzarūnī, 53–54, 82, 132, 137, 189; *Risāla*, 182

Balyānī, Imām al-dīn Maḥmūd Kāzarūnī, 54, 101, 176
Bānhbīna, 128–30, 139. *See also* Sammas
Barakī, Jalāl al-dīn, 55
Baranī, Aḥmad, 166–67, 171
Baranī, Żiyā' al-dīn, 16–17, 29, 125–27; *Ma'āṣir-i Jalālī,* 126; *Ṣaḥīfa-yi na't-i Muḥammadī,* 126; *Tārīkh-i Fīrōz Shāhī,* 125, 127, 132
Baṯwah, 144
bay'at, 34, 94–98, 150. See also *khirqa*
Bengal, 132, 135, 146, 178
Bhakkar, 19–20, 22, 54, 78
Bhatnēr, 126
Bhaṯṯī, Aḥmad Bahā' al-dīn b. Ya'qūb, 9, 59, 145, 165; *Khizānat al-fawā'id al-Jalālīya,* 9, 30–31, 44, 52, 59, 64, 70–72, 74–76, 80, 91, 94, 105, 116, 126, 132, 145, 165–66, 174, 176, 178–79.
Bhopal, 145–46
Bhutto, Zulfiqar Ali, 147
Bihar, 33, 60, 135–36
Bisṭāmī, Bāyazīd, 79, 116
Bolan Pass, 20, 54
British rule in India, 1, 109
Bukhara, 15–17, 19, 108, 174, 176
Bukhārī, 'Abdallāh, 114, 144, 167
Bukhārī, Abū al-Mu'ayyad 'Alī, 16
Bukhārī, Aḥmad Kabīr, 19–20, 22–24, 27–28, 34–35, 44, 52, 58, 60, 68–69, 79, 86, 114–15, 127, 145–46, 152, 174, 178–79
Bukhārī, 'Alī al-Akbar, 114
Bukhārī, Awḥād al-dīn 'Alī, 17, 23
Bukhārī, Bahā' al-dīn, 19
Bukhārī, Fayżallāh b. Nāṣir al-dīn Maḥmūd, 145
Bukhārī, Ḥāmid, 138–39
Bukhārī, Ja'far, 17
Bukhārī, Jalāl al-dīn Makhdūm-i jahāniyān: descendants, 114, 144–45; disciples, 145–46; displays of humility, 24, 45, 47, 60, 120–22, 150; doctrines and teachings (*see individual topics*); family origins, 15–18; *malfūẓāt,* 7–9, 70–75, 165–68 (*see also individual titles*); marriage and sexuality, 114–15; masters and teachers, 23–28, 30–36, 41–55, 58–60, 157–64; meetings with contemporary saints, 135–37; names and titles, 6, 15–17, 35–36, 37, 51, 76, 109, 121, 148, 170, 175, 177–78, 192n1; personal finances, 50, 107; relations with secular powers, 29–36, 58–59, 125–31, 133–35, 137–43; spurious travelogues, 36–37, 46, 131, 170–71; textual study, 23, 48, 50–51, 53; tomb, 146–48; travels, 35, 37–58, 131–35, 137–43, 148, 170, 173–76; visionary and miraculous experiences, 45–46, 49, 51, 59–60, 84–85, 121, 130, 175; use of vernacular language, 111
Bukhārī, Jalāl al-dīn Surkh-pōsh, 15–22
Bukhārī, Muḥammad Bāqir b. 'Uṯmān, 193n10; *Jawāhir al-awliyā',* 91, 132, 193n10
Bukhārī, Nāṣir al-dīn Maḥmūd, 114, 138, 107, 144–45
Bukhārī, Qāsim, 17
Bukhārī, Ṣadr al-dīn Muḥammad, 18–19, 22, 157
Bukhārī, Ṣadr al-dīn Muḥammad Rājū-qattāl, 18, 22, 104, 112–14, 141, 144, 179
Bukhārī, wife of Jalāl al-dīn Makhdūm-i jahāniyān, 50, 52, 84, 114–16, 119, 138
Bulliet, Richard, 92
Burhān al-dīn 'Abdallāh Quṭb-i 'ālam, 28, 45, 55, 114, 136, 144–45; *Jāmi' al-ṭuruq,* 145
Burhān al-dīn Gharīb, 33, 70, 182
Bushehr, 54

caste, 17–18
Central Asia, 2, 40, 43, 71, 74, 108, 135
chilla. See seclusion
China, 39, 77
Chirāgh-i Dihlī. *See* Naṣīr al-dīn Maḥmūd
Chishtīya, 2, 4, 53, 29, 31, 34, 36, 55, 138, 146, 152, 153, 160, 173; practices, 32, 68, 84, 101; policy on gifts and patronage, 24, 32, 103, 105–6; relations with the state, 29, 32, 58; rivalry with the Suhrawardīya, 21, 31–33, 48, 58, 84, 103. *See also* Naṣīr al-dīn Maḥmūd Chirāgh-i Dihlī
Chishtī, 'Abd al-Raḥmān, 178–79
Chishtī, Muḥyi al-dīn 'Alī b. Aḥmad, 53
Chishtī, Mu'īn al-dīn Sijzī, 17, 21, 53, 56, 120
Chishtī, Quṭb al-dīn Mawdūd, 53
Chittagong, 146
Christianity, 89–92, 107, 109, 144
"common" people, 49, 71, 78, 97–98, 111–12, 116, 118–19, 121, 166
Companions of the Cave, 89

conversion, religious, 2, 10, 16, 108–14, 148
Cornell, Vincent, 119–20

Damascus, 49, 116, 132–33
Dārā Shukōh, 154
Dargāh Qadam-i Sharīf, 132, 138, 171
Daryā Khān, 134. *See also* Ẓafar Khān, Khān-i a'ẓam
Dātā Darbār, 147
Dātā Ganj Bakhsh. *See* Hujwīrī
Dā'ūd b. Burhān al-dīn 'Abdallāh Quṭb-i 'ālam, 145
Dāwar Malik, 143
Dawlatābād, 29
Deccan, 33, 60, 153
Delhi, 9, 19, 29, 32, 34–35, 39, 53, 55, 57–60, 67, 76, 78–79, 83, 86, 104, 107–8, 110, 112, 114–16, 119, 128, 130–43, 146, 153, 166–67, 171, 177–79
Delhi Sultanate, 2, 3, 6, 16, 19–20, 29, 34, 40, 47, 50, 56, 58, 110, 119, 126–28, 131, 141, 143, 147.
devil, 64, 77–79, 116–18, 134, 152
Dhuhaybī, Faqīh Baṣṣāl Jamāl al-dīn al-, 42, 51, 106
Digby, Simon, 29, 149
Dihlawī, 'Abd al-Ḥaqq Muḥaddis̱, 135, 175–79
Dimashqī, Quṭb al-dīn al-, 48, 116; *al Risāla al-Makkīya*, 48, 67–68, 100, 169, 182
disease, 52; Black Death, 36; cholera, 88; epilepsy, 90
Divine Names, 50, 65, 68, 82, 89, 111, 115
dreams and visions, 19, 23, 25, 28, 35, 45, 49–52, 54–55, 85, 102, 121, 131, 150, 156, 174
du'ā', 64, 87–92, 95–97, 111, 143. *See also* prayer
al-Durr al-naẓīm fī khawāṣṣ al-Qur'ān al-'aẓīm (Yāfi'ī), 91

Eaton, Richard, 109
economics, 103–7; endowments, 22, 50, 105–6, 115, 130–31, 132, 153; gifts and donations, 22, 24–25, 32, 53, 100, 103–7, 131, 133, 139, 149; loans, 53, 87, 133, 106–7, 141; taxation, 59, 104, 127, 141; trade (*see* merchants); work, 50, 106–7
ecstasy, 5–6, 27, 33, 79, 84–85, 149–50, 152, 156
emotion, 5, 27, 79, 84–85
Egypt, 37, 40–41, 118, 170
Ernst, Carl, 70, 73

Fakhr al-dīn S̱ānī, 136–37
faqīh, 63–65, 76–77. *See also* 'ulama
Faqīh Baṣṣāl. *See* Dhuhaybī
Farajī, Shihāb al-dīn al-, 69
Farīd al-dīn Mas'ūd Ganj-i shakar, 21, 32–33, 47, 56, 103, 119, 146–47, 165
Fars, 52
fasting, 5, 50, 81–82, 88, 116, 140, 149
fatāwā, 36, 65–66, 73–75, 80, 104, 185–87
Fatāwā-yi Fīrōz Shāhī. See *Fiqh-i Fīrōz Shāhī*
Fatāwā al-khānīya (Awzjandī), 104, 185
Fatḥ Khān b. Fīrōz Shāh, 76
Fāṭima b. Badr al-dīn Ḥusaynī Bhakkarī, 19
Fāṭima b. Muḥammad, 126
fiqh. *See* law, Islamic
Fiqh-i Fīrōz Shāhī, 74–75
Firdawsīya, 33
Firishta, Abū al-Qāsim, 177–78
Fīrōz Shāh Tughluq, 58–59, 74, 116, 119, 126–32, 138–39; relations with Jalāl al-dīn Bukhārī, 4, 52, 59, 78, 104, 110, 112, 125, 129, 133–34, 138–43, 151; religious attitudes, 4, 17, 41, 59, 79, 104, 153, 210n52
food, 24, 83, 87, 139, 145; from one's *pīr*, 26–27, 50, 52; from supernatural sources, 25, 37, 49, 78, 116, 118, 174, 177; legality of, 26, 81, 103–4, 131, 204

Gabriel, 78, 134
Ghaws̱ī Shaṭṭārī, Muḥammad, 175–76
Ghaythī, Muḥammad b. 'Ubayd al-, 51
Ghazālī, Abū Ḥāmid al-, 65, 73, 84
Ghazni, 19, 54, 132
Ghaznawī, Badr al-dīn, 143
Ghaznawī, Muḥammad, 145, 166; *Tuḥfat al-sarā'ir*, 9, 91, 116, 132–35, 145, 166, 181
Ghiyās̱ al-dīn. *See* Tughluq, Ghiyās̱ al-dīn; Tughluq Shāh
Ghurid Dynasty, 19
Gīlānī, 'Abd al-Qādir b. Muḥammad Ghaws̱, 148
Gīlānī, Muḥammad Ghaws̱, 148
Gīlānī, Muḥyi al-dīn 'Abd al-Qādir al-, 48, 69, 90, 100, 116, 148, 173, 176–77
Gillani, Makhdoom Syed Zafar Husain, 148

Gīsūdarāz, Muḥammad Ḥusaynī, 17, 60, 118, 210n53
Glossary of the Tribes and Castes of Punjab and the North-West Frontier Province (Rose), 109
Graham, William, 72
Gujarat, 54, 58, 114, 134, 136, 144–45, 178
Gulzār-i abrār (Ghawsī), 175–77
Gulshan-i Ibrāhīmī (Firishta),177–78

Habib, Mohammad, 126
hadith, 2, 4, 23, 26, 36, 39, 41–42, 44, 57, 63–68, 71–73, 76, 80, 82, 86, 94, 99–100, 106, 126, 138, 150, 152–53, 165–67, 169
hagiography. See *tazkiras*; *malfūẓāt*
hair: ritual cut, 44, 53–54, 69, 95–96, 98; matted, 45, 79; shaved, 79
Hajj. *See* pilgrimage: to the Ka'ba
halal and haram, 24, 82, 103–5
Ḥallāj, Manṣūr al-, 79
Hamadānī, 'Alī, 17, 33, 60, 113, 118, 135, 137, 176; *Risāla-yi Hamadānīya,* 135
Hamadānī, 'Ayn al-qużāt, 73
Ḥamīd al-dīn Abū al-Waqt Maḥmūd Samarqandī, 53, 69, 160–61, 164, 169, 200n76, 218n3
Ḥamza, Amīr, 170
Ḥanafism, 16, 23, 36, 40, 42–43, 60, 65, 74, 97, 108
Hangī, Rukn al-dīn al-, 54
Hansawī, Quṭb al-dīn Munawwar, 55
haram. *See* halal and haram
Hardy, Peter, 125
Hārūn al-Rashīd, 170
Ḥasan, Khwāja, 139
Ḥasan b. 'Alī, Imām, 99, 126
Ḥasan Muḥammad, 179
Ḥasanid Sharifs, 40–41, 197n8
Ḥaẓīra-yi Fīrōz Khān, 132, 138. *See also* Dargāh Qadam-i Sharīf
Hejaz, 39, 41–43, 47–48, 51–52, 66, 132, 153, 174, 177
Hermansen, Marcia, 173
al-Hidāya (al-Marghīnānī), 23, 26–27, 67–68, 74, 186
Hind and Hindūstān, 19, 21, 41, 59–60, 115. *See also* South Asia; India, Republic of
Hindawī, 110–12
Hindi, 110
Hindus, 110, 112–13, 115, 119, 146, 175, 178
Hindu Nationalism, 155
Hinduism, 2, 10, 18, 89, 119, 154, 177
Hīr (Wāris̱ Shāh), 21
A History of Sufism in India (Rizvi), 10
Hodgson, Marshall, 2
Hormuz, 41, 54, 197n9
Hujwīrī, 'Alī Dātā Ganj Bakhsh, 147; *Kashf al-maḥjūb,* 73, 147. *See also* Dātā Darbār
Ḥusāmī (Akhsīkātī), 67, 185
Ḥusayn, Sajjād, 9, 73, 165–66
Ḥusayn b. 'Alī, Imām, 18, 99, 126, 164
Ḥusaynī, Abū 'Abdallāh 'Alā' al-dīn: investiture by Bukhārī, 100, 101; instructions to his readers, 81; *Jāmi' al-'ulūm,* 9, 35, 45–46, 52, 59, 64, 67, 81, 84, 89, 97–98, 100, 101, 106, 110–12, 114, 116, 118, 121, 132–34, 137–39, 141–43, 145, 165–66, 168–69, 176, 179
Ḥusaynī, Badr al-dīn Bhakkarī, 18–19
Ḥusaynid Sharifs, 40–41

Ibn al-'Arabī, Muḥyi al-dīn, 5–6, 49–50, 85, 119
Ibn Baṭṭūṭa, Abū 'Abdallāh Muḥammad, 16, 29, 37, 39–40, 45, 53–54, 56–58, 101
Ibn al-Ḥājib, 51
Ibn Māhrū, 'Ayn al-mulk, 127–30; *Inshā'-i Māhrū,* 127–29
Ibn al-Sā'ātī, 67, 187
Ibn Taymīya, Taqī al-dīn, 49
ignorance, 40, 49, 63–64, 78, 80, 90, 93, 110–11, 118, 134, 140, 152
ijāzat, 3, 34–35, 44, 58, 66, 68, 94, 99, 150, 174, 201n106. See also *khirqas*
Ikhtiyār Khān, 145
Ilkhānid dynasty, 52–53
'ilm, 4, 26, 63–65, 76–78, 81, 117, 135, 140, 170
India. *See* South Asia; India, Republic of; Pakistan
India, Republic of, 9, 155
Indian sub-continent. *See* South Asia
Indus River, 19–20, 22, 39, 54, 111, 128, 143, 147–48
initiation. See *khirqas*
Īnjū, Abū Isḥāq b. Muḥammad Shāh, 53
Inshā'-i Māhrū (Ibn Māhrū), 127–29
inspiration, 78, 117, 211n71
intertextuality, 72–74
Īrajī, Yūsuf Bud'h, 146

Iran, 2, 4, 37, 39–40, 52, 57, 66, 133
Iraq, 2, 4, 15, 45, 52, 132, 133
'Irāqī, Fakhr al-dīn, 20
Iṣfahānī, Najm al-dīn, 42, 50
Islam, 4, 39–40, 147, 153–55: intellectual traditions of, 2, 23, 26, 64–71, 73; conversion to, 2, 10, 108–14, 148; scholarship on, 1–2, 5, 43–44
Islam, Riazul, 128–30
Islamicate civilization, 56–57
i'tikāf. *See* seclusion
I'timād al-murīdīn (Sirāj al-dīn Muḥammad Shāh-i 'ālam), 176–77, 179, 219n22

Jackson, Paul, 79, 136
Jackson, Peter, 141
Jām Jūnā, 128–30. *See also* Sammas
Jamāl al-dīn Uchchī, 21, 24–27, 29, 47, 60, 67, 90, 104, 116, 152, 174, 177
Jamāl al-dīn Ma'barī, 143, 201n106
Jamālī, 146; *Siyar al-'ārifīn*, 9, 24, 112–13, 134, 146, 173–79
Jāmi' al-ṣaghīr (al-Shaybānī), 74
Jāmi' al-ṭuruq (Burhān al-dīn 'Abdallāh Quṭb-i 'ālam), 145
Jāmi' al-'ulūm (Ḥusaynī), 9, 35, 45–46, 52, 59, 64, 67, 81, 84, 89, 97–98, 100–101, 106, 110, 112, 114, 116, 118, 121, 132–34, 137–39, 141–43, 145, 165–66, 168, 169, 176, 179.
Jāmi'-i quṭbī. See *Manāqib-i quṭbī*
Jawāb-i nuh su'āl (Najm al-dīn Kubrā), 99–100
Jawāhir al-awliyā' (Bukhārī, Muḥammad Bāqir), 91, 132
Jawnā Shāh, Khān-i jahān, 107, 134, 141–43
Jawnpūr, 146, 178
Jeddah, 39, 175
Jesus, 45, 89
jinns, 6, 25, 49, 86, 90, 92, 117–18, 135
Jīwarī, 'Alā' al-dīn, 143
Judaism, 89

Ka'b al-Aḥbār, 133
Ka'ba, 41, 47–50, 116–17, 121
Kabir, 56
Kabīr al-dīn Ismā'īl, 146
kāfirs. *See* unbelievers
Kāfiya (Ibn al-Ḥājib), 51
Kākawī, 'Izz, 79
Kalābādhī, Muḥammad b. Isḥāq al-, 65, 67, 183
kalām. *See* theology
Kamāl al-dīn, Khwāja 'Allāma, 178–79
Kanz al-wuṣūl (Pazdawī), 23, 26, 67–68
Kara, 135, 146, 166
karāmāt. *See* saints: wonders performed by
kasb. *See* economics: work
Kāshānī, 'Abd al-Razzāq, 135
Kāshānī, Rukn al-dīn, 70; *Shamā'il al-atqiyā'*, 70–75; *Rumūz al-wālihīn*, 73
Kashf al-maḥjūb (Hujwīrī), 73, 147
Kashmir, 33, 37, 145, 170
Kāzarūn, 44, 53–54, 57, 63, 137
Kāzarūnī, Abū Isḥāq, 53–54
Kāzarūnī, Amīn al-dīn. *See* Balyānī, Amīn al-dīn
Kāzarūnī, Imām al-dīn. *See* Balyānī, Imām al-dīn
Kāzarūnīya, 24, 53–55
khalwat. *See* seclusion
khān-i jahān. *See* Maqbūl Tilangī; Jawnā Shāh
khānqāhs, 26–27, 76, 81–82; economics of, 103–7; in Arabia, 115, 151; in Multan, 20, 26; in Sīwistān, 28–30, 34, 176; in Uch, 20, 22, 24, 130–31, 145
Khaṣṣāf, Abū Bakr Aḥmad al-, 69
Khayr al-majālis (Ḥamīd Qalandar), 34
khil'at, 20, 30–31
khirqas, 20, 23, 33–34, 36, 76, 81, 93–102, 150, 152; analogous to books, 68–69, 99–100; from multiple orders, 33–34, 36, 42, 44–45, 54–55; protective powers of, 31, 33, 100; related paraphernalia, 44, 54, 101; rituals of investiture, 44, 54, 94–99, 150; from specific shaykhs and orders (*see individual names*); types of, 93, 100–102.
Khizāna-yi jawāhir-i Jalālīya ('Abbāsī), 9, 86, 145, 167–68
Khizānat al-fawā'id al-Jalāliya (Bhaṯṯī), 9, 30–31, 44, 52, 59, 64, 70–72, 74–76, 80, 91, 94, 105, 116, 126, 132, 145, 165–66, 174, 176, 178–79
Khiżr, 21–22, 45, 50, 69, 87, 118, 142
Khiżr Khān, 131
Khiżr (of Sīwistān), 121
Khulāṣat al-alfāẓ jāmi' al-'ulūm. See *Jāmi' al-'ulūm*
Khulāṣat al-mafākhir (Yāfi'ī), 48
Khurāsān, 21, 41, 54, 132–33
Khurāsānī, Hamza, 82

Khwurd, Mīr, 119
Khyber Pass, 133
Kichawcha, 135
Kirmānī, Jalāl al-dīn, 42
Kirmānī, Shihāb al-dīn Abū Sa'īd, 50, 53, 69
Kitāb adab al-qāżī al-Khaṣṣāf (al-Khaṣṣāf), 69
Kitāb al-muttafiq wa al-muftariq (al-Baghdādī), 67, 187
Kubrā, Najm al-dīn, 55; *Jawāb-i nuh su'āl,* 99–100. *See also* Kubrawīya
Kubrawīya, 33, 53, 55, 113, 161

Lahārī, 39
Lahore, 145, 147
Laḥsā, 41, 52, 197n9
Lak'hnawī, 'Abd al-Ḥayy, 19, 114
Lak'hnawī, Qiwām al-dīn, 146
Lā'l Shāhbāz Qalandar. *See* Marwandī, 'Uṣmān
Laṭā'if-i Ashrafī (Niẓām Gharīb Yamanī), 85, 145, 178
law, Islamic, 2–4, 6, 23, 26, 36, 40, 42–43, 49, 53, 59, 63–67, 70–80, 84–87, 93, 95, 98, 104, 110, 113–14, 116, 138, 140, 148, 150, 152–53, 154–56
Lawrence, Bruce, 10, 149–52, 173

Ma'āṣir-i Jalālī (Baranī), 126–27
Madārik al-tanzīl (al-Nasafī), 67–68
madrasas, 2–3, 26–27, 41–44, 50, 53, 59, 63–64, 66, 68, 70–71, 76, 132, 138–39, 153, 156
Maghribī, Bābā Isḥāq, 60, 136
Maghribīya, 136
magic, 91–93
magic squares, 90–91
Maḥmūd of Ghazni, 19
Maḥmūd Khān, 143
Majālis-i Ḥusaynīya (Muḥammad b. Ḥasan), 179
Majd al-dīn al-Baghdādī, 53, 56
Majd al-dīn, Mawlānā, 26
Majma' al-baḥrayn (Ibn al-Sā'ātī), 67, 187
Makkī, Abū Ṭālib, 73; *Qūt al-qulūb,* 46, 73, 183
Maktūbāt-i dō ṣadī (Manērī), 77–80
malangs. See *qalandars*
Malfūẓāt-i Makhdūm-i jahāniyān, 9, 129–30, 168
Malik 'Alī, 134, 143
Malik Mardān, Naṣīr al-mulk Dawlat, 104–5, 130–31
Mamluk Empire, 40–42
Manāqib al-aṣfiyā', 79
Manāqib-i Makhdūm-i jahāniyān. See *Malfūẓāt-i Makhdūm-i jahāniyān*
Manāqib-i quṭbī (Mu'izz al-dīn Rasūl-dār), 138, 145, 168, 174–75, 178
Manērī, Sharaf al-dīn, 33, 60, 77–80, 88, 98, 118, 135–37; *Maktūbāt-i dō ṣadī,* 77–80
Mānikpūrī, Rukn al-dīn Rājā, 141
Maqbūl Tilangī, Khān-i jahān, 134, 175, 178,
Marghīnānī, Burhān al-dīn al-, 67; *al-Hidāya* 23, 26–27, 67–68, 74, 186
Ma'rūf, Sayyid, 140, 143
Marwandī, 'Uṣmān Lāl Shāhbāz Qalandar, 20–21, 147
Maṣābīḥ al-sunna (Baghawī), 23, 53, 67–68, 169, 184, 203n17
Mashāriq al-anwār (al-Ṣaghānī), 67, 169, 179, 184, 203n17
Mashhad, 19
Maṭarī, 'Afīf al-dīn al-, 24–25, 42–48, 50–52, 56–57, 59–60, 68, 75, 77, 80, 86, 116, 169–70, 175–77
maẕhab, 16, 41–43, 63, 74, 97. *See also* Ḥanafism; Shāfi'ism
Maẓhar-i Jalālī (Shāh Ṣalāḥ al-dīn), 16
Mecca, 4, 16, 19, 28–30, 35–36, 37, 39–42, 44, 46–51, 53, 56, 58, 63, 67–68, 86, 105–8, 114, 116, 118, 137, 148, 151–52, 169–70, 175, 177
Medina, 4, 16–17, 19, 35–36, 37, 39–48, 50–51, 63, 67–68, 76–77, 86, 114, 116, 131–33, 151–52, 169, 176, 178
merchants, 37, 39, 50, 56, 105–6, 108, 115, 118, 149
Middle East, 40, 44, 56–57
Miftāḥ al-jinān (Muḥammad Mujīr), 70–75
Mīnā, Shaykh, 146
miracles. *See* saints: wonders performed by
Mir'āt al-asrār ('Abd al-Raḥmān Chishtī), 178–79.
Mir'āt al-jinān (Yāfi'ī), 42, 44
Mirṣād al-'ibād (Rāzī, Najm al-dīn Dāyā), 73, 183
Mongols, 1, 19–20, 36, 65, 88, 128, 143, 147
Morocco, 56
Mortel, Richard, 40
Mubārak Khān, 141, 143
Mughal Empire, 1–2, 9, 154, 173
Muḥammad b. Fīrōz Shāh, 145

Muḥammad b. Ḥasan Muḥammad, 179
Muḥammad b. Qāsim, 19
Muḥammad b. Tughluq, 4, 17, 29–35, 39, 58, 86, 91, 100, 125–28, 131, 134, 141, 143, 176, 178–79
Muḥammad Bihāmad Khānī, 176; *Tārīkh-i Muḥammadī,* 176, 179, 218n16
Muḥammad Mujīr b. Wajīh al-dīn, 70; *Miftāḥ al-jinān,* 70–75
Muḥammad, the Prophet, 19, 40, 41, 64–65, 77–78, 89, 97, 101, 103, 112–13; descent from, 4, 15–17, 41, 45–46, 90, 108, 126–27, 130–31, 151, 173, 177 (*see also* sayyids); example of, 5, 40, 86, 95–96, 98, 114, 150; footprint of, 131–32, 138, 171 (*see also* Dargāh Qadam-i sharīf); khirqa from, 50, 55, 69, 93, 99; mosque of, 42, 44–45, 51, 76, 133; prayer from, 50, 89; tomb of, 45–47, 50, 86, 170, 177; voice of, 45–46, 86, 121, 131, 148, 170, 174, 177–78; *ẕikr* from, 82
Mu'izz al-dīn Rasūl-dār, 138, 145, 168; *Manāqib-i quṭbī,* 138, 145, 168, 174–75, 178
Multan, 19–22, 26–29, 64, 66, 68
Muqarrar-nāma, 79–80
Mūsa, Shaykh, 26
Musāfir-nāma, 171. See also *Safar-nāma*
music. *See samā'*
Muṭī' al-imām, 136
Muẓaffar Shāh Wajīh al-mulk Ẓafar Khān, 145

Nagōrī, Ḥamīd al-dīn, 143
namāz, 5, 27, 45, 47, 49, 52, 65, 78–80, 81–83, 86–89, 91, 97, 102, 112–13, 115–16, 140, 142, 151–52, 167, 170, 212n82. *See also* prayer
Nanak, Guru, 56
Naqshbandīya, 117
Nasafī, Hāfiẓ al-dīn Abū al-Barakāt al-, 67; *'Aqīdat al-Nasafī,* 67, 188; *Madārik al-tanzīl,* 67–68, 189
Naṣā'iḥ-i Makhdūm-i jahāniyān. See *Muqarrar-nāma*
Nāṣir al-dīn Abū al-Ḥasan Maḥmūd Daryā-nōsh, 145
Nāṣir al-dīn b. Iltutmish, 19
Naṣīr al-dīn Maḥmūd Chirāgh-i Dihlī, 17, 21, 24, 29–31, 33–36, 43–44, 46–49, 58–60, 70, 86, 91, 96, 98, 100, 106, 120, 128, 131, 138, 173, 175–79
Naṣīr al-dīn Maḥmūd Shāh, 143
Nawāhūn, 112–13, 134, 175
al-Nawawī, 43, 182, 184
Niẓām al-dīn Awliyā', 17, 26, 31–33, 54–55, 98, 126, 138, 143, 165
Nizami, Khaliq Ahmad, 10, 32, 58, 66, 103, 166
North Africa, 57
Nūr Quṭb-i 'ālam b. 'Alā' al-Ḥaqq, 178
Nūshirwān, 170

Padwick, Constance, 91–92
Pakistan, 1, 6, 9–10, 19, 21, 111, 146–48, 154–55, 217n4, 217n5
Pakpattan. *See* Ajūdhān
panch pīr, 21–22
Pandua, 178
Panjnad Barrage, 148
Pazdawī, Abū al-Ḥasan, 23; *Kanz al-wuṣūl,* 23, 26, 67–68, 187, 203n17
Persia. *See* Iran
Persian Gulf, 52, 54
Persian language, 2, 4, 23, 39, 56–57, 70–71, 74–75, 89, 97, 110–12, 115; translations from Arabic, 39, 48, 50, 67, 70–71, 74, 169. *See also* language
pilgrimage: to the Ka'ba, 4, 29, 35, 37, 41, 48–50, 55–56, 82, 104, 106–7, 110, 116–17, 131, 169–70, 175, 200n76; to other sites, 2, 41, 44–47, 50, 57
poetry and verse, 6, 33, 48, 71–73, 80, 84, 111, 126, 149, 155, 165, 167, 190
prayer: efficacy of, 6, 30, 31, 33, 49, 87–93, 97, 102, 116, 119, 129–30, 155; formulas for, 5–6, 9, 31, 33, 39, 50, 88–89, 91, 111–12, 119, 167; funerary, 28, 43, 59–60, 178, 201n102; litanies (see *awrād*); ritual (see *namāz*); supplications (see *du'ā'*)
Punjab, 1, 19, 22, 127, 147–48, 216n19, 217n5
Punjabi language, 21, 111

Qabāchā, 147
Qādirī, Muḥammad Ayyūb, 10
Qādirīya, 33, 42, 48, 51, 55, 148, 173. *See also* Gīlānī, Muḥyi al-dīn 'Abd al-Qādir
Qāf, Mount, 37, 148, 170
qalandars, 21, 24, 85, 114, 193n4, 204n60, 207n69
al-Qaṣīda al-Shāṭibīya (al-Shāṭibī), 48, 189
Qāsim, Sayyid, 30

Qaṭīf, 41, 52, 197n9
Qiwām al-dīn, 53, 200n78
Qiwām al-dīn Lak'hnawī, 146
Qiwām al-dīn Muḥammad b. Ẓahīr al-dīn, 201n106
Qudūrī, Abū al-Ḥusayn al-, 67, 187, 203n17
Quran, 21, 72–73, 88–90, 92, 95–98, 106, 116, 207n72; commentary on, 23, 63–65, 67, 71–72, 76, 85, 152, 167, 189; recitation and reading of, 42, 81, 83–84, 87–90, 95, 97; study of, 2, 4, 23, 26, 39, 41–42, 44, 48, 63–64, 71–73; talismanic powers of, 87–91
Qushayrī, Abū al-Qāsim al-, 65, 73, 183
Qūt al-qulūb (Makkī), 46, 73, 183
quṭb, 17, 48, 51, 59, 76, 121, 170, 211n77. *See also* saints
Quṭb al-dīn Ż Kākī, 17, 138, 143
Quṭb-i ʿālam. *See* Burhān al-dīn ʿAbdallāh

Rābiʿa al-ʿAdawīya, 88
Rāḥat al-qulūb, 165, 217n2
Raḥmān Bābā, 217n4
Rajasthan, 21
Rasūlid Dynasty, 40
Rawḍat al-rayāḥīn (Yāfiʿī), 48–49, 182
Rāzī, Najm al-dīn Dāyā, 73, 183
Red Sea, 39
retreats. *See* seclusion
Rifāʿī, Aḥmad, 44, 45, 55, 198n27
Rifāʿī, Aḥmad Kūchak, 45, 198n27
Rifāʿīya, 33, 42, 44–45, 55, 79
Risāla (Shams al-dīn Masʿūd Mashhadī), 177, 179
Risāla-yi Hamadānīya (Hamadānī, ʿAlī), 135
al-Risāla al-Makkīya (Dimashqī, Quṭb al-dīn al-) 48, 65, 67–68, 100, 169, 183
Risāla Makkīya Jalālīya (Bukhārī), 169, 200n76,
al-Risāla al-Qushayrīya (Qushayrī), 65, 73, 183
Riżawī, Muḥammad b. Jalāl-shāhī, 168; *Sawāl ō jawāb*, 19, 168, 194n15
Rizvi, Sayyid Athar Abbas, 10
Rose, H. A., 109
Rukn al-dīn Abū al-Fatḥ Multānī, 20–21, 26–30, 34–36, 43–44, 46–49, 51–55, 60, 64, 68, 76, 86, 90, 95, 98, 106, 112, 119–21, 130, 141, 146, 150, 152, 157, 169–70, 173–78, 196n78, 199n61, 200n76, 200n78
Rumūz al-wālihīn (Kāshānī, Rukn al-dīn), 73

Sadhāran. *See* Muẓaffar Shāh
Ṣadr al-dīn ʿĀrif Multānī, 20–21, 24, 28, 90, 95, 105, 157, 175, 205n7, 212n82
Ṣadr al-dīn, Pīr, 193n9
Ṣadr al-dīn, Shaykh al-islām, 128, 139–40, 143, 213n11
ṣadr-i jahān, 139–40, 142
Safar-nāma, 36, 37, 46, 131, 169–71
Ṣaghānī, Raḍī al-dīn al-, 67; *Mashāriq al-anwār*, 67, 169, 179, 184, 203n17
Ṣaḥīfa-yi naʿt-i Muḥammadī (Baranī), 126–27
saints, 103, 115–21; false, 78–80, 118, 134, 152; female, 109, 112, 115–16, 118–20; hereditary, 22–23; hidden, 120; ranks of, 112, 211n77; insight of, 3, 5, 24, 52, 78, 80, 104, 135, 150, 152; territories of, 20–22, 120–21; *wilāyat* vs. *walāyat*, 119–20; wonders performed by, 6, 21, 25, 45–47, 49, 86–87, 90–92, 100, 107, 109, 113, 116–21, 149–50, 174–75. See also *abdāl; quṭb*
Sakhāwat, Mirzā, 10
Sālār Bud'h, 146
ṣalāt. See *namāz*
samāʿ, 32, 84, 102
Samāʿ al-dīn, Shaykh, 112, 146, 174
Ṣamarāt al-quds min shajarāt al-uns (Badakhshī), 176–77
Samarkand, 54, 132
Sammas, 20, 128–30, 218n9
Sarandīb, Mount, 37, 108, 148, 170
Sārang, Shaykh, 146
Sārangpūr, 146
Sarwar, Ghulām, 9, 165–66, 201n102
Sawāl ō jawāb (Riżawī), 19, 168, 194n15
Sayyid Dynasty, 131
sayyids, 4, 15–18, 23, 27, 40–41, 45–46, 52, 60, 76, 90, 108, 114, 121, 126–27, 131, 139, 151, 152, 177–78, 193n11, 198n32, 198n35
Schimmel, Annemarie, 10, 149
seclusion, 5, 43, 51, 59–60, 81–85, 88, 102, 116, 137, 150, 152, 175
Sehwan, 20, 22, 30, 147. *See also* Sīwistān
sexuality, 96, 114–15, 151
Shabānkāreh, 52–53, 57, 68
Shāfiʿism, 16, 41–43, 48, 60, 65, 197n17, 201n102
Shāh Buḏā, 145
Shāh-i ʿālam. *See* Sirāj al-dīn Muḥammad
Shamāʾil al-atqiyāʾ (Kāshānī), 70–73, 75

Shams al-dīn Mas'ūd Mashhadī 'Irāqī, 53, 107, 118, 133, 141; *Risāla*, 177, 179
Shams al-dīn Muḥammad b. Yaḥyā Awadhī, 54–55, 160
Sharaf al-dīn Sāmī, 145
Shari'a. *See* law, Islamic
Sharif, Nawaz, 147, 216n19
Sharif, Shahbaz, 147, 216n19
Sharīfa b. Farīd al-dīn Mas'ūd, Bībī, 119
sharīfs. *See* Ḥasanid Sharifs; Ḥusaynid Sharifs; *sayyids*
Sharqī Dynasty, 178
Shāshī, Qaffāl al-, 43, 189
Shāṭibī, Abū al-Qāsim al-, 48, 189, 199n48
Shaṭṭārīya, 173, 205n7
al-Shaybānī, Imām Muḥammad, 74, 186, 187
shaykh al-islām, 30, 34–35, 44, 58, 91, 107–8
Shihāb al-dīn Ḥaqq-gūy, 136
Shi'ism, 15–16, 40–41, 52, 126, 139, 148, 151, 193n4, 193n9, 193n10
Shiraz, 37, 52–54, 56, 66, 84
Shirāzī, Maḥmūd b. Muḥammad, 145
siḥr, 92. *See also* magic
Sikandar b. Mas'ūd, 145, 215n9
Simnānī, 'Alā' al-dawla, 135
Simnānī, Ashraf Jahāngīr, 17, 49–50, 60, 85, 98, 118–19, 135, 137, 145, 178, 205n7
Sinai, Mount, 37, 170
Sind, 19–22, 28, 30, 34, 39, 51–52, 54, 56, 58, 60, 97, 111–12, 127–28, 147–48, 167, 193n4, 213n7, 218n9
Sindhi, 111
Siraiki, 111
Sirāj al-dīn b. Khwāja Kamāl al-dīn, 178–79
Sirāj al-dīn Muḥammad Shāh-i 'ālam, 54, 114, 137, 144–45, 176, 179; *I'timād al-murīdīn*, 176–77, 179, 219n22
Sirāj al-hidāya, 9, 54, 70–75, 111, 121, 129–30, 132–34, 166–67, 171, 176
Sīstān, 54
Sīwistān, 28, 30, 34–35, 37, 39, 116, 120–21, 213n7. *See also* Sehwan
Siyar al-'ārifīn (Jamālī), 9, 24, 112–13, 134, 146, 173–75, 177–79
South Asia, 1–4, 15, 19, 35–37, 39, 49–50, 54, 56, 58, 107–8, 125, 135, 138, 178; Islam in, 1–2, 16–17, 37, 39–40, 42–44, 60, 68, 71, 74–76, 89, 108–12, 140, 147, 149, 153–55, 193, 217n5; languages of, 57, 71, 110–11; in relation to Middle East and Central Asia, 1, 2, 4–5, 39–41, 43–44, 46–50, 89, 97, 108, 115, 153–54, 171; Sufism in, 2–9, 17, 20–21, 24, 26, 31–33, 36, 42–43, 47, 49–50, 53, 55, 60, 70, 72, 80, 91, 105, 109, 120, 125, 145, 152–55, 173, 175, 204n60, 205n7, 217n5
Southeast Asia, 4, 37
Staal, Frits, 97
Stewart, Devin, 16
Suhrawardī, Shihāb al-dīn 'Umar al-, 5–6, 20, 32, 44, 50–53, 65, 67–69, 82, 98, 100, 157–59, 176, 182–84; *'Awārif al-ma'ārif*, 6, 32, 51, 53, 67–68, 73, 84, 98, 100, 182; *Awrād*, 68, 182
Suhrawardī, Yaḥyā Maqtūl al-, 50
Suhrawardī, Żiyā' al-dīn Abū al-Najīb al-, 69, 157–59, 161, 188
Suhrawardīya, 2, 4, 20–21, 42, 57, 60, 153, 169, 173, 177; Bukhārī's affiliation with, 1–2, 4, 6, 15, 23, 28–29, 34–36, 42, 44, 48, 50–51, 54–55, 57, 60, 68–69, 102, 125, 138, 152, 157–59, 173, 175, 179; establishment in Multan, 19–21, 26, 28, 48, 53, 116, 153, 174, 177, 179; policy on gifts and donations, 24, 32, 35, 103; practices and teachings, 6, 32, 35, 50, 82, 84; relations with the state, 32, 128; rivalry with Chishtīya, 21, 24, 31–34, 55, 84, 102, 103, 138, 179
Sumras, 19–20, 58, 218n9
Sunnism, 41, 43–44, 56, 93, 148, 151, 153; of the Bukhārī sayyids, 16, 193n10; in Bukhārī's teachings, 4, 16, 36, 41, 43–44, 65, 68, 89, 110, 148, 151
Sutlej River, 22

al-Ta'arruf lī madhhab ahl al-taṣawwuf (Kalābādhī), 65, 67, 183
Tabriz, 132–33
tafsīr. *See* Quran: commentary on
Taghī, 127
Tāj al-dīn Aḥmad Mu'īn Siyāh-pōsh 'Alawī, 167, 169, 205n63
Tāj al-dīn Bhakkarī, 145
Tāj al-dīn Muḥammad, Mawlānā, 84
Tāj al-dīn Muḥammad Lūr Fārsī, 134. *See also* Ẓafar Khān, Khān-i a'ẓam
Taliban, 154, 217n4
Tangiers, 37
taqīya, 16, 193n9

Tārīkh-i Firishta. See *Gulshan-i Ibrāhīmī*
Tārīkh-i Fīrōz Shāhī ('Afif), 59, 128–30, 132–33, 141–42
Tārīkh-i Fīrōz Shāhī (Baranī), 125, 127, 132
Tārīkh-i Muḥammadī (Muḥammad Bihāmad Khānī), 176, 179, 218n16
Taseer, Salmaan, 217n5
Ṭawāshī, Ṣāḥib Ḥālī Nūr al-dīn 'Alī al-, 42, 51
ta'wīz, 5, 6, 21, 31, 33, 49, 90–93, 102, 121, 151, 155, 198n32
tazkiras, 8–10, 44, 54; accounts of Bukhārī, 26, 28, 36, 37, 39, 46, 68, 112–13, 131, 134–35, 137, 145, 167, 173–79; compared to *malfūẓāt*, 8–10, 25–26, 46, 54, 173–74; tropes and themes, 25–26, 113, 173–74
Tazkira-yi awliyā'-i Aḥmadābād (Miṣbāḥī), 145
Tazkira-yi ḥazrat sayyid Jalāl al-dīn Makhdūm-i jahāniyān Jahāngasht (Sakhāwat), 10
Thatta, 19, 20, 58, 86, 116, 120, 128–30, 134, 167, 218n9
theology, 4, 23, 32, 42, 44, 50, 63–65, 67, 71, 85, 149, 188
travel, 37–38, 50, 55–57
Tughluq, Ghiyās al-dīn, 24
Tughluq Shāh, 143
Tuḥfat al-sarā'ir (Ghaznawī, Muḥammad), 9, 91, 116, 132–35, 145, 166, 181
Turābī, 117–18
Tustarī, Sharaf al-dīn Maḥmūd Shāh, 52–53, 68, 82, 158, 176, 200n73

Uch, 1, 6, 9, 15–16, 19–36, 39, 49–55, 58–60, 69, 76, 78, 83, 86, 88, 104–5, 108–9, 111, 113–14, 116, 118, 125, 127, 129, 132–35, 138, 141–43, 144–48, 157, 165, 167, 173–79, 193n9, 195n35, 201n106, 209n33.
Udaypūr, 21
'ulama, 2–4, 17, 36, 40–42, 44, 59, 63, 65–66, 68, 70, 75–78, 80, 99, 116, 125, 134–35, 137–38, 140, 152, 154–56, 169, 179, 212n82
'Umayyad Dynasty, 19
unbelievers, 34, 78, 80, 110
United States of America, The, 147, 154
Urdu, 110
Uṣūl-i Pazdawī. See *Kanz al-wuṣūl*

Vatva, 144
verse. *See* poetry

waqfs. *See* economics: endowments
Wāriṣ Shāh, 21
women, 106, 133; converts, 109, 112, 115–16; disciples, 49, 96, 98–99, 109, 112, 115–16; saints, 49, 109, 112, 115–16, 118–20, 129; shaykhs, 119–20; wives and concubines, 17, 19, 22, 50, 84, 114–16, 138

Yāfi'ī, 'Abdallāh b. Asad al-, 24–25, 42–44, 46–52, 56–57, 60, 68, 75, 91, 93, 101, 108, 116, 174–77; *al-Durr al-naẓīm fī khawāṣṣ al-Qur'ān al-'aẓīm*, 91; *Mir'āt al-jinān*, 42, 44; *Rawḍat al-rayāḥīn*, 48–49, 183; *Khulāṣat al-mafākhir*, 48
Yazīd, 139
Yemen, 25–26, 39–42, 51, 57, 108, 132, 152, 158

Ẓafar Khān, Khān-i a'ẓam, 132, 134, 215n4
Ẓafar Khān (son of Fīrōz Shāh), 134, 143
Ẓafar Khān Wajīh al-mulk. *See* Muẓaffar Shāh
Zahra b. Badr al-dīn Ḥusaynī Bhakkarī, 19
ẕikr, 5, 44–45, 53–54, 81–83, 95, 97, 102, 111, 150, 170, 205n7
Ẕikr al-aṣfiyā' (Aḥmadpūrī), 178–79